Reflections of a
WHALE-WATCHER

Jake & Rhea –

Thanks for all you've done
with Biological Journeys.

It's been a great trip!

Dan

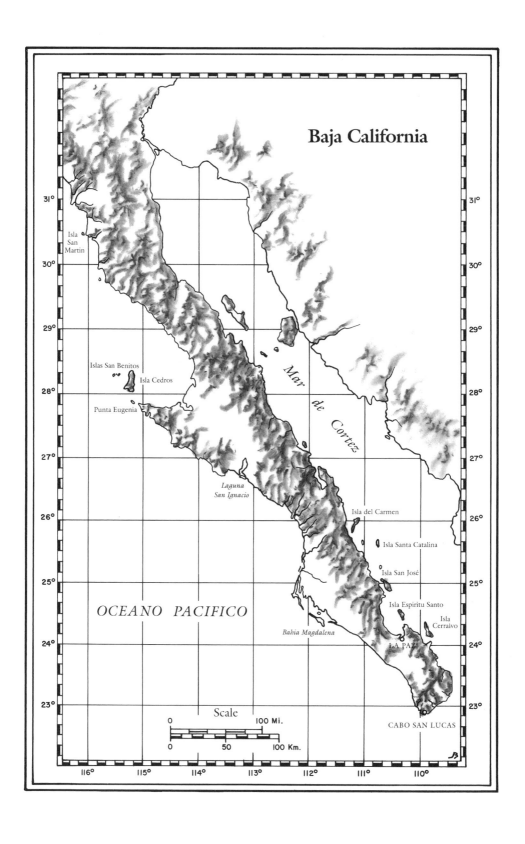

Baja California

31°

Isla
San
Martin

30°

29°

Islas San Benitos

Isla Cedros

28°

Punta Eugenia

Mar

27°

de

Cortez

Laguna
San Ignacio

Isla del Carmen

26°

Isla Santa Catalina

Isla San José

25°

Isla Espiritu Santo

Isla
Cerralvo

OCEANO PACIFICO

Bahia Magdalena

LA PAZ

24°

23°

Scale

0   100 Mi.

0   50   100 Km.

CABO SAN LUCAS

Reflections of a
WHALE-
WATCHER

Michelle A. Gilders

INDIANA UNIVERSITY PRESS

Bloomington · Indianapolis

"Whales Weep Not!" by D. H. Lawrence, from *The Complete Poems of D. H. Lawrence* by D. H. Lawrence, edited by V. de Sola Pinto and F. W. Roberts. Copyright © 1964, 1971 by Angelo Ravagli and C. M. Weekley, Executors of the Estate of Frieda Lawrence Ravagli. Used by permission of Viking Penguin, a division of Penguin Books USA Inc.

Lines from "News for the Delphic Oracle" are reprinted with permission of Simon & Schuster from *The Poems of W. B. Yeats: A New Edition*, edited by Richard J. Finneran. Copyright 1940 by Georgie Yeats, renewed 1968 by Bertha Georgie Yeats, Michael Butler Yeats, and Anne Yeats.

The paper used in this publication meets the minimum requirements of American National Standard for Information Sciences—Permanence of Paper for Printed Library Materials, ANSI Z39.48-1984.

Manufactured in the United States of America

Library of Congress Cataloging-in-Publication Data

Gilders, Michelle A., date
    Reflections of a whale-watcher / Michelle A. Gilders.
      p.   cm.
    Includes bibliographical references (p.   ) and index.
    ISBN 0-253-32572-2 (cl : alk. paper)
    1. Whales—Mexico—California, Gulf of.   2. Whale watching—
Mexico—California, Gulf of.   3. Gilders, Michelle A., date—
Journeys—Mexico—California, Gulf of.   4. Natural history—Mexico—
Baja California Sur.   5. California, Gulf of (Mexico)   I. Title.
QL737.C4G395   1995
599.5—dc20
[B]   94-38745

1 2 3 4 5 00 99 98 97 96 95

To my mother, for everything

Omnis natura, inquantum natura est, bonum est.
　　　—Augustine

You see things, and say why?
But I dream things that never were,
And I say why not?
　　　—George Bernard Shaw

Contents

List of Maps

Preface

The first time I saw a whale, I looked into its eye and saw myself reflected. We meet these leviathans at the interface of two worlds—one two-dimensional and limited by technology, the other three-dimensional and seemingly limited only by our imaginations.

The tales I relate in this book reflect several years of seeking out encounters with whales and dolphins in the waters of Baja California, Mexico. I set out with no preconceptions or undue expectations, simply as an amateur whale-watcher wanting to achieve some level of contact with these remarkable creatures.

These animals stir our imaginations and our consciences. They have graced the pages of myths and legends through millennia. We can learn some of the wonders of the world through observing their lives.

In 1851, Herman Melville wrote in *Moby Dick*, "If God were a fish, he'd be a whale." When you are sitting in a five-meter skiff, hand outstretched in what must be the most amazing of all human-animal encounters, or find yourself adrift in the Pacific Ocean surrounded by the largest animal ever to have graced the Earth, you are inclined to agree. In fact, you are certain of it.

So as you read the words that follow, see beyond the physical animal. Look through a child's eyes into the eye of the whale and see yourself reflected.

Acknowledgments

To be able to write about whales and to experience them in their natural habitat requires the combined assistance of countless people. Without those who have helped me, none of this would have been possible.

I would like to thank all of those people, known and unknown, who have campaigned tirelessly over the years to "Save the Whale." Without them my writings would be about history and museums instead of living, breathing beings. So to those who have marched, donated money or time, and especially to those who placed themselves at risk to secure a future for Cetacea, and to perpetuate an ideal, I say thank you.

Baja California Sur is a remarkable place. Nowhere else on Earth provides for such intense whale-watching experiences. I extend my deepest gratitude to the Mexican government for their judicious protection of the breeding and birthing lagoons of the gray whale.

To meet with whales on their terms requires traveling great distances and taking to the water. It requires the patience and knowledge of captain and crew. And it requires enthusiasm. I would like to thank the crews of the *Don José* (1989, 1991, 1992) and the *Searcher* (1990) and the captains of both vessels, José Luzano and Joe Herring. Without their guiding hands at the wheel, our experiences afloat would have been the poorer.

I would like to extend my thanks to everyone at Biological Journeys for their commitment to providing such once-in-a-lifetime voyages—they truly are unique! To Ron LeValley and Ronn Storro-Paterson, co-owners, thank you for all your help. And to the guides on each trip—Mason Weinrich (1989, 1991), John Kipping (1990), and Ron LeValley (1992)—your knowledge and enthusiasm were infectious. Heather Angel (1989, 1992) and Diane Gendron (1992) also added their wealth of knowledge to the excursions.

Thanks go to J. J. Wilson for his encouragement, and for his review of the manuscript from its earliest beginnings; Ron LeValley and Mason Weinrich for casting scientific and knowledgeable eyes over the contents; Patty Bielawski and Jennifer Purl for their interest and enthusiasm. Jim Barnes created the wonderful maps, and Steve Lombard provided his usual brand of invaluable assistance along the way. All of the photographs were taken by the author.

Finally, all my love goes to my family—to Valerie, Brian, and Chris, for their support and help over the years as I have headed out on my own in search of whales.

Reflections of a

WHALE-
WATCHER

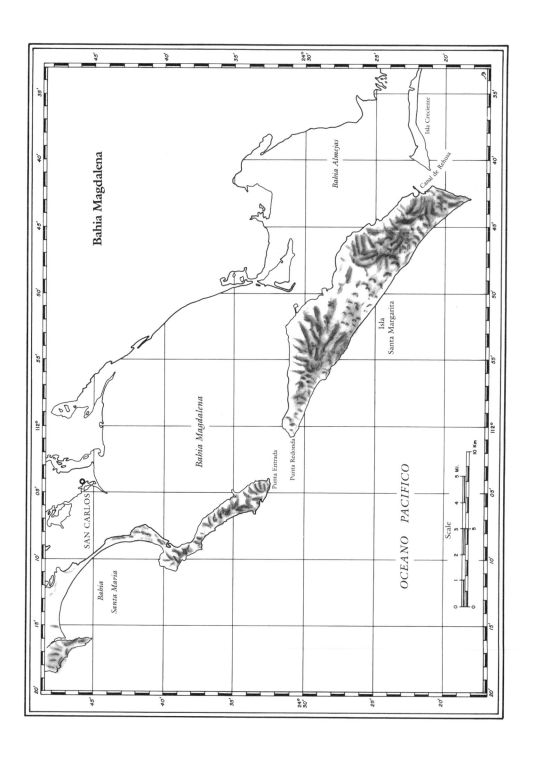

Bahia Magdalena

SAN CARLOS

112°

Bahia
Santa Maria

Bahia Magdalena

Punta Entrada
Punta Redonda

OCEANO PACIFICO

Isla
Santa Margarita

Bahia Almejas

Canal de Rehusa

Isla Creciente

112°

Scale

0   1   2   3   4   5 Mi.

0   5   10 Km

1

Whales, Whales, Whales

They say the sea is cold, but the sea contains
the hottest blood of all, and the wildest,
the most urgent.

All the whales in the wider deeps, hot are they,
as they urge on and on, and dive beneath the icebergs.
The right whales, the sperm-whales, the hammerheads, the killers
there they blow, there they blow,
hot wild white breath out of the sea!
                                        —D. H. Lawrence

My first sight of Baja, framed by the aircraft window, was of a beautiful jewel set between two azure seas. From 7,000 meters the mountains and valleys drifted to the sea in soft, dusky lines that disguised the harsh reality of this desert land. The mountain peaks were etched by the millennia of past rains, tricking the eye into believing that the gullies held water still, whereas in truth my window gazes far into the past.

From the plane the steep-sided mountains became gently rolling hills, and the distance from the Sea of Cortez to the Pacific Ocean traversable in a single day. Aircraft travel distorts relationships in time and space. But no matter how small the mountain, artificial structures are diminished many times over—just as the first space missions opened humankind's eyes to the singular beauty and fragility of the planet, so aircraft travel enables the everyday traveler to experience something of the immensity of nature and the smallness of humanity.

The flight went quickly; the air was calm, with clouds occasionally whispering about the wings or molding the shapes of this changeling landscape. On the approach to La Paz, the plane banked left to fly over the Sea of Cortez, providing a perfect aerial view of the islands that the voyage would encounter. Isla Cerralvo, Los Islotes, Espiritu Santo—names to conjure up an ancient empire shrouded in the blues and greens of a perfect sea. No jewel could have a more beautiful setting than that afforded the Baja Peninsula by these aquamarine waters.

My reasons for visiting Baja, though, had little to do with the physical beauty of this arid land; the mountains that I wanted to see were living—magnificent leviathans called to its shores to breed and birth. So as the plane flew along the backbone of the peninsula, revealing lagoons and inlets frame by frame through the porthole, I fancied that the shadows and breakers hid whales.

Baja California, Mexico, is truly a contradiction in biology and geography: lifeless desert and life-filled lagoons. Here you see nature's design amplified, with the smallest and the largest crowded together. There is nothing gentle about Baja. Life for human and nonhuman alike is beautiful, but harsh. The life force clings to a narrow fringe, a blaze of color and passion amid the golden browns and blues of the coast.

This is where my journey took me, a journey into the heart of nature—the biggest heart of all—and into the soul of humanity. For in nature we find a purpose to life, a value and wonder to cherish in a modern world.

Any journey begins before the land is even reached. The mind rushes ahead of the body with equal measures of anticipation and anxiety. You fear that what you see will disappoint, and that the emotions that you believe you have will be exposed as fraud. You travel with strangers across the expanse of ocean that separates lands that separate oceans and feel as though hurrying to a rendezvous with someone you have never met—only read about, seen pictures of, and visualized in dreams. The love affair has been carried on at a distance, and now you have the opportunity to fulfill the dream with reality.

As you travel, the first stage of the journey is entirely visual. Then all five senses are overrun, and emotions are fired with a seemingly inexplicable fever of anticipation and wonder. When there is time to reflect, you are able to delve deep into the awakening of feelings of such intensity that you are taken aback at their source: a land and its animals that at once seem so alien and yet so familiar.

All my life I have been fascinated by the natural world. In our increasingly ordered and carefully arranged lives, there is a need to be able to experience the beauty and wildness of places where the human hand has only scratched at the surface or passed over completely, whether in deference or ignorance. The voyages of past discovery combined with modern capabilities have simultaneously opened up the world to us individually, and yet closed many of the adventures that perhaps in the past we would have been driven to undertake.

The essence of new lands has been removed. The nobility of Yosemite, the Grand Canyon, and Death Valley has not been lost because of their accessibility, but they have been tamed by the populace; Hetch Hetchy Valley has been flooded, the Colorado River dammed, and Death Valley conquered by the air-conditioned car. Animals too have been "tamed," or at least corralled, in game reserves, zoos, aquariums, parklands. So much of the unexpected, the sheer spontaneity, of the natural world has been corrupted and controlled, forced into shapes that fit the modern traveler's requirements; when you stare in awe at the monolithic El Capitan from Yosemite Valley, it loses none of its grandeur, but from the safety of the tarmac road and tourist trolley, it has lost its danger and much of its wildness. To comprehend the past glories of such places, we are forced to review the writings of those who were the last to witness the untamed wilderness: the journals of John Muir, Major John Powell, Meriwether Lewis and William Clark.

In our modern world there are few places that capture this prehuman spirit, among them Alaska, Antarctica, Siberia, and the hot deserts of the world. They are the inimical places that taunt people with their climatic hostility. But even these are now being tamed as the riches that drive our world are discovered within their midst. We will undoubtedly learn that to conquer the spirit of the natural world, we must first conquer our own.

It was with these thoughts that I arrived in Baja for the first time. It was February 1989—the year of the *Exxon Valdez* oil spill, the year events began to unfold in Eastern Europe that ultimately changed the face of the world. This was the year that I cemented my relationship with nature.

This was the year I touched a whale.

Twenty-two whale-watchers gathered in La Paz for the voyage—people separated by nationality, culture, background, and age were united by a simple fascination with whales. The term *whale-watcher* has been adopted to refer to lay enthusiasts whose amateur status certainly does not detract from their knowledge or appreciation of these most remarkable of mammals. Where the scientist may be restricted by logic and impartial observation, the amateur whale-watcher need make no apology for emotional enthrallment and wide-eyed wonder.

From La Paz we traveled by coach 240 kilometers northward to Bahia Magdalena. We were traveling at that special time when day turns to night. The giant cardon cacti stood like sentinels in the failing light, their thorns catching the last embers of sunlight before turning to silhouettes on the horizon. The bright burnished yellows and occasional bursts of green in the desert, the flurry of blue jay and red cardinal, all were gradually subdued. What an absence of water fails to do is achieved daily by the setting sun.

Our passage along the potholed road, past the shrines and crosses that punctuate the roadside (silent monuments to long-distant miracles and present tragedies), was observed with the detachment that only turkey vultures seem able to achieve. These large birds herald the planes as they land at La Paz, making use of the updrafts over the runway. Here they are ubiquitous road ornaments, perhaps awaiting the prelude to another white cross. But most of the time they are resigned to their uncomfortable posts atop the cacti, only rarely taking to the air with languid wing beats if a car or bus passes too close to their perch.

To see Baja from the road, however fleetingly, is a memorable experience. Most of our journey was at twilight, when the darkness envelops the hills and gullies and the night plays shadows among boulders and cacti. However, the illumination offered by the stars and moon, unimpeded by the glow of urban lights, gives the observer a view of past, present, and future, for the interior is a landscape that appears, to our eyes, immutable and unchanging.

As I gaze out of my window at the birds and plants that have made this land their own—and have given past explorers cause to condemn the land as useless, a land of thorns, poisonous to all humanity—I am glad that the creatures and land that repel others captivate me and draw me in to explore. Here, nature is hard, but it is also very much alive and free. We have grown too far from such places, if not in distance then in spirit. This world of ours has simultaneously separated us from a close connection with the land, and given us the opportunity to examine it more closely.

Occasionally the coach headlights sent a jackrabbit darting for cover, and once, briefly, the lights caught the reflective glare in the eyes of a coyote. Finally, after four or five hours, the coach pulled off the road at the northern end of Bahia Magdalena. We had arrived.

We stepped onto the shore of the largest lagoon in Baja. We might as well have stepped into another world, or perhaps into the distant past of our own, when the marks of people were transient, subdued, and dwarfed by natural wonders. We are strangers to this land, and certainly strangers to this experience and to each other. Our belongings were piled together on the sand, and we talked nervously—wondering aloud what it was that drew us to a deserted beach, far from civilization, on an unyieldingly black night. The waters of the lagoon offered no definition, no depth or perspective to the expanse. It was as if the light from the stars and moon were pulled into the depths, a terrestrial black hole with no reflection, no ripple, and complete silence.

Isolated in the darkness, dwarfed by the night, an oasis of reflection and light surrounded the twenty-seven-meter *Don José* anchored in the bay. The vessel's lights caught the wing movements of a night-heron and a group of three brown pelicans, but they passed quickly out of range in this darkly eclipsed world.

As we waited on the sand, our eyes were drawn skyward. I have never seen a night sky as clear as those I witnessed in Baja. The combination of cloudless skies, a dry atmosphere, and an absence of all but the smallest of human settlements brings a limitless expanse of space into view.

I could see the universe and imagine it punctuated with life. The names we have given the stars conjure up a supernatural past, of gods and heroes, of creatures with powers over men. Perseus, Capella, Cassiopeia, Andromeda, Pegasus, Pleiades, Betelgeuse. Each holds a tale of wonder and lives in prehistory. They tell of a time before science dispelled imagination. One story relates how the huntsman of the gods found the door to the sun in the mountains. He journeyed into its heart and found the souls of the dead. As punishment for what he had seen, the huntsman was transformed and achieved immortality in the heavens. I looked upon Orion and smiled.

Our links to the stars have waxed and waned through the ages, mirroring the strength and weakness of the moon that now hung overhead. From believing our world to be the center of the universe with so many lights adorning the roof of creation, we have come to understand a little of the distance, the depth, and the scale of what we see above. I am still not sure which view is more frightening—that we are at the center of some master plan, or that we are tiny, insignificant components in a universe beyond our comprehension.

I am staring into time itself. Some of the stars I can see died millennia ago; perhaps their worlds did too. As I turn around, the constellations take up different positions and the stars' brightness varies with that classic twinkle. I am beginning to feel dizzy; my head is bent back to take in the expanse, and my neck is starting to ache. If there were time, I should like to lie on the sand and stare for hours into the night. I wonder if there is anyone looking back. I hope so.

We loaded the skiffs and set out toward the *Don José,* the outboard motors creating an unwelcome intrusion into this primeval world. The lagoon breeze smelled so fresh, and the skiffs sent up swirling currents of water and a light salt spray. Once on board the custom-built ship, I stood silently on the deck staring back into the night. I am reminded of the first line in John Muir's journal of his thousand-mile walk: "John Muir, Earth-planet, Universe." The water was gently lapping against the gunnels, and in the distance the occasional cry of a loon broke the stillness. This is Planet Ocean.

At dawn the horizon looked as though the embers of a coal fire had been gently stoked, creating a palette of orange, red, and yellow across the sky. As we ate breakfast, pairs of bottlenose dolphins swam close to the ship, occasionally slapping their small gray flukes on the water's surface, sounding a report like a gunshot. In the distance a gray whale blew, its heart-shaped exhalation just visible hanging suspended in the early morning air.

We were anchored near Pueblo Lopez Mateos, and the small fishing boats and "pangas" were silhouetted by the morning light. The dawn cloud dispersed rapidly, and out across the bay, the calm expanse of water reached to a horizon marked by sand dunes. Blue water, blue sky, golden dunes—the simple colors of a desert where ocean and land blend together.

For the next week we would cruise Baja California Sur. Two days would be spent in the sheltered waters of Bahia Magdalena and close encounters with gray whales; the rest of the voyage would take us into the Pacific, around Cabo San Lucas, and into the Sea of Cortez, always in search of whales. The itinerary, our shipboard naturalist Mason explained, was summarized by the F word: F is for flexibility.

As the *Don José* was being prepared for departure, we had the chance to look her over and establish our bearings for the week ahead. Our arrival the night before had provided little opportunity to gain a perspective of the scale or visual impression of the vessel. But under the bright desert sun, her stout beams and surprising comfort were evident. The *Don José* was predominantly white with dark wood trim, although the railings and crow's nest were painted a bright canary yellow. She was approaching her first decade, having been launched in July 1979. Señor Don José v Aboroa had fashioned twenty-seven meters of solid craftsmanship, which had been perfected for wilderness travel.

The main deck held four of the cabins (we did not call them staterooms after the first night), the galley, and the main seating area, which contained an assemblage of marine artifacts—bones, feathers, and shells that color the shores of Baja. The vessel's stern had an easily reached boarding platform, and under one of the benches was the all-important cooler box and the beer. The bow tapered to a neat point and contained the mechanics for anchor and chain. Both fore and aft there were steps to the upper deck that was used as the small boat-storage area. Also on the upper deck were four additional staterooms, the captain's cabin, and the helm. A ladder provided access up to the whale-watching deck and crow's nest. It was the whale-watching deck above the wheelhouse (rapidly abbreviated to the w-w deck) that was to be our main focus when we were not in one of the three five-meter skiffs or "pangas." The *Don José* was a proud, compact little ship that provided us with a level of comfort and a degree of spaciousness that belied her statistics.

The w-w deck gave us an unobstructed 360 degree view of the bay. From our anchorage the blows were distant and the whales amorphous shapes of gray— no dorsal fins, slate-smooth, iceberg animals slipping beneath the waters with hardly a ripple. I wondered momentarily whether all our visions of whales would be like this—distant and detached, witnessed by observers at the fringes of a shallow marine world. But this was only the beginning; we were being drawn in, crossing that narrow line between observer and participant.

After breakfast we left Pueblo Lopez Mateos and headed deeper into the bay; as we cruised, we began to see more whales. The dolphins were still with us, occasionally joining our bow in twos or threes, and breaking the surface ahead of us were a gray whale mother and calf, dappled backs and shades of gray.

Standing atop the w-w deck, we were awed by this desert fringed in green. Our route was bordered by a bank of red mangrove, an extensive thicket of dense growth six or eight meters high. The leaves and white wood gave the vegetation a dry, mottled appearance, although in places the leaves were dark and verdant, truly suggestive of a subtropical paradise.

Sitting high in the mangrove branches, and circling overhead, magnificent frigatebirds spread their wings. These large, piratical seabirds are reminiscent of pterodactyls. Watching their slow glides on upcurrents, you soon realize that dinosaurs are alive and well in the present, and have taken the form of these feathered creatures. Mariners named the birds after their swift warships. The analogy is fitting. When feeding, frigates either skim the surface of the water with their hooked beaks, snapping them shut when they hit a fish, or, more dramatically, they harass other birds, forcing them to disgorge their food in midflight, then swooping down to claim their regurgitated booty.

Among the mangroves, we could make out the white-breasted females and the distinctive juveniles, which also sport white heads and necks. A flash of orange singled out the lone black male perched among the females and young. As we passed by, he turned and half-inflated his bright orange-red throat pouch, the gesture of a pirate welcoming us into a treasured land.

It is simple moments such as this that focus your mind on the reality of the natural world. Until this point I had not really witnessed nature that had not in one way or another been manipulated by people. Western Europe is so controlled that the spontaneity has been lost. But here in the extravagant gesture of this tropical bird was an introduction to the real world, away from construction, manipulation, and control. The television images of exotic creatures and far-flung places were now in front of me, unimpeded by the technology of our time (save the camera that I chronically overused during the trip). At the conclusion of every journey that I have been on, people have bemoaned having to return to the "real world," when it is the "real world" that they are leaving behind.

The clarity of this February day was astounding. Even the breeze in Baja feels different from that in other places. It cleanses the skin, the heart, and the soul. Letting the early morning air in Baja permeate your thoughts is like allowing yourself to be transported to a place where you are the only travelers, and where what you are seeing has been seen by no other eyes. What I am going to relate in the pages that follow is what these eyes saw, and my interpretations of those images—others aboard the ship may have seen different things, thought different thoughts; those standing right next to me may have entirely different recollections of the same events. My images of Baja are an amalgam of thoughts during and after the event, of changing perceptions, and of relating past histories and future potential to what we have in the present.

With whales this means dealing with the past horrors that have been inflicted upon them, the present captives that entertain us, and the future, when we must decide whether commercial exploitation or benign understanding is what we seek. In Bahia Magdalena these questions are of more than academic interest.

This population of gray whales was decimated twice in the space of less than one hundred years, driven to the brink of extinction. It was here in Bahia Magdalena that Captain Charles Scammon discovered his "desert whale," and it was after whaling in Baja that Scammon introduced the explosive harpoon to ease the whalers' task.

Our horizons were limited by the mangroves, so that as we traveled it was as if the world went no further than these green borders. In a way that was true. To our backs were the terrestrial deserts of Baja, and in front of us, on the other side of the bay, were the marine deserts of the tropical deep Pacific. Only at the fringes, the interfaces, was life luxuriant.

As we entered deeper water, the *Don José* dropped anchor, and the three pangas were lowered from the vessel. It was about nine when we entered the small pangas for the first time and set off into the bay, driven by a small outboard in the capable hands of our panga driver, Hector.

The weather was perfect. The bay was like glass, with only an occasional dark squall coloring the surface with ripples. It is hard to describe the feeling of being in a small five-meter wooden panga out in a bay with minimal power and a couple of oars. The animals that we were seeking inhabited a world beyond our perception, hidden from our eyes. The blows, arched backs, and flukes that we could observe from a distance were only fleeting glimpses of a routine and interactions taking place below us. The only time we are able to observe these whales is when they return to the surface to breathe, reinforcing in our own minds the one tangible link between our species—that we are both air-breathing mammals.

As we motored slowly through the water, we watched the whales blow in the distance, trying to gauge where the activity was centered. With the *Don José* at rest two kilometers away, and the horizon marked by dunes, we began to follow an adult gray whale that had surfaced a couple of hundred meters distant. As we followed we could note the routine. Surface, blow, one, two, three, four, fluke, dive, down, one, two, three, four minutes, surface, blow. Down, one, two. Suddenly the count was interrupted as 20,000 kilograms of gray exploded from the water; three-quarters of the animal cleared the surface. It turned and twisted, the small paddle-shaped flipper mottled white by barnacles at its side. The thirteen-meter leviathan plunged into the water, landing on its back in a maelstrom of foaming spray. Although the animal was perhaps two hundred meters away, our small craft was dwarfed by the aerial spectacle.

Why whales breach is a mystery: to dislodge parasites; to signal other whales; to reinforce territorial boundaries; to signal displeasure or simple exuberance—no one knows. All that is clear is that the energy required to push a 20,000-kilogram animal out of the water is probably tremendous, and the biology of energetics tells us that the event must "mean" something to the animal. There must be some benefit to the expenditure of all that valuable energy. Consideration of the bioenergetics of the breaching gray, however, was not central to our appreciation of the event. The gray had afforded us our first look at the animal as a whole, in all its dramatic, exuberant fashion.

The gray whale is a rotund animal, which some even call ungainly. It is a mysticete—a "mustached whale" with fibrous baleen instead of teeth to sift its food from the ocean water. The world's cetaceans belong to two groups: the mysticetes or baleen whales include, in addition to the gray, the blue, fin, humpback, bowhead, great right, pygmy right, sei, minke, and the elusive Bryde's whale; and the odontocetes are the familiar toothed whales such as the bottlenose dolphin, orca, and sperm whale. Worldwide there are currently some 80 identified cetacean species in the oceans, ranging in size from the 1.3-meter harbor porpoise to the 33-meter-plus blue whale. Among the cetaceans the gray is medium-sized, reaching between 11.5 and 15 meters in length and weighing anywhere from 20,000 to 37,000 kilograms—by any standards a true leviathan.

So, what are the characteristics required by a biologically "successful" whale? There are some fairly obvious differences between marine and terrestrial mammals. It is important to remember that the change from terrestrial to marine took place gradually over many millions of years. For a long time the pre-cetacean had four legs and probably returned to shallow estuaries and coasts to give birth.

Cetaceans are entirely aquatic. They inhabit all the oceans of the world, and some of the river and lake systems. Their tail flukes are set in the horizontal plane, unlike the tails of fish, such as sharks, which are vertical. It is the up-and-down movement of the tail that propels the cetacean through the water. In some species, such as the blue whale, the strength and speed of the animal are clearly apparent from the thick muscles of the tail stock leading to the flukes.

Other obvious features are the torpedo-like body shape (more so in some whales than others), the front limbs modified to pectoral flippers, the absence of visible hind limbs, and the presence of a dorsal fin (in many species). Cetaceans also have no external ears or ear muscles, and they do not have scales or gills. They lack a covering of fur, although many mysticete whales do have sensitive hairs on their rostrums or snouts, and embryonic cetaceans show a more extensive hair covering that disappears as the fetus develops. Most cetaceans do not have sweat or sebaceous glands; instead they have a thick layer of blubber fat and oil beneath their skin that is used for insulation, heat regulation, and energy storage.

Cetaceans are air-breathing mammals. Their aquatic lifestyle has resulted in the evolution of a unique body shape in the mammalian world. The sirenians (manatees and dugongs) are certainly large, blubbery sea mammals, but they are missing the one feature of cetaceans that could be said to govern much of their behavior: the blowhole. All cetaceans possess a blowhole at the apex of the head. Odontocetes, such as the bottlenose dolphin, have a single blowhole, while the mysticetes, including the gray whale and the humpback, have a double blowhole. As the first pre-cetacean took to the water, evolution over the millennia gradually moved the nostrils from the front of the head to the top, making swimming and breathing much easier. In contrast to other mammals, the whale's blowhole has a direct connection with the lungs, so a suckling calf cannot get milk into its lungs as perhaps a human child might.

Cetaceans have been able to attain their large size through the supportive medium of the oceans. The blue whale is possibly the largest animal ever to have lived on Earth, perhaps larger than any of the dinosaurs (although recent finds may yet relegate the animal to second place). An animal the size of a blue whale would be unlikely to be able to move about on land, and probably would not have been able to find sufficient food to sustain itself. The largest of the dinosaurs were vegetarian, while all cetaceans eat other animals. The odontocetes hunt fish, squid, and in certain cases other cetaceans, while the mysticetes, being essentially marine grazers, still feed on other animals, fish or zooplankton. While the huge land-based dinosaurs probably had to feed continuously, the mysticetes are using a rich protein source that gives the majority the freedom of not being tied to their food resource all the time. The blue whale is an important exception; its bulk dictates year-round feeding. Many of the migratory great whales feed principally during the summer in high temperate or polar waters, moving toward the equator in the winter to give birth and raise their offspring. During this time they feed only opportunistically in the warmer, less productive waters. This migratory habitat would have been denied the larger dinosaurs simply because they could not go for so long without access to major food supplies. Whether the smaller terrestrial dinosaurs migrated over great distances is still hotly debated.

The past and future evolution of cetaceans has attracted a great deal of attention, particularly as our knowledge of genetics has increased. Much of the debate has been centered around whether these eighty species consist of numerous subspecies, or even whether other species have yet to be described. It has been suggested that there are genetically distinct populations of pygmy blue and minke whales.

The poles-to-tropics migrations of many baleen whales clearly indicate that in time the Northern and Southern Hemisphere populations, as well as the geographically isolated Atlantic and Pacific ocean stocks, would go their own way from an evolutionary standpoint. Similarly, the geographic isolation of many toothed whales suggests that evolutionary divergence is a distinct possibility. The variations that we are witness to in genetic analyses and slight color or size differences appear to lend support to this theory. So even if these whales are not yet different species, evolutionary theory strongly suggests that eventually they will be.

The past evolution of cetaceans is still poorly understood. Fossils of identifiable cetaceans have been found to range from the middle Eocene (45 to 38 million years ago) to recent times, and discoveries in northern Pakistan of the archaeocetes *Pakicetus* and *Ambulocetus* have now pushed this date back to 50 million years ago. It is believed that the early ancestors of modern-day whales diverged from the Creodontia, an extinct order of terrestrial carnivores, at the end of the Cretaceous (65 million years ago) and entered the sea in the Paleocene (55 million years ago). Creodonts are known as archaic carnivores; they are not the true carnivores that we recognize today, but were more likely intermediate between carnivores and ungulates. The earliest known fossil cetaceans have been placed in the extinct suborder Archaeoceti. These ancient whales had symmetrical skulls and clearly differentiated teeth. Fossils recognizable as Odontoceti have been found in the upper Eocene (30 million years ago), and the Mysticeti in the lower Oligocene (38 to 25 million years ago). Further divergence occurred during the Miocene (24 to 5 million years ago), and by the beginning of the Pliocene, 2 million years ago, the major families were in existence.

What could have caused that land-dwelling pre-cetacean to take to the waters? The location of several important fossil finds suggests that the transition from terrestrial to aquatic took place at the edges of the ancient Tethys Sea. This sea was located where the Mediterranean Sea and the Asian subcontinent now lie. The world of 65 to 55 million years ago was very different from the world of today, in terms of both the placement of the continents and seas and the prevailing climate.

Fifty-five million years ago the major continents were nearing their present positions, but South America had yet to fuse with the North, India was still racing northward to crash into the Asian continent, and Australia and Antarctica were still one over the South Pole. Sea level was high throughout most of the Cretaceous. In fact, it was higher than at any other time in the history of the Earth. The oceans were probably 200 to 250 meters higher during the late Cretaceous than they are at present. Earth was truly a marine planet, with only about 18 percent of the surface not covered by water. Not only were the large oceans deeper than today, but many of the continents were inundated by shallow seas.

So the Creodont terrestrial carnivore inhabited a world dominated by deep oceans and shallow continental seas. The oceans were incredibly productive, and the climate was warm and equable worldwide. Tropical conditions extended to 45 degrees north, and temperate conditions prevailed all the way to the poles. Many of the tropical continents were arid and dry. Marine life flourished in upwelling regions, including reeflike structures built by rudist bivalves. The oceans were full of snails, corals, ammonites, plesiosaurs and ichthyosaurs, sharks and rays. On land the placental mammals were emerging, and above them flew pterosaurs.

But at the close of the Cretaceous something happened that resulted in mass extinctions. The cause is unknown. Perhaps an asteroid hit the Earth and sent dust and particles into the air, disrupting plant photosynthesis and severely impacting the food chain. Perhaps the gradually shifting continents and climate change were altering the available habitats so that some species were unable to adapt in time and suffered the ultimate evolutionary setback. Whatever the cause, the ramifications were felt on land and in the oceans. The terrestrial dinosaurs vanished, and in the oceans only 13 percent of the planktonic foraminifera survived. The ammonites disappeared, as did the plesiosaurs, ichthyosaurs, and rudist bivalves.

This became the world of the Creodont. The arid terrestrial conditions and the high productivity of the surrounding waters that dominated the planet probably drew this group of archaic carnivores initially to the estuaries and shallows, and over millions of years into the deep oceans. The Cretaceous extinctions removed the large marine reptiles from the scene, thus eliminating an important competitor. As time passed, the continents took up their present positions, the sea level fell as the world entered ice age after ice age, and the marine mammals that had taken to the waters were segregated and isolated across the world. Temperatures fell, and the evolving baleen whales moved poleward to feed on the concentrations of zooplankton; however, they still returned to the tropics to breed and give birth, thus establishing the migrations that continue to this day.

The geological record suggests that it was the odontocetes that evolved first from those Creodonton ancestors, and that mysticetes emerged from odontocete stock. This is by no means certain, and some researchers have hypothesized different origins for these whales. It is interesting, however, that mysticete fetuses during their *in utero* development have teeth that are later lost as the baleen forms, a clear example of the classic concept "ontogeny recapitulates phylogeny," which simply states that early fetal development mirrors the evolutionary ancestry of the species. Therefore it seems reasonable to conclude that the ancestors of mysticetes did have teeth. Furthermore, mysticete fetuses exhibit polydonty and homodonty—which means that their ancestors must have also possessed this dental diversity, a characteristic shown by odontocete ancestors.

Our breaching gray whale is the only species in the Cetacea family Eschrichtidae, and among the great whales is believed to be the most primitive. Some researchers see the gray as intermediate between the right whales in the family Balaenidae and the sleek rorquals of the family Balaenopteridae, which includes the blue whale. *Rorqual* is a Norwegian term that means "furrow whale" or "tube whale," and refers to the throat grooves that identify whales in the Balaenopteridae family. Right whales, such as the bowhead of the Arctic, lack these distinctive throat grooves, while the Balaenopteridae have varying numbers, from a low of fourteen in the humpback to upwards of ninety-four in the blue. The gray whale has only two to five grooves. These throat grooves serve to increase the whale's ability to expand its throat while feeding, and thus increase its intake of krill or fish. Another feature that appears to be an afterthought in the gray whale is the dorsal fin. The gray has a small hump leading to a series of knuckles along the lower back. The right whales completely lack a dorsal fin, while in the rorquals the sickle-shaped fin acts as a keel, adding control to their rapid swimming speed. To view a diving gray whale closely is to be left with the impression of something prehistoric and primeval living in the oceans.

Despite its ancient stock, the gray whale almost appears to offer us a snapshot of a species in flux. We can observe whale species at other ends of the evolutionary spectrum: the right whales, which have evolved to bulky size, huge mouths, and extensive baleen. If you like analogies, the right whales are the ocean liners of cetaceans, while the rorquals have trimmed down and developed the sleek, fast racing-boat model. The grays are simply the weekender's pleasure craft—without the bulk of a liner, but without the speed of the racing boat. It seems somehow fitting that it is these unprepossessing animals that have now earned the title of "the friendly whales."

The gray whale was first scientifically described in 1725 by the Honorable Paul Dudley. Noting the animal's mottled gray appearance and the profusion of parasitic attachments, he named it the "scrag whale." The definition of *scrag* is "a thin or scrawny person or animal." It is difficult to see that image in the rotund gray whale, and there is even some doubt that it was a gray that Dudley described; however, he may have been referring to the parasitic growths that cover the whale, or the specimen that he examined may have been in particularly poor condition. Through the years the whale has been known by various names, mainly descriptive, such that it is often difficult to determine whether two sources are actually describing the same species. The gray whale has been called "rip sack," in reference to the method used to flense the animal on deck, and "mussel digger," referring to its bottom-feeding habits (although it does not feed on mussels). The knuckles along its back led to the Dutch name *knabbelvisch,* the German *knotenfish,* and the French *baleine á six bosses.* However, it was the gray mottling color that eventually gave name to the species. In 1864 the whale was officially classified as *Eshrichtitus robustus,* the gray whale.

The knabbelvisch breached again. It almost appeared to happen in slow motion, then gained momentum until the foaming water cascaded about the spot where the whale disappeared. I can still hear the whale-watchers in the panga cheering the animal on. Applause for a thunderclap.

We left the breaching whale and began to follow a cow-calf pair who had surfaced a little to our starboard side (or, in the terms adopted by consensus, at three o'clock).

The mother and calf surfaced in unison, creating swirling eddies of water around them. Their white plumed blows exploded into the atmosphere. The clear blue water magnified our vision of the depths, and we could see the animals well below the surface as they rose to refill their lungs. A line of pelicans flew across our bow, wings beating in turn, their images reflected in the water— a temporary distraction.

The calf was obviously curious about us. She circled the panga slowly, almost stopping as she turned to face us. When within five meters of the panga she faded into the water, plunging into the depths. Moments later she surfaced in exactly the same place, head held high above the water, effectively standing on her tail. She stayed in this controlled position for perhaps thirty seconds before sinking slowly downward.

Some term this action a *spy-hop,* and at times this clearly describes the curious behavior. Others are less convinced of the observational component and use the term *high head up* to describe the action, thus leaving interpretation a little less defined. Both are probably accurate. On occasion the animals raise their heads so far out of the water that they can get a clear view of the world around them, while at others it seems that only the tip of the rostrum, or snout, is exposed, with the eye remaining below the waterline. In the latter case some observers believe that the high head up simply provides the animal with an easy way of maneuvering in the shallows.

These enclosed, protected waters along the Baja California coast—Laguna Guerrero Negro, Laguna Ojo de Liebre, Laguna San Ignacio, and Bahia Magdalena—are vital to the survival of the gray whale. These whales are perpetuating an age-old migration from the cold, food-rich Arctic waters off Alaska to the warm, tropical ones off the California and Mexican coasts. The warm, shallow lagoons may offer little to the whales by way of food, but the protected bays are essential for the young calves to grow and mature away from the rigors of the open ocean and the chill of northern waters. The young calves lack a well-developed layer of insulating blubber and would not be able to survive life in the frigid, though productive, north.

The 18,000-kilometer round-trip migration undertaken by the gray whale is one of the longest made by any mammal, bettered only by a Southern Hemisphere population of humpback whales. Only when the calves have put on their insulating layer of blubber and enough weight to last them on the long trek north does the return migration to Alaska take place. Before then the calves are reliant on their dams for nourishment, and their dams reliant on the store of fat they were able to build up during the Alaskan summer.

The lagoons are a nursery ground for the young whales, away from the threats of sharks and orca, and in part away from the advances of male grays that will attempt to mate with available females at every opportunity.

The calf gamboling about us now was probably a month old, and in length more than a match for our panga. When mother and calf were seen side by side, the differences between them were dramatic. The mother, at thirteen meters in length, was some three times her youngster's size. The difference in coloration was also marked. At times the mother appeared slate black, with numerous barnacle encrustations around her head, flukes, and flippers, while the calf was a much lighter shade of gray, and the sun created a subtle mottling pattern on her back. The calf was too young to have acquired many barnacles, and her skin was clear and unblemished.

The youngster stayed close to her dam, the cow moderating her movements, keeping time and speed suited to the calf's abilities. They were often so close that they touched at the surface, a gentle stroking of flippers between gargantuans.

Captain Scammon, whaler and naturalist, noted similar activities in the lagoons. His touching words paint a picture of parental bonds through terrible adversity. On defending young from harm: "The movements of the mother are sympathetically suited to the necessities of her dependent offspring. It is rare that the dam will forsake her young one, when molested." Watching the mother tending to her young calf, it is well to consider the history of these lagoons and the history of human encounters with gray whales—to think of the methodology of whaling; to consider what whaling actually involved and the toll it took, on human and whale alike.

In his 1874 book *Marine Mammals of the Northwestern Coast of North America,* Scammon writes of a gray whale fishery that is simultaneously horrific where it concerns the slaughter and the hardships and dangers associated with the industry. After detailing the statistics of whales caught in the region, and following the delicate haunting line drawing of a gray whale fetus, Scammon relates some of his observations:

> If the whale is struck it dashes about, lashing the water into foam, oftentimes staving the boats. . . . The officer . . . watches a favorable opportunity to shoot a bomb-lance. Should this enter a vital part and explode, it kills instantly, but it is not often this good luck occurs; more frequently two or three bombs are shot, which paralyze the animal to some extent.

The calf swam close to our panga, circling, with the cow in close attendance.

> In darting the lance at the mother, the young one, in its gambols, will get in the way of the weapon, and receive the wound, instead of the intended victim. In such instances, the parent animal in her frenzy, will chase the boats, and overtaking them, will overturn them with her head, or dash them in pieces with a stroke of her ponderous flukes.

The gray whale gained a fierce reputation among the California whalers. The females would place themselves in danger to protect their calves. They staved in boats. Men died for oil and blubber. Whalers called the whales devilfish.

Even up until the 1970s, people feared close encounters with gray whale cows with their calves. The females are highly protective, and skiff operators know better than to separate a mother from her calf. However, other incidents over the last two decades have tempered this fear, and the devilfish has earned the new title "the friendly whale." Perhaps they have forgiven us.

Friendly gray whales were first described in 1975. The unexpected incidents occurred in Laguna San Ignacio, to the north of Bahia Magdalena. Initially close approaches by whales were met with concern, and the human response was usually to get out of the water. But gradually, as the approaches continued, people began to relax in the presence of whales. What is surprising, given the gray whales' history, is that friendlies are often cow-calf pairs, although all sexes and age classes seem to participate. Some encounters have even involved a mother soliciting attention from skiffs, and pushing her calf toward the out-stretched hands of people. During the early eighties, practically every vessel entering Laguna San Ignacio was rewarded with close, friendly encounters. People touched the whales, and the whales touched the hearts of people.

Friendly behavior continues to be common in San Ignacio and has also been recorded in other areas in Baja, including Laguna Guerrero Negro, Laguna Ojo de Liebre (Scammon's Lagoon), and Bahia Magdalena. "Friendlies" have even been encountered on the northerly stretches of their migration, along the shores of Oregon. However, it is Laguna San Ignacio that almost guarantees friendly encounters. In the other lagoons and bays, friendlies are rarer, and nobody enters Bahia Magdalena expecting such a reward.

As the whales circled our panga, we were not thinking of the statistics of encounters, or of the proportion of friendlies seen in respective bays and lagoons. We were entirely focused on these animals, just as they seemed intrigued by our presence. To observe whales closely is a momentous reward in itself. To think of reaching out and touching one can at times seem an imposition. But the barrier between observer and observed was breaking down; observers were becoming participants in this curious dance of whales and skiff.

The whales kept their distance at between three and six meters, although at times it was clear that they were swimming directly under us. We were still motoring slowly, and when we were not moving, the engine continued to turn over.

The sky was a deep blue you think cannot exist in nature. The same sky looked down over the first whaling season in this bay, during the winter of 1845–46. Only two vessels entered the bay that year; the *Hibernia* and the *United States* took 32 gray whales between them. They were the first gray whales ever killed by westerners. In the seasons that followed, the numbers taken increased. Sixty-two to 68 whales were killed in each of the nine years to 1854. The peak period of whaling for grays, 1854–1865, averaged 486 whales every year, and even as the whaling industry declined, the kill still averaged 214 each year until 1874. For every 10 whales captured, at least 1 was killed and lost. In the space of thirty years, the gray whale population was decimated.

As Scammon related, the strategy was often to hunt females with calves. The majority of gray whales taken were females, and the number of calves killed was never recorded. The gray whale slaughter never even had the pretense of sustainability. The heart of the herd, the future generations, was cut out on the decks of flensing boats. But think now of the present.

The calf before us was a comical representation of a swimming whale. The young calf would bring her entire head up clear of the water as she surfaced, revealing the line of jaw and mouth and the small eye set far back in the head; her body was at an acute angle rather than horizontal in the water. This action was in marked contrast to the smooth, rolling motion of the cow. It was as if the young whale were always trying to see what was above the surface. Or perhaps she was simply overshooting her role of surface, breathe, and dive. Whatever the reason, the calf gave the impression of being a novice swimmer under tutelage.

Other actions by the calf demonstrated the universality of parent-child relationships. Occasionally the mother would lie at the surface, logging, breathing quietly, as if resting. The calf would swim around a little, approaching her mother, rolling onto her side or back, playing at blowing bubbles. Then, bored at being left alone, she would swim to her mother and push herself on top of her, covering her blowhole. It has to be said that preventing your parent from breathing is probably a very effective way of getting the attention that you think you deserve. The cow seemed to take this exuberance in good spirits; she simply sank into the water, dislodging her infant.

We followed the whales a short distance as they began to move off. They were picking up speed, and the calf peeled back and forth across our bow—a bow-riding 1,000-kilogram whale. Suddenly Hector bought the panga to an abrupt halt. The calf stopped ahead of us and brought her head high up clear of the water, right in front of us. The back of her head was highlighted by the sun; the bivalve blowhole was open to the fresh incoming air, the dark intricate mottling patterns on her skin glistened, and the white line of the bottom jaw could be seen from above. She may have been able to see us behind her, since a whale's eyes are set quite a long way back on each side, but the reason for this sudden "high head up" was unclear. She was probably just playing tag with our small panga. Without a ripple, the calf relaxed her position and sank beneath the waves.

In many of the encounters that I have experienced, it seems that there comes a time when both parties realize that the moment has passed, and the encounter is over. The cow surfaced next to her calf. The change of mood was clear. As they began to swim away, they paid no attention to our panga. Their movements were determined; their curiosity was settled. We were of no further interest. It was time to leave the whales alone to do what whales do when humans are not observing.

It was about noon when we returned to the *Don José*. To say that we were elated by what we had witnessed on our first day would be an understatement. When close to nonhuman animals, it is difficult not to apply human emotions and perceptions to those beings, because they are the methods by which we interpret the world. I cannot prove that others feel the same way as I do about things external to myself, but I can conclude that because I am aware of something, then other people must also be aware. Whether nonhuman animals are sentient, whether they have the power of sense perception or sensation, whether they are conscious, is still hotly debated. A number of studies, particularly with other primates, suggest that animals are very perceptive about things external to themselves, although in some cases they do not appear to know what it is that they know. In other words, they are unable to apply their knowledge to new situations, and do not attribute their own thoughts to other members of their species.

It is difficult to determine whether whales, such as the gray whale, are sentient in the way that we are. Each species has evolved to fit a certain niche, and is supremely adapted to survival in that environment. The ability of an animal to survive is a function of its awareness in that domain. Thus the whale is aware of its world and is undoubtedly curious about anything that enters it. Whether they are able to pass on information to other individuals or to learn from experience is uncertain, although anecdotal tales suggest that to place arbitrary limits on the whales' sentient ability reflects more on our perceptions than on theirs. The marine world is so different from our own—three-dimensional rather than two-, auditory rather than visual—that we are constrained in our ability to gather information about the interactions of marine species. We know so little, so we cannot exclude any possibility.

A number of psychologists have examined thought processes, and our own ability to interpret relationships. One thought-provoking idea was espoused by the late Gregory Bateson. Bateson, known for his controversial views on Larmarckian evolution and the link between mental and physical processes, considered the thought processes of schizophrenics. When asked to establish relationships between objects or living things, schizophrenics are unable to do so. There are two syllogisms that are useful in evaluating perceptions and the way that we categorize different things and events. The first is known as Barbara, and reads:

> Men die,
> Socrates is a man,
> Socrates will die.

The other is commonly (or irreverently) known as "syllogism in grass," and reads:

Grass dies.
Men die.
Men are grass.

As Bateson pointed out, "syllogism in grass" is also the way that poets and schizophrenics think, and the way that Bateson himself saw the world. The difference between the two syllogisms is more than simple semantics. The correct term for "syllogism in grass" is *affirming the consequent*. Some may use the term *metaphor* more easily.

The Barbara syllogism identifies Socrates as a member of a class, and what befalls members of that class will ultimately befall Socrates. On the other hand, the grass syllogism is concerned with predicates, that is, with the part of the sentence or clause that contains the verbal group. It is the verbal group that indicates the occurrence or performance of an action, or the existence of a state or condition. In other words, under "syllogism in grass," the state or condition of the grass is translated to other living things. What it is, so we are. What befalls it will befall us. In Bateson's words, "That which dies is equal to that other thing which dies."

Bateson's view was that since the Barbara syllogism requires subjects, it cannot be applied to the biological world until the evolution of language and the separation of subjects from predicates, an occurrence that took place at most several hundred thousand years ago. Bateson therefore suggests that until that time, there were only syllogisms in grass.

We cannot assume that other animals are excluded from the class that we have determined for ourselves. By looking beyond the semantics, we can see that when we remove the barriers that we are taught early in life, about our place in the order of things and our relationships with others, we can reconsider the true relationships between different life forms. "Syllogism in grass" simply takes this relationship to its ultimate conclusion.

It is time that we stopped looking at the differences between creatures and began to look in greater depth at the similarities. Perhaps the schizophrenic and the poet are able to see clearly what years of anthropocentric conditioning have driven from our own minds. Perhaps their perception of the world is more accurate. After all, we are alive, and we think; it is truly a liberty to suggest that those factors are precluded from other living things just because we possess them. We are still restricted by a narrow creationist viewpoint that retains humankind as the apex of life. The ability to think and evaluate is an evolutionary progression, but we should never forget that evolution is blind and has no end product. We may feel safer excluding the possibility of other organisms thinking and feeling in the way that we do, or in some other way for that matter, but that does not make it so.

The whales that we had watched during the morning were keenly aware of our presence. They knew how to keep pace with the panga, to stay just out of arm's reach. They knew that we did not pose a threat, and they treated us accordingly. They were curious and playful. The calf was highly observant of the world around her, us included. But in the end they satisfied their curiosity and left us with a feeling that we had been in the presence of animals that did "know" what they knew—that probably knew more than we give them credit for.

Aboard the *Don José* we could only gaze back into the lagoon and watch the blows approach and disappear as the whales traveled and interacted out of sight, beyond our perception, beyond our ability to understand. Our first entry into the bay had heralded contact that before this moment had been in the domain of dreams. How do you even attempt to relate how that feels? It is as if you become privileged to see what others cannot, to witness lives that exist regardless, or in spite, of our interference. It is humbling in this anthropocentric world to be faced with such a fact. Perhaps if we can begin to think along those lines, realize that other animals are not commodities to be used and sold to the highest bidder, that animals have lives that do not revolve around our own, that they live and die in their own world—then we may begin to understand what it is to be nonhuman. And what it is to *be* human.

After reliving the morning's events over lunch, we returned to the pangas and prepared to go ashore. The sun was now high, and the heat was only mildly ameliorated by the soft coastal breeze. The pangas took us to a small embayment within the larger bay complex. As we stepped onto the beach, we felt the sand envelop our feet. Hot sand, almost scorching, drifted between toes as we sank up to our ankles in the fine grains of this silica shore.

The dune-desert environment is a harsh one; some may even call it hostile. To us, maybe. But to say that the environment is harsh when speaking of the animals that inhabit the area is to misunderstand the evolutionary process. An environment is harsh only to the poorly adapted, and they do not survive. In classic evolutionary terms, desert evolution and adaptation is truly the survival of the fittest. The result is species supremely adapted to this land. The sand was molded into forms and shapes that would befit a gallery in Soho—the grand artistic designs of nature: sculpted rocks, shadows on sand ripples, the sun beating down on weathered sticks and bleached driftwood. The surf gently shaped the ephemeral shoreline—a straight beach, now curving, now a bay or an inlet. Ever changing, and ever remaining the same. Over time and over centuries, the cycles of life are shaped by the cycles of the lifeless. The physical shapes the biological. Evolution is captured before our eyes.

We drifted along the beach, our minds and thoughts blown in different directions, just as the tiniest grains of sand are blown through time. We looked at the intricacies before us, the smallest of patterns in the sand—the tiny marks of bombardier beetles scuttling along the beach, the line of a side-blotched lizard's tail left imprinted as the animal vanished with a flurry. And in the distance, beyond the dunes, the blow of the desert whale. Imagine the scene one hundred or more years ago, standing on the dunes, out of sight of the bay, and still able to see the plume of the whale punctuate the horizon. The smallest and the largest of this desert land beheld in a single moment.

We followed the line of a small channel cutting into the dune system. The water, no more than fifteen centimeters deep, felt warm and soothing as we waded in the shallows. The sun reflected starbursts off the surface and created dappled patterns on the sand below.

Sea hares dotted the area. Gelatinous creatures, these mollusks are marine snails in the same class, Gastropoda, as terrestrial snails and slugs. Sea hares, Aplysiidae, are the only members of the order Aplysiomorpha. The species before us was predominantly speckled brown, with lime-green markings about the head and flanks. It was undoubtedly sluglike in appearance, and moved slowly across the substrate. The animal was fairly large, as we could see when we rescued one that had strayed into a drying pool of water and was in danger of fatal desiccation. To hold it in the palm of your hand is to feel as though the animal will disintegrate and flow between your fingers, like some amoebic being that re-forms itself from fragments and molds itself to new life.

The statistics associated with the sea hare are remarkable. This creature can produce more than twenty million eggs at one time. Every individual creates the potential for twenty million more lives at each mating. Furthermore, the sea hare is a hermaphrodite, both male and female in the same gelatinous mold. Lines of mating sea hares have been seen, with each animal simultaneously fertilizing and being fertilized—a chain of procreation in the sea that spawned life on Earth. If a mate is lacking, the animal is even able to fertilize itself.

It is by looking at creatures such as the sea hare that it is possible to gain a true appreciation of the simplicity and wonder of evolution, and the geniuses who elucidated its message: Charles Darwin and Alfred Russel Wallace. Independently these two men hypothesized a process that could explain the diversity and adaptation that they encountered around the world. They laid the bedrock of evolutionary biology that today shapes the way we perceive the natural world, and our place in it. They developed the theory on the origin of species through natural selection. They explain why the world is not knee deep in sea hares.

Evolutionary theory holds that every individual is attempting to maximize its reproductive success. The goal, if that word can be used in this context, is to perpetuate your genes—the genetic make-up that makes you what you are, or our sea hare what it is. If you do not succeed in mating successfully, and ensuring that some of your offspring survive to adulthood and procreate themselves, then your genes will go no further than your generation, and you will be the last of your kind.

The sea hare is known as an r-selected animal. Ecologists generally recognize two reproductive strategies, r-selected and k-selected. "R" strategists produce literally millions of offspring. These offspring are highly vulnerable, and the production of vast numbers ensures that even if 99.9 percent are lost through predation or as a result of harsh environmental conditions, some at least will reach adulthood. The strategy is to swamp the environment with young, in the knowledge that some will slip through the survival net. In contrast, a k-selected animal produces only few offspring, perhaps one at a time, like the gray whale, and expends a great deal of energy and time on that single offspring to ensure its survival. Both strategies fit the evolutionary requirement; only the fittest survive to reproduce, while the others blend into the food chain to support other organisms in their quest for evolutionary success. For the sea hare the most vulnerable time is when the young are part of the mass of zooplankton in the waters, while the whale faces relatively even threats throughout its life.

In simple terms, Darwin noted that living organisms, such as our sea hare, have the potential to increase at an accelerating rate, but it is also apparent that the numbers of a particular species remain remarkably constant. Therefore, hypothesized Darwin, there must be a "struggle for existence" between those organisms for the finite resources that they all require to survive. Since all organisms differ from each other in some way, not all are equally adept at gaining access to those resources; some will be better than others. So, through competition, it is the best-adapted organisms that will gain access to those finite resources and breed, thus passing on their genes to future generations. Survival of the fittest, the best-adapted, removes the poorly adapted, and results in the natural selection of individual characteristics, genes, that convey the highest reproductive success rate.

Evolution is not static, nor does it have an endpoint or direction. Those species that exist today have adapted to the stresses of the environment in their own genetic past. As the environment changes, evolution continues to remove the poorly adapted and streamline the genetic base, forming new species that are capable of survival under the existing conditions. Extinction is a natural process, whereby the poorly adapted organisms are replaced by others better adapted to those conditions. It is natural variation supplemented by genetic mutations within a species that provides the raw material for evolution to act upon.

In his text *On the Origin of Species,* first published in 1859, Charles Darwin waxed lyrical on the evolutionary theme: "So it is that the great Tree of Life fills with its dead and broken branches the crust of the earth, and covers the surface with its ever-branching and beautiful ramifications." In such eloquent terms we were given insight into the process that shaped, and continues to shape, the lives that we witness around us—the sea hare, the whale, and fellow whale-watchers. We can only guess at the direction that evolution will take us in the future.

We left our sea hare to its watery domain and continued procreation, and scaled some of the dunes behind us, sinking calf-deep in silky sand. From the top of the sand dune we could survey the mangrove complex bordering the far side of the inlet.

In the distance, far above our heads, we could make out the form of an osprey flying toward us. The plumage of the bird was distinctive: dark brown back and wings, white underbelly, and a prominent dark eye strip. As the bird flew overhead, the sun glinted off the scales of a fish tightly clasped in its talons. We could almost hear the wind whisper around the feathers. A short distance away the wing beats slowed, then stopped, and the bird glided down, an occasional beat steadying its descent. The osprey is one of those birds whose description you feel should be punctuated with adjectives such as *noble, powerful,* and *agile*—the fish eagle with the deadly touch.

We elected to trek across the sands to see if the bird was nesting nearby. Walking up and down sand dunes is a tiring business. The steep face of each dune crumbles and cascades with each step. Feet and sneakers sink into suffocating grains that seem to grasp the limb and restrain it. It took far longer than anticipated to reach the spot where the eagle had landed. And even then, well, all dunes look very much alike. We milled around for a short while, trying to decide if indeed this was the place. There was no sign of the bird or its fish, simply a dune and a scattering of plants casting linear slivers of shade. Tired under the sun, we rested there among the dunes, trying to take advantage of what meager shade was offered by the sloping angles of the dunes, and failing.

How to take it all in. To let the heat and the sensation of the place become what you are. To experience the desert and its life for what it really is. To feel the remoteness and the tenacity of the life around you. To live the uncertainty and the vulnerability. To feel Baja—as the people once did, and people did live here.

Baja has a history in its past peoples. They found the desert land and survived. They no longer live here, but there are signs and memories of their existence in the plants and animals. Few signs remain of their passing—shell middens on beaches, occasional cave paintings, and simple tools made from granite chips and flakes. The native population crashed when Western missionaries and Spanish conquistadors arrived in the region. When the Jesuit missionaries came here at the end of the seventeenth century, some 50,000 Indians remained, already reduced by disease spread by the conquerors. When the Jesuits left seventy years later, there were only 10,000 Indians, and by the early nineteenth century they had all but disappeared, fallen to disease and intolerance.

As we crossed the dunes, infrequent plants were scattered among the depressions. These plants were the lifeblood of the Pericu Indians. Two of the pitaya cactus species were particularly important to their culture and survival: pitaya dulce and pitaya agria.

The pitaya dulce, which translates to "sweet pitaya" but in English is known as the organ pipe cactus, stands up to eight meters tall and is made up of numerous heavily ribbed vertical trunks. This pitaya produces a sweet, watermelon-colored, spiny fruit that grows to about the size of a tennis ball. The fruits ripen in late summer and autumn and were prized by the natives. They used a cardon rib with a hook to harvest them, and the harvest was so widespread and so intense that missionaries noted that only during this time was hunger abated. It was a joyful time when different tribes came together to feast, trade, and marry.

Missionaries who came to the region saw the pitaya harvest and the attendant festivities as profanities and did their best to discourage the practices. Particularly aberrant to the outsiders was the so-called "second harvest." During this roughly two-month period of plenty, the natives would defecate at one particular spot. Later they would gather their dried feces to collect the small black pitaya seeds that had passed through their intestinal tracts undigested. The Indians ground these seeds into a paste that was eaten as a pozole.

This "second harvest" gave the people a nutritious boost long after the first harvest had been exhausted. In such ways the desert people were able to survive conditions that would kill the less versatile and the less adaptable.

The second staple cactus was pitaya agria, or sour pitaya. This cactus grows into an impenetrable mass of stems and thorns that thread around each other like tendrils, a pattern of growth that gives the plant its other name: gamboling cactus. The fruit of this plant was also favored by the natives. It has slightly narcotic properties and was crushed and thrown into the water to stupefy fish.

We left these desert thorns and returned to the inlet where there were cool waters to wade in and sprinkle over taut, dry skin. The mangroves on the other side of the water were alive with color and sound. Birds darted around the lush green vegetation, their colorful plumage and shrill tunes adding to the image of an oasis of life in the desert. Back among the dunes, the only colors to oppose the golden hue of the sand were the varying green shades of the cacti—enveloped in thorns and daggers that decry the harshness of this land as the plant hides and protects the moisture it holds within. Here in the mangroves, we could behold the delicate steps of long-legged aviators—the white ibis, dowitchers, wandering tattlers, greater yellowlegs, willet, plovers and sandpipers, great blue heron, and tiny snowy egret. And surveying the scene from on high, the magnificent frigatebird and osprey. A spiraling array of bird life lifts the mind and soul to new heights, lets you imagine what it would be like to soar on upcurrents and dive into the waters' depths, to catch a fish with razor talons, or simply to see through a bird's eyes. We all need to consider the impossible, because when we realize that we will never soar, then it becomes even more vital that we protect those who can. Without them, we cannot even imagine.

It was almost four when we finally returned to the *Don José.* The sun sets quickly in this part of the world, and we knew that we had less than two hours of good whale-watching left before the sun would sink into the bay and douse the flames of the desert. Roughly half of the ship's complement elected to stay on board, while the remainder, myself included, made the crossing from deck to panga once again, and pushed off into the bay.

The two pangas separated as we left our mooring, and we each began our search for whales. Hector continually scanned the water, sunglasses shielding his eyes. He directed the panga with ease, obviously seeing more than we were able to, and using his years of experience to supplement visual clues with intuition. We motored for ten minutes or so, catching only brief glimpses of whale spouts in the distance. Hector cut the motor and let the engine turn over gently. We drifted slightly in the light breeze, just listening to the sounds around us: the teasing lap of water against the panga, the cries of distant birds, and the occasional whoosh of an exhalation carried in the wind. Hands fingered the water, and we savored the tranquil moment.

Looking back, I am still not sure where they came from. Hector must have seen them in front of us, under the water. But until they surfaced, the rest of us were blind to their presence. We had been stationary for about five minutes when they came up underneath us—a gray whale mother and calf. Next to us, touching us, and letting us touch them.

I always wonder what the whales are doing when we cannot see them. Many people have a view of whales propagated by the sight of vast skeletons or models hung from the ceilings of museum galleries, or the mental picture of stranded behemoths on a beach, their form distorted by unyielding gravity. The first whale that I ever saw as a child was suspended from the ceiling of the British Museum of Natural History, a mighty blue whale of plastic and fiberglass—a lifeless, static embodiment of leviathan. It was enough to enthrall me. But to appreciate the whale, one must see the animal in its three-dimensional habitat, flowing, flying, in an all-embracing, all-supporting medium. Gray whales may not be the most streamlined or graceful of the great whales, but underwater they glide and turn, stand on heads or tails, and roll and twist, weightless in their own world. In water their bulk is no constraint. They are not limited as were the reptilian dinosaurs on land. In the ocean, leviathans rule.

Perhaps the whales had been lying in the deep, and as they turned upward they saw our silhouette in the sun. Out of curiosity they decided to approach. They could just as easily have faded into the bay and surfaced out of sight or far in the distance. We would never have known that two animals weighing perhaps 30,000 kilograms between them had been so close.

There were six of us in the panga, each reaching out to touch a whale more than twice the length of our vessel. They nuzzled the boat. The calf in particular seemed intrigued by the Yamaha engine. He would approach the panga from the stern and hang motionless inches from the safely enclosed prop, mesmerized by the gentle emission of sounds close to the whale's own frequencies.

The encounter was unyielding. Cow and calf jostled each other to approach our craft. And those in the panga bumped and jostled each other as we all tried to reach out and touch these curious creatures. What is it like to touch a whale? The intensity of the moment is such that it is an event I have to consider in hindsight. On subsequent trips I have tried to control my thoughts, to examine the feelings and sensations as they occur. But as soon as an encounter begins, control is lost and you become consumed in the moment. You are touching a whale. Your outstretched hand, backed by a body and frame adapted to a terrestrial existence, is making physical contact with a thirteen-meter, 25,000-kilogram marine mammal whose ancestors took to the seas when your own pre-primate antecedents were scurrying around on the forest floor eating insects. As the calf surfaces next to the panga and your hand runs along his back, rubs the head and rostrum, and you stare into the eye that beholds everything that is happening, you feel a link that goes beyond evolutionary kinship. The skin feels like an inflated wetsuit, slightly rubbery, soft and pliant. You feel the sensation of a living animal beneath your fingers, and the calf seems equally aware of your presence. He bumps against the side of the boat as you strain to touch. You rub his rostrum, and the calf seems to push up toward you, encouraging your actions. You rub harder, and the calf cavorts like a playful puppy—a five-meter, 1,000-kilogram puppy. If you relax your rubbing or softly caress the whale, he slowly moves away to find someone less cautious in expressing affection. The harder you rub, the longer he'll stay.

The encounter is a wet one. The whales bounce around the panga, sending small waves and spray over the gunnels. As you reach out to touch, the boat rocks up and down, its movements exaggerated by the closeness of the whales, and more water flows into the craft. As the whales pass underneath, hands follow, delving into the water. Hands, elbows, up to your shoulders in warm Baja water, with fingertips on whale.

Hector signaled to the other panga that we had friendlies by waving one of the oars above his head. The second boat responded in kind, and began to motor in our direction. In moments they were by our side. Mason yelled over, "Did you touch a whale?" The cheer that went up from our vessel was all the affirmation required.

The whales' curiosity seemed only to increase with the new addition to their world. The rest of the encounter (which probably lasted ninety minutes) involved the whales moving from one panga to the other, playing with both, splitting their time equally between the craft.

On occasion both animals sat up in the water, raising their heads. This was the same spy-hopping or high-head-up maneuver that we had seen from the other calf that morning. But these whales more usually pushed only the tips of their rostrums above the water. When the calf tried this maneuver, the sun glistened and reflected off the tiny dimples surrounding each hair follicle, and the slightly crossed upper and lower jaw made the youngster look almost quizzical.

The hairs on the gray whale are undoubtedly important for a bottom-feeding animal, providing vital sensory data on the bottom and the animals' position. The sensitivity of the hairs on the whales' rostrums may also explain why they are so keen to present them for physical contact.

Gray whales have an assortment of parasitic attachments that adorn their skin. The cow before us was well covered with encrustations of barnacles and whale lice, and the smooth, dark-skinned calf would soon take on the mottled, light gray appearance of his dam. Whales show a similar type of predisposition to either left or right as humans, so just as we may be left- or right-handed, so whales are left- or right-"baleened." When bottom feeding, the whales consistently favor either their left or right side for rolling onto before taking a bite out of the mud bottom. This right- or left-"handed" action means that barnacles tend to become dislodged from whichever side the animal rolls onto. With most animals, then, the distribution of barnacles on either side of the head is different—one side having significantly fewer attachments than the other. Just like humans, the majority of whales appear to be "right-handed."

As the whales continued to circle our pangas, playing with outstretched hands, Mason pointed out the circular barnacle scars on the cow's paddle-like flippers, and when close we were able to stare in wonder at the profusion of cyamids, or whale lice, that cluster around barnacles and lesions on the whales' skin.

Whale lice are small, pinkish crustaceans. Three species are commonly found on the gray whale: *Cyamus ceti, C. kessleri,* and *C. scammoni.* Of these three species, two are found only on the gray whale, and for all the parasites, including the barnacles, the whale is their world; when the whale dies, so do they. Evolution has resulted in parallel paths for these creatures. The longevity of the whale and the reproductive fecundity of the parasites have resulted in the evolution of species-specific, and in rarer cases individual-specific, parasites. The barnacle *Cryptolepas rhachianecti* is also found only on the gray whale.

The lice are formidable-looking parasites and have vicious gripping mandibles that can inflict severe bites on their host. They feed on the living whale, but probably serve a useful function in cleaning wounds and lesions of decaying tissue, thus preventing infection. However, the sight of a mass of lice collected around barnacles with mandibles clasped to whale flesh is still uncomfortable. Given the sensitivity that the whales seem to show to the slightest human touch, it is startling to imagine what sensation the barnacles and lice create. Perhaps breaching to remove parasites is not quite so unlikely a theory when you remember that caribou stampede to avoid mosquitoes, and people react in similar fashion if plagued by midges, mosquitoes, or noseeums.

The young calf continued to show the most interest in us. The cow allowed herself to be touched, but on the whole she was more distant around the boats, often positioning herself midway between the pangas as the calf went from one to the other. It was as though the cow were simply overseeing the process, keeping an eye on how things were going, but letting her calf approach us as close as he wanted. We were always careful not to get between mother and young, but she never showed any obvious anxiety no matter how close we were to her offspring.

The calf would blow bubbles underwater next to the panga; oftentimes it seemed that he was doing his best to soak us when he finally surfaced to blow. Too often for simple coincidence, a perfect camera shot was ruined by the ejection of warm whale breath and atomized water droplets at 112 kilometers an hour seconds before the shutter was clicked. It became a running joke in our panga over who would be next to sample "whale snot." Perhaps it is a reflection on the people in our vessel that to be thus doused was taken as a matter of pride; after all, how many people can state that they have been on the receiving end of an exhaling whale?

In the *Log from the Sea of Cortez,* John Steinbeck, in one of his only references to whales in the book, wrote: "A school of whales went by, one of them so close that the spray from his blow-hole came over our deck. There is nothing so evil-smelling as a whale anyway, and a whale's breath is frightfully sickening. It smells of complete decay." Surely a damning indictment of cetacean oral hygiene. Ancient mariners believed that just the smell of a whale's breath was fatal, and Steinbeck's colorful words certainly suggest that he shared that view. Whale breath certainly has a fishy taint to it, particularly if the whale has been feeding, but nothing so strong that it would turn the stomach of a dedicated whale-watcher.

The young calf rolled over onto one side. There was an immense dark shadow beneath—the cow was holding him up. The calf was partly raised out of the water on his mother's back, and the length of the animal cleared the surface. Water swirled around his head, and his dimples reflected sunlight. The calf's eye watched us intently, moving to take a long look at each of us. The moment was charged: eye-to-eye contact with a leviathan.

Loren Eiseley, anthropologist and naturalist, wrote in *The Unexpected Universe:*

> It is possible that for the soul to come to its true self it needs the help and recognition of the [animal]. It craves that empathy clinging between man and beast, that nagging shadow of remembrance which, try as we may to deny it, asserts our unity with life and does more. Paradoxically, it establishes, in the end, our own humanity. One does not meet oneself until one catches the reflection from an eye other than human.

For the first time, I looked into the eye of a whale and saw myself reflected. That moment more than any other, more than the actual physical contact, was the pivotal moment of the trip—the rare chance to gaze into the eye of another animal and perhaps get an idea of what it is that they see in us. Our humanity hangs on tenuous threads. Our own history shows that we are capable of great atrocities against our own kind, let alone against the nonhuman. But out here in a small boat with nothing between us, all things are equal.

Scammon told of whalers taking calves and using them to gain a shot at the mother:

> Sometimes the calf is fastened to instead of the cow. In such instances the mother may . . . stav[e] the boats. . . . One instance occurred in Magdalena Lagoon, in 1857, where, after several boats had been staved, they being near the beach, the men in those remaining afloat managed to pick up their swimming comrade, and in the meantime, to run the line to the shore, hauling the calf into as shallow water as would float the dam, she keeping near her troubled young one, giving the gunner a good chance for a shot with his bomb-gun from the beach.

But now there was only trust, the mother raising up her youngster to be greeted with outstretched arms from conspecifics in mind. This lagoon was a far cry from the fiberglass whales in the musty museums of my childhood. Here there were no artificial lights or colors, no strings. And here the eyes of whales moved and reflected images of people. To touch a whale was to feel a leviathan tremble at your fingertips, to feel the warm wash of water across a dappled back, and the exhalation of moist air from deep within upon your face. This was Baja.

The night was spent dreaming fitfully of whales. Swimming through turquoise waters, legs fused into flukes and arms molded to flippers. Flying among whales, breaking the water's surface to breathe clean, fresh air into thirsty lungs. Dreams punctuated by whales exhaling near the ship, adding loose reality to synaptic images. In Buddhist philosophy it is said that when you dream, you are surprised by your dream, its content and intensity, but that the dream is you. You are both subject and object, you are yourself and you are the dream. In Baja when in the awakened state, you feel as though the dream continues, that the world around you is part of you and apart from you. Subject, object, observer, and participant. Om.

In the morning we entered the pangas as the dawn light filtered through the high cirrus clouds. The horizon was tinged pink, and as we neared the mangrove swamp, the rising sun lit up the backdrop as though a thousand forest fires were contained within. The air was cool and still. Nothing stirred. The only sound as we entered the mangrove channels was the gentle hum of the outboards. The water was unbelievably calm. To simply compare the surface to a mirror is to ignore the depth of the image before us. The channels reflected the deep azure of the sky to perfection, and holding the seams of the scene together were the mangroves themselves—double images joined at the roots. Even the pangas were mirrored, creating a double-edged world. The scarcity of color in this environment was solved in part by the doubling effect of the reflection; suddenly all around us looked green. Blue and green and yellow and brown and yellow and green and blue.

As we motored through this oasis at the fringes of the lagoon, we passed close to a low exposed cliff face. The red sandstone was painted in desert hues and topped by gamboling cactus. The harsh call of a loggerhead shrike cut the silence. Ripples in the channel created by our wake formed a surreal image of color and shapes in the shallows, magnifying and distorting reflected images. This was natural artistry.

Approaching the face of the mangroves, you are struck by the impenetrable thicket of dense growth. It was almost impossible to tell where real merged into reflection. The thicket was the deepest of greens, dark and inaccessible. The occasional bird could be seen darting among the canopy, and it could be drawn into the open with a gentle "pish, pish, pish." The small yellow bird would fly directly upward from its perch to look in the direction of the noise, then fly back into the thicket, becoming visible only in motion, darting between waxy leaves. The mangrove warbler used to be classified as a distinct species, but is now known simply as *Dendroica petechia,* the common yellow warbler.

The mangroves' dense root system extends both above and below water level, providing vital shelter for marine and land animals that share the swamp. At the base of the mangroves we watched a small green-backed heron. The bird sported a greenish-black cap, chestnut brown neck and breast, and gray-blue wings. With long yellow legs the squat heron picked its way between stems and roots, eyes concentrated on the water searching for the telltale shadows of fish.

Our eyes followed those of the heron into the dark silty waters below. The water was filled with floating organic particles, and the sediment was heavily covered with twigs, leaves, and detritus. The decomposition of this material creates an organic soup that flows through the swamp. This rich nutrient base feeds the diversity of fish and invertebrate life found in its midst. The prolific mangrove ecosystem provides habitat for more than 2,000 species of fish, invertebrates, and epiphytic plants, and both directly and indirectly supports coastal and open-ocean fisheries around the world.

As we motored through the silt-laden water, schools of fish flashed in the sunlight as they detoured around our vessel. The narrow mangrove channels broadened to an expanse of open water, and a great blue heron stood out ahead of us. The large gray-blue bird with a distinctive yellow bill and streaks of black down its throat watched us closely, and only when we got within six meters did the bird languidly take to the air, showing off black primaries trimming broad wings. The "v"-shaped flight of the heron was matched in reflection.

From high in the mangrove canopy, mourning doves called out in a sorrowful voice. Beyond them the cirrus clouds swirled in high-altitude wind currents, and the moon became increasingly obscured as the sun rose higher and higher in the sky. Belted kingfishers dressed in gray-blue plumage and punk-like crests darted by our boats, and northern pintails, wigeons, and ruddy ducks began to emerge from the mangroves.

As we began to motor back into Bahia Magdalena proper, a white ibis was highlighted among the green. In full breeding plumage, the bird had pure white plumes and red face and legs framed by lush green. We re-entered the bay and passed a sandbank at the neck of the swamp. Brown pelicans and double-crested cormorants were massed together on the shoreline. Cormorants with outstretched wings had the appearance of priests giving benediction, while the pelicans stared nonchalantly at our passage. We had returned to the true desert environ. Sand dunes now eclipsed our view, rather than mangroves, and the color combination returned to gold, brown, and blue.

As we motored toward the *Don José,* we could see a shape in the water ahead. There were no discerning features from the object, and no disturbance in the calm water, only a long gray countenance. It was a gray whale in characteristic "logging" position. The whale was simply resting at the surface with its blowhole above the water. Whales are voluntary breathers. Unlike humans, all cetaceans have to be conscious to breathe. If they were to go into a deep sleep, they would suffocate, as they would if knocked unconscious. This means that whales do not sleep in the way that we recognize. They must always be awake enough to "remember" to breathe. We steered clear of the animal and returned to breakfast, although we were already full on the sights and sounds of this tropical paradise.

The lagoon was spread out before us like a carpet, fluid with the ebb and flow of life cycles cradled in its midst. The panga buoyed us along at water level. Whale-watching has a certain image in people's minds. But just consider what it is that you see first, and best, when traveling behind whales in a small craft—the blowhole. Staring down the nostrils of a whale may not have the romantic vision of staring into its eye, but whale-watchers will take what they can get. I can certainly vouch for the fact that I have looked into far more whale nostrils than whale eyes!

We followed animal after animal, watching heart-shaped exhalations hang in the morning air. The *Don José* was at anchor on the horizon. Whales breached in the distance, punctuating the silence with pistol shots of tonnage hitting water. As whales dove close to the panga, they lifted broad tail flukes clear of the water. The trailing edges of these flukes were often scratched and abraded. On a number of individuals it was possible to see clear white striations—the mark of orca. To witness the concerted, organized attack on a great whale by a pod of orca must surely be one of the most awesome natural events still to be seen in the world's oceans.

As the whales continued their dives the flukes disappeared, leaving a swirl-ing slick of smooth water known as the "footprint" or "flukeprint." This flukeprint is created by the vortices set up by the upthrust of the flukes, and when the whale is shallow-swimming these flukeprints appear on the water's surface as indications of where the whale was, rather than where it is now. By carefully judging the whales' swimming speed and watching for the appearance of flukeprints, it is possible to prepare for a whale before it surfaces—a trick that whalers rapidly learned in the lagoons of bygone years.

All cetaceans leave flukeprints; the larger the whale, the larger the flukeprint, and vice versa. For many smaller cetaceans, such as the dolphins, the flukeprint is too small and too fleeting to be visible except under very calm conditions. In whaling times the flukeprint was believed to be the result of whale oils—liter-ally a mini oil slick—and this continued to be taken as dogma until scientists took samples of the flukeprint area and discovered that the "slick" was simply seawater.

At length we began to follow a cow-calf pair, memories of the previous day's encounter refusing to abate. Both animals were boisterous. They circled our panga at a distance, then began to approach closer and closer with each pass. They swam under our bow, swirling water around the boat. We were still mo-toring slowly and the calf began to race ahead, almost as if playing tag with our small craft. The young animal cleared the water in front of us in half-breaches, once, twice, three times, four. At times the half-breach was a true side sweep of the animal's body across the surface of the water, while at others the exuberance was more akin to a high head up that slowly slipped sideways. The calf was sur-rounded by swirling currents of her own making—flukeprints and eddies creating patterns on the calm waters of the bay. After the fourth half-breach the calf disappeared. The cow was also out of sight. We had been so mesmerized by the calf's actions that we had lost track of her dam.

Within seconds the calf breached, full, within fifteen meters of our vessel. I was sitting square in the middle of the panga so that the breach was directly in front of me. The calf filled the camera frame, a silver-gray arc of motion reflected in a lagoon of astonishing blue. The breach seemed to last for the longest time, and I have relived the moment often as I gaze at the best breaching gray whale photograph that I have ever taken. The dappling gray coloration of the calf, the flow of water off flippers and flanks, the line of the head, and the power of the movement generated by this six-meter animal are imprinted in my memory just as the colors and motion were captured permanently by Kodachrome.

As the calf powered back into the water, she turned and headed straight toward the panga. We were ready for another close encounter; cameras were stowed and hands outstretched. The calf raced over, creating a small wake off her own "bow." She was probably within two meters of us when we lost our footing. The panga rolled dramatically and we clutched at the sides to regain our balance. The thirteen-meter cow was right next to the boat; she had not touched our craft but had rolled next to us, generating a wave action that knocked us back and sent her calf swimming 180 degrees in the opposite direction. With that accomplished, the cow sank beneath us and resurfaced fifty meters away with her calf. It is quite a ride to feel the force of a full-grown whale, especially when you realize that the force was so controlled. And it is sobering to know that with one blow from a tail fluke or flipper, we could have ended up in the water. Just imagine the ride that devilfish gave the whalers.

Despite the cow's actions, no one in the panga felt that we were ever in any danger. I have never felt threatened when close to whales. They always seem so aware of our presence, and the encounter is so much a matter of their choice that potentially conflicting episodes are avoided simply by the whale sinking beneath the boat and resurfacing at some distance—when that happens, the encounter is over and there is no pursuit. I have been in skiffs when whales lifted us clear of the water on their backs and then lowered us down, as if to check how much we weighed, and I have been on boats when whales came over to rub themselves along our hull. I have also seen a cow leave a calf with one skiff, swim over to another vessel that was flouting the etiquette rules of whale-watching, and soak them with one well-aimed tail slap before going back to the first skiff to retrieve her calf and leave. Apparently sometimes even whales get annoyed at tourists.

Late afternoon found us ashore again, among dunes and cacti and the silhouettes of islands and barriers in the distance. We hiked leisurely across the sandbars that separated the Pacific Ocean from the protected waters of the bay. The light was incredibly diffuse, so that peaks and islands on the horizon merged and blended into the soft clouds above and the silky gray texture of the waters at their feet. The light cloud cover also reduced the intensity of the desert sun. Members of our group jogged along the beach, taking full advantage of the expanse to stretch legs and minds confined to a twenty-seven-meter ship.

The silica gold beach was dotted with shells and debris that may have drifted halfway round the world. In places we found scallop shells piled high—relics from days long gone when local Indians used these sandbars and beaches to gather shellfish. Clam shells half covered by sand and set among undulating "sand waves" provided a natural artistic commentary. Everything around us was a sculpture brushed and painted by the hand of sand, sea, and air.

Bombardier beetles and side-blotched lizards scurried ahead of us, dodging attempts to corral them for photographs. The small, rotund black beetles with abdomens raised in defense raced off to the concealing cover of cactus thickets, leaving tiny paired footprints in neat tracks across the sand—marks so ephemeral that the slightest breeze washed them from sight.

A greater yellowlegs picked its way along the shoreline, probing the mud and sand for invertebrates. The contents of an open scallop shell gently washed by dying waves were being quietly devoured by small green whelks in a captivatingly macabre scene. Whelks from a wide area around the shell were drawn to the feast, the tiny mollusks moving remarkably fast across the silt, and hoisting their calcareous enclosed bodies into the larger shell of the less fortunate scallop.

Farther down the beach we found the remnants of the larger marine animal that had drawn us to this place. A number of gray whale vertebrae littered the sand. The whale bone was covered by barnacles and other parasitic growths. It crumbled at a touch, the porosity of the bone giving it no lasting strength. Whale bones are spongy in texture, and in living animals the cavities are filled with oil. To see such a detached bone, out of the context of the whole animal, leaves one with a strange sensation. From our position on the beach looking back into the bay, we could occasionally see blows from living whales, and here in front of us were the remains of one of those leviathans. It is like looking at a human femur in biology class and trying to imagine the person it came from. An impossible task.

To see any animal in death, whether whole or in part, it is difficult to get a sense of the real animal. This was further reinforced on our slender barrier beach with the discovery of a bottlenose dolphin skull. The dolphin skull is telescoped to support the evident "beak" that the bottlenose sports. To hold the skull in your hands, feel the line of the jaw, the points of the teeth, and the rim of the blowhole, and to cradle in your hands the body of the skull that once contained a 1,500-gram brain—perhaps then we can consider what the animal was like in life.

We have all witnessed the antics of dolphins, either in the wild, in aquariums, or on television. These animals are the embodiment of grace, playfulness, and strength. To see the dolphin's skull, which is so light and delicate, so sculptured, one cannot help wondering what thoughts it once enclosed.

The dolphin skull returned to the *Don José* with us, and was presented to the ship's crew. It was placed in a position of prominence along with the myriad other artifacts that the vessel had picked up on its voyages. Once again this dolphin would travel the waters of Baja.

The *Don José* headed southward between Isla de Santa Margarita and Isla Magdalena. The breeze was distinctly cooling. We had planned to depart the bay at first dawn, but our permits had been delayed and we spent part of the morning cruising, while we awaited word from the port authorities that our papers were in order.

We cruised close to red mangroves that clung to the islands. Magnificent frigatebirds dotted the branches, and even brown pelicans took roost in the trees. As we passed the pelicans, they took to the air and plunged into the water, surfacing with distended throat pouches.

Finally our papers were approved. As we left Bahia Magdalena, the whales blew all around us, a picket fence of blows. Wherever we looked, white breaths of life punctuated the air. In this main channel the whaling ships would congregate and the longboats pushed off in search of whales. Here the catch was pulled in, the animals were flensed, and the blubber and bones were rendered to oil. Here, in the bays and lagoons of Baja, we almost lost the gray whale.

As we headed out for the deep water of the Pacific, a large cruise ship entered the bay. Looking more like an ocean liner than a whale-watching vessel, this ship was on charter to the New York Museum of Natural History. I can't help thinking that our small group had a more personal and "up-close" view of the bay that would be denied this huge vessel and the hundred or more people on board. They may have had staterooms and dining halls, but there is something to be said for spending your voyage on a ship only slightly larger than the animals that you are seeking.

I turned back toward the bay, reflecting on the ties between the living things that we had observed. It is impossible to imagine that the peaceful scenes before us could ever have been otherwise, that people came to the lagoons for any other purpose than to observe and wonder at the diversity of life—the gelatinous sea hare and the graceful osprey, the darting side-blotched lizard and the scurrying bombardier beetle, the piratical frigatebird and the comical pelican, and at the center of this grand show of life—leviathan, the devilfish. I had touched the soul of the peninsula's ecosystem and united with the heart of this desert land. I had seen the bleached bones on the shore, stepped among the remnants of the sea's creatures, and beheld the living behemoth. I touched the whale, and the whale touched me.

> The large bays and lagoons, where these animals once congregated, brought forth and nurtured their young, are already nearly deserted. The mammoth bones of the California Gray lie bleached on the shores of those silvery waters, and are scattered along the broken coasts, from Siberia to the Gulf of California; and ere long it may be questioned whether this mammal will not be numbered among the extinct species of the Pacific. (Scammon, 1874)

Between 1845 and 1874, whalers caught more than 7,000 gray whales, killing more than 8,000 to land that number, principally cows. They hit at the reproductive core of the species, leaving the breeding and birthing lagoons deserted. In just eleven whaling seasons, the majority of the lagoons were abandoned by the whalers as nonprofitable. Whaling in Bahia Magdalena lasted longer, the large enclave offering a more sizable population. But after thirty years and 2,200 dead whales, Bahia Magdalena was abandoned. What was left of the population, perhaps 2,500 animals, maybe as many as 4,000, slowly began to recover, only to succumb to a thankfully short-lived return of the factory ships in the early twentieth century.

The Eastern Pacific stock of gray whales has continued to recover and today numbers approximately 22,000 animals, probably equivalent to the pre-whaling population. The United States has now reclassified the gray whale under its Endangered Species Act. The whale is classed as threatened rather than endangered. Eventually it will be removed from the list entirely. The other stocks of gray whales have not been so lucky. The Atlantic population became extinct between three hundred and six hundred years ago. The Western Pacific stock has been reduced to very small numbers and was believed to be extinct, but a few scattered sightings suggest that a few tens, perhaps a hundred animals remain there.

Twice in less than one hundred years, gray whales have been taken to the brink.

The Pacific Ocean was spread out before us. Baja framed one horizon, while the other reached to infinity. The ocean was calm and peaceful, with only the occasional wave tripping over into a whitecap. In the distance the water looked as though it were darkened by a squall. Then the ocean began to boil around us, and foaming water engulfed our bow and stern. Two or three hundred common dolphins churned the ocean into a maelstrom. The dolphins plowed through the water, sending up streams of salt spray and darting ahead of our bow as though propelled by an invisible force. White flanks flashed in the silver water, and gray dorsal fins cut through the waves.

Dolphins are spellbinding to observe. They are sizable creatures in their own right, although certainly not in the same league as the great whales. Their speed, complex brains, social relationships, and beauty combine to create a certain image in our minds: power and playfulness in a slate-gray body.

The first dolphins that I ever saw were in the Brighton Aquarium in southern England. Those animals were bottlenose dolphins, and they were housed in a glorified swimming pool. The two dolphins performed routines for public gratification and were condemned to an early death from infection and boredom. The animals that were bowriding the *Don José* bore about as much resemblance to the Brighton dolphins as a shadow does to the sun.

Leaning over the bow, we watched in fascination as dolphins wove in and out of our path, sometimes only inches from the vessel. As the animals swung away from the bow, they hit the surface and their valve blowholes snapped open. We could hear the sharp intake of breath moments before the animals submerged. As we watched, so occasionally the dolphins watched us. They turned onto their sides, still maintaining their set distance from the bow, and gazed intently up in our direction, their eyes following ours. Then just as unexpectedly they were gone.

The *Don José* continued south, parallel to a Baja coast punctuated with peaks and canyons. The burnt colors of the coast baked in the sun, russets and golden browns—tired colors that suggest a potential for life if only fresh water could anoint the ground.

We were making fairly good time despite the delays of the morning, but it would be dark when we reached Cabo San Lucas and the fingertip of the Baja Peninsula. We sat on the w-w deck enjoying the passage and the remoteness of our situation. The wind off the Pacific was cold enough that most people on the ship were wrapped in windbreakers and sweaters as we crossed the Tropic of Capricorn. The occasional black storm-petrel followed our wake, and curious California and Bonaparte's gulls flew low overhead. For hours we lounged on the deck, luxuriating in the tranquillity of the ocean.

Toward early afternoon José, our captain, abruptly changed direction, and we began to head almost due west. He had seen a blow on the horizon, probably three kilometers distant. We held our breath and strained to see the blows for ourselves, but what experienced eyes saw eluded us. To see a blow from more than three kilometers away, even on a calm day, is suggestive to a whale-watcher. Only one species of whale produces a blow that explodes more than eight meters into the air.

We motored toward the whales and watched as the white plumes grew closer. Within the hour we were close to them. José brought the vessel almost to idle, and we spent another few minutes on slow approach. The whales disappeared from view frequently, and for long moments we feared that they had vanished, leaving us alone surrounded only by an expanse of ocean.

But suddenly they were with us, and the *Don José* was among the whales, dwarfed by them—seven blue whales, *Balaenoptera musculus*, probably the largest animal ever to have graced Planet Earth.

The statistics on blue whales are staggering. It is almost impossible to comprehend that such an animal even exists; they are capable of reaching over 33 meters in length, weighing up to 190,000 kilograms, with arteries so large that a small child could crawl through them. At birth the blue whale is already huge at 7 meters and weighing 2,000 kilograms. It was these immense creatures that bore the brunt of Antarctic commercial whaling operations in the twentieth century. A pre-whaling population of close to 230,000 contrasts dramatically with the current, probably optimistic, estimates of 10,000 animals—6 percent of the original stock. In 1989 the International Whaling Commission revealed census data that suggested the population was only 500 in the Southern Hemisphere, and less than 2,000 in the Northern Hemisphere. If these figures are to be believed, after almost thirty years of complete protection, the future of the blue whale looks very bleak indeed.

The seven whales were surface-feeding and lunging. With one mouthful they tripled their volume before expelling the water through sieve-like baleen, retaining the sought-after krill. Bright red krill dotted the water around us. We joined this feeding group quietly, and José cut our engines so that we idled among them.

In the open ocean, the most startling feature of the blue whale when observed "up-close and personal" is the color. A blue whale in the water is simply quite unbelievably blue.

The calm Pacific cradled us in their midst, the sea for once living up to her name. The ocean carried no swell, and now that we were stationary, the heat of the sun permeated our windbreakers and clothing. The w-w deck was baking in the sun. We discarded excess clothing in record time and stood atop the ship, awed by the immensity around us. When a whale swam under our ship, its head and a good third of its body emerged on the port side while much of the body and the flukes trailed well behind to our starboard. The w-w deck offered unobstructed views. There were no barriers, no walls or guards; we could lean over the edge and stare as blue water revealed blue whale. Below the water the whales looked as though surrounded by an aura, a blue-green shadow that was visible before the body of the whale could be discerned. Occasionally we saw a shadow appear and then fade as the whales sank deep into the abyss.

As the whales surface-lunged with open mouths, their throat grooves expanded as they drew in water and then streamed it out through baleen. Seven 26.5-meter whales with a combined mass of more than 500,000 kilograms create a sizable effect, and we were soon on the receiving end of all of that displaced mass. Our steady footing on the w-w deck was no more. The swell generated by half a million kilograms of lunging whale tossed our vessel into troughs and peaks. The ship listed dramatically, and those of us on the deck fell from side to side, tripping across our own feet, trying to retain balance and cameras while not wishing to miss a moment of the display in front of us. More than once we almost joined the whales in the water below—and in the heat and intensity of the moment it was almost tempting.

The blows hung in the still air for the longest time. It was as though our captivation and enthrallment had been translated to a living embodiment of exclamation. As the whales surfaced, we watched as the broad, flat rostrums characteristic of the rorquals slid through the water. As an animal began to dive, its dappled gray-blue back seemed to be at the surface forever. Only as the last third of the body came into view could we see the tiny sickle-shaped dorsal fin. For such an immense animal the small dorsal appears incongruous, but the streamlining of the whale's body is such that even a small dorsal fin is a sufficient "keel" to allow careful control over speed and direction.

Rorquals are known for their rapid swimming speed; blue whales can swim more than thirty kilometers per hour if alarmed—an ability that protected them from whaling until the advent of steamships. However, with the arrival of steam, the blue whales' bulk and size effectively signed the animals' death warrant. There were 328,177 blue whales killed in the Antarctic from 1909 to 1965. Protection from the slaughter came only in 1966, when the animal was believed to be commercially and possibly even biologically extinct. Such a conclusion may yet be the fate of these creatures. Recent revelations by the Russian government of significant blue whale takes through the 1960s may explain why populations have yet to recover.

As we stared ahead of us, only two of the whales were at the surface, and the sun glinted silver off their skin. Remoras clung to the animals' flanks and dorsal fin, and straight ahead a huge flukeprint appeared on the water's surface. The smooth slick of water covered an area much larger than the flukeprints that rise from the stirrings of gray whales. Another flukeprint appeared a little farther ahead, and then another. The whale surfaced in his own wake, the explosion of air from his lungs like a cannon shot.

We stayed with these serene sea mammoths until they faded into the blue water, their aura no longer beckoned, and flukeprints ceased to give warning of an imminent surfacing.

The size of a blue whale is staggering to the mind, and they seem possessed of a gentleness that belies their immensity. The blue whale not only gives us a view of a part of nature separate from our own world, but also provides an insight into our own minds and our ability to relate to the natural world and its components.

In the space of little more than fifty years, 328,177 blue whales died in the Antarctic—328,177 of the largest animals ever to have lived on Earth died to provide oils for margarine. We almost lost the opportunity to begin to unravel the mysteries contained in a 4,500-gram brain; to understand why almost none of the whales killed was ever found to have a malignant tumor; or to learn how the eye of the whale survives permanent contact with ice water without damaging effect. Or simply to look upon the blue whale and feel small.

The oceans are vast expanses of water—all inhabited by cetaceans, but past practices have depleted numbers to such an extent that when we search the horizon for blows, we cannot always be sure of finding them. This trip was my first whale-watch, and I was faced with the ultimate: the blue whale.

Whale-watching is a very personal experience. There is so much time for reflection that you get to know yourself better than you ever thought possible. Out on the ocean, with no distractions, you are forced to think for yourself and consider your own life and the lives of those around you. There are no guarantees that you will see whales at all. But no one can look at a whale without hope for the future, for them and for us. The landmarks that we judge our lives by, the bearings we use to pass through our terrestrial world, have no meaning here. This is a separate planet; this is Ocean.

As the sun faded to the west, two immense slate animals surfaced to our starboard. The two fin whales blew twice and vanished into the dying light. Second in size only to the blue, the fin whales gave us just one tantalizing glimpse of their dark frames and then were gone, leaving only the burst of adrenaline that they precipitated in our minds, and the hopeful anticipation of a longer encounter in the future.

We traveled for a good portion of the night, finally dropping anchor at Cabo San Lucas around one in the morning. We were here in search of the humpback whales that often congregate at Gorda Bank following their summer repast in Central California or Alaska.

When we awoke, Cabo San Lucas was laid out before us like a banquet. The town and marina are a typical tourist locale. Hotels rimmed the cove, complete and incomplete, preparing for the masses. The harbor was filled with brash, colorful boats that had sailed the world and settled in Cabo. Fishing boats departed at dawn crowded with tourists in search of marlin and trophies to take back to cities where a little bit of the exotic and wilderness was sorely needed. The town and surrounding area had a "buzz" for which we were unprepared. A voyage on a ship viewing whales is cathartic and cleansing. When you return to civilization, the "buzz" no longer appeals and you yearn for open water and a horizon of mountains or ocean instead of hotels and masts.

As we ate breakfast, we watched as boats raced around buoys, towing skiers or parasailers to new heights and speeds. The colors of the town left us wide-eyed—red, blue, and yellow sails; chrome, white, and golden hulls. And people: sailing, talking across moorings; fishermen meandering between vessels with fresh catches to impart to the hungry or curious. Towering over this cacophony of noise, activity, and smells were the Friars, huge pillars and arches of granite that mark the Cape of Baja California.

We were to leave Cabo early and head out onto the shallow waters of Gorda Bank. But as we were rapidly learning, the best-made plans are soon laid to rest. The engine of our proud little vessel choked and lay idle. Instead of leaving with the fishing vessels, we would remain in port amid the variety and confusion of a *turista de la ciudad*.

Alternative plans were rapidly implemented, and as our crew worked to correct the mechanical problems, we took to the pangas for a closer look at the Friars. There was a possibility of seeing whales, and we took a hydrophone with us. At least we might be comforted by the sounds of whales, even if they remained out of sight.

The Friars dominate the area. When one thinks of Cabo, it is the Friars that give the thought substance. There are three of them. The largest is near shore and sports an arch cut from its mass by the never-ending action of the waves that wash through the striations and crevices at the heart of each monolith. The second and third are single solid blocks of granite, with deep creases in rock and cubic structures formed by fractures and stresses within. All three show a gradation in color from top to bottom. The pinnacles appear baked white in the sun, as do any ledges or prominent points. From a distance the monolithic Friars appear as lifeless granite extrusions from the ocean. When you approach, the striations and crevices reveal that life has more than a tenuous hold here, and that where water and sun work in combination, even the most barren of sites are capable of supporting a community of life. Anywhere that birds are able to settle has the crisp white covering of guano that provides limited fertilization to the site. In some of the crevices and niches a dash of green is visible, taking advantage of any nutrients returned to the rock by birds feeding in the ocean depths. Closer to the water line is the dark rim of ocean life that regular dousing supports—barnacles, mussels, and the associated scurrying life.

We rounded the Friars. The granite revealed caves and caverns molded by the elements, past and present. California sea lions basked on the rocks, their coats varying from near black to gold. They watched as we passed by, but nothing stirred them. We headed back toward open water, determined to find whales in these waters. Our range was limited by the capacity of the small outboards on the pangas, so we positioned ourselves a few kilometers offshore. The sun was unrelenting on the open boats, and we were restricted in our movements so that all we could do was sit and watch and wait.

The hydrophone was lowered into the water and we listened. Occasionally sounds rose from the depths, and at times it was difficult to know whether they came from the microphone or through the wooden boards under our feet. The sounds were haunting—songs of whales many kilometers distant; deep, guttural sounds that seem to human ears to come from sages beyond our ability to understand. What science tells us is that only male humpback whales sing, and then only in the winter months when they ply the warm waters in search of a mate. But what science also tells us is that humpback songs are the most complex produced by any animal, and we have no idea what they really mean, what information they are meant to convey, or why they change on an annual basis.

The sky was cloudless, and the waters that mix between the Pacific Ocean and the Golfo de California were so calm that we hardly drifted even when the motor was turned off to conserve the little fuel that we had on board.

We sat in the panga talking quietly. The hours passed and the day drew long. Once as we gazed into the waters around us, a mammalian eye looked back, and a bottlenose dolphin surfaced briefly at our bow before disappearing into the depths. An idle panga did not offer much sport. We listened to the underwater world and the eerie calls and moans of behemoths, imagining the sight of the singing whale hanging motionless in the depths, and as through unknown means the sounds propagate through the oceans of the world. We were joined in our contemplation by a brown pelican and an immature one-eyed glaucous-winged gull. The appearance of these birds struck a chord with the whale-watchers who had been poised with cameras for any cetacean surfacing. These two avian emissaries must have been some of the most photographed individuals on the Baja Peninsula. But even these curious birds soon departed when they realized that we would offer no food.

The hydrophone had grown quiet, and our throats parched. Everyone was still in good spirits, but the conversation had faded. We were ready to return to the *Don José* and investigate the status of the engine. The three pangas brought their Yamaha engines to life and turned toward the harbor.

To our port side, beyond the Friars, a heart-shaped blow answered the day's prayers; at least three gray whales had made an appearance on the far side of the cape. Gray whales weren't quite what we were looking for, but several hours in a panga with only eye-to-eye contact with a pelican and a dolphin demanded action. We changed course toward them.

The now-familiar countenance of the whales—gray mottled skin, knuckles running toward the tail stock, and the heart-shaped blow—were in front of us again. With the Friars in the background, the scene was startlingly prehistoric. The whales were keeping close to shore, and the deep swell from the Pacific buoyed us up, or lowered us into troughs that obscured our view and turned distant boats into invisible phantoms. The whales seemed intent on whatever business keeps whales occupied, and it was soon apparent that the only way we could get close would be active pursuit, and that was not our aim. Whale-watching requires unobtrusive observation; pursuit interferes with that aim, and any behavior that you elicit is tainted and worthless.

We returned to the *Don José* satisfied in part by seeing the gray whales, but still hoping against hope that the next blows we saw would be humpbacks. The engine had been resuscitated, and we pulled out of the protected waters of Cabo San Lucas at about 1:00 P.M. Radio conversations with other boats offered promises of whales on Gorda Bank, and we allowed our hearts some hope that the day was not yet over.

As we rounded the peninsula heading into the Golfo de California or Sea of Cortez proper, we began to encounter a weather system that would shroud the *Don José* in fog and coat everything with clinging droplets wrung from saturated air. In the distance just before the start of the seemingly impenetrable white fog bank, three misty blows lifted from the water and merged with the clinging mist.

We watched as the whales moved in unison and began to dive with the rounded back action and raising of huge, ponderous flukes so characteristic of humpbacks. We approached slowly and began to observe some of the very apparent drama that was unfolding before us.

There were three animals. The largest and most placid of the three we took to be the female, and throughout most of the encounter she was distant from the other whales. The second whale, only slightly smaller than the female, we took to be the escort male, while the third, smaller animal we characterized as a young male interloper.

Initially all three animals were closely aligned, surfacing, blowing, and diving together. The female was closest to us on the port side of the vessel, the escort male was next to her, and on his far side was the smaller male. Every move made by the smaller of the two males was matched by the escort. Attempts by the young male to approach the female were confounded at every turn with massive exhalations and reverberating sounds that we could hear clearly above the water. The animals lifted their flukes at each dive, and water streamed off the trailing edges in the classic *Megaptera* fashion. The dives were shallow, and none of the animals stayed below the surface for more than ninety seconds before cracking the silence with a cannon-shot breath.

As the two males vied for position close to the female, we could feel the combat between them. The fog was building, and at times all three animals disappeared into the whiteout around us. We could hear the commotion and imagine actual physical contact between the males. At one surfacing close to the *Don José* we saw that one of the whales had been bloodied, and I have no doubt that these "gentle giants" had come to blows beneath the surface.

The female up to this point had been a passive participant in the combat that seemed to be holding her as the prize. Now she had separated herself from proximity to the males and lay belly up, lashing her huge white pectoral flippers on the surface of the water with resounding crashes. It is these long, tapering flippers, perhaps 4.5 meters in length, that have given the humpback whale its scientific name: *Megaptera noveangliae*—big-winged New Englander. Repeatedly the flippers were lifted clear of the water and slapped down. Crash after crash provided the feminine comment on the gladiator whales that were fighting for her favors.

The young male repeatedly tried to outrun his adversary, but he was turned at every attempt. As we watched the animals battle, the escort disappeared from view and the youngster seemed to have his chance. As the young male began to swim toward his goal, a huge wall of bubbles broke the surface, creating a long, narrow blue-green shadow that was reminiscent of the surfacing blue whales we had watched the day before. The young humpback veered off course deflected by the bubbles, and the escort surfaced near the female seeming to have won the tournament.

Suddenly everything was quiet. The escort and his female were off to our starboard side, while the young male had last surfaced to our port. We were turned toward the two whales when the female powered clear of the water directly in front of us, a full breach that saw the animal swirl water into a maelstrom and rotate 360 degrees before falling onto her back surrounded by a tumult of white water and a cataclysmic thunderclap. The game was afoot once more. The escort left the side of his mate to settle matters with the interloper conclusively. As he returned to the battle arena venting air and sounds that seemed as though they emanated from the bowels of the Earth, the fog descended and our view of the world became white. We could hear the whales around us, and we could only imagine the strategies, bubble walls, flipper slapping, or breaches that would settle the encounter and deliver the victor to the female.

We were soon forced to navigate on instruments, leaving the whales to fight their own battles and settle their own scores. But what an insight we had been afforded in our brief encounter with these big-winged New Englanders of Baja!

All landmarks vanished and we cruised through a world devoid of sights, punctuated only by the sounds of foghorns from our vessel and vessels that we could not see. We could have been anywhere in the world at this moment; why do tales of the *Mary Celeste* and the Bermuda Triangle spring to mind? Hopes of seeing the humpbacks disappeared into the fog, and we settled into cabins or galley to browse through books, play cards, or talk over the events of previous days and the last few hours. The type of encounter that we had witnessed is not often relayed. Popular books often retell much that should be contained in the realms of myths and legends surrounding these magnificent beasts.

Four of the more frequently told "myths" spring to mind. The first is that these animals are "gentle giants," a remarkably anthropomorphic term that assumes placidity as a prerequisite to size. The second is that whales are monogamous, the third concerns the role of the "third" whale, and the fourth involves the actual mating process of leviathans, what takes place and how.

Observations of whales are confounded by the fact that they spend more than 70 percent of their time below the water's surface, with the result that people have had a tendency to read more than they should into sparse encounters. Like all "fish stories," tales often grow in the retelling so that what was first noted in curiosity is interpreted and reinterpreted until the story becomes dogma and irrefutable fact based on tenuous evidence.

The perception of whales as "gentle giants" is one that sits well on the human intellect. Perhaps in reflection of the way that the human race has treated whales over the past centuries, we feel that justification is needed to change our view of the animals as commodities to be used by an industrial hungry world; so we have this image of the gentle paragon in the ocean depths, a gentle giant wronged by a product-oriented society. But is our enthrallment and protection of these animals dependent on their fulfilling this image? Stories of devilfish and Moby Dick suggest that we can move beyond such an idealistic vision. Orca have become the darlings of aquariums without having to shed their "killer" image. However, it is likely that the great whales, which are essentially the cows of the sea, will always have a place in our hearts and minds as gentle creatures that will not respond with deadly force unless so threatened. And to a species such as ours, that is a virtue.

The second and third myths relate to the supposed monogamy of whales and the role of the third whale. It has become popular to view whales, which are held up in the media and popular books as intelligent mammals, marine versions of ourselves, as monogamous, mating for life and living in discrete family units: mother whale, father whale, and baby whale. This idealistic image of marine parental bonds is a reflection more of our social structure than of theirs.

The idea of a parental unit was given credence because in several species, a third animal was often seen with mother and calf. In some instances this whale was called the "aunty" whale and was believed to be a female who would assist the mother as required. In certain dolphin species an "aunty" is often seen in attendance at the birth, sometimes assisting the young calf to the surface and its first breath of air. But in other cases, involving great whales, the third whale was believed to be a male, the father of the calf and the female's permanent partner. Through detailed observation over a number of years, it is now known that whales such as humpbacks are not monogamous, and females are not seen with the same male "escort" over successive years. It has been noted that fin and blue whales are frequently seen in pairs, but they are also often seen in cow-calf pairs or singly. We simply do not have enough information to determine whether or not these animals are monogamous. With what we know about humpback, orca, and gray whales, as well as some of the smaller cetaceans, we could suppose that the other rorquals are not monogamous, but more study is needed to be sure.

It can be said with some certainty that when the baleen whales are seen in groups, whether they are blues, humpbacks, or grays, it is because they are each using the same resources, rather than forming any cohesive permanent alliance or family unit. As our knowledge of the smaller cetaceans increases, we are also beginning to reinterpret our understanding of their social structure and organization. The vast schools of dolphins seen in the oceans of the world are not permanent associations, but form and disintegrate with remarkable frequency. Among the whales, perhaps our most detailed knowledge and understanding of sociality comes from the resident pods of orca found in the coastal waters of Puget Sound and Vancouver Island. Only these whales, as far as we know, have the type of family organization that has been popularized for other species. But even here the typical family unit is not present; each animal stays with the pod that it is born into, and mating occurs only between pods. The young orca is raised by its mother with her family—the father stays with his mother in their pod.

The orca of Washington State and British Columbia probably represent a unique social organization within the Cetacea. The typical orca is the wide-ranging, transient individual that is adept at pack-hunting other whales and marine mammals. The high biological productivity of the resident orcas' habitat has removed the imperative to move continually through the oceans in search of food, and thus has allowed the evolution of a complex social structure. In the majority of whale species, the basic social unit is mother and calf. Other associations are usually fluid and transient. Further information will allow us to interpret more fully how frequently such associations form, for example between cooperatively feeding humpbacks, but for now there is no scientific reason to assume that the schools and pods of whales that we witness while traveling across the vast plains of open ocean are any different from the herds of wildebeest or zebra that move en masse across the Serengeti.

The final myth is an interesting one to deal with because it is based entirely on supposition, plus a great deal of imagination. The issue is how whales mate. The vision of a coupling between leviathans is certainly a daunting one, and it has spawned remarkable tales that should perhaps adorn the pages of a submarine kama sutra. First we can deal with the gray whale and the mystery that seems to surround this animal's attempts at procreation.

In numerous texts on whales you will find reference to the "pas de trois" of mating gray whales. The following account by Lyall Watson (1981) is typical:

> In the early morning there is much spyhopping and circling, intensified around midday as the whales break up into trios composed of two males and a single female. Only one male is involved in actual mating. He can usually be identified by a single flipper which is held up motionless above the surface of the water, presumably as a signal. The female approaches with a delicate touch display, caressing the male with her flippers until they come to lie belly-to-belly in very shallow water. The other male remains in close attendance, taking an upright position on the far side of the female and apparently forms a prop or wedge.

Unfortunately this neat story contains only a single truth: gray whales mate belly to belly, as do all cetaceans. The rest of the account is insupportable on purely biological grounds.

Observations of gray whales and others indicate that cetacean mating behavior can be divided into two distinct types—external and internal competition. Humpback whales are examples of the former, and gray whales of the latter. In the humpback whale the key to mating success is in the display and active competition between males, just as we witnessed near Gorda Bank. The victor in the battle likely mates with the female, and she probably mates only with that victor. The gray whale does not practice such selection. The female gray mates with multiple suitors, and the competition is both external and internal—between the sperm of different males, and between the males before the sex act. Certainly observers in the lagoons of Baja witnessed females surrounded by multiple males, often two, but what they were witness to was not some altruistic act by the second male but an interaction that has the female mating with each animal in turn.

Consider for the moment what it would mean if the interaction between the gray whales were truly altruistic. The second male would be actively assisting the first to mate successfully and pass on his genetic traits to the next generation, to the detriment of the second male's own attempts to do so. From the point of view of evolutionary genetics, such an act makes sense only if the two males share a genetic heritage, i.e., they are brothers. If the two males are less than brothers, then the second male's genes will rapidly be purged from the gene pool because such altruistic acts usually go unrewarded in nature. If the second male is relying on a reciprocal act by the first at a later stage, then the outcome remains the same because the scales will always be weighed against him—he offered the service, was taken advantage of, and there is nothing to force the recipient of such a gift to return the favor. Evolution and survival are selfish entities.

The procreation of humpback whales has also received anecdotal embellishment over the years. A drawing is often included in books to depict what no one has seen: mating humpback whales. The sketch shows two humpbacks standing upright in the water, with flippers embracing. No one has ever witnessed such a scene. We know that all whales mate belly to belly, and such a picture may represent true events, but a review of past writings indicates that these two mating/spy-hopping whales represent a distortion of tales told over centuries.

Humpbacks are known to spy-hop and are perhaps the most aerial of cetaceans. Journals of whaling captains and travelers speak of seeing many humpbacks spy-hopping on the southern whaling grounds; often the whales were close together. Delicate and surprisingly accurate plates are included in these publications. But over the years the same drawings were redrawn and reinterpreted. Gradually, spy-hopping humpbacks viewing whaling vessels became mating whales embracing in a double spy-hop.

The light was failing fast under the fog when we were roused again from our bunks and seats, from thoughts of "pas de trois" and altruistic cetaceans, with the cry of "Whales off the bow." We rushed to the w-w deck and were faced with a sight that reinforced the fact that sea voyages still reveal the new and the unknown to the curious. The fog had cleared sufficiently to provide a fair amount of visibility, although the saturated air continued to coat everything with a fine layer of droplets. Ahead of the *Don José* were the characteristic slicks of turbulence that form the whales' flukeprint, and just ahead of those were three gray whales. The animals were swimming in point formation at the surface, with mouths agape and yellow baleen clearly visible.

The whales were skimming, filter-feeding along the surface. We could hardly believe it. Gray whales are bottom-feeders. They earned their descriptive alternative name of "mussel digger" because of their predilection for taking huge bites out of the mud bottom and straining mud and water through baleen to retrieve crustaceans. Surface skim-feeding is simply not something associated with them. The right whales are the skimmers, the rorquals are the gulpers, and the grays are the bottom-feeders.

The fog bank was still ahead of us, and our view of the skimmer was eclipsed as we re-entered the mist. We were left to wonder what other mysteries whales may hold. Despite centuries of scrutiny to capture their oil and meat, we still know surprisingly little about them. Under such conditions it is not wise to discount or endorse anything entirely, regardless of the apparent credentials that such statements appear to contain. Categorical statements of fact can be notoriously incorrect.

The whale-watching day had closed with an expression of power and exuberance from a humpback and a sight that had reinforced our need to understand more about the whales of this strange blue-green planet. Our world is dominated by bipedal terrestrial mammals that have the potential to threaten all other forms of life including their own. There is immense and unfathomable value in learning from the other products of four billion years of evolution that may well be unique in this universe.

We traveled through part of the night shrouded in fog, and the morning found us anchored in a protected cove at Los Frailes, the southernmost coral reef in Baja California and the Northern Hemisphere. The fog had lifted and the cove was bathed in sunlight, although a chill breeze persisted in dropping the temperatures near the coast.

Los Frailes is located on the Sea of Cortez side of the Baja Peninsula, approximately 130 kilometers south of La Paz, where our journey through Baja had begun just five days earlier. There was a small encampment of fishermen and their families at Bahia Los Frailes, which means "Monks' Bay." The sandstone ridge around the cove was a rich red and the vegetation sparse, in dramatic contrast to the mangroves that border the edge of Bahia Magdalena.

After breakfast we took the pangas to shore, planning to hike through the desert and then take to the water and snorkel with Baja's subsea life. As we stepped onto the sandy shore, turkey vultures landed some fifteen meters away to investigate. They are ungainly birds at best, and it is difficult to look favorably upon their naked red heads and dull black plumage. Turkey vultures are scavengers and survivors. They clean up the debris of life around them. Their mere presence imparts a feeling of defensiveness over the subject of their interest, and we moved on, leaving the vultures to pick through the latest additions to the drift line.

We had landed at the far left of the beach, and we walked past the fish camp trailers and upturned boats toward the rocky cliff at the other end of the bay. The fishermen shouted greetings, and their dogs barked surprise notice of the presence of strangers along their isolated stretch of beach. The cartilaginous bodies of inflated puffers littered the drift line along with crab carapaces, urchins, and miscellaneous debris that was stamped with trade names from half a world away.

We left our snorkeling equipment at the base of the granite blocks that marked the foot of the cliff, and followed the trail into the interior and hills behind the bay. The vegetation was dominated by the cacti: pitaya dulce, pitaya agria, cardon, and barrel cactus. At our feet numerous small hedgehog cacti and the aptly named jumping cholla made walking through the underbrush a painful business.

Picking our way through the trails, we scared up a black-tailed jackrabbit, and a northern mockingbird let out a cry, alerting all to our presence. The sun was oppressively hot, and there was no doubt that our hike would be cut short.

Despite liberal supplies of sunscreen we were soon suffering from burns. While traveling around the Cape, I had severely burned my ankles, and walking through cholla and other thorny vegetation was soon too much to bear. Our group began to scatter, most in search of shade. Above us the turkey vultures watched with inquisitive eyes. Costa's hummingbirds darted around, and the occasional northern cardinal flew into thickets that hid the plumage of this most unsubtle of birds.

A hawk flew low overhead and landed in a cardon barbon cactus heavy with the dying remnants of its fruit and a few white flowers. These thickly barbed fruits were used as hairbrushes by the Indians of the region. Unlike those of the larger cardon pelon, the fruits are neither fleshy nor edible. They are covered with yellowish-brown bristles and are much larger than the fruits of other cardon cousins. The Indians also made use of the skeleton of the plant. The dried ribs were used as building materials or to manufacture fishing poles or spears in a land where wood is a rare commodity.

The hills around us were now wrapped in mist, and the cardons that dotted the slopes began to fade from view or take on the appearance of phantom shadows in the fog. The *Don José* had vanished, as had the fishing camp at the far end of the beach. The fog had smothered only certain parts of the shoreline, and where we sat at the base of the granite cliff the sun still baked the rocks and scorched already red skin. The turkey vultures were picking at the fish discarded by the camp, and the fog presented an eerie backdrop to their ghostly deliberations.

The blanket of fog and the cold breeze streaming from its midst had significantly dropped the temperature of the water. It would take brave souls to enter the water now. The light was becoming increasingly poor as the fog stretched over the sun, and the blue water became a steely gray that would transform the colorful array of life below to uniformity before our eyes. A few of our number, those with wetsuits, entered the water, and others without attempted to follow. The water was simply too cold and the light too poor. The snorkeling session was brief.

We returned to the *Don José* and another day with the potential to be cloaked in white. Los Frailes was left behind hidden in the mist as though it had been a figment of our imaginations in this changeling land. As we headed into the Sea of Cortez the fog stayed behind us, clinging to the shoreline as though attempting to protect the land from prying eyes and those wishing to map the shore or use landmarks for navigation. Early maps of the region were dotted with imaginary islands that disappeared when approached, merging with clouds or water, or that faded as mirages into the distant desert. Temperature inversions created alien landscapes that fooled the eye, and shifting sandbars and barrier islands presented real changes to a coastline that offered more challenges to early explorers than many other regions of the world.

Ahead of us the horizon was clear, and we could see the coast of mainland Mexico across the narrow sea born of the rupture of the San Andreas fault five or six million years ago. We were heading northward toward Isla Cerralvo and Isla Espiritu Santo. En route we hoped to see more whales, perhaps fin or Bryde's, but our luck seemed to leave us and during the remainder of the day we saw only distant heart-shaped blows from grays. At one point our vessel was joined by a huge school of bottlenose dolphins. Three or four hundred animals massed together amid churning white water of their own making. They rode our bow for a short time, allowing us to watch the precision of their swimming— and to imagine what it would be like to enter the water just once and become a dolphin.

Then they left us to plow the waters independently, drawing us closer to the world that we had so deliberately left behind. The remainder of the day was quiet and thoughtful. The fog intermittently cloaked the land, and the distant horizon was replaced by low white clouds.

Toward dusk we approached the sloping grandeur of Isla Espiritu Santo, Island of the Holy Spirit. We pulled into a safe harbor and dropped anchor. Our trip was coming to a close. The morning would see us ashore among rock pools and caves searching for Steinbeck's sally lightfoot crabs. Early afternoon we would spend at Los Islotes with the California sea lions that treat this rocky outcrop to the north of Espiritu Santo as their home. From Los Islotes we would push on to La Paz, ready to face the human world with a deeper understanding of the natural world we seem to have forsaken.

Isla Espiritu Santo is set into the Sea of Cortez in a sequence of sloping layers intersected with aqua-blue coves and indentations. It is a remarkably picturesque island. In the morning we entered our three pangas, and our crew directed the small vessels to shore. We landed at the stretch of beach that separates Isla Espiritu Santo from Isla Partida. On some maps Partida is marked as a separate and distinct island, on others as an extension of Espiritu Santo. When we returned later that morning, we would see why.

The bow of each panga was beached against the large boulders, and we left the boats glad for the dry landing. Around us were scattered the grinning heads of hammerhead sharks. Each was small, perhaps twenty centimeters across, and after looking up and down the beach I rapidly lost count of the numbers spread out before us. Sharks have had to put up with unsubstantiated fears cultivated by media and films as well as the pressures from fishermen who use them for bait or to provide sharkskin to the fashion industry. Somehow through the explosion of concern for marine life, particularly the whales and dolphins, sharks have been exempt. They do not fit the profile of photogenic, benign creatures ripe for salvation from a cruel world. One day I hope that will change.

Scattered at intervals among the boulders were puffers and the skeletons of numerous other fish—skeletal forms that were once colorful visions in pools and reefs. A short distance down the beach was the fishing camp. The fishermen were playing volleyball over a net strung between two drought-stricken trees, and we waved greetings as we headed into the island.

The volcanic geologic structure of Espiritu Santo cuts the island into slivers marked by bays and indentations. Giant cardon cactus stood masterfully over a landscape punctuated by small, low-lying xerophytic plants. The huge ribbed trunks stretched skyward. We were presented with vast, towering specimens that cast linear shadows. Some individual cacti were more than eleven meters high, with multiple vertical trunks. The coloration of these immense trunks ranged from gray to dark green, depending on their age and the amount of photosynthetic chlorophyll contained within each rib. Each trunk is able to expand its ribs to take in water whenever it is available. Such methods, combined with shallow roots designed to spread out and catch any rainfall, are among the adaptations that have evolved to enable these plants to survive in such an unyieldingly hot climate.

Many of the cacti were heavily gnawed around their base, a sign of the black jackrabbits so prevalent on the island, and the upper reaches of the trunks were punctuated with holes used by myriad species of birds ranging from woodpeckers to owls. The giant cardon acts like a multistory apartment building for the creatures in the area, every level providing some essential service, accommodation, or food.

It was this cardon, not the type we had seen earlier, that formed a staple part of the Indians' diet in this region. Missionaries reported that the local Indians either would grind the fruit into a paste to eat, or would run water through the ground fruit and drink the resulting liquid. Where the pitaya dulce offered a choice, the cardon was never an important food source; however, it continues to be used for its antiseptic properties, and its skeleton, the dried ribs, is used extensively as a building material just as was the smaller cardon barbon.

We continued our hike, which was shortened by the profusion of life that drew our eyes to the ground and into the undergrowth. We set out toward a cliff face bordering one of the bays. Our footing was upset by large unstable boulders, and more than once we were forced to steady our steps with hands against the ground. We were approaching the place where the cliff met the sea in a meandering confusion of huge black boulders interspersed with caves and rock pools, and we made our way along rocks made slick with water and weed.

The caves carved out of the rock by the action of the sea were alive with scurrying creatures. The light was dim in many, but some of the more open caverns revealed the source of the movement we were catching in our peripheral vision, sally lightfoot crabs, the bane of John Steinbeck:

> Everyone who has seen them has been delighted with them. The very name they are called by reflects the delight of the name. . . . They have remarkable eyes and an extremely fast reaction time. . . . They are exceedingly hard to catch. . . . They appear to read the mind of their hunter. . . . When you plunge at them, they seem to disappear in little puffs of blue smoke—at any rate, they disappear. . . . They are very beautiful, with clear brilliant colors, reds and blues and warm browns.

We did not attempt to test Steinbeck's testimony, and simply watched the crabs as they scuttled around, always just out of reach. Even in the dark of the caves and crevices that they made their hiding places, the colors that adorned their carapaces were stunning. The reds and blues were of an intensity that is not often seen in the natural world, and certainly are not the colors that we generally associate with these armored marine creatures.

As we picked our way back along the shore to firmer ground, the black boulders we clambered over seemed to come alive as thousands of isopods ran in waves from our feet. These cockroach-size crustaceans glistened black in the sunlight, moving as one unit in response to ocean waves or human feet.

The stench of decay reached us as we moved up the rocky shore. It was not the marine decay of weed or mollusks, but the smell of a mammalian corpse. Overlying a number of the smooth rocks was the barely identifiable body of a toothed whale. We had passed close to the carcass on the way down the beach, but only on our return did the wind carry the decay to our senses. The head and jaws were reasonably intact, but the rest of the carcass appeared to have disintegrated long before it found shore. The whale did not have a beak, but instead a smoothly rounded jawline. The teeth, those that remained, were large and conical, evenly placed in a disconcerting smile within the open jaws. The animal was a member of the subfamily Globicephalinae, which includes pilot whales and orca. Given its size and our location, it was probably a shortfin pilot whale.

There is a certain fascination in viewing death—not just the macabre aspects of decay and disintegration of what was once lithe and agile, but beyond that, a consideration of what life entails. The emergence of various religions over the eons of human evolution has resulted in an unnatural view of death and the processes that it involves. Without death there would be no life. The cyclical nature of the world depends on the return of nutrients and elements to the ecosystem and their reuse by other life forms. Death and decay are the ultimate in recycling and sustainable resource management. It may be something that humans would rather not think about, but our deaths secure a future for others, however insignificant we may consider those creatures, the microbes and bacteria. Without them plants would not have access to essential nitrogen, phosphorus, and potassium, and without plants the entire oxygen–carbon dioxide cycle would collapse, with obvious consequences. Our deaths secure life directly and indirectly for all other life forms on this planet, and when you think about it, that is rather comforting.

We headed back toward the fishing camp. Small brown ground squirrels darted off into the undergrowth startled at our presence, and common terns, yellow-footed gulls, and Brandt's cormorants wheeled overhead. We were soon back at the cove where we had landed upon the Holy Spirit. The *Don José* was anchored in the cove, and the pangas were launched in response to our waves. But now we were faced with a problem. Isla Partida had been set loose from Isla Espiritu Santo by the rising tide, but it was still too shallow for the pangas to reach us. We would have to wade out until the water was deep enough for the boats to reach us and support our weight. A number of our group were wearing jeans, and even those in shorts soon found themselves waist-deep in water with cameras held high. It was one of those moments when initially you think that you can make the trip back without getting too wet, so jeans and shorts are turned up. Then as the water gets deeper and deeper, until it is lapping about your waist, the only concern is to keep moving across the sandy bottom with camera and film safe and dry.

We were soon spread out, wading toward the waiting boats. Those of us toward the head of the line could clearly see the sandy bottom dotted with sea hares, and could step accordingly. But as we passed by, the sand was churned and visibility disappeared. I still cringe when I think of those poor sea hares and the expressions on the faces of our barefooted waders as they stepped sight unseen upon the sand. As we reached the boats I had also given thought to the numbers of hammerheads we had seen on the beach, and I am prone to as many irrational thoughts as the next person. The sharks had been small, but I could just imagine the confusion and panic if one had been spotted. Such thoughts simply reinforce the view that in water we are out of our depth in more ways than one.

Terrestrial animals can make adaptations to the water, and we can learn to be at one with the isotonic fluid that gave us life at the beginning of time. But it seems that the barrier between marine and terrestrial will always exist. We are no longer evolving as other organisms continue to do. Our evolution is cultural and intellectual rather than physical. Future technology may lead us to develop or create new races; to colonize new worlds, either in inner space or outer space. But such changes are gross in nature and apart from us as human beings. We have to deal with the marine world as we are now, not in the expectation or hope of what we could be in centuries to come. We need to look at it and see the differences and the similarities of life, and to learn from both.

Sharks and whales have borne the brunt of misunderstanding. Let us hope that neither will ever be dismissed so easily again in a future of our making.

We dropped anchor off the two small rocky outcrops that form Los Islotes at the northern end of Espiritu Santo. Los Islotes was stained white with guano. Birds crowded the ledges and filled the sky above us. One of the islands sloped dramatically downward, and a few cardon cacti maintained a tenuous hold upon the incline. At the base of the rocks California sea lions congregated, basking in the sun, lying on top of each other, and swimming lazily in the water. These sea lions were of the subspecies *californianus* which breeds throughout Baja, and are classified as *Zalophus californianus californianus*. They are coastal animals, rarely seen more than sixteen kilometers offshore.

We had planned to enter the water but, as had occurred at Los Frailes, it was too cold, and we had to settle for seeing the islands and marine mammals from the pangas. We circled the rocks staring skyward at the spiraling frigatebirds. Turrets of rock pushed upward along the rise of the islands, resembling immense salt encrustations in a dying lake. Blue-footed boobies with their streaked head plumage and startlingly blue feet settled on several ledges. However, most of the birds above us were the drabber brown boobies that flew from ledge to ledge, settling wherever sufficient room allowed them to land and nest.

Several Brandt's cormorants held wings to the drying power of the sun, and black oystercatchers scurried among the tidepools. As the waves lapped against the shore, sally lightfoot crabs moved as a unit, their brightly colored carapaces flashing in the sunlight. The tide line was marked by the dark stain of marine life and the protrusions of weed and mollusks. The sea lions lounged on the rocks in complete relaxation, their coats baked golden brown, and a few swam in the cool waters as we cruised past.

Occasionally immature males and female sea lions dove under our panga, curiously following our wake or meandering across our path. As they hit the surface after a dive, their nostrils would open and the inrush of air was reminiscent of those larger marine mammals that had captivated us over the last few days. Sea lions make frequent dives during the day to feed on cephalopods and small fish. They may make over 150 dives per trip to depths averaging 37 meters, and in captivity sea lions have been trained to retrieve objects at depths of 250 meters.

The water was clear enough for us to see to the bottom up to the point where the rocky outcrop plunged into the abyss. We could see the brightly colored tropical fish and corals that invited us to look closer, as in those days long since past when the sirens called to sailors to join them in the life-affirming waters, only to find that life and death were one in the oceans.

We could see the huge bulls, weighing from 200 to 400 kilograms, with necks and ruffs that clearly demonstrated the power the animal held in its muscles. The females were less than half that size. Adult males maintain their territories from May to August. We were witnessing the nonbreeding-season segregation of males and females. The young males were crowded toward one end of the island and the females to the other; larger males were scattered about, often on their own. During the summer, the adult males establish their territories when the females are already present on the beach or rocks. Each male then battles for and defends his territory from the incursions of other males, often patrolling the water in front of his harem, barking at potential trespassers.

It seems that all marine mammals share a harrowing past in connection with humans. The California sea lion was hunted for skin and oil, as well as internal organs that were valued in the East for their purported medicinal properties. Its whiskers were even used as pipecleaners. Just as the whales suffered dramatic population declines, so did the sea lion; complete herds were exterminated. In 1938, surveys counted just 2,020 animals along the entire California coastline. Today, under careful protection, some 74,000 animals live in Norte California and 83,000 in Mexico.

Occasionally a young male would surface too close to a more dominant male, and there followed posturing, barking, and commotion among the animals until the interloper was forced back into the water. None of the encounters that we observed resulted in direct combat, but the scars we saw indicated that it was always an option. Other encounters were more benign. Animals left the water to find a place to lie in the sun, only to find that their path took them over the bodies of those already in place, resulting in scuffles and barked recriminations.

We circumnavigated the islands, peering into crevices and caves, watching the movements of invertebrates among the tide, and the laconic activity of sea lions. Several of the females were suckling large pups from the previous year's season. When the females return to the beaches to breed, they birth their single pups from the previous year's mating, and are almost immediately ready to mate again. The young pups grow rapidly and form large nursery groups when their mothers are out at sea feeding. The link between mother and pup is principally an acoustic one, the female responding to a pup whose bleat she recognizes, although she also responds to its scent and will prevent impostors from nursing.

In the distance, back toward the sloping grandeur of the Holy Spirit, two blows told us that whales were in these waters. They were far in the distance, beyond our reach. We watched as the two animals surfaced again; and then they were gone. The dive action of the animals had revealed a small, sickle-like dorsal fin and no flukes. The animals were smaller than gray whales, probably twelve meters in length. In all likelihood this was our first view of Bryde's whales (pronounced Broo-dus; named after the Norwegian consul to South Africa who built the first whaling factory in Durban in 1909). These elusive whales resemble sei and minke whales, but are geographically restricted to tropical waters defined by the twenty-degree isotherm. It is typical to see just one or two blows before the animal sinks from view and vanishes in the depths.

Our group returned to the *Don José* with the sounds and smells of Los Islotes and its sea lions still strong in our nostrils.

The city of La Paz was four or five hours over the horizon. As the Sea of Cortez stretched out ahead of us, we packed our belongings and checked plane tickets to homes that seemed more than miles away. Just when everything was carefully stowed came the heartwarming cry, "Dolphins on the bow!" A tumultuous school of common dolphins appeared out of the depths, acting as pilots to lost souls aboard our vessel. For once, by accident rather than design, we could watch the power of these animals without thinking of that perfect camera shot. Instead we could allow our minds to capture the memory of how light, sea, and animal merged into one inspiring sight.

The dolphins were the medicine that we all needed to end our voyage. The sounds of their breathing, the snap of the blowhole on the bow, and the sight of the animal turning upward to stare at us—those are memories to keep for a lifetime. We parted company after about twenty minutes, but many of us stayed on the bow or the w-w deck staring at the fading white water that marked the moving school, and then just staring into the depths around us or to the horizon. What we are able to see about us is a mere shadow of what is contained within.

We were standing atop the w-w deck as we entered Bahia de la Paz and passed the Pemex refinery and other burgeoning signs of civilization. We followed the path laid out by the large metallic green and red buoys flagged by cormorants, and mentally prepared ourselves for the bustle of the life we had so intentionally left behind. Then we began to notice that the harbor was alive. The water swirled and parted to reveal dappled backs and shades of gray. The whales had returned to Bahia de la Paz for the first time since the whaling ships had plied these waters.

First we saw one gray whale, then two, three, five. As we scanned the waters, the whales multiplied to twenty, thirty, or more. Ahead of us two gray whales blew and lay at the surface, blocking our way forward. José cut the engines and we idled, watching the quiet, slow maneuvers of the leviathans.

The whales eventually moved slowly out of the shipping lane, and we continued on our path. The day was drawing to a close and the sun was beginning to set. The last embers of light hit the dark gray waters of Bahia de la Paz and sent flashes of orange and red into the depths.

As we approached the dock, a gray whale breached three times in the distance, silhouetted in the sunlight. We watched in silence at the type of finale that completes dreams and rarely enters reality. If Poseidon, brother of Zeus, exists, then he was watching over us on our voyage.

Darkness eventually took the harbor from our eyes, and the whales vanished into the night as phantoms and spirits of another world. The stars of heaven opened up above us and we were transported to a new world of light and darkness, of life and death united in a universe beyond our understanding. It was a melancholy moment, but one that could be lifted by remembrance of days past and of days still to come. We were home. To the land that is washed and sustained by Planet Ocean.

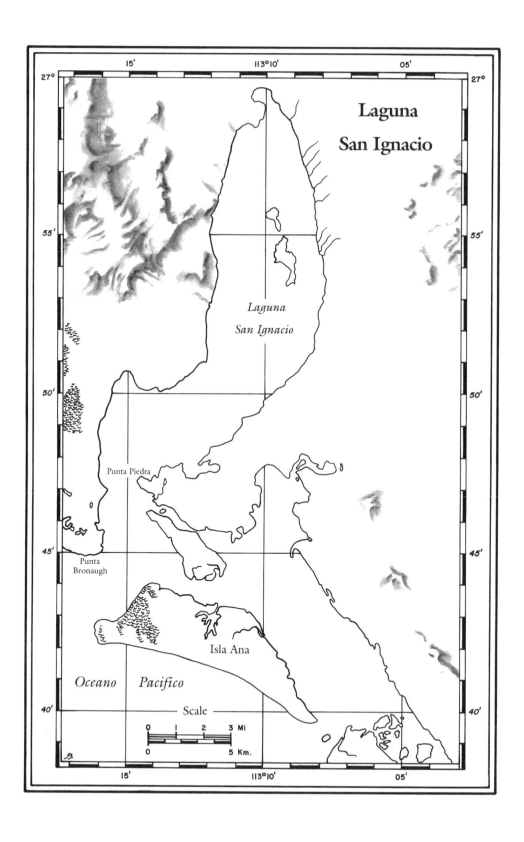

2

Gray Water, Gray Whales

The very air here is miraculous,
and outlines of reality change with
the moment. . . . A dream hangs over the
whole region, a brooding kind of hallucination.
—John Steinbeck, 1951

It is impossible to resist the pull of something that unites with your soul, that reflects the thoughts and feelings you have in your mind's eye. I returned to Baja almost exactly one year after my first voyage. Once more I used modern technology to take me across oceans to desert. Once more I wanted to immerse myself in the body and soul of Baja, to discover and learn more of this land—and its whales.

This voyage began in the southernmost city in American California, the naval port of San Diego. Here the golden people of Southern California live their golden lives, draining the water from north and east, trying to deny that they live in a desert land. These people are separated from the Pericu Indians by more than time.

In the huge bay of San Diego the naval ships lie at anchor, vast gray behemoths of man's creation. Before the city was here, before the people moved west, that other gray behemoth made use of this bay. Now the gray whales pass by San Diego on their route south, and no longer do they enter to bring their calves into the world. Now they rely on the warm, almost peopleless Baja California Sur.

I traveled to San Diego from Seattle, Washington. I had visited the Northwest to see the ancient forests and the snow-brushed mountains. Walking in the moist, temperate rainforest, I had seen tiny black shrew moles and black-tailed Sitka deer. I watched sunrises across mist-laden trees and saw night fall in the company of stars and the curious wildlife that had lost their fear of people.

On the flight south, green forests were replaced by straight-edged fields of cultivation and mammoth projects to capture water and funnel it to bustling cities. During the flight to San Diego over Mount Shasta, Lake Tahoe, Yosemite, then Los Angeles and the irrigated, distorted desert, the natural order vanished. I was in a world of manufactured desires and things that changed from being luxuries to necessities in decades rather than generations. The Promised Land of citrus fruit and Silicon Valley, of swimming pools and green lawns, is surrounded by desert that ultimately will reclaim its own.

The irrigation channels and flooded valleys looked like aberrations on the landscape, but even the most immense of projects somehow looked small in the context of all that we could see from 11,500 meters. The human footprint is small and temporary, and however we may criticize and defend against the changes that occur, it is satisfying to know that the winds of time will slowly and completely eradicate every blemish and blot that has been perpetrated against this land. We will not be around to witness this cleansing, but it will happen.

Once in San Diego I found myself at Fisherman's Landing and the *Searcher*, home for the next week as we looked for whales amid the glow of a desert sun, the cradling security of El Pacifico, and the protected waters of Laguna San Ignacio. The voyage would also be punctuated by island stops at Todos Santos, San Benitos, Cedros, and San Martin in search of sea lions and elephant seals, endemics and exotics.

The weather was typically Californian. The city skyline and the masts of the marina were topped by a clear blue sky, with only high cirrus clouds adding a subtle softening tone to the azure coloring. The temperature was a climatic shock. Only hours earlier I had been immersed in the rain and snow of Washington.

I left my bags aboard the *Searcher* and walked leisurely around the marina, taking in the sounds, smells, and activity of this marine metropolis. We were due to leave port at midnight, and the afternoon offered the promise of birding amid the affluent fishing-folk of the bay.

Western grebes abounded in the marina. Their red eyes flashed in the sunlight, and they watched carefully as the day's catch was gutted on the boats. At the suggestion of danger the birds were gone, their slender bodies plummeting into the depths with hardly a ripple remaining on the surface.

Along the artificial shoreline, least sandpipers scuttled along the high tide line, picking their way diligently through the debris left by the waves. Tiny birds, they appeared too delicate to survive the many pressures of life. Even more remarkable is that this twelve-centimeter, light brown bird spends its summers on the Alaskan tundra, venturing south to the warm Pacific coast only when the long northern days fade into cold and darkness.

Even among the bustling humanity of the marina, wildlife abounded in a spiraling array of noisy, arrogant winged fauna. Forster's terns circled the fishing boats overhead, followed by Heering, Thayer's, California, and western gulls. And moving from vessel to vessel, favorite among the crews, a pair of mallards plowed the docks as though the royalty of the marina's bird life.

As the sun set behind the boats, silhouetting the masts and stays against a cloudless sky, all prospective whale-watchers returned to the *Searcher*. We were introduced to the ship and its crew: Captain Joe Herring; Chris, Bob, and Newman, our skiff drivers; and Mitch, our cook. John Kipping, an old-school California radical with an *Earth First!* mentality, would be our guide and naturalist for the week aboard the thirty-five-meter chartered fishing vessel.

We relaxed toward the stern, awaiting the moment when the lines would be dropped and we would begin sailing south. Crested black-crowned night-herons alighted on the ship, and we became witness to an entertaining dance between herons and the prey that had attracted them, the anchovies held captive in the bait tanks on the stern.

The immature birds, first to approach, were bold and forthright individuals. The floodlights highlighted their buff coloration, flecked with light spots and olive brown streaks. The birds' pale yellow eyes followed the movements in the tanks with precision. The herons would stand on the edge of the bait tank and peer into the water, straightening their necks and creating a straight line from beak to legs, giving maximum strike force as they hit the water. When a bird drew back its weapon, more often than not a small, wriggling fish was gripped securely in its bill. The bird would then carefully manipulate the catch, gently but forcefully grinding the fish and maneuvering the tiny animal until it was positioned headfirst. Then with a throwback of the head and a shivering motion of the gullet, the fish was gone and the heron could return to fishing.

As the night progressed, the glossy black adult birds began to appear, initially in the darkness beyond the lights. Occasionally one would settle on the back railing, the distinctive white tapering crest almost fluorescent under the lights. This twelve-centimeter-long crest is absent in the younger birds, but it makes the adults truly reminiscent of birds of paradise.

Whenever the mature birds attempted to encroach directly on the bait tank, the juveniles responded aggressively with loud barks and flapping wings. The adult birds always seemed to get the worst of any confrontation with their offspring. At one time seven herons were crowded on the stern, the juveniles on the tanks, the adult birds relegated to the railing and jetty. The crested birds flew silently around the ship, their gray wings caught in the marina lights like ghosts on the edge of life, unable to land but continually flying in search of a landing spot. Avian Flying Dutchmen.

Only when the juveniles were sated by their dips into the bait tank and left of their own accord were the adults able to show off their fishing skills. The crested birds would spread their wings silently over the tanks, as if shading the fish from the glare of the floodlights and enticing them into striking distance.

This dance of the fish herons was carried on silently, with only an occasional bark of consternation.

Under the floodlights we were able to get a good look at the adults. They were distinguished-looking birds—medium-sized herons with short, thick necks. The birds had a glossy blackish-green crown and back, gray wings and tail, and a white face and underparts. The large red eyes certainly looked as though they should impart good night vision to these predatory fishers. The legs were slender and pale, while the feet were distinctively large, with three long toes pointing forward and one straight back in typical exaggerated avian fashion.

Eventually the birds had their fill of live wriggling fish, and they slowly flew off, gray wings taking them silently into the night. Soon only a single adult bird remained, taking advantage of the total absence of competition to make up his share of the catch. Throughout the rest of the evening, until the ship left the dock at midnight, the birds continued to come and go. The squabbling between juveniles seemed to increase, and once, briefly, a snowy egret felt the brunt of their brusque manner over the bait tank.

As we left the marina, we passed other floodlit patches on the jetty, and numerous caches of bait, the focus of intense bird activity. Night-herons, pelicans, and egrets were all taking advantage of corralled living food placed so carefully by their human captors, and rapidly being converted from fish into bird.

We traveled through the night, and at dawn found ourselves approaching Islas Todos Santos, All Saints' Island. It was St. Patrick's Day.

The sun rose at six, revealing calm blue seas, and on the horizon the barren countenance of Todos Santos. This was my first morning back in Baja. One full year had passed since I was last here. I can remember every moment, replay all the images in my mind, instance by instance. I can taste the desert air in my lungs, feel the crisp heat of the sun on my skin, and sense the whales from the deep at the ends of my fingertips.

I stood on the deck of the *Searcher* and stared into the depths and to the horizon. There was such familiarity in these waters. Then they appeared. A group of thirty or more common dolphins passed by, pausing briefly to porpoise on our bow and in our wake, their hourglass coloration flashing beneath the waves. They glanced in our direction, perhaps looking up to the people on the bow, and vanished. Witnessing such an encounter is always exhilarating. It reaffirms that these waters are alive and vibrant, that the cycle of life, perhaps even intelligence, inhabits the oceans.

The encounter also does more—it demonstrates that we are far from these oceans in spirit and body. We are the aliens dependent on surface vessels to take us across bodies of water. The water's surface is a ceiling to them and a floor to us, a membranous barrier to intraspecific understanding. Perhaps that is why some are drawn to the depths. So many look to the stars for contact, but it is the inner space, the oceans, that offer the immediacy of scientific gratification to the curious. Simply allow yourself to enter the water, in spirit and body, and the wonders of life are revealed.

We drew closer to Islas Todos Santos, and Cassin's auklets fled from our path. As we approached one group of three of these squat little birds, they glanced backward and began to swim faster and faster. They seemed to realize that we were approaching too rapidly, and they tried to take to the air. The birds flapped their wings and ran across the surface of the water, feet tripping in the waves and wings beating, trying to get the lift necessary to raise their rotund bulks out of the water. When auklets feed on the fry that forms their staple diet, they eat so much at a single instance that for a while they are quite incapable of flight. In desperation the birds dove into the water with an audible plop, and we could see them flying through the depths, trailing bubbles.

As we neared the island, a few California sea lions basked in the sun. Several raised flippers clear of the water to warm themselves in a posture known as jugging. Sea lion flippers are well served by blood vessels; when feeling cold, the animals lift their flippers into the air, allowing the breeze to warm them. Several of the sea lions had been fishing, and the remnants of their catch attracted ring-billed and western gulls that wheeled overhead and alighted in the water for scraps.

We dropped anchor at Islas Todos Santos at 6:45 A.M. After breakfast the aluminum skiffs were launched, and we landed on the island. As we pulled ashore, the sun caught the white paint on one of the rocks:

    WELCOME IN GOD WE TRUST
    Y TODOS SANTOS
    VI/XI/LXXV

Islas Todos Santos is a small island off the coast of Baja California Norte near Ensenada. The island inhabitants frequent a small, temporary fishing village, where they cure their catch and dry algae on the windswept and sun-scorched hillsides.

Black oystercatchers dodged the incoming waves amid the boulders, and six harbor seals watched us from the water, their heads bobbing gently in the swell. At the far end of the beach was a small slate-gray dappled seal pup, its umbilical scar still clearly visible. A group of western gulls were relentlessly harassing it, pecking and squabbling over the lone and forlorn individual. Perhaps the mother was one of the heads bobbing in the surf, cautiously watching our movements, or maybe the youngster was alone, abandoned and unsure.

Innumerable crushed purple sea urchins were scattered across the beach. The urchin feed on kelp, and in turn are preyed upon by the fishermen, who farm the creatures commercially, selling the gonads to Japan. The forces of commercial bargaining reach even to Baja and its desert islands. Kelp flies swarmed about our feet, covering the decaying vegetation on the tide line, and buzzing our heads as we delayed on the shore. We made our way up the cliff as the seals slapped warnings on the water's surface. Western gulls covered the hillside, white dots among the green vegetation, and interspersed between them, occasional white crosses punctuated the slope, marking the point of some accidental death.

This body of rock was a creation of the tectonic forces of the region. We could make out five clearly cut marine terraces. They were formed roughly 100,000 years apart as the land shifted and the sea level rose and fell over time, responding to the global shifts in magma and the polar icecaps as the blue-green planet that is our home traveled through the universe in defined cycles that stretch the imagination.

We could look upon the volcanic rocks, the gray waki, and the foraminifera fossils imprisoned in the chert and imagine the pressures that shaped this land and the life upon it. The foraminifera are an order of plankton that literally wander the oceans of the world (the term derives from the Greek *planktos,* meaning "wandering" or "drifting," the same root that gives us the word planet). Plankton have been in existence since the Cambrian period, 570 million years ago. Despite their tiny dimensions, these single-celled animals have hard shells of calcium carbonate that is precipitated into forms and shapes that are staggeringly beautiful. They look like living snowflakes. When these animated sculptures die, their calcareous bodies form the chalk with which we are all so familiar, and under certain conditions, when huge pressures are exerted on the delicate structures, marble is created. So much of the art of the world is carved from these wandering organic snowflakes.

We walked through the small village on the hillside. Only six shacks made up this temporary dwelling. Each of the buildings was built of corrugated sheet and panels from wooden crates stamped with brand names familiar to consumers the world over. Tarpaulin covered sections of the structures, and one or two had an open awning from which people and dogs watched as we passed by.

In front of one of the shacks was a twelve-by-six-meter red rectangle of epiphytic algae, drying under the sun for export to the East. It was a harsh, windblown existence where everything had a use and nothing was thrown away. The people greeted us warmly, not overly curious about our presence, but with apparent humor as we peered at the plants about our feet and snapped photographs of the views and animals with which they lived their lives.

We stared in wonder at the native plant species that tripped and speared our feet. Gamboling cactus, the pitaya agria, and prickly pear abounded. Golden-crowned and sage sparrows darted about as we trekked across to the west side of the island, and a black phoebe flushed from the undergrowth.

In places, the terraces were well stocked with vegetation. From a distance Islas Todos Santos had appeared nearly barren, but at our feet were delicate communities of plants, both native and foreign, that had a grip on this rock. Desert mallow, pickleweed, and ice plants held forth in the shallow soil and crevices of the boulders, their fleshy stems and specialized adaptations allowing them to survive in habitats devoid of essential nutrients and smothered in salt. Cliff spurge, a plant well adapted to this region, was everywhere. Poisonous milky white sap flows from the stem when broken, a useful defense employed in modern times against the European rabbits and hares that have invaded these islands. Further, the spurge is often completely leafless, investing in its small, ovate leaves only following rare rainfalls; in this manner the plant can avoid serious water loss through transpiration in time of drought but is still able to photosynthesize. Flashes of color on the island were provided by the endemic yellow poppy, its small flower contrasting with the gray-green skeletal stem and leaves, and at our feet the distinctive flowers of *Mirabilis* blazed purple.

The poisonous nature of the spurge was matched by an onion-like plant with purple flower heads that we often saw growing out of its center, or through the heart of the prickly boxthorn. This onion plant is laced with toxic alkaloids that protect it from being grazed and seem to inhibit the growth of certain plants around it, thus restricting the competition it faces for limited desert resources.

Between these salt-loving adaptive and hardy plants were the bones of animals that had died far below us along the shore, carried here by scavenging gulls. Harbor seal vertebrae had been picked clean and glimmered white among the green of the plants and dusty browns of the soil.

Far below us, bright green surf grass covered the rocks along the shoreline. Surf grass is prime feed for the black brant that flee Alaska at the onset of winter and find sanctuary along this golden coast. Pelicans launched themselves into the surf from guano-covered rocks, and far beyond the surf line a gray whale blew and lifted its flukes clear of the water. The animal was heading south. It was our first sighting of a great whale on the voyage, and we stared at the place the whale dove.

White surf crashed over the rocks, cascading into pools and creating swirling currents and eddies along the shore. We continued our pedestrian circumnavigation of the island. We were at the mouth of Bahia de Todos Santos, so that to the east and south the horizon was marked by the gray silhouettes of mainland mountains. A low mist seemed to hug the ocean about us, and a haze shrouded the mountains in the distance. Only as we sat and leisurely gazed around did we realize the source of this haze. To the north the bustling cities of San Diego and Los Angeles were exporting more than tourists to Baja. Smog in the wilderness—a sad commentary on the transboundary nature of pollution, and that one nation's actions can directly affect the purity and preservation of another.

As we sat and contemplated the pervasiveness of the air around us, western gulls postured on the side of the hill. Among the low-lying vegetation on the west side of the island, the gulls were pairing up for the summer. Or rather they were re-pairing, reaffirming the link between individuals who mate for life. The birds bobbed and wove around each other, nodding heads in greeting or passing gifts of greenery from bill to bill. The growth of shrubs on the west side of the island was restricted due to its windswept aspect and the activity of the gulls. The birds trample the vegetation, never allowing the larger plants to gain a foothold. The result was a perfect landing strip, allowing the gulls to take full advantage of the upcurrents off the cliff face.

We were overlooking the eroded coves that punctuated the western shore. The cove below us was frequented by fifteen or twenty harbor seals who peered at us with large cow eyes. A wandering tattler scurried over the rocks at the base of the cliff, weaving between waves on long yellow legs. Farther out in the cove we could see brown pelicans wheeling over the water, plunging in with arrow-like precision and surfacing with distended bills. The light revealed the source of the avian interest: a school of opal-eyed perch were massed over anchovies, their flanks flashing in the sunlight at every turn. We watched as the pelicans dove repeatedly on the massed fish, surfacing with a shake of their massive bills and seeming to have the arrogant gleam of success in their eyes. A large orange shape beneath the waves distracted us temporarily from the pelicans, and a garibaldi fish revealed itself to us briefly before settling deeper in the water column.

On the eastern side of the island, grasses and shrubbery reached above knee height. Songbirds called and darted from the concealing mass of plants. Red-breasted house finches whistled their characteristic three-note phrases, and horned larks sang above our heads. The tangled mass and the color of plants were stunning. Lemonade berry bushes stood two to three meters high, sporting their scented leaves and reddish berries that can slake a thirst. The boxthorn held up its small white blooms and supported a lichen used in the last century to make dyes. The lichen and boxthorn exist in a symbiotic relationship whereby the host plant provides a substrate, protection, and water, while the symbiont provides essential nutrients that it is able to assimilate more rapidly than its host. Such are the intimate ties in nature.

As we walked the trails, the fishhook cactus, *Mammillaria,* revealed itself to us, painfully. The plant is just a few centimeters high and consists of clustered stems and hooked spines that, once embedded, are difficult to remove. They were clustered on the paths, probably transported there as seeds by the hooves of animals and the feet or clothing of people, ready to harass and prick new generations of visitors.

Occasionally we stopped to overturn a rock or stone and peer beneath it for signs of slithering life. One stone revealed a western blue-tailed skink. The skink had a striped body and a distinctive red marking under its chin. Our reptile had lost its blue tail and was in the process of regrowing the appendage. But this replacement would not be blue. After a single escape from danger, the tiny reptile loses the reason for its name and enters reptilian anonymity. A second rock heralded a scorpion all of two centimeters long. We temporarily corralled it in a lunchbox and watched as it snapped its pincers and arched its stinger high over its segmented back—a wondrously malevolent-looking creature.

The desert was in full-scented bloom around us. In shades of yellow: the California poppy, the tubular flowers of the coastal agave or century plant, the prickly pear, and the large flowers of coreopsis, the sea dahlia. In shades of red: the hummingbird-pollinated Indian paintbrush. In shades of pink: the desert mallow. And in shades of purple: the "blue dick" or desert hyacinth, *Mirabilis,* the desert lavender, and *Mammillaria.*

Between Islas Todos Santos and the mainland, a school of common dolphins churned the water as though a tiny maelstrom had been generated by unseen forces beneath the waves. Onshore we were entertained by the laughing cries of the western gulls that grew to crescendos after slow and labored starts, by the darting olive-colored orange-crowned warbler, and by the whining calls of rufous-sided towhees.

The east side of the island had marked topography, and we sat beneath an extrusion of rock that reached far above our heads. Pitaya agria and prickly pear massed around us, and the carpet at our feet was painted in pastel pinks and reds. At length we returned to the cove where our trek had begun, and looked down at the *Searcher.* The harbor seals raised their heads to watch us as we approached, and again several slapped warnings on the water.

We returned to our vessel. With us came the kelp flies, persistent, buzzing, and irritating companions that remained with us for the rest of the voyage. We toasted St. Patrick and All Saints' Island at lunch as we sailed south toward Islas San Benitos and the elephant seal colony, some 440 kilometers distant. The journey took approximately eighteen hours of sailing time, and we traveled through the night.

Just after lunch we spotted a northbound gray whale, and changed course to follow him. We watched his movements carefully, counting blows and noting surfacing and dive times. He was moving fast and surfacing infrequently, and we soon turned to resume our journey south. At least we knew that whales were in these waters.

We were seven kilometers offshore, and the landscape to the east was still muted and obscured by haze so the land appeared to shift and change before our eyes. The mountains merged into the high cirrus clouds above, confounding the line between real and unreal, rock and phantom. A flock of surf scoters raced past us, northward-bound with the whale to Alaska, and a northern fulmar skimmed the water.

Within half an hour of the first gray whale sighting, we began to see more blows on the horizon, distant shapes of gray and bursts of steam rising from the water. We were joined fleetingly by eight Pacific white-sided dolphins, who briefly rode our stern waves to starboard before peeling off and ending a flirtation that could not have lasted more than two minutes. Still, they left us standing and leaning over the rail crying out for more.

A few common loons dove as our wake disturbed them, their elegant bodies visible flying through the water, and black-vented shearwaters darted about the ship. Otherwise the afternoon passed quietly, and we took the opportunity to talk with each other and introduce ourselves to the comforts of the thirty-five-meter vessel.

The cabins were located below deck and were linked to the captain by intercom so that all could be roused from their bunks should whales be seen. The galley occupied most of the first deck, while the helm and small boat-storage area were on the second. The vessel had no rooftop observation area as did the *Don José*, but instead offered a panoramic view in front of the helm, and from the crow's nest. There were sixteen of us aboard the vessel, plus crew and guide. It was a comfortable number for a craft of this size, few enough that the skiffs were not crowded and conversation during the week came around to everyone.

We journeyed south, savoring our excursion into this new world. The hike had been long and the previous night's sleep brief, so the afternoon was leisurely and lazy. We were roused from our bunks only once as the sun hung low in the sky. Fifteen or twenty common dolphins rode our bow, sending rainbows across the surf. The animals porpoised effortlessly by our side, clearing the water, weaving about our bulky vessel like messengers from Poseidon. They were drawing us into their watery world, tempting us, like the sirens of old, to make the transition from air to aqueous in a single motion, magical, musical dancers in the waves.

At six we gathered on the stern and watched as the sun slowly lowered to the horizon. No cloud hindered the view, and as the last embers hit the water, the fading spectrum of light passed before our eyes. The green flash emanated from the last crescent of the sun as the light faded and died, buried in the Pacific until tomorrow. In the morning the sun would resurrect itself and again warm the embers of the Earth and provide the energy that drives the planet. These age-old mysteries captivated Copernicus and his contemporaries, and they sought to observe and explain. The result is that today we forget the marvel of such a daily occurrence, the rising and setting of the sun. If it stopped one day, we would surely notice.

Darkness enveloped the *Searcher* within half an hour of the sun's sinking to the west. The weather turned distinctly brisk, and the waves threw bioluminescent whitecaps into ever-deepening troughs. The night sky above us was startlingly clear. Jupiter, Saturn, and Orion stood out among the innumerable unnamed or unknown constellations, and in the sea around us the bioluminescence created a vision of stars captured and imprisoned in the water. It was a vision of two universes, above and below, mirror images of living lights, and lights that may be warming other lives on other planets. Henry David Thoreau wrote, "Heaven is under our feet as well as over our heads." We were stargazers sailing through a new universe that reached out below us in three dimensions, that lit up as we passed through it and revealed shapes and forms as alien to us as those we could expect to find on a blue-green planet in some far-off corner of a distant solar system. The *Searcher* could not have been better named.

We were fast approaching our rendezvous at the three islands that make up Islas San Benitos to the north of the much larger Isla Cedros. As we ate breakfast, we were interrupted by a group of porpoising California sea lion pups who surfaced briefly around our vessel like some multiheaded serpent or medusa. The chocolate-colored pups streaked through the water, trailing bubbles, and cleared the surface in leaps and bounds as they raced toward the island.

It was eight before we stepped ashore, and the day was already heating up. We landed at the fishing village on the shore. It was a typical Baja encampment—wooden shacks of corrugated iron and boarding, everything and nothing used to create a village. Those who had constructed the town obviously had a dry sense of humor, particularly considering the tour boats that stop to see the elephant seal colony. One shack had HOTEL painted in large blue letters on the side wall.

Rubbish littered the sand and dust. The small settlement had generated quite a garbage dump, and western gulls and common ravens squabbled over fish skeletons and organic scraps. Two burros were wandering the village, and approached in anticipation of handouts. Each wore a tin can on its left foreleg—at first we thought by accident, but on closer inspection it appeared to be by design. They were curious animals, and followed as we paced the village. As the burros picked at the garbage, we noticed another presence among the dirt: a weaner elephant seal. The forlorn-looking yearling was alone and seemed quite despondent. He was in molt, and flies buzzed his dark, watery eyes. As we approached he raised his head and bleated with a half-open mouth. One of the burros entered on the scene and sniffed the youngster, so that for one split second, on the beach at Islas San Benitos, burro and weaner elephant seal kissed.

We were planning to circumnavigate the island, and began to follow one of the trails leading out of the camp. The trail was dotted with jumping cholla, that painful, well-adapted cactus that seems to leap upon the uninitiated and impale with all the tenacity that a vegetative object can muster to ensure its passage and transportation to new ground. All around us, along the trail, around the bushes, and in the undergrowth, the ground was pitted with small burrows. We stepped carefully to avoid the entrances to the subterranean lairs, as well as trying to gauge where the tunnels were so that our weight would not cause some cavernous collapse. Our passage flushed one of the burrows' inhabitants, and the black storm-petrel half ran, half flew from our feet until it took to the air and disappeared.

We crossed a short peninsula on the island, and as we approached the far shore, we began to hear and smell, rather than see, what we had come for. At first it was as though they were invisible, and then they were obvious, and they were everywhere. After all, how do you hide something the size of an elephant seal? These animals live up to their gargantuan name. Adult males can weigh in at over 2,700 kilograms and measure 6.5 meters in length, while females are half that size. But it is more than size that gives the animal its name.

The northern elephant seal, along with the whales of the region, faced broad-scale slaughter in the late 1800s. One large male could be rendered to give 560 liters of oil. It is only through luck that the species survived at all. In 1892 a group of scientists found what they believed were the last eight surviving northern elephant seals; they killed seven of them. The rationale for such an action escapes me. Luckily they missed a small but viable seal colony on Isla Guadalupe, and in 1911, 125 animals were censused there. Today the population has rebounded under international protection, and some 100,000 animals have regained their former range.

The long-term implications of the species having to go through such a forced genetic bottleneck are unknown. The drastically reduced gene pool may well have restricted the species' long-term viability by limiting the population's ability to respond to environmental change. A sudden change in food supply, water temperature, or any other environmental variable could potentially present the species with an evolutionary hurdle that it is no longer adapted to overcome. Undoubtedly we will not know until it is too late.

The northern elephant seal, one of the largest of the earless seals (exceeded in size only by its southern cousins), is today found all along the California coast, from American Norte to Mexican Baja. The seal breeds at the island rookeries of Año Nuevo, the Farallons, and the Channel Islands to the north, and in Baja on the islands of San Miguel, San Nicholas, Guadalupe, and of course Islas San Benitos. Released from hunting pressure, the animals are even beginning to re-establish rookeries on the mainland.

They are captivating animals. Despite the past slaughter, the seals do not appear to treat humans as a threat, and the social structure of the rookeries is fascinating to watch. The seals have the photogenic appeal of large, dark, watery eyes topped by sparse eyebrows, ripples of blubbery fat, and a contented, laid-back attitude toward life. The animals are also incredibly vocal, producing sounds that range in pitch from squeals to deep belches, from rumbling roars to delicate, pathetic whimpers. And then there is that nose.

All elephant seals, at least young males and all females, have a slightly fleshy pug nose, delicately trimmed by whiskers. As the males mature, however, the pug nose is transformed into a fleshy, dangling, lumpy, resonating proboscis that may be up to sixty centimeters long. Present only in the mature males, the elephant seal's nose is a secondary sexual characteristic, much like the plumes on birds of paradise or the narwhal's tusk. The larger the male's nose, the more dominant the animal, and the more females he will be able to mate with.

The male elephant seal uses his proboscis to amplify the sounds he makes, and it is often the noises generated by a male that decide the winner during a challenge rather than any direct physical contact. Thus, elephant seals use their noses in much the same way that gorillas beat their chests. The larger the seal, the bigger his nose, and the louder the noise he can make. All the posturing and roars are meant to reduce the chance of direct, possibly harmful, physical encounters. A small or immature male just entering the mating game should be well aware of his opponents' abilities before they ever come to blows, and so mismatched confrontations are avoided. All because of that nose.

We stepped among the seals along the shoreline. The ocean was a rich sapphire blue, and the waves lapped gently against the slopping shore, or crashed against the rocky granite outcrops between which were nestled seals. There were about a dozen females and immature males in this cove. Most were dozing in the sun, epitomizing the slightly derogatory term often applied to these blubbery animals: "beach maggots." They were not really asleep, and as we walked by they opened teary eyes and gurgled or whimpered. Only if we approached too close would an animal raise its head, open its mouth to reveal an impressive array of teeth and a bright pink palate, and bark, or more precisely bleat, and such a high-pitched bleat that we could hardly believe that the sound emanated from such rotund Falstaffian creatures. But most of the movement and sounds coming from the seals were directed at each other, and we hardly elicited a reaction.

Several seals were lying head to tail, and we were able to observe the comical posturing and sniping between animals as one moved to a slightly more comfortable position in the sand, only to hit the animal sleeping behind it in the face with a misplaced flipper. The offended seal would raise its head back in open-mouthed dismay and a deep-throated gurgle, ripples of skin folding along its neck, only to return to dozing seconds later, slightly rearranged, but seemingly too tired to move.

Some animals lay along the tide line, allowing each wave to wash under them, while others moved from the sea up the beach with massive peristaltic blubbery rhythms rippling through their bodies. The animals were every shade from black to light tan, and several looked as though they had begun to molt. It was usual to see two or more seals huddled together as they slept, as though these marine mammoths hate to sleep alone. They were often positioned either head to head or head to tail, sometimes creating the distant image of a two-headed beast.

Most of the seals were covered with sand and small pieces of gravel. The seals are fairly dexterous with their foreflippers, using them to scoop up the gravelly material around them and fling it upon their own backs. In doing so they often hit their companion, resulting in more whimpers and bleats of recrimination or open-mouthed, pink-palated silent pleas of protest. The reasons behind the sand bath may be multiple: to shoo away the persistent and immensely irritating kelp flies that hover around their tear-filled eyes, to reduce the impact of the heat of the sun on their exposed backs, or to cool the animals' skin. Whatever the reason or purpose, the elephant seal is the only pinniped to engage in this activity.

The northern elephant seal is also the deepest-diving of the pinnipeds. It feeds mainly on deep-water and bottom-dwelling organisms such as squid, elasmobranch, and teleost fish. Average dives are to depths of 350 to 650 meters, although the deepest dive ever recorded was to 894 meters (more than 2,600 feet).

Our movements along the beach were being closely matched by a common raven. The slate-black bird picked through the bands of kelp on the beach, poking at the remains of sea creatures long since dead and disintegrated. He was unperturbed by the number of people surrounding him on the beach, often only a meter away; after all, he had the ultimate ability—flight. The sea is an incredible provider, both to those who enter its depths and to those who wait at its periphery and take what it regurgitates. Other birds followed the raven's lead. Savannah sparrows darted from rocks to tide pools to drift line, scavenging whatever was available. These small brown sparrows are common on the mainland, but here they are evolving to take advantage of ecological niches, new ways of life, that are unoccupied on the isolated islands. Through such adaptive radiation, the sparrows are evolving down a path similar to that of the famous finches of the Galapagos. The savannah sparrows of Islas San Benitos even feed on seal carcasses.

We continued on the coastal trail, sending up clouds of kelp flies from the seaweed, with savannah sparrows darting about our feet. As we followed the slightly elevated trail, we wove between granite outcrops, and upon rounding one we came face to face with a very surprised-looking elephant seal. She stared at us, and we stared back. Her mouth opened slightly to reveal well-developed canines, and her eyes reflected quizzical curiosity rather than fear. Those large eyes, so much larger than ours, seemed to hold only trust. She simply stared at us, obviously not quite sure what we were, and certainly not treating us as a threat. She whimpered slightly, but otherwise made no sound.

She was beautiful. Her coat was a light tan color and completely unblemished. Her eyes were clear and black, glinting in the sunlight, and delicate whiskers covered her fleshy nose. Her eyebrows seemed raised in surprise, and as we walked by she watched closely, but without ever giving up her position on the trail.

The next cove was home to twenty or thirty more seals, overlooked by an osprey eyrie set high on a granite promontory. As in the previous location, the principal pastime for these animals was sleep, basking under the sun. Most of the animals lay on their stomachs, sneezing each breath as they opened their nostrils, but others lay more on their sides or backs, contented grins on their round faces. The kelp flies were everywhere, in the seaweed and on the faces of these angelic cherubs. One young weaner stared at us without recognition as kelp flies swarmed about his head, drinking the tears that flowed continuously from his eyes. Occasionally the seals would flinch and shake their heads, or paw at their muzzles with foreflippers, but generally they were resigned to the buzzing insistence of the flies and ignored them.

At the center of this large group was a full-grown adult male elephant seal. He was surrounded by his harem, and dwarfed every individual. He was probably 6.5 meters long, and his long nose hung limply in the sand. The season was late, mating was done for the year, and the bull was at rest. The adults of both sexes were already beginning to leave for the open sea, and soon only the newly weaned pups would remain on shore.

The time of intense activity on the beach occurs in late November or early December, when the mature males arrive on shore and vie for dominance. The bulls do not defend a specific territory as do other pinniped species, but establish a hierarchy of dominance among themselves. The males are extremely vocal at this time, inflating their snouts through muscular action and blood pressure, effectively amplifying their roars. Should the posturing and vocal threats not settle the issue of dominance, then the animals come to bloody blows. When fighting, the males rear up and battle chest to chest, ripping at each other with canines, biting at the fleshy nose and neck. The winner becomes the alpha male of the beach and guards his harem of twenty-five to fifty females from the incursions of lesser, beta, males, who loiter at the periphery of the alpha male's territory.

When the females arrive on the beach they are pregnant, and they pup within a week. Less than three weeks later they mate again. Mature females essentially spend all of their adult life pregnant. Following the birth of their offspring, the cows feed their pups with incredibly rich milk, and the 30-to-45-kilogram pups quadruple their birth weight in just a month. Over the same period the fasting cow may lose 320 kilograms in support of her youngster. Life is tough for the black-coated pup during its early days. Mortality is high, and as many as 40 percent of the pups will not survive the first few months. Some will fall victim to battling males who crush them unseen beneath 2,500-kilogram weights; others will be separated from their mothers, whom they link with at birth via a distinctive and individually identifiable bonding call, and starve. There are many accidents that can befall such a dependent baby. However, there are also some particularly astute pups on the beach, who steal milk from other cows. These so-called "super-weaners" can put on 180 kilograms in a single month.

When they reach about four weeks of age, the pups are abruptly weaned. The cows head for open water, simply abandoning their young and leaving them to learn to swim and feed themselves. The weaners lose the black coats of puphood and turn silvery gray. They remain on the beach until April or May, and then they too head for the open ocean.

As we walked back to the trail, the sounds of the colony followed us, the groans, belches, whistles, yawns, sneezes and snuffles, whines and whimpers, the sound of blubber on gravel, and gravel being flung upon blubber, carried by Pacific breezes. An elephant seal colony is never totally silent, even when every individual seems to be asleep.

Two osprey nests overlooked the sleeping pinnipeds, and as we hiked toward them a bird on one of the nests screamed a rapid warning, *kywe kywe kywe,* and swiveled its head to watch us. Its partner was skimming the water out to sea, and returned to the nest with empty talons. The two birds clicked beaks, and the newly returned parent bent gently down into the nest. For a second we could make out the fluffy white form of the chick. The nest itself was an avian engineering phenomenon. Ospreys return year after year to their eyries, building them into a mansion of avian architecture. The nest was probably two meters high, a mass of intertwined twigs and sticks mottled white with guano.

The ospreys had an incredible view of this volcanic and tortured island—a tortured landscape in terms of both its geologic history and the scorching climatic pressure that bakes the plants to dry, fragile crisps that crack underfoot and snap at a touch. The coastline was dominated by black granite tinged with the grays and oranges of crusty lichen, while at our backs the hills had been rounded out by time. Typical desert plants dotted the hillsides. Boxthorn grew in clumps, but the most conspicuous plant was an alkali heath, Palmer's frankenia. Frankenia is a blue-gray, multibranched low perennial shrub with a woody crown and roots. Salt crystals cover its leaves. The plant is alleopathic, meaning that it produces chemicals that diffuse from the roots and inhibit the growth of other plants within a certain radius. In this manner the plant is able to restrict the growth of other plants that would compete for the limited desert water and soil nutrients. The visual result is a hillside dotted with evenly spaced blue-gray vegetation.

Growing out of the geometric shapes of the islands' rocks were several coastal agaves in full bloom. This species of agave has large, glossy leaves arranged in a rosette close to the ground. Each leaf is fleshy and succulent and terminates in sharp spines edged with teeth. From the center of this spiral rosette of leaves shoots the single flower stalk, perhaps four meters high, which branches at its apex as though pointing roots toward the sky. Each terminus is tipped with brilliant orange tubular flowers.

The agave grows slowly, putting its reserves into the spiraling pointed leaves for years, then suddenly redirecting its energies and producing the towering stalk of flowers. After the plant has put forth this splash of procreative color, it dies. Oftentimes another plant will grow up in its place, repeating the long growth cycle, and giving rise to the belief that the agave flowers but once every one hundred years: the century plant.

In places the island turned red and russet as the volcanic rocks were exposed by the eons of erosion. The fossilized foraminifera were compressed into the cherts and quartz of the island, and the plants held tenuous hold in this soil of ancient life now giving new muted life to the desert. Constrained only by the lack of water, waiting to burst forth in a cacophony of color, when . . .

One of the agaves above us was a perch to one of the fish eagles devouring its most recent catch. We watched as the osprey picked at the fish, and silvery scales fell from the blooms to litter the ground with cartilaginous offerings.

The sun was baking, and the hike was getting more strenuous as we stepped heavily on the unstable scree and shales. Our trail came out to a cliff top, and we sat and ate lunch while watching the elephant seals on the beach below. Tiny yellow rock daisies took hold in the slip scree, along with some of the frankenia and cliff spurge, and in the rock pools below an American oystercatcher picked its way between boulders, both granite and living. Omnipresent ospreys soared overhead, *kyweing* our presence.

At length we scrambled down the cliff to walk the beach and look at the seals. As we reached the beach, it was obvious that we were to see something that none of us had expected: asphalt. The black rocks around us were not the natural colors of the granite that we had seen earlier. The hard, black coating here was solidified oil from some dumping or spill that had come unseen and silent upon the beach. When we could not tell, but the elephant seals on this beach were speckled with oil. None of the animals were heavily coated, but all had their bellies daubed with black dots and streaks from pulling themselves across the tainted gravel. It was sad to see, and impossible to do anything about. Perhaps a passing ship had washed bilge water from its tanks and illegally discharged its waste in these waters, unknowing or uncaring as to what would happen when the oil hit shore. The seals did not understand and did not care. They were busy with their lives, and only when ours infringes upon theirs do their squawks of indignation become more than idle noises.

A few young males and females bent their heads over gravelly backs to watch our movements, and some mouthed their feelings of discontent, but most returned to doing what they are best at, throwing gravel and moving their bulks around in undulating fashion. A minor squabble between two animals broke out in the surf, and for a moment 1,000 kilograms of combined bodies seemed to grapple in confrontation as the animals raised themselves up, chest to chest, and wove around each other, mouths agape, but never actually coming into physical contact. Then the animals collapsed onto the sand next to each other and went back to sleep, honor having been satisfied.

Back on the trail, the raven had returned. In a split second while the ospreys had both been away from the eyrie fishing, the raven had snatched the chick. The black bird was now feasting on a rocky ledge above our heads. Ospreys are majestic birds, the sight of which lifts the soul to new heights. To see the dark raven devouring the hope of the next generation bordered on the horrific, but ravens have to live, and the carelessness of the ospreys had given the raven the opportunity to reap the benefits for itself and its offspring. Still, there is something about seeing an animal preying upon one that is not normally at its level on the food chain that is disconcerting and intensely macabre. With involuntary shivers and glances toward the now-empty eyrie, we left the cliff.

As at the beginning of the trail, the path was pocketed with burrows, but these were larger, home to the Cassin's auklets that run from boats, tripping across waves when their rotund bodies deny them lift. The trail led us to a maritime graveyard. Dashed against the volcanic rocks was a vast tuna seiner, heavily listing to starboard. The vessel had run aground here in February 1989 following a fierce Pacific storm. Perhaps it was this vessel that now leaked black oil and tar on the nearby beaches, staining the life of the island. Time would eventually remove the stain and crush the iron of the vessel's hull, rusting the bolts and supports until the ship crumbled into the surf, perhaps creating a new reef for life to cover.

Behind us we were alerted to yet another osprey eyrie by the eagle eyes of the bird and its distinctive alarm call. The tide was washing into the black pools, and sally lightfoot crabs danced between crevices, their brash reds and blues contrasting dramatically with the black of the shoreline. As we jumped from rock to rock among the pools, the crabs ran ahead of us like Steinbeck's "little puffs of blue smoke." We felt the challenge, and wanted to look more upon this crustacean. Where Steinbeck had failed so often, we determined to succeed.

We watched the crabs move from pool to pool, trying to see how we could corner one. The sally lightfoots were new arrivals to this island. Only with the warming of the 1986 El Niño current were conditions conducive to a northward expansion of the animals' range. John Kipping, our naturalist, made repeated attempts at capture, but at the slightest flinch, the crabs evaporated from sight. Eventually we managed to corner one in a crevice. In moments we had one of these elusive, ghostly crabs that seem to inhabit another dimension in our own world, held securely in our hands. John Steinbeck's characterization of the moment of capture is classic: "Eventually we did catch a few Sallys, but we think they were the halt and the blind, the simpletons of their species. With reasonably well-balanced and non-neurotic Lightfoots we stood no chance."

We held our neurotic specimen to the light. The crab was slightly larger than a man's hand. Held carefully but securely, it made no move, save for the stalked eyes rotating to watch its human captors. The crab's carapace and legs were a deep, dark red, speckled with blue dots, while its underside was a lighter yellow-red. The crab was immensely patient with us, and we petted it gently to feel the shell, so familiar to us as people but so alien to us as a species.

At length we returned the crab to its pool. It hesitated momentarily on the side of a rock, then scurried away, clicking its legs and claws against the volcanic shale, and vanished into the labyrinth of pools.

We poked around in the tide pools for a while longer, peering at mollusks of all shapes and sizes, anemones waving tentacles in the underwater breezes, and chitons locked in place on the rocks. Chitons are oval plated creatures that have remained unchanged since Cambrian times, 600 to 500 million years ago, evolutionarily secure in a cushioned marine environment. They reminded me of the trilobites frozen into rocks I collected as a child. Chitons are grazers, rasping algae from the surface of rocks, their "coat-of-mail" shells securing them against predators. They are our window to a past that is too often locked in stone instead of alive, moving, and vibrant.

A more contemporary evolutionary experiment barked at us from a distant pool: a fully maned bull California sea lion. In comparison with the chitons this is an infant species, a species whose ancestors entered these warm waters a mere 25 million years ago, yet still ancient in terms of human biological and cultural evolution.

A lighthouse was positioned high above us, and we hiked upward. The path was lined with stocky barrel cactus adorned with bright red blooms and more agaves. Rufous hummingbirds darted between flowers, their colors dazzling in the sunlight. The hike was strenuous, but when we reached the top, the view of the wreck and to the horizon was simply breathtaking.

From a distance the lighthouse's white-daubed tower had appeared intact and in fine condition, but as we reached the base of the tower, the ground was sprinkled with glass. We climbed the spiral steps to the top, peering through the round porthole windows. The light was smashed and the windows were gone; small beads of mercury collected on the wooden floor, and abandoned tins were piled high on the boards.

The landscape around the lighthouse was barren compared to the vegetation elsewhere on the island. Agaves, barrel cactus, frankenia, jumping cholla, and cliff spurge dominated. The ground was baked hard, and the only movement was the occasional side-blotched lizard dashing to shade.

We began our descent back down toward the fishing village. We had almost circumnavigated the island, and now the distant islands that complete Islas San Benitos were visible ahead of us, white breakers crashing on their shores. The well-marked trail was punctuated by the dead white flower stalks of the agave, and the occasional white-framed cliff spurge devoid of leaves. Violet-green swallows flew overhead on bent wings, and the smell and sound of the salt waves reached us on high.

As we headed down, we looked out upon a tidal pool complex inhabited by half-submerged elephant seals, their coats darkened by the water. The beach area was crowded with animals, perhaps fifty or sixty. In the water, swimming in the depths, was a bull elephant seal. He looked to be patrolling the access to the beach, and as he turned toward shore, he dipped his nose into the water and blew air through his chamber. Bubbles frothed up in the water, and it sounded as though someone were blowing through a straw at the bottom of a glass—a very big glass. The females on the beach largely ignored this loud display and continued their own squabbling.

The bull began to approach the dozing females, most of whom were aligned with heads toward the ocean. His movements were slow and deliberate; it was like watching a 2,500-kilogram slug pull itself along with quiet determination. The bull swam as close to shore as he could, then stopped abruptly. He was grounded on the sloping beach, still about two meters from dry land. The bull hesitated, lifted himself up in the surf line, and waited until a wave crashed to shore. With the momentum and lift provided by the water, he shuffled forward. As the wave washed back, he flopped heavily onto the still-submerged sandy gravel. This process was repeated five or six times, the bull gaining ground on the beach with each wave.

As he finally pulled himself ashore, the beach awoke in a cacophony of sound. The females who had been dozing quietly awoke, and the beach came alive as they turned and fled from the advancing male. Several of the largest females seemed to move with incredible speed, their bodies rippling and undulating in blubbery motion as they took up positions high on the beach, almost to the cliff face. It was entertaining to watch the evident distaste and mistrust the females had of the newly arrived male, but they need not have worried. The male was evidently exhausted by his efforts, and he collapsed in the surf line and went to sleep. Five minutes later all was quiet again as the rearranged seals settled down and the waves continued to lap beneath the bulk of the male.

The *Searcher* was in the channel below us, and we hurried down, stepping carefully along a narrow ledge rimming the bay, past a fisherman bringing in crab pots. We waited while the skiffs were sent out from the *Searcher*, and within half an hour we were steaming south. Once more we traveled through the night, along the coastline of the Desierto de Vizcaino, past Punta de San Pedro, Bahia de Asuncion, and Bahia de San Hipolito, until we reached Bahia de Ballenas and the breaker entrance to Laguna San Ignacio.

The wind whipped around the *Searcher* and raised the white-capped waves to new heights as they stormed over the unseen shifting sandbars that defied our maps. A few gray whales blew around us, seeking their own way through the maelstrom. One of the skiffs was lowered into the water and sent ahead to find a channel to the inner sanctuary.

The wind swept tails of white from the waves in front of us, and they galloped forward as if a stampeding herd of horses had been let loose in some fresh new pasture. There is a tale in Irish prehistory of Manannan, son of Lir, Lord of the Sea. Manannan's vessel, the *Ocean-sweeper*, obeyed the thoughts of those who sailed in her, but had neither oar nor sail. The Celts called the white-crested waves of surf the Horses of Manannan, and Manannan himself was garbed in a great cloak which, chameleon-like, could transform to any shade or color. Truly this was a sight to lead to those great legends of magical sorcerers and supernatural beings.

The *Searcher* responded to the silent commands of the helm, and slowly followed the aluminum skiff through the breakers. As we reached the channel, the *Searcher* was borne up by the swell and we surfed through the white-winged Horses of Manannan. For a few tense minutes it seemed as though we were at the mercy of the riptide currents and the mesmerism of this changeling world, rather than under the control of a wheel and helm.

Whales traveled through with us, close to our port side, and as we headed into the calmer protected waters of the lagoon, the whales slowly spread out ahead of us. They were the visual evidence that the tales of pilot whales and leviathans helping mariners in distress are founded in more than the myth and legend of the ocean-weary traveler.

It was 8:30 A.M., and the waters about us lay calm and mirrored. We were in the lower portion of Laguna San Ignacio, with Isla Ana to our starboard and Punta Bronaugh on the mainland to our port. The lagoon snakes into the Desierto de Vizcaino on the mainland and is a true desert inlet, receiving no freshwater runoff from the surrounding region. Our activity was to be centered in the lower lagoon as far north as Punta Piedra. Farther north, the middle, upper, and north ends of the lagoon were off limits to vessels to protect the seclusion of pregnant near-term females and newborn calves who favored these "nursery" areas early in the season. Our area to the south would be visited by females with older calves, and the young and more mature males who enter the lagoon to mate with available females.

Charles Scammon, discoverer of Laguna Ojo de Liebre and prolific whaler in Bahia Magdalena, was also the first to enter Laguna San Ignacio. This calving and mating area was also known as Laguna Ballenas, Lagoon of Whales. Scammon entered these waters during the winter of 1859–60 with three tenders and barks. Bahia Magdalena was already in decline, and the whalers were looking elsewhere to fill their wooden barrels and holds. Scammon and his colleagues took many whales during this and subsequent seasons, both within the lagoon proper and in the adjacent bay. During the fourteen years of the most active whaling, some 400 to 440 whales were killed annually; as in Bahia Magdalena, most of the whales were females, and the number of calves killed was not recorded. As in Bahia Magdalena, this level of whaling activity was not sustainable.

We sailed onward. A pair of bottlenose dolphins swam close by, cruising the waters and curious about this new addition to their environment. Their small gray flukes slapped the water as they passed, and their sleek gray bodies appeared and disappeared as they merged with the water below us. In the distance a congregation of western gulls wheeled and dove over a dark form lying still in the water. It was the bloated body of a gray whale, now the fetid prey of cawing seabirds—a natural and yet unnatural vision of a great leviathan. Brown pelicans skimmed the water, and flocks of sandpipers turned and whirled overhead in the singular motion of many.

The *Searcher* was motoring steadily, and we approached two whales that were lounging in our path. The captain brought the vessel to a near-stop, and the whales logged silently at the surface within meters of the ship. The *Searcher's* gears idled in neutral, but we were still drifting toward the whales. Captain Herring kicked the vessel into reverse, and the whales awoke from their dozing. With a double-fluke slap on the water's surface, they churned the water white and dove from sight.

We went over the plan for the next few days in the lagoon. Each morning and afternoon half of the group would take to the skiffs and ply the waters, while the other half of our complement would step ashore and hike across dunes and tidal pools. Thus we would alternate from ship to shore, half a day with each, always hoping that the good luck of those first out on the water would remain for those who followed.

We entered the skiffs after breakfast. Three and a half hours of intimate whale-watching was to follow. There were five of us to a skiff, including the driver, giving us ample room for our camera equipment and rain gear, and of course to lean precariously over the side and get soaking wet should the opportunity present itself. The three skiffs headed in different directions, all seeking whales, all to encounter separate experiences.

The surface of the lagoon was unblemished by the rippling effect of the wind, and the three-to-four-kilometer-wide channel stretched away from us in all directions, rimmed by the low sand dunes and intertidal flats so characteristic of Baja. We motored gently across the bay for about an hour. The sun was baking us into dozing silence, with pelicans and surf scoters our only close encounters. In the distance a spy-hopping gray whale brought its head clear of the water to look in our direction as if playing hide-and-seek, then vanished beneath the steel-blue waters.

Once a mother and calf pair surfaced close to our skiff, but they ignored us and continued on their travels. We watched as the vast mammoth gray backs rolled in the water revealing mottled markings, and the whales sent up steaming plumes of breath as their blowholes snapped open to the warm desert air.

As time passed, we dragged hands and feet in the cooling water and sunned ourselves as the unseen whales played whatever games they play with curious visitors. Our friends in the other two skiffs waved oars high over their heads; they had friendlies. How tempting to leave our independent search and encroach on their experience. Any consideration of combining forces with the other skiffs was abandoned as a cow-calf pair surfaced to our starboard and began to play around us. The whales kept their distance, always out of arm's reach, but at times directly below us. One of the other two skiffs raised an oar again; to confirm that we had seen them and understood the message, we responded in kind. We would stay with our whales.

Whale-watchers get incredibly proprietary about the source of their fascination. We could have joined our colleagues and "touched down" with their whales, but these animals in front of us were ours; an encounter with them was our own, no one else's. This was our experience, however brief, however effectual, however realized in the minds of whale and whale-watcher. The sum of the experience is in the isolation, in the knowledge that what you see and feel is personal and private. There is no need to see, feel, and touch everything with your eyes, mind, and hands, as long as your heart is open. Eventually our two elusive and cautious whales faded from view and we were left alone. But we had been so close that hearts and minds touched what eluded hands and fingers.

The other two skiffs had separated, and we began to motor over toward the spot that had held their interest for so long. We were still some distance off when two large adult gray whales approached, dwarfing our skiff with their thirteen-meter-plus lengths. They spy-hopped a few tens of meters away, both animals bringing their heads clear of the water. Slowly they sank beneath the ripples and hovered under our skiff, turning to look up at us silhouetted in the sunlight. We gazed into the water at them, mesmerized by the shape, form, and color of these living embodiments of Neptune and Proteus. Then they sank deeper into the water column and vanished in the green-blue waters. No sooner had the two full-grown whales disappeared from view than we were suddenly in an audience with a mother and calf. They came straight to us, unerring and definite in their movements. Perhaps these were the whales that had captivated our colleagues, or perhaps they were simply the curious and the inquisitive. Just like us.

As the cow and calf approached, their barnacled dark forms reached out toward us below the water. The clarity was startling as these marine phantoms materialized and faded below. The cow probably measured thirteen to fourteen meters in length, and her calf less than half that. For one moment they were distant, then they changed course and, like huge silent torpedoes, they reached us. Hands stretched out to meet them, to introduce them to our world as best we could.

Ask me to describe the emotions of the experience and I cannot. Ask me to say how I felt during the encounter, and I can only smile and laugh at remembering the episode. How does it feel to be in love? That is how it feels to touch a whale. Sheer elation.

The cow let us touch first, then she nudged up against the skiff, rubbing herself against us. I ran my hand over her back, across barnacles and whale lice, feeling the pliant nature of the skin overlying blubber and the rough, angular sharpness of each living parasite. The whale hung next to our skiff as we rubbed hard along her head and back. Below the water, the line of her jaw and the moving curious eye held our hearts, and she watched us. She sank deeper in the water under our skiff, and our hands and arms followed as far as we could, constrained by our surface existence, wanting so much to enter the warm, nurturing waters and swim with the whales, wanting to communicate with more than a touch.

As the cow moved beyond our reach, the calf approached. He circled the skiff, occasionally cocking his head clear of the water, or blowing bubbles. The calf cut a dark, sleek shape with his dimpled head and twin white blowholes. He circled the skiff slowly, playfully, more often than not approaching from the stern, nuzzling the Yamaha engine as if it were some long-lost relative.

The young calf settled beneath our craft, gently rocking the wooden skiff across his back. His rostrum protruded next to our tapering bow, and I scrambled to lean over the side and watch his antics. Occasionally both animals surfaced together on the same side of the skiff, and they rubbed and leaned against each other as we reached out to them.

Slowly the game changed, and the cow and calf began to play more together than with us. The calf would raise his head and rest it across his mother's back, buoyed up by her bulk. The other skiffs were approaching, and with them appeared more blows. Within moments the three skiffs were grouped together, and we were surrounded. Six whales played between our boats, three cow-calf pairs blew softly in the desert air, dousing boats in whale breath, raising pointed rostrums and rounded pectorals clear of the water. How small do you feel in a five-meter skiff, surrounded by six whales whose combined length of fifty-five meters translates to hundreds of thousands of kilograms? Small. Very small.

The water was ideally calm, and the heat of the day was ameliorated as we plunged arms into the water following whales. But often we just sat and watched as the whales seemed to dance in the arena of water between us. One of the calves settled in close by, his dam just a little further out. We reached out in practiced fashion, rubbing hard down the animal's head and back, always watchful to avoid blowhole, flippers, or flukes. But this encounter was different; the young animal was incredibly observant. He held his head inches below the water, the sun setting starbursts over his dappled patterns, and his eye looked intensely at each of us staring down at him. We watched as his eye moved from person to person, focusing on each of us with a vision of humanity reflected without and within. Then the whale opened his mouth.

We stared for a moment, initially not quite sure what we were seeing. The calf opened his jaws about thirty centimeters, revealing coarse yellow baleen hanging from his palate. The water was washing over the baleen, and we continued to run our hands over his head. One of our group shouted over to Kipping, "He's opened his mouth, what should we do?"

"Don't put your hand in."

We laughed. Who in their right mind would place hand and arm in the mouth of a whale, even one without teeth?

Seconds later we were reaching into the whale's mouth with definite motions and caressing the fibrous baleen. The calf responded with enthusiasm. He rocked his head back and forth in the water, sending small waves into our skiff, and we continued to rub. After we were thoroughly soaked, the calf began to pull slowly away from the side of the skiff, so that we had to lean further and further out of it to reach him; eventually we could not, and our hands and arms returned to our sides. Only then did the whale snap his jaws closed.

What an experience! Not quite Jonah in the belly of the whale, or on a par with putting one's head in a lion's mouth. But still, how many people can say that they have even had the opportunity to feel the baleen of a living whale, and seemingly at the whale's request?

The morning was drawing to a close, and the skiffs were due back at the *Searcher.* Our companions took their leave of the whales, but we delayed. The votes in our skiff lauded whales over lunch, shade, and a rest stop with a vengeance. The six whales were less intrigued by a single skiff and a single engine, and two of the pairs moved off, leaving us with a single mother and calf. But these animals certainly made up in playfulness and exuberance what they lacked in numbers. The calf gamboled around us as only whales can gambol. He launched himself into calf half-breaches as he lunged left and right. The cow rolled and splashed the water's surface as her calf slapped the water with small flukes and blew underwater bubbles that frothed to the surface in boiling pockets of foam.

The animals soon seemed self-absorbed, and after delaying as long as possible, we began to head slowly back to the *Searcher.* As soon as the engine was revved, the whales broke off their games and began to follow us. We were not moving fast, certainly not fast enough to generate a significant wake, and they soon caught up, cutting off our advance by descending beneath the skiff and surfacing in front.

Newman idled the motor, and we petted cow and calf some more as they determined to monopolize the skiff and those held captive in her. The whales jostled each other to reach us, and for ten more minutes we entertained. Then Newman brought the engine back to life, and the chase was repeated. Once again the whales outran us. We accelerated, and so did they. We stopped, admittedly glad to be apprehended. The whales bumped the bottom of the skiff, rubbed themselves along the gunnels, and hung motionless inches from the motor.

After more minutes, the engine was kicked into action. We had to return to our vessel, much as we and they wanted the encounter to continue. Inevitably the whales followed; perhaps they thought this was some kind of new game to play with surface visitors. They were certainly the most persistent and pushiest friendlies that I have ever known. Newman accelerated the skiff until a billowing surf was raised from our bow and the whales could not catch us. For the longest time, though, almost until we reached the *Searcher,* we could see the blows of the two whales following our wake, in search of their partners in a game of tag across the reaches of Laguna San Ignacio.

After lunch we began our terrestrial exploration of the lagoon complex. The sloping, patterned sand beach was intersected by the hard, angular extrusions of black shale, and we picked among the crevices examining the life and death that had found a place here.

Gray whale ribs and vertebrae littered the sand and shales. Their smooth porcelain lines ran across the granular beach like huge punctuation marks in the literature of life. Lying among the whale's vertebrae was the perfection of a bottlenose dolphin skull. The wind and lagoon breezes had molded the sand around the bones, so that they appeared integral to the beach, as though the sand had engulfed the living animal and only now did time release the remains. Or perhaps it was a vision of a beach that itself was alive, a part of the animal that now lay across it. However baked and desolate this beach appeared, harbinger of the dead and decayed, it was still very much alive.

Windblown tenacious plants grew between the rocks and bones, spurge and pickleweed and the occasional stunted mangrove setting long shadows among the dunes. A curlew poked its long, curved beak into the wet sand along the shore, and Caspian terns wheeled over our heads. White moon snails slimed their way in search of clams, ready to bore into their muscle tissue and digest the living prey. And iridescent green tiger beetles and ghost shrimps left tiny interlaced tracks that vanished with each advancing wave.

We walked the beach, our feet folding into the warm sand, and crossed the high tide line into a low spartina salt marsh. Spartina is the most productive plant in the world, and also among the most inedible; only through the degrading power of the microfauna does the plant release its nutrients to the world. We stopped to watch the delicate workings of a spineback mangrove spider in one stunted tree. The colorful spider measured about one and a half centimeters across its yellow-green carapace, marked with distinctive black spots. From each corner of the polygonally shaped carapace projected a short red spine, six in all, so that the spider looked like some garish plant propagule as it repaired and extended the orb web hung between two branches.

Behind the loose band of red mangroves, the flats were dominated by salicornia, the pickleweed or jelly bean plant. This low branching plant has bulbous succulent stems and scale-like leaves. It is startlingly green, and to look at the plant gives one the impression that some submarine coral animal has finally returned to the land.

An osprey passed overhead, flying out toward the lagoon in search of fish, its wings in silent beat and talons glinting in the sunlight. A Virginia rail called from the interior of the mangroves, *kid kid kidick kidick,* but remained out of sight. And a greater yellowlegs darted along the lagoon shore as we meandered along the creeks and canals that cut their way through the dunes and grasses.

Nothing was in a straight line; everything before us was curved and smooth, the meandering designs of nature where straight edges or angles are muted by time and activity. A mixture of salt grasses crowded the flats, and the sandy textured material at their base was punctuated with the holes of fiddler crabs.

We walked along the front of a mangrove bank, our feet washing in the shallow waters. The elusive rail dashed from its hiding place, while the less secretive of the mangroves' inhabitants—green-backed herons, mangrove warblers, and tricolored herons—permitted us a more leisurely account of their presence. A white-veined butterfly wafted through the air, its delicate lines and powdery wings seeming out of place. Ephemeral life takes hold amid the heat and sand, life which through our eyes appears so small or brittle that survival is an impossibility. The butterfly, sea hare, and rail exist in an environment that would eliminate us from the gene pool in a geologic microsecond. Evolution and adaptation are marvelous processes, for they have given rise to a Pandora's box of life and form.

Along the beach we could make out the signs of a coyote, and whimbrels and Curlews continued to call across the lagoon. Flocks of sandpipers massed along the shoreline, taking to the air in a single sweeping motion. They flew as a single unit low over our heads, their wings setting up a rush through the still air. Shells and patterned sand lay at our feet as the surf lapped the edge of the beach. Nowhere does natural artistry exist in such perfection as on desert shores where the harsh physical environment shapes all with a delicate brush.

It was close to sunset when we found ourselves back on board the *Searcher* listening to our colleagues relate their encounters with whales. Still, we took to the skiffs as the sun lay low on the horizon, and the brash, bright colors of the desert were softened by the fading light. There was a slight swell, and the water had darkened. A few clouds had come in across the lagoon, and they hung in surreal patterns against the intensely blue darkening sky, as though some huge white-winged bird were hovering gracefully over the *Searcher.* We watched as a few whales surfaced nearby, their flukeprints swirling the water into a smooth, circular slick with each well-timed fluke movement, and two or three bottlenose dolphins inspected us briefly as the sun hit the horizon, sending out flashes of orange to tint the clouds on the periphery of the lagoon.

We returned to the *Searcher* as the dying light of the sun turned the waters black. The sun was directly behind the vessel, and the silhouetted ship looked as though it were surrounded by an aurora of light stretching across the horizon and up into the sky. The entire color spectrum was visible, from yellow and orange to purple and the darkness of night.

At 8:30 Captain Joe Herring turned off the generator, and we stared into the sky as the lights of other worlds were revealed. The lagoon was silent to us; then our ears became accustomed to the sounds, just as our eyes were now accustomed to the dark. Whales exhaled in the distance, an unseen arctic loon cried out from the blackness, and from the shore the eerie call of the coyote shot through the night.

Joe fired off two bright flares that illuminated the night around us, catching brown pelicans and ring-billed gulls in ghostly luminescence. As the artificial light faded, our eyes returned to the night, and we stayed on deck for the longest time, savoring silence and darkness. Eventually we turned to our bunks, sated from a day filled with whales.

We awoke at 4:25 A.M. as the *Searcher* shuddered from a blow to the hull. A logging gray whale had hit the ship, or perhaps it was a nighttime friendly simply trying to garner some attention from the vessel's sleeping inhabitants. We slept on, dreaming of whales and water, herons and ospreys, white bleached bones and patterned sand.

At 6 A.M. we watched as a single gray whale, perhaps the same individual who had awakened us just an hour and a half earlier, approached the ship. One of the crewmen tried to reach the whale with a long-handled broom, offering a back rub, but the animal remained just out of reach, and eventually drifted away. It was another perfect Baja day; the waters of the lagoon were calm and glassy, and wispy clouds filtered the sun's rays, creating a slightly hazy effect across the lagoon.

Half the ship's complement headed into the mangroves before breakfast to bird-watch as the sun rose and the birds emerged in full dawn chorus. The rest of us remained aboard the *Searcher,* standing out on the bow as the crew pulled up the anchor and we sailed toward Punta Piedra, Rocky Point, the furthest location to which we could venture in the lagoon. Another ship was entering the area and we wanted to distance ourselves.

We reached Punta Piedra and dropped anchor, just as another whale ventured close to our bow. The crew were ready; they knew this whale by name. Over the years that whale-watching vessels had been entering the lagoon, she had been seeking out ships with two main aims: to receive a back rub with a broom, and to get hosed down with water—hence her nickname, Hoser.

Hoser swam slowly alongside the ship, and one of the crew leaned over the side with the broom while another prepared the hose. The whale blew just off our bow and lounged in the water as Newman rubbed along her back with the hard-bristled broom. Then the hose was brought to the side of the ship, and water splashed at the whale in long, refreshing dribbles. She stayed within a meter of our starboard side, always remaining in reach of the broom and careful not to stray, until evidently the itch was satisfied and Hoser sank into the water and vanished.

The skiffs returned from the mangroves and were tied in place behind the *Searcher.* While we were preparing to venture ashore, two mother-calf pairs approached from behind, attempting to play with the boats bouncing gently in the swell. But with no people to offer a scratch and no gurgling engines to nuzzle, they soon drifted off. We loaded up the skiffs as the second ship permitted to enter Laguna San Ignacio came into sight. Our strategy failed; the *Polaris Deluxe* dropped anchor next to us and lowered three rubber zodiacs into the water. We had company.

By 8:30 we had landed at Punta Piedra. Kayakers make frequent use of this area during the whale-watching season, and we found traces of their camp—fire-scorched rocks and the occasional bottlecap. Bleached bones and green turtle carapaces littered the beach. Each carapace lay in the sand like a carefully arranged still life, and delicate shadow lines were drawn in the sand by the slender stalks of vegetation. The turtle shells looked taut and strained in the desert sun, cracks and holes appearing between segments. When you look at the shape and form of the cover, it is hard to imagine the kind of animal that once hid within. They are gone now, as so many of the *caguama,* the green turtles, have gone, to support the poachers' trade. But they are now slowly beginning to return to these waters through the judicious protection of the Mexican government, just as the gray whale has returned.

We tripped over the compacted black sedimentary deposits along the beach that splintered and impaled us, revealing fossilized shells from times long since past. Black brant swam in the shallows feeding on the threads of eel grass, and ring-billed gulls and double-crested cormorants crossed the lagoon high above our heads. A curlew cried out in distinctive tones, and a loggerhead shrike darted from the red-flowered ocotillo it was using to impale and store its prey.

The rock pools captured between the crusty black shales were teeming with life in miniature. Bright green seaweed coated the surface of the glistening rocks, and sea anemones hid among the crevices. Each soft-bodied creature was covered in pieces of carefully collected reflective white shells that served to reduce the exposure of the fluid animal to the desiccating rays of the sun when the waters receded. When disturbed by inquiring fingers, the anemone squirts a jet of water from its single opening—startling the inquisitive and detracting the potential predator.

Dunlin and least sandpipers scurried between the pools, along the gently sloping shoreline, and across the exposed tidal mud flats punctuated by ghost shrimp burrows, the tasty prey of curlew, white ibis, and egrets. These erect birds stood out as sentinels in the shallow water, watching our passage with a nonchalance bred of indifference. We picked at the rocks to reveal shore crabs, and found more bones of a once great whale scattered at our feet. This whale had come ashore just two short years ago, a young gray found by passing travelers lying across the rocks that now held only crushed and fractured pieces. How strange to realize that something so large can disintegrate and decay to practically nothing. Whales appear inviolable, here now and forever, long-lived gargantuans threatened only by the lance. What drove this youngster ashore? Illness, storm, or misguided adventure? We know only that he never grew up, and that instead of contributing to the biological environment of this world, he is an integral part of the physical, the landscape. Immortality in a sense, enshrined in stone, preserved by the desert air, but silenced by the shore and the oppressive force of gravity.

Looking out over the lagoon, we saw the three skiffs from the *Searcher*. The aluminum boats were huddled together, with people reaching over the side into the water to touch what we could not see but could surely imagine.

Back on shore, the beach was broken by a slight rise in elevation, and we climbed over the shales. In the distance a large, dark object seemed to merge with the rocks, and we headed over to investigate this change in the lie of the sand and shale. As we neared, the shape turned to whale, and the rocks held up the carcass of a fourteen-meter female gray.

The animal's head was pointed down the beach toward us, its jaws slightly askew and drawing long shadows across the sand. The back half of the whale was slightly raised on the black shales, and the limp flukes lay placidly among the boulders. The animal was lying on its back, the small pectoral flippers hanging loosely down at the sides. The entire carcass had a deflated look about it, as though when life was extinguished from the body it took something else, something highly visible, from the whale. The half-closed blood-red eye stared sightlessly out at us, the pupil full and black, glazed and lifeless, so different from the living, curious visions we had seen earlier. The whale had not been ashore long and was largely intact, although coyotes had begun to tear at its side, and gulls to peck at the skin. The whale looked so large that even this slightly unnatural vision, as though this were not quite a whale, seemed to strike us dumb, and we stood slightly back from the animal, silent, out of some reverence perhaps, or respect.

As time passed, this immense carcass in front of us would fade and collapse, leaving only bones stretched across the sand as evidence that something great had found this place to die. Perhaps the skeleton would remain here, whole, and reveal the inner self of the whale, or perhaps the waves and currents would remove the animal in part and spread it across the lagoon, scattering substance to the four winds and tides until the whole becomes part of all around us, and the whale returns to the water.

The light lagoon breeze was with us as we left the whale, and the smell of death and decay followed us down the beach. A nauseating sickness that we could taste turned the stomach and reconfirmed in our minds the link between death, decay, and everything that we fear and view as disgusting or unpleasant. The return of the animal to the soil, the air, and the water becomes something that we all try to deny, because the manifestation of the process becomes something to avoid all contact with.

We recoiled from the malodorousness of the whale by crossing from the shore into the desert proper. We walked across a barren, flat land, sparsely vegetated and stretching out in front of us as though to the hills in the distance. The sun was beating down relentlessly, and we were exposed to the maximum amount of desert heat against the backs of our legs and necks. The dry sand was covered in a loose crust of salt crystals that our feet broke through with each step, sinking into the soft shell-filled sand. Occasionally the vegetation increased in patches, but the greenery was deceptive and hidden by thorns.

The carefully dug-out den of a coyote was nestled in a mound of soft sand beyond the dunes. The den was abandoned now, but once would have held yelping pups whose first view of the world would have been through this opening. Jumping cholla backed the den, and I wondered how the young, naive pups would have dealt with their first encounter with such a prickly neighbor.

The den was not entirely deserted. Almost hidden in the undulations of the sand was the conical trap of an ant lion. This cleverly constructed pit was designed to catch the ants that scurried across the grains of sand. When an ant met the crater it would slip downward toward the waiting mouth of the ant lion protruding from the center. Should the ant try to scramble up the sides of the slippery cone, the ant lion would begin to spew grains of sand at the unfortunate individual, until it plummeted inevitably to its fate, providing the ant lion with justification for its name. We stood momentarily next to the crater wondering whether we would get to witness this display of predatory passion, and some even began to search for an unsuspecting ant. But compassion won out and we moved on, content with an imaginative description of the event rather than any visual confirmation.

The expanse of the desert spread out before us—the patchy vegetation, thorns of *Mammillaria* and cholla, and the succulence of the jelly bean plant. The only movement, beyond our own steps, was the flickering of the side-blotched lizard. Ahead, the sandy dry desert was transformed into the dark green of mangroves, washed by the cooling shallow waters of the lagoon. The lightly clouded sky was reflected in the shallows, as were the banks of mangroves, and again we waded in the water searching out sea hares and moon snails. We sat along the curving beach and mud flats and watched as the bird life of the area emerged and delicate white-veined butterflies fluttered in the breeze. Mangrove warblers darted deep in the heart of the trees, while the reddish egrets, great blue herons, curlews, least and western sandpipers plied the shore and probed the shallows. In places the verdant mangroves were pale and encrusted with the hanging fibrous growth of lichen. This growth gave the plants a diseased and subdued appearance, as though they were under silent attack by some creeping epiphytic plague.

Back on the beach, we could watch the skiffs grouped closely on the lagoon, the three from the *Searcher* and the three zodiacs from the *Deluxe*. All aboard were captivated by whales around them. And all the whales appeared to be friendlies. It was eleven o'clock, and we would have to wait for the afternoon before heading out ourselves.

We lay on the beach waiting for the skiffs to return us to the *Searcher*. Occasionally the water close to shore erupted with tiny white-foamed splashes as three bottlenose dolphins swam along the beachfront. They slapped their flukes on the water's surface, sounding short reports that carried on the wind and punctuated our dozing. Our beach was dominated by scallop shells. On either side of the cove the sand was uncluttered, so this narrow section of curved and serrated scallops had the appearance of a midden. The shells were spread across the beach, only one or two deep, their colors and light and dark contrasts an artistic picture of abstraction. The breeze was beginning to pick up, coming across the lagoon from the west. As the wind built, the glass lagoon would darken, and the swells would grow and whitecaps tip into ever-deepening troughs. We looked longingly at the skiffs.

After lunch we were well rested from our hike and stimulated by tales of the morning's friendlies. We entered the skiffs as the wind whistled around the *Searcher*, creating swells across the lagoon. As we had many times before, we set off across the expanse of Laguna San Ignacio in search of the whales. With the *Searcher* on our starboard side, a gray whale breached three times within two hundred meters, sending streaming water and an explosion of sound in our direction.

We followed the whale at a distance of two to three hundred meters, watching as flukes and dappled pectorals were raised clear of the water and the animal rolled at the surface, churning and side-slapping the water with flukes. The zodiacs had not returned, and for a short while we had the lagoon to ourselves.

Almost on cue, a mother-calf pair approached, and our three small craft congregated about the whales. Mother and offspring nuzzled the vessels; the calf eagerly bobbed in the water, rostrum held high as we petted her bulbous head. The cow rested alongside the skiff, leaving just enough room for her calf to slide in between. The result was that the calf felt outstretched human hands and the comforting security of mother whale at the same moment.

Loren Eiseley wrote of the whale in *The Unexpected Universe:*

> It is not known whether the small eyes placed yards apart on opposite sides of their huge heads can co-ordinate the meaning of two sights at once. If not, that

great solitary beast, with all its hoary antiquity written in the weapons ranged along its back, saw, as it floundered in its death throes, two separate worlds. It saw with one dimming affectionate eye the ancient mother, the heaving expanse of the universal sea. With the other it glimpsed the indescribable foreboding the approaching shape of man, the messenger of death and change. So it was that the dying whale in its dissociated vision had arrived, momentarily, at the one true place where the nature of the past mingles with the onrush of the future and is borne down forever into darkness. It is an instant to remember, for it will come, in turn, to man.

This young calf in front of us could behold both human and whale in a single moment, perhaps linking the two, aware now that humans did not necessarily bring death and the red seas of years past.

Our solitude was soon interrupted as we watched the *Deluxe* discharge her rubbery craft into the lagoon, and they powered over. The whales' loyalty was instantly compromised. The zodiacs were more fun than our static, unyielding aluminum skiffs. Zodiacs bounced in the waves, they could be lifted and bumped, they yielded to pressure, and they probably felt similar to whales, pliant and rubbery. Our whales moved off to play with these new toys, and the zodiacs' occupants braced themselves for a more benign version of the Nantucket sleighride.

We watched and followed, but the whales were drawn further away, only occasionally returning to proffer themselves to us before swimming back to the bouncy rubber toys, like oversized puppies playing with a plastic bone. We had to be content with our brief encounter. The wind continued to build, and the waves rose over the gunnels, soaking everything in the skiffs but drenching those in the zodiacs. Back on the *Searcher* we talked grudgingly about the fact that the *Deluxe* had "stolen" our whales, however willingly they had deserted. As I have said before, whale-watchers are incredibly proprietary about their whales.

With sunrise lighting the sky like a fireball, we began our final day in the lagoon. The dawn light was streaming diffusely through the high clouds, and we headed into the mangroves that rimmed the inlet. A heavy, dark fog bank hung over the lagoon, creating an eerie backdrop to the mangroves and giving the early morning light a surreal quality. It was the kind of light that hurts the eyes, giving the observer a headache and the air a tangible quality, an oppressive, pre-storm feeling.

The protected inlet waters surrounding the mangroves were among the calmest we had during the voyage. Our skiffs were mirrored in the water, as were the mangroves, but the fog turned the water a steel, cold gray, and the atmosphere was brooding. We followed the channels between the mangroves, occasionally cutting the motor to savor the silence and listen to the birds deep in the undergrowth. We could hear the fog, silent, dark, and impenetrable—the fog of moors and legend.

A double-crested cormorant stood tall on a stick protruding from the water. The bird took to the air with a powerful beat of dark wings, and fish darted under our skiff, while others picked at the woody stems of the mangroves, flooded by rising water. The stems reflected symmetrical patterns in the water, patterns that moved and merged as the ripples from our passing lapped the shore.

The mangroves became less prevalent as we continued along the channel. We soon came upon a flat expanse of salt-loving vegetation dominated by sedges and pickleweed, upon which were feeding four white ibis in full breeding plumage. The birds stood out vividly on the green background. The adults were pure white with red legs and a bright scarlet face and bill. A single juvenile among them had much more understated plumage: brown wings, white underparts, and slightly rosy legs and bill. As the skiff drew close to shore, the adult birds took to the air, showing off their black-tipped primaries. The juvenile ignored us and continued to pick its way through the undergrowth.

We landed on a sandbar toward the periphery of the vegetated embayment, and stepped from the skiffs to stand and look across the lagoon and back into the mangroves—such diametrically opposed worlds of color and content. Coyote tracks crisscrossed the sand dunes, and sparse windblown grasses took tenuous hold.

As we headed back into the lagoon, we passed close to a sandbar crowded with brown pelicans and a lone snowy egret. A single gray whale surfaced close by, rounding its broad back before leisurely fluking and sinking from view. We hurried back to the *Searcher.*

During the previous two days we thought we had determined the whales' general daily routine. During the morning, when the lagoon was like glass with a soft offshore breeze barely strong enough to ruffle a pelican's feathers, the whales were intensely curious. In the afternoon the westerly wind would pick up, darkening the lagoon, and the whales seemed preoccupied with the roughening waters and made little contact with our skiffs.

The fog was lifting, and the high clouds were burning off. The day looked certain to be baking hot and glassy calm. We were prepared for an intensive whale-watching session.

The lagoon was unusually quiet when we launched the skiffs. Few whales broke the surface, and even fewer approached our craft. Brown pelicans flew in formation over our heads, gliding down to skim the water, wing beats starting in peristaltic motion. Surf scoters clumsily took to the air, tripping across the water with labored effort. Occasionally a whale spy-hopped a couple of hundred meters distant, as if pinpointing our position. But the only whales that came within ten meters were intent on travel and ignored us. We watched as their dappled gray backs and flukes rose slowly from the calm water, breaking silently through the glass barrier, superbly reflected and translucent, dripping water and exploding mist into the still air. We began to feel distinctly out of favor, and the high expectations that we'd had at breakfast plummeted.

We dragged feet and hands in the water, trying to subdue the baking effects of the sun. As we dipped our hands over the side, steam literally rose from our skin as the water droplets evaporated in the desert air. Two bottlenose dolphins blew next to the skiff, and we scrambled to sit up and encourage their approach. The tiny dorsal fins cut through the water as the dolphins circled our vessel. Newman hit the accelerator and the engine roared to life. The bow lifted and we sped forward, pushing a wave. The dolphins darted into position and rode the bow as we gained speed. I leaned over, watching as the two dolphins wove back and forth, changing positions frequently, and turning to look up at me without missing a beat. Stretched out toward the bow I was prone next to the dolphins, inches away. Bottlenose dolphins are large animals. These were at least 3.5 meters long, and probably weighed in at 250 kilograms. They moved effortlessly, capable of faster speeds than we and considerably greater artistry; they seemed to moderate their actions to suit our abilities.

As we raced and played with the dolphins, the commotion attracted the attention of the gray whales nearby, and several spy-hopped to look in our direction. We continued our high-speed antics for about twenty minutes, then the dolphins peeled off and left us alone.

During the remainder of the morning a few whales passed by, but none came forward to investigate, and we returned to the *Searcher.* Preparations for the afternoon were somewhat muted. The wind had picked up rapidly, and it was going to be very rough, and very wet.

The *Searcher* was anchored toward the mouth of the lagoon. The huge breakers we had crossed coming in were clearly visible, forming a seemingly impenetrable surf line across the entrance. We loaded up the skiffs, and in full wet-weather gear headed out toward a sandbank where the blue of the lagoon was transformed into the muddy brown of silt and shallowness. This was a site favored by the whales. Ahead of us we could see an incredible thrashing and foaming of water. Pectoral flippers and flukes were being thrown in every direction. For a moment we thought we had interrupted a mating couple. But as the water settled, we were able to make out a mother-calf pair. We were witnessing a lesson in bottom-feeding.

The young calf was probably seven to nine weeks old and five to six meters in length. Her dark skin was as yet unblemished by barnacles, and the dimples on her head glistened in the sunlight. She raised her head repeatedly clear of the water's surface. Her three throat grooves were distended, and she rocked her head back and forth, mouth opening and closing, water and mud streaming from her jaws, and short, yellow baleen clearly visible. Eventually, tired from the effort, she would crash back into the water with deliberate force, sending up thunderclaps of white surf, or sink beneath the surface leaving only a swirling eddy of water. Her mother was always close, and the calf, following such exertion, would often rush to her side and lie across the adult's back.

Continuing the apparent lesson, her mother would sink beneath the surface and dive, lifting her broad flukes clear of the water, imitated in her actions by the calf. The adult's flukes hung in the air, and we could only imagine events on the shallow, silty floor of the lagoon. When mother and calf returned to the surface again, both were streaming mud and water from their jaws. At times both animals brought their heads together at the surface, throat grooves expanded and rostrums rocking back and forth in the waves.

The whales were so preoccupied with their feeding lesson that we approached easily to within a few meters. At times when the mother dove, she did so within a meter of our skiff. Although largely indifferent to our presence, the pair would occasionally break off their lesson and inspect us, swimming repeatedly under the skiff, rolling over, and circling, always just out of arm's reach. Seasoned tourist-teasers.

It was astounding to watch the lesson unfold before us. It is difficult to avoid anthropomorphic characterizations in such a situation. To describe actions and events, it is easier for us to be able to ascribe some kind of meaning that allows those not present to interpret what it is that we witnessed. It is true that we cannot interpret the actions of whales in exactly the same manner that we would the actions of a human parent with her child, but it is equally true that the limits of our knowledge mean that we cannot assume that such characterizations are not accurate. Indeed, anecdotal observation and the role of the observer are important components that should not be disregarded simply because they cannot be rigorously tested.

In their fascinating book on the social lives and motives of green vervet monkeys in Africa, Dorothy Cheney and Robert Seyfarth discuss whether mental states (motive, belief, desire, vigor, and love) really exist in the mind of any animal. Perhaps, they say, these states are "artifacts, invented by ethologists as the best means of describing what they have seen. When we watch non-human primates and analyze their social behavior, do we have their minds or ours under the microscope?" The same may be true for those who profess to study whales. It may be that the description says more of the observer than of the observed, but again I believe this is a legitimate application. The way we treat the natural world and those who inhabit it is as much a function of belief and anthropomorphic interpretation as it is of scientific, testable truth.

We were soaked. Every time the whales passed under our skiff, we reached out to touch them. We were up to our shoulders in water chilled by turbulence, and fully clothed in wet-weather gear. As we leaned over the side, the combined action of whales and wind filled the skiff repeatedly with water, until our packs and camera bags were swimming.

The plan for the afternoon was to allow two sessions out in the skiffs for final observations of gray whales. It was soon time for us to return and permit our colleagues the chance to get the wet and windy treatment. Luckily our demeanor was a discouragement to several, and while they elected to pass on the final sojourn, I took my place once again in the skiff. Wet, wind, and cold were not sufficient reason to miss the opportunity of a lifetime.

We headed out to the same spot on the shallow sandbank. The whales were still there, but the intensity of the moment had gone, and we found that we could not get as close as before. For some reason they were warier, and we did not press our intrusion.

Other blows were becoming visible among the waves, and we continued to cross the midsection of the outer lagoon. We encountered another mother-calf pair who traveled with us, between two of the skiffs, while the third vessel followed. The waves swelled and rolled while the calf cavorted, performing aerial antics and backflips across the surface. Dark shadows beneath allowed us to track the young whale as he passed underneath, while lighter, ghostly pale images revealed the position of the barnacle-speckled adult. Skiffs and whales were one in this wet world of continual motion. The whales jostled each other, surfacing between us to blow and lounge at the surface before continuing on, or coming closer to investigate. After about an hour the game changed. Suddenly, imperceptibly, we were participants. The mother and calf approached the skiffs, taking turns from one to the other. Those in the skiffs leaned precariously over the side to touch their whale, unbalancing the vessels and forcing our skiff drivers to act as ballast toward the bow or stern, depending on the focus of activity. Those captivated by the moment leaned toward the raised rostrum of the calf, to the cheers and laughter of others in the audience, and kissed the whale.

As the whales approached our skiff, the young calf surfaced directly off our starboard side, blowing instantly and soaking every camera pointed in his direction, as well as dousing all in pungent whale breath. The calf raced from skiff to skiff, and the cow offered herself to the outstretched hands of whale-watchers. Then two more blows identified whales nearby; in moments we were joined by a second mother-calf pair.

Four whales crowded our skiffs. As they surfaced, the waves washed off broad backs, displaced in white foam and cascading rivulets. The cows stayed close to their offspring, but showed no undue concern if temporarily separated by the skiffs. We stretched out our hands to touch these gentle, curious creatures, and the cows nudged their offspring toward us. The young devilfish rolled against the gunnels and closed their eyes as we rubbed head and back and caressed the short, yellow baleen in the open, inviting mouth.

As one of the young whales pushed against the skiff with urgent movements, protruding her rostrum clear of the water and occasionally turning her head to look at us, I couldn't resist the impulse. I leaned over, rubbing the calf smoothly down her head, pressing hard onto the skin and blubbery layer, feeling the lice and barnacles that were beginning to adorn her slate-dark body. And I kissed the whale. Her head continued to bob up and down in the surf, and water flowed freely into the skiff. I kissed her again. Of course I also kissed the whale lice, but that doesn't sound as good, and the experience is certainly not one to dwell upon.

Looking back, it was a crazy way to spend a vacation. Traveling the world to get soaking wet, to alternately bake and freeze in an unyielding climate, and to try to touch, let alone kiss, a whale. But whenever I think of the experience, watch the video footage or look at the slides, I end up grinning from ear to ear, and I remember that life is about gathering experiences. And this has to be among the best there is.

As we caressed and petted and kissed the four whales around us, and were regularly doused in water and whale breath, John Kipping, our enthusiastic guide, summed up the afternoon as "continuous hard-core whale petting." There is no other way to describe it.

Unfortunately, all experiences must come to an end. It is also true that the great experiences are the rare ones, the ones that we cannot repeat or capture— experiences that live on as memories and in the remembrance of a touch at the end of a fingertip, or the feel of water across skin; the look in the eye of the whale, and in the eye of the whale-watcher.

We were to leave Laguna San Ignacio on the high tide, and that required an early departure. With much regret we left our friendly, exuberant whales and boarded our vessel as the light was fading and setting starbursts across the water. Once again it was we rather than the whales who had to break off the en-counter, and return to that other world where people and whales rarely meet under such amicable circumstances.

The passage out through the breaker channel was considerably easier than our entrance, and we were soon heading northward toward Isla Cedros.

At dawn we were greeted by bowriding common dolphins as the sun filled the Baja sky with the glare and brightness that we had come to expect. We dropped anchor on the protected east side of Isla Cedros and prepared to go ashore. Our original destination had been Laguna Ojo de Liebre, but this year the lagoon was closed to vessels, and Isla Cedros was to be our consolation.

Isla Cedros is a sizable island, 32 kilometers long and reaching 1,300 meters into the sky. It even has its own freshwater supply high up in the mountains. The island is situated at the mouth of Bahia de Sebastian Vizcaino, which guards the entrance to Laguna Ojo de Liebre, Scammon's Lagoon. Although Bahia Magdalena, Laguna Ojo de Liebre, and Laguna San Ignacio were the focus of whaling activity, the region between Isla Cedros and Islas San Benitos to the northeast was also heavily exploited by the alongshore whalemen. These waters gave whalers the chance of pursuit as whales entered and left both Laguna San Ignacio to the south and Laguna Ojo de Liebre, as well as of pursuing their prize into the shallow waters of the lagoon system itself. Every island along the coast of Baja became a sheltered haven for whaling vessels as they awaited the passage of whales close to shore in the kelp beds. Cedros, with its freshwater springs, was a favored anchorage.

The size and topography of the island impart some interesting ecological and climatic characteristics. At one point in its long history, when much of the world was imprisoned in ice, the sea level fell, linking disjunct islands to mainland, creating land bridges between peninsula and great plains across the shallow expanses of bays and lagoons, and Isla Cedros was connected to the mainland. The result is that even today the biota of the island reflect this past unification.

High in the mountains that provide the backbone of the island, a pine forest exists, evidence of cooler and moister times, surviving now as a result of local conditions that give rise to an almost permanent fog across the mountains, which rains life-sustaining moisture on the forest. Throughout the rest of the island, across the cliffs and floodplain, desert plants predominate, reflecting the current climatic conditions. Thus, Isla Cedros captures across its lands vegetative indicators of the prevailing climates both past and present.

From the *Searcher,* Isla Cedros looked rocky and inhibiting, the highest points shrouded in cloud and fog. Striations and crevices bisected the hills, the different-colored formations, rich in copper and magnesium, baking and dry under the sun. The rock formations showed the contortions of millennia, of pressure and heat, and the force of the ocean and wind.

We landed on the beach and stepped out onto large, black, rounded pebbles, sculpted and molded by the motion of Pacific waves. Caspian terns and western gulls circled over our heads as we began to explore the shoreward extension of the island. Brown *Macrocystis* kelp littered the beach, and the tide line was cluttered with driftwood and the other discarded refuse of the sea. Everything along the tide line moved with the crawling insistence of microlife: amphipods, sand fleas, and the myriad of the unnamed.

Behind us, beyond the flash-flood plain, the cliffs and hillsides were punctuated by agave and alleopathic plants. Isla Cedros has a significant proportion of endemic plant and animal species that serve as evidence both of a long separation from the mainland, and that such a connection did at one time exist. Thus, the island has an endemic species of deer and a tree frog and rattlesnake found nowhere else in the world. Even the common side-blotched lizards found across the region show slight differences on these isolated islands. All serve as evidence of evolution and island speciation in progress at our feet.

Islands such as Cedros are also invaluable stops for small birds, giving them the opportunity to rest and recuperate during long migrations. Speciation on the island may well have been accelerated by migratory species stopping on the island and remaining.

The floodplain was a broad expanse of mud and low interspersed vegetation corralled by a gully that reached toward the center of the island. The mud was thick and dry, creating neat, mathematically perfect polygons. During massive floods this plain channeled the debris and mud down toward the beach, so that as the pressure behind the torrent died, everything collected at its mouth—the bones of trees and animals, boulders and rocks from the heart of the island, all moved by the force of water in the desert.

Across the mud flats were the familiar blue-gray frankenia plants and a small shrub, the California saltbush, known locally as chamizo or the shad scale bush. This saltbush grows well in saline soils and is covered with minute scales instead of leaves. It is an example of desert perfection, the scale-like leaves reducing moisture loss through evapotranspiration. At intervals larger plants lifted themselves two meters above us. They were sumac shrubs. On Islas San Benitos we had seen the lemonade berry bush, hiedra; here on Cedros we had two endemic sumacs, *Rhus integrifolia cedrosensis,* a variety similar to hiedra, and *Rhus lentii,* the sugar bush, lentisco. Both varieties had long, narrow leaves and bright red berries adorning the apex of each branch. A northern mockingbird called stridently from one of the shrubs, *check, check, check,* and flashed its white wing patches as it flew to a more distant perch. A couple of black-throated sparrows darted deep within the protected cover of the plants, and a male Costa's hummingbird landed momentarily on one of the sugar bushes, his violet breast adding a burst of color among the green, and adding to the deep color of the plant's own fruit.

We walked up one of the long gullies eroded by the infrequent flash floods and leading toward the center of the island. Our path meandered around the tall stalks of coastal agaves, the majority white and dry, but some topped by brilliant yellow flowers. Intricate patterns were carved in the mud by water that had long since evaporated or been absorbed by the parched inhabitants. Gray-white mottled wood showing the contortions of growth lay on the ground, as if some silent still life had been placed so carefully by the hand of nature, casting shadows and reflecting light.

Most of the plants hugged the ground, their growth squat and made dwarf by desert deficiencies. Bursage, commonly known as burro-weed, was liberally spread across the flats, half dead, half alive, its intertwined gray-green stems wrapping around each other like some vegetative kama sutra. The tiny bur-fruit clung to clothing as we passed by, further spreading this early colonizer that thrives on the temporary and the disturbed. In places the intense green of broom baccharis stood out against the subdued colors of most of the other plants. This plant, like the bursage, is adapted to disturbed sites. It is nearly leaf-less, with angled branches topped with broomlike tufts of verdant green. The Indians of the region used to chew these branches to relieve toothache, and swatches of branches were tied up to make the broom of its name.

Rock daisy, white forget-me-not, and bush snapdragon were interlaced between rocks and driftwood, adding tiny splashes of color to a desert robbed of intensity by the combined action of time, sun, and flood. Incongruously we found the small but thriving form of a California juniper on the mud flats. Juniper is a fragrant, evergreen shrub and is found at high elevations on Cedros. This bright green, be-coned individual had obviously sprung up through the germination of an errant seed blown from the higher reaches of the island. We watched groundsel under attack by aphids, the endemic cactus *Cochemia pondii* with its clustered spiny stems and signs of emerging red blooms, and the dusty miller plant, soft and woolly, the blue-gray lair of a crab spider awaiting the unwary insect. Each plant illustrated the desert way—the interrelationship between plant and insect, animal and bird, and heat and sun.

The deficiencies of the desert soil are dealt with in part by specialized adaptations of the plants. Both the endemic lupine, with its tiny purple flower, and the other legumes found on the island are able to "fix" nitrogen in the soil. Each legume holds microscopic nitrogen-fixing bacteria in special nodules on its roots. It is these bacteria that convert nitrogen gas from the atmosphere into the accessible nitrates that can subsequently be used by both the legume and other plants in the vital manufacture of protein required for growth and reproduction.

Ahead of us was a large bush, rounded in growth, almost spherical, and topped by yellow flowers which, combined with the yellow-green of the small oval leaves, gave the plant a subtle glowing aura. It was the goatnut shrub, jojoba. This remarkable plant can be viewed, indirectly, as a savior of the very animals that I had journeyed south to see. In many regions of the world the plant is cultivated for the commercial production of oil. Jojoba oil has many of the same chemical properties and uses as spermaceti oil, and as such has served as a substitute for whale oil in many commercial and industrial products. The discovery of jojoba, along with the rising environmental consciousness of governments and their people and the obvious long-term economic suicide of the whaling industry through stock mismanagement, provided the whales with the avenue of escape at a time when straightforward ethical and moral ideology was not a sufficient motivator. The jojoba may live for 100 years or more, and with "whale oil" flowing through its vegetative veins, it is an analogous leviathan of land and soil.

We continued down the gully through a box canyon. The elephant trees now appeared in force along the sides of the hills, away from the infrequent but destructive flow of the waters. Their newly emerging leaves reflected golden in the sunlight. A tree such as this could hold the golden fleece and satisfy the desires of the argonauts, and all those who follow their dreams. The elephant tree is classified in the same family as the sumac shrubs, lemonade berry and sugar bush. But, this species is visually distinct, with its contorted, bulbous trunk flaking and peeling bark. It lives up to its scientific name, *Pachycormus discolor:* a pachyderm among plants. Locally the tree is known as copalquin or the torote blanco. It is my favorite plant; its gentle strength, its firmness and resilience to the elements, and the golden leaves all provide visual evidence of beauty and survival in an otherwise inhospitable place. This elephant's trunk is a mastery of texture and shape and form. It makes a person think of the long term, the old and the wise. If plants have their sage, then it would be fitting to place the elephant tree in that position.

The elephant tree is drought-deciduous, putting forth its energies into photosynthetic leaves only after the rains. All those trees around us were now doing just that, so that every tree was shrouded in the golden aura of life and growth following life-affirming rains. Eventually these trees would turn their energies to flowers, and the golden trees would be tinged with deep-pink flowers hiding their propagules within and setting forth seed to start the next generation of sages across this ancient island.

Drought had captured and held Isla Cedros for a number of years now, and this was reflected by the placement and wide spacing of plants. Those plants that abounded, the cliff spurge and daisy-like brittlebush, desert mallow, barrel cactus, and more of the nitrogen-fixing legumes, were rarely in flower. The lack of rains had sapped much of the energy required, so that the blanket of spring color that we might have expected stepping onto the island toward the end of March was largely absent. Only occasionally did we see the yellow of the brittlebush and mallow, the red of the barrel cactus, and the purple of the lupine. In future years perhaps the rains would release earlier to flood the valley with life translated to color, but for now we were seeing the desert as it was, and as it will be, until climates change and fronts shift to create a milder regime over this land. Picking between the rocks and plants, searching for lizards and spiders, we found the hoof and femur of one of the Cedros Island mule deer that inhabit the hills and feed on the sparse vegetation. The tendons and much of the fur were still attached, and the hoof looked so small cradled in our hands.

We meandered along a three-to-five-meter exposed cliff face at the side of the gully showing the compacted layers of sediment and rock from flash floods that must have occurred over centuries. Coarse material overlay fine, and fine overlay coarse as we mentally mapped the layers in our mind and tried to translate what we saw into actual events long since past. In the top layer of sediment we could see the roots of the desert plants penetrating into the depths. Most of the roots were only in the uppermost layers, shallow to capture the maximum amount of water before evaporation, and other plants stole what each individual requires for survival.

We sat in the shade created by this erosion, the only substantial shade that we had been able to find along the trail. It felt good to hide from the oppressive sun, and we took long drinks from canteens already warm. The occasional hummingbird darted by, and other birds soon became visible in flight and sound. The ever-present mockingbird sang from its perch in an elephant tree, golden-crowned sparrows cut the silence with their plaintive trill calls, and unseen rufous-sided towhees whined in the distance. Malevolent-looking ravens circled overhead, and the breeze caught the wings of a West Coast lady butterfly and brought her near.

Our search through the undergrowth for reptilian life was successful, and we flushed a rock lizard, a *Petrosaurus,* from beneath a sugar bush. It was about thirty centimeters long, and its body was covered in spots. We managed to corral it and eventually capture the animal. Who says dinosaurs are extinct? We held in our hands a distant relative of those creatures that dominated our world for 150 million years. Our saurian was brontosaurus or tyrannosaurus in miniature. The birds may be the true descendants of the dinosaur lineage, but the lizards win on appearance.

The canyon was marked by clearly visible striations and geologic features in the rocks and hills. In places the layers of sedimentary rock were almost vertical, silent witness to the intense pressures and manipulation that they had been subject to before even our *Petrosaurus's* ancestors had progressed to their ultimate fate. How difficult it is for our minds to consider the forces that are required to transform rock, to mold stone as a child molds modeling clay, to lift mountains and create caverns and trenches on the ocean floor. It is in rocks such as these that people have discovered fossilized whales from the Miocene that resemble the gray whales of today. It is in rocks in other places, other lands, that we can unfurl our own past.

Further along the path a section of sedimentary rock was exposed. The fractures and shapes revealed in stone took on the image of some cubist painting. Staring at the perfection of these natural cubes carved of stone, I realized that everything that humans can invent or lift from their imagination is somewhere mirrored in nature. Thus the cubist art of Pablo Picasso and Georges Braque is reflected outside the expression of human ingenuity. Even Picasso's other abstract paintings seem strangely familiar to those who have gazed intently at the face of the flatfish.

Back toward the beach, the ravens croaked overhead, contrasting with the delicate call of an unseen orange-crowned warbler. The outwash of the floodplain was clogged with the dry mud of the inner slopes, and the crushed remains of purple sea urchins littered the ground—evidence of either the scattering nature of scavenging gulls or the flooding capability of the tide. An osprey surveyed the beach from on high, clipping the surface of the water with curled talons. It came up empty and swung around to repeat the action. Eventually it vanished from sight, journeying to other hunting grounds.

The *Searcher* was at anchor in the bay. A bank of gray fog hugged the horizon behind it. The skiffs landed on the beach of smooth rounded stones, and we returned for lunch. When the anchor was lifted, we began to cruise along the eastern side of the island toward the beaches favored by California sea lions and elephant seals. The vanguard drew us on as sea lions bobbed in our wake.

The water was sparklingly clear under the skiffs. Sounds and smells emanated from the mammals massed on the beach. The water was aqua-green, and the ripples and flow magnified the fish and sand patterns on the bottom. As we neared the golden cove, the sea lions raced into the water, churning the nearshore white and loud with barks and splashes. Erect heads lifted clear of the water next to us, eyes bright and ears alert. Others swam, gliding under the skiff, rolling their streamlined bodies to gaze up at us open-mouthed, bubbles glistening on wet fur and billowing from nostrils and mouth.

Some of the animals that remained ashore on the sand raised their heads to watch their fellows play. But most slept and baked in the sun. Elephant seals lay still on the beach, in their element in the water but on land inhibited by gravity. A bull sea lion, head crowned white with a sagittal crest and sporting a thick, muscular neck of pure strength, bent his head back to watch us. Two jet-black sea lions were curled at the shore, each nibbling at hide, flipper, fur, and skin, perfect duplicate images reflecting light on dark.

Moving from one side of the beach to the other, we passed nesting Brandt's cormorants on the guano-spotted cliffs fringing the cove, and local fishermen stood on the boulders, casting line into the waters. We moved back toward the *Searcher* while animals continued to porpoise along the surface, imitating those other familiar marine mammals. Two sea lions stood high on a rock jutting from the shallows, bobbing around each other with mouths agape and red, barks and squeaks and whines projected with indignation.

Back on board the *Searcher,* people fished quietly from the stern, and the bank of fog on the horizon began to envelop the island until the mountains vanished. We left our anchorage at three that afternoon. The *Deluxe* had passed on word of blue whales to the north end of Isla Cedros, just thirteen kilometers away. Our course was changed and we ventured toward the fog. As we traveled further from Cedros, the calm blue waters that surrounded the island and the sun that roasted everything under it disappeared like an ephemeral cloud. I was standing on the top deck outside the wheelhouse, binoculars in hand. Ahead of the *Searcher* the wind had whipped the water into a frenzy, and the calm ocean was transformed into a maelstrom. The water changed color as though from white to black, so dramatic was the transition. Behind us Isla Cedros was almost completely hidden, and the *Searcher* plowed into a wall of cloud. Spray and waves lifted over our bow and even to the wheelhouse, soaking the windows and me with well-aimed throws.

We searched the rough waters for whales. The island was now just a memory, and our attention was focused on the violent motion of the vessel and the troughs and peaks of the waves that threw white threads of water across the surface, confounding our ability to spot the telltale blow of whales. The wind would have obliterated any exhalation in seconds, and the fog and clouds had so reduced the available light that sky, clouds, and sea seemed to merge into the same shade of gray that caused eyes to squint and redden. The motion of waves and of the ship undoubtedly further reduced our ability to detect the movements of whales. Only through luck, and because it passed so close to our starboard side, did we spot the humpback whale that fluked twice before disappearing into the gray nothingness surrounding us.

The day was at an end, and the light was largely gone when we were roused from the galley and the shelter of the inner reaches of the vessel. A group of three or four blue whales were in front of us. These whales were not the intense blue that sun and calm seas project, but a steely mottled gray that mirrored all around us. Under the poor light we could barely make out the blows that hung momentarily in the air and the brief surfacings that were obscured by crashing waves. Occasionally one of the animals passed close to our bow as it dove, and we could see the distinctive, small sickle-shaped dorsal fin set far down the broad, expansive back. A couple of times we were able to make out the large blow and body of a whale closely followed on its flanks by a much smaller animal—a blue whale cow and calf. A sight for sore eyes.

By six o'clock the light had failed, and the *Searcher* continued to rock in the waves as we progressed northward, leaving the blue whales to merge with the sea. A mother and calf blue whale. Hope for the future.

We arrived at Isla San Martin the following morning. The depressing gray weather of the evening and night remained. When we landed on the black shores of the island, a haunting world greeted us. The cloud cover was complete and the air saturated. A dead sea lion lay on the black sand, its fatal wounds harried by common ravens. Sandpipers and godwits picked their way along the shoreline, and a red-throated loon called as though from beyond reality.

Atop the black sand lay the huge spherical and oval lava rocks that had been sent forth from the center of the Earth 10,000 or 15,000 years ago with a force that we can only imagine, but sadly are also trying to duplicate. The landscape of Isla San Martin was dominated by the cinder craters that punctuated the skyline, further visual evidence of the power of magma and lava beneath our feet. This place was such a contrast to the bright desert colors and shades that we had been used to in our travels. It was a strange place to end a trip of this kind. Bleak, desolate, depressed, even. Monochromatic, silent and brooding under the surface, as though the cinder cones could at any moment reveal what had happened so many centuries before. There was an intensity here, but so different from the intensity of feelings that arose in the lagoons. Here the feelings were of foreboding, a feeling that the past was not that far behind us, and that a simple crack at the surface could return us to the lava flow and bloodletting that once darkened the skies and waters of Baja.

The vast oval lava rocks were piled high in an artificial-looking though natural ridge stretching along the coast. Many of the lower boulders were stained and crusted with orange and yellow lichen. Between some of the rocks, ice plant and the purple-flowered sea rocket had taken hold. The sea rocket is an exotic here; it has spread rapidly throughout the region following its accidental introduction to the Golden Gate Park in Northern California. Seeds of the plant contaminated batches of sand dune grasses imported from Europe to stabilize the dune systems. Now the sea rocket has spread and invaded far and wide. This plant was not the only alien on desolate Isla San Martin.

As we wandered over the almost lunar landscape, cats followed our steps. During the tenth century, when the Saxon kings ruled England and scholars of the day thought the sun and planets circled the Earth, abalone divers from China lived here, and the cats came with them. Being from such ancient stock imparts a certain ancestral honor to these felines, an honor that seems reflected in their gait and attitude. Or perhaps that is simply born of feline indifference to human observation.

We climbed to the top of the boulder ridge and looked out over the black water. Harbor seals peered up at us like lost souls from the abyss, imprisoned in this darkling world. The ghosts of whalers and their tenders would be at home here—as would the souls of whales.

I would be intrigued to know how much of my recollection about Isla San Martin is a function and reflection of the weather on that day. Perhaps if the sun had been bright and the sky and waters blue, the description would have been different. Foreboding black sand and tide pools might have become brilliant jet pools of sparkling light. Monochromatic, brooding visions transformed to contrasting vividness of light and dark. Perhaps the description was also a function of the trip coming to an end, the knowledge that the whales were vanishing and that it would be a number of months before I could see, hear, and feel these sensations again. Whatever the reasons, Isla San Martin did not have the attractiveness and color, in reality or interpretation, of earlier locations.

Back down on the flat, cholla dogged our feet. Its spines added substance to our feelings. More benign evening primrose radiated across the ground in spiraling tendrils sporting delicate yellow flowers. We climbed toward the cinder cones, wandering along cliff faces looking at spiders hung between cholla spines, lichen adding crusty color to rocks, and listening to the alert cries of horned larks. The seals watched as we hiked high above the shoreline, occasionally sending scree tumbling downward. We sat on the boulders, looking south to where we had journeyed from, and north to where we were heading, and whence we came. This was the transition, the place where a change in mind and attitude overcame us. My thoughts were already rushing ahead. The happenings of the last few days were confined to memories. So soon.

It is of value to be faced with a juxtaposition of emotions. It requires a conviction and effort to examine the relationships between them—how they feed off each other and allow each to grow and flourish, or perish and die, depending on the strength of both and the character of the participants.

As we headed back into U.S. waters, two gray whales spouted in the distance. Gray on gray.

The mark of life in the exhaled breath. An affirmation of life in water and on land. Whale-watching with heart and mind. And spirit.

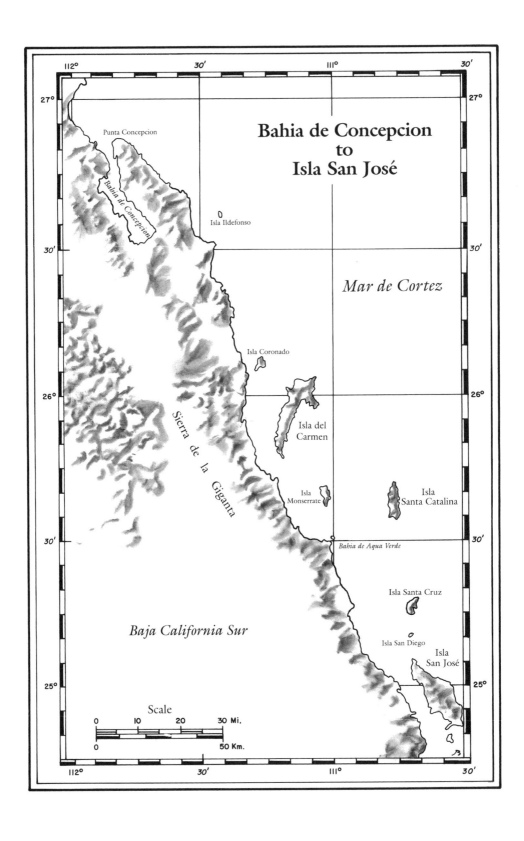

Bahia de Concepcion
to
Isla San José

Punta Concepcion

Bahia de Concepcion

Isla Ildefonso

Mar de Cortez

Isla Coronado

Isla del
Carmen

Sierra de la Giganta

Isla
Monserrate

Isla
Santa Catalina

Bahia de Aqua Verde

Isla Santa Cruz

Baja California Sur

Isla San Diego

Isla
San José

Scale

| 0 | 10 | 20 | 30 Mi. |

| 0 | | 50 Km. |

27° 30' 111° 30'

26°

30'

25°

3

Blue Water, Blue Whales

*A fabulous presence emerged, and the world took
on a whole new dimension. Centuries of immobility
suddenly unfurled, the granite was moving,
swimming, breathing! I can still see the prow of
that living Nautilus curling back the sea, the water
streaming down its hulk, the peaceable jaws. I can still
hear the swish of spray, the mighty, measured panting
of its breathing apparatus. . . All I know is that,
ever since that encounter, nothing has been quite
the same. Secretly, I've had to date everything as
happening before or after that whale.*
                                        —*Samivel, 1976*

In August 1990 I moved from England to Alaska, and al-
though not deliberate in motive, I suddenly found myself doing the same annual
journey as the surf scoters and the northern fulmars, the humpbacks and the
grays—from Alaska to Baja.

In March 1991 I returned to the Sea of Cortez for the express purpose of
spending more time with blue whales. My previous encounters in 1989 and
1990 had been brief but tantalizing. On this trip they would be the focus.

In reality, we do not know much about these blues. We do not know where
they go when they leave the warm waters of the Golfo de California, or where
they breed. Many of these animals probably reach the Farallons off the coast of
Northern California, and some may head as far north as the Gulf of Alaska. All
we know for certain is that the inglorious days of whaling devastated the world's
population, and today few blues roam the oceans.

When I arrived in La Paz, the weather was perfect Baja: clear blue skies, day-
time temperatures of 24 to 27° C, and nighttime temperatures of 13 to 15° C. A

nice change from Alaska. Once again the voyage was based on the quiet elegance of the *Don José*. The afternoon was spent aboard the vessel or around the harbor. We watched the magnificent frigatebirds, brown pelicans, and yellow-footed gulls overhead, and the snowy egrets, great blue herons, curlews, and sandpipers pick their way along the shoreline. Only José, the captain, remained from the 1989 trip, and I introduced myself to the other members of the crew: Luis, the first mate; Hernan; Felix; Roberto, the cook; and César, the cook's mate.

From the deck of the vessel we could peer over the side at the sparkling water and the occasional school of graybar grunts. Surreally, the bird life that buzzed the deck of the *Don José* was joined by a bright blue budgerigar, which alighted momentarily on the deck and vanished in a flurry of azure feathers.

The night was spent at anchor in the harbor, listening to the sounds of a bustling city, dogs and music from the shore, and in the morning at daybreak the urgent crows of cockerels. We eagerly awaited our departure when we would head into the jewel of Mexico, Baja California Sur and the emerald waters of the Sea of Cortez. These waters hid whales that revealed themselves to the patient with ease, and that permitted close encounters to the enthusiastic and the reverent.

Our small group of fourteen was guided once again by Mason Weinrich. Mason had so skillfully led the 1989 voyage that in whale-watching circles it was still spoken of as "The Trip." This voyage would be confined to the southern portion of the Sea of Cortez. We would travel northward to Isla San Francisco, Isla San José, Isla Santa Catalina, and Isla Monserrate, taking refuge frequently in Bahia de Aqua Verde, before heading south again to Isla Espiritu Santo and Los Islotes, and returning to Bahia de la Paz.

The morning was topped by a sky of desert perfection, clear blue sky devoid even of high cirrus clouds. As we left the harbor, the vessels around us were reflected in dual images of color and form. We worked our way through the buoy-marked channel. Bottlenose dolphins joined our bow and wake, the bright sun reflecting off slate-gray dorsal fins. The red and green buoys were colorful perches for double-crested cormorants, and on one, three California sea lions lounged in the drying light of the sun until black coats turned golden.

The Pemex refinery discharged gray-brown smoke into the air. The discoloration was carried softly on the light breeze and stretched across the line of the mountains and the bay, visual evidence of the energetic transformation that was occurring within, and that ultimately drives the town, the boats, and the planes.

Magnificent frigatebirds circled high over our heads, rarely beating their wings, simply gliding on the upcurrents, creating a piratical black outline against the blue sky. An osprey was perched on one of the overhead power cables near the refinery, watching the goings on with intense curiosity. The hooked beak of this winged predator was clearly visible in profile.

The water in Bahia de La Paz was glass calm, the wind rippling the surface, in places creating delicate patterns and dappling the surface in lines, curves, and reflection. As we turned into the wind, the water darkened and a light squall danced around our ship. A brown booby flew low in front of us, the light reflecting brashly off its white breast, and a frigatebird began to chase an elegant tern in an attempt to force the small bird to disgorge its catch. Cardon cactus dotted the hillsides on the mainland, creating a speckled pattern of green across the brown and dusty hills and valleys. The sun was reflecting starbursts off the water, and alternately lit and subdued the landscape in patterns of light and shadow.

A fishing panga near the shore was drawing in nets heavy with fish, and the water surrounding the vessel was a maelstrom of birds vying for position. Hundreds of yellow-footed, California, and laughing gulls cawed and flapped their wings, while brown pelicans lifted distended bills from the deep.

Beyond the confines of the bay, and distant from the muting effects of the refinery emissions, we could see forever. Visibility was at least fifty kilometers, and the entire length of the Sea of Cortez seemed laid out before us. Six brown pelicans descended in formation, wings beating in unison as they alighted on the water next to a California sea lion. The sea lion had a large fish clamped between strong jaws, and it now dove and leaped and barked at the birds in an attempt to drive them from its bounty. We cut the motor and watched. The sea lion was too fast for the pelicans, but the birds' persistence was paying off in the form of scraps dropped from the animal's mouth. The motion of the *Don José* was no longer washing us with a cooling breeze, and the sun beat upon the w-w deck with a desert ferocity. The engine idled, and we listened to the wind and the water lapping against the ship. Occasionally a gull flew close by and cawed, and we could hear the whoosh of air between crafted and well-preened feathers. Another sound distracted us: that of a wave running up the sand and pebbles of a beach, tipping into breakers and transforming motion into sound. But there was no beach. Ahead of the ship, just a few meters away, the flat, calm water bubbled and darkened, and we heard the rush of the wave again. The tiny fins of fish clipped the surface, and a dark mass raced across the surface, generating the sound of breakers in their synchronized and frantic motion. Something from below, unseen, was herding the fish back and forth, frothing the surface with panic. The pelicans were instantly attracted to the motion and dove on the school, surfacing frequently to shake their heads and swallow their catch, water running from oversized bills.

The fish continued to swarm until their tormentor descended into the deep, and they were no longer driven along the surface. The sound faded, and we continued on, the wind driving subtlety from our ears, but permitting the raucous gulls to intrude. The few squalls that had darkened the water's surface vanished, and the sea took on the appearance of rippling satin of the deepest blue. The rocks that formed the hills of the mainland revealed the strata of geologic time and pressures, contrasting in dramatic fashion with the blue of sea and sky. As we left Bahia de la Paz entering the Sea of Cortez, we passed a long, tapering colonial jellyfish floating along the surface, and two California sea lions lay at rest close by, their flippers held clear of the water to warm their blood in the air.

We passed the morning in luxurious leisure, lying on the w-w deck under the sun, watching the gulls follow our wake and black-vented shearwaters alternately glide and beat their sculpted wings close to the water's surface. These small, dusky birds would glide in easy motion, then beat their wings five times and return to glide, occasionally tripping along the water with delicate steps.

In the distance a Bryde's whale blew and vanished from sight, in typical Bryde's fashion. It was our first tantalizing glimpse of a great whale, and my first of the year. Still the water and air around us were full of life.

As the *Don José* cut through the gentle ripples of the wind, tiny fins in multiples of two were held clear of the water. These small twin fins were the wing tips of mobulas, a variety of manta. Each animal was one to two meters across, and as it hung suspended just below the surface, each tip of the broad expanse of the "wings" emerged above the water, resembling the dorsals of sharks, but more rounded.

We watched as the rays, often in groups of two or three, lay basking at the surface, their dark forms clearly visible in the calm waters. Their distinctive bat-like shape was topped and tailed with a long spearlike tail to the rear and twin horns projecting forward from the head. Just as the gray whale earned its name of devilfish from the whalers as a result of its tenacity, so the mobula earned the same name, because of its physical characteristics; to the fishermen of the region the mobulas' horns were the sign of the devil. The mobulas' counter-shading was revealed as they leapt from the water executing double and triple twists with amazing deftness and then re-entering the water with a resounding splash. The top of the ray was slate gray, while beneath the animal was creamy white—perfect camouflage for its environment, rendering the ray invisible when viewed from above or below. We know less about the "breaching" of mobulas than we do of breaching whales. Some have suggested that, like whales, the rays leap to remove parasites, while others suggest that the leap followed by such a dramatic splash is used to stun or scare their prey. The truth is that we don't know.

Comically, the ray's mouth can be seen in a downturned curve in mid-leap, resembling the tragedy mask of theater. In reality, the Mobulidae, especially the huge Pacific manta, have reason to reflect such an image. The Pacific manta used to be widespread in these waters but is now a rarity. The wingspan of this species could exceed 6.5 meters, and the animal weighed more than 1,600 kilograms. In years past the mantas were hunted by fishermen for bait, and few of the giants can be seen in modern times. The smaller mobulas continue to be common, but are also taken for bait in some areas.

As the bow of the *Don José* passed close to several mobulas, their wing tips flattened, and with powerful downward beats of flexible wings they propelled themselves from our path. They flew through the water, descending into the depths and merging their dark wings with the dark water hidden from the penetrating sunlight.

Isla Espiritu Santo was to our starboard; the guano-covered pinnacles of Los Islotes were visible to the north, familiar from previous years, and destination of a later date on this voyage. We were still heading north, but toward eleven we turned south to close in on a group of brown pelicans, gulls, and shearwaters that were massed over a school of fish. The familiar yellow-footed and California gulls were joined by the more distinctive Heermann's and black-headed Bonaparte's gulls. Heermann's gulls are probably the most beautiful of these winged mariners. They are a delicate frosty gray color with a black tail and a white trailing edge to the wings. Their white head contrasts dramatically with the blood-red bill. Even the immatures are distinctive, making them unique in the annals of immature gull identification. The youngsters are dark brown with a clear mottling pattern across the feathers. During the voyage, immature Heermann's would often follow our wake and glide gently alongside the w-w deck.

Sooty and pink-footed shearwaters darted between the larger gulls, descending to the water to dance across the waves, their bent wings giving speed and art of motion denied the larger birds.

At length we began to head toward Isla Espiritu Santo, drawn by the long white plume of a whale near the island. Three large thresher sharks were grouped at the surface and moved off with slow, deliberate side sweeps of their heavy tails as we passed. Each shark was about three meters long, with a massive scythe-like caudal fin extending behind it. They moved with ease through the water, their method of motion so different from that of whales and dolphins, their attitude so different. They captivated us with the horror that human conditioning has imparted.

A few interesting if somewhat obscure facts may better illustrate why sharks seem so alien to us. Sharks evolved more than 300 million years ago during the middle Devonian period, well before mammals began to dominate the land and finally took to the sea. Sixty million years ago all the major shark families had appeared, and in the subsequent passage of time there has been little change in shape or form. Today there are some 350 species of sharks. It may be notable that the term *shark*, the word that can perhaps strike fear into more people than any other, derives from a term used to denote unscrupulous people, principally a person who swindled sailors. So it seems that we have named sharks based on our own perceptions of human behavior!

The tenacity and voraciousness of sharks have been widely reported. Bull sharks have been known to chase their prey onto land. A 2.5-meter shark exerts 22,500 kilograms per square centimeter of pressure with its jaws. Sharks can detect 1 part of blood in 100 million parts of water, and two-thirds of their brain's weight is used for smelling. Sharks never sleep, and their eyes glow in the dark like a cat's. A shark can swallow anything up to half its size in a single gulp. They have no sense of pain, and will continue to function, even attacking and feeding, while being disemboweled. When in a feeding frenzy, as well as biting and eating fellow sharks, individuals have even been known to take a bite out of their own bodies. And finally, sand sharks are the only animals that are known to eat one another before they are born; a shark researcher was once bitten by a sand shark embryo while studying its mother.

Sharks known for attacks on people include the tiger, mako, hammerhead, gray nurse, dusky, great blue, brown, lemon, reef, whitetip, blacktip, sand, porbeagle, bullshark, and, of course, the great white. Even so, there are an average of only twenty-eight shark attacks reported each year, and few of these are fatal. The chance of being attacked by a shark is fifty times less than that of being struck by lightning.

But our view of sharks continues to be bound by fear. We treat them so differently from other predators that occasionally take people as prey. Our views of lions, tigers, polar bears, and grizzlies are so different from those directed toward sharks, crocodiles, anacondas, and vipers. Is it purely a function of blood? Do we understand the motives of the warm-blooded predator more because we can see ourselves in the same role? Is our misunderstanding of the cold-blooded a matter of evolution rather than a fear of death, which after all can come from any of these species?

The great white we fear and kill at every opportunity; the killer whale we hold up as a fine example of cooperative deadly hunting. Is this simply an expression of a pro-mammalian bias? Or of something else, something deeper in our psyche, that sees the shark, a part of a world to which we can make only trivial excursions, as simply a manifestation of something more, our own limitations in a submarine world? The other deadly nonmammalian predators inhabit similarly inimical worlds, of river depths, tropical jungles, or dry deserts. Our inability to survive in many of those places compounds our fears, and they take on the shapes and forms of the creatures that we can least identify with and feel sympathy for: the reptilian, the piscine, and the arthropodal.

Another blow burst from the water toward Isla Espiritu Santo, and we began to move in that direction. The water's surface was stippled by the wind, and the calm, silky blue water revealed mobula after mobula, twin fins projecting into the air. The occasional sea lion porpoised near our vessel, and ahead Espiritu Santo transported us to a past of volcanics and immense subterranean pressures.

The waters were quiet; the whale that had drawn us toward the island had vanished into the impenetrable depths. José turned the ship back toward Isla San Francisco, and with black storm-petrels, Heermann's gulls, and shearwaters following our wake, we pulled into the curving sandy bay on the south side of the island.

Isla San Francisco is a sloping, red volcanic extrusion from the floor of the Sea of Cortez. Red- and green-colored rocks are exposed at the surface, and the russet cliffs and scree slopes are dappled with evenly spaced vegetation. The gently curved beach and the shallow water were painted in shimmering patterns by the sunlight, and water lapped the shore with gentle motion and no appreciable wave action.

The *Don José* dropped her anchor and we prepared to enter the water from the beach. We were wearing short wetsuits, but initially the water felt cool, too cool. Curiosity eventually won out, and I walked into the water and lay face down, peering through my mask into a meter of liquid life. I can vividly remember the sound of my own breathing—the sound of life, my life, passing through a narrow plastic tube from enveloping water to open air. It sounded loud, coarse. As I swam, I occasionally held my breath to block out the intrusion of my own lungs and relished in the silence. I watched as the tiny pulsating comb jellies glided past my mask, the sunlight hitting their bodies, transforming them into tiny, living prisms of color. I was concentrating so hard on the tiny visions inches from my mask that the first time I saw a large fish swim underneath me, I was so surprised that I began to hyperventilate.

Having regained some semblance of composure (if the snorkel had not been in my mouth, I probably would have been grinning from ear to ear), I returned to the water, breathing slow, controlled breaths. I began to swim along the beach toward the point where the red boulders entered the water, creating a multitude of hiding places and anchors for the colorful array of life that blossoms in this warm, sun-blessed land.

Fish of all shapes, sizes, forms, and colors moved and wafted across my field of vision—unknown, unnamed creatures, colors seemingly found only in the water, prevented from excursions to land by the harshness of the air and the brashness of the sun. All below me was suspended by the gentle hand of the ocean, buoyed up and caressed by the currents, protected from the extremes of temperature, shielded from the unyielding and desiccating sun. Here, animal and plant seemed to merge into one kind, evolution and adaptation creating animals as plants and plants as animals in this metropolis of interconnections, where the actions of one are countered or matched by the actions of another, where the balance of the ecosystem is a function of the ocean working with and through the diversity of form.

Evolution began on this world 4 billion years ago, in the water. It is a time that we know little about, and can imagine even less. In the oceans we can literally see the largest and the smallest of all the living things that have appeared on this planet, the blue whale and the single-celled microorganism.

We can see the grotesque and the exquisite, the colorless and those that blaze color.

Approximately 20 percent of the Earth's organisms are aquatic, perhaps even more. We do not know exactly how many that is; there are some 20,000 known species of fish, but perhaps 20,000 more have yet to be described. There are 31,250 known species of protozoa, 5,000 species of sponges, 9,400 species of sea anemones and jellyfish, 100 species of comb jellies, 130 species of endoprocta, 2,000 species of rotifers, kinorhynchs, and gastrotrichs, 260 species of lampshells, 4,000 species of moss animals, 11 species of horseshoe worms, 6,350 species of flatworms and ribbon worms, 12,000 species of roundworms, 700 species of spiny-headed worms, and 80 species of horsehair worms.

There are 11,500 species of segmented worms, 459 species of echiurans, priapulans, and sipunculans, 150 species of beard worms, 70 species of arrow worms, 90 species of acorn worms. There are 39,000 species of crustaceans, which includes 8,400 species of copepods, 1,025 species of barnacles, 23,000 species of shrimps. There are 500 species of sea spiders and 4 species of horseshoe crabs; there are 400 species of water bears and 90 of tongue worms. There are 80,000 to 100,000 species of mollusks, including 500 species of chitons, 60,000 to 75,000 species of slugs and snails, and 15,000 to 20,000 species of clams and mussels. There are 6,000 species of starfish, sea lilies, and sea urchins, and 2,000 species of sea squirts and lancelets.

Adding the world's whales, pinnipeds, and sirenians hardly makes a dent in the total. How many more fish and marine invertebrates are currently unseen, unknown? Eventually the figure will probably double, maybe even triple.

We can enter that world of mollusks, echinoderms, and copepods, and look at the magnificent coral reefs built from living animals and decorated with the flowers of the marine kingdom. But we are always on the fringes of that otherworldly place. How strange must we black-coated snorkelers look to these animals, our silhouettes temporarily blocking out the sun as we swim over them, our breath resonating through the water, hands and legs flaying in uncoordinated fashion as the terrestrial animal in us tries to conform to a three-dimensional world of near-zero gravity where terrestrial perspective vanishes.

A group of Mexican goatfish moved in unison across the rocks strewn across the floor of the bay, their yellow lateral line and fins matched motion for motion throughout the school. The shimmering silver of mullet flashed by, catching the light with every turn of their slender bodies.

I moved over the rocks, peering into the crevices between boulders, into the recesses that hid shy fish from the gaze of both the curious and the predatory. Reef cornetfish swam in jerky motion, their arrow-like bodies moved by almost invisible caudal fins. Each fish was about a meter long and occasionally pointed downward, permitting the tiny mouth to poke and pick at the growth beneath it. Sea pens and fans, gorgonians in yellow and red, and feather duster polychaetes flowered in the depths, animal in the form of plant, adding color and intricacy to the boulders over which other animals only swam.

I stretched out a hand toward a school of Panamic sergeant major fish, their rank denoted by the distinctive black stripes that bisected each fish. They moved on, unaware or unperturbed by the intrusion. King angelfish swam close to the boulders, a royal fish of turquoise and yellow, marked by a vertical white bar behind the pectoral fin. A number of lone juveniles moved slowly by, their turquoise bodies heavily mottled with yellow that would soon fade with age.

Against the dark red and shadows of the boulders, a stunningly iridescent blue fish darted from side to side. There were many of them close to the rocks; only seven centimeters or so in length, they were undeniably one of the most gloriously attired fish on the reef. They were juvenile Cortez damselfish. If any adults were present among the boulders, I did not see them, for when mature the fish lose their color and become a uniform dull brown. In most species, the young are camouflaged and hidden. As juveniles they are vulnerable to attack. But damselfish juveniles seem to court attention, while the adults fade into the background. It is a remarkable reversal of coloration to which we infer some unknown purpose. I hope that some things will always remain mysteries. Mystery adds interest and heightens curiosity. It limits knowledge but stimulates imagination.

The dichotomy of the damselfish was more than matched by the Cortez rainbow wrasse. The yellow, black, and red striped females abounded, but far fewer of the tricolor blue, yellow, and purple secondary males were present. Wrasses are well known as the "personal cleaners" of the deep, often swimming inside large fishes' mouths to clean debris from the jaws and gills. But these wrasses exhibit another, even more remarkable characteristic. They are all born female. The secondary male is just that, secondary. Through unknown mechanisms that may be related to water temperature, salinity, sunlight, or density-dependent characteristics, female rainbow wrasses can transform themselves into males when necessary. When not required for mating, rainbow wrasses are predominantly female.

Many fish show coloration characteristics similar to those of their terrestrial counterparts, the birds, where color is often based on sex. Slightly to one side of the wrasse, a female Pacific boxfish hovered as though in midair. The male and female boxfish have distinctive, though very different, coloration. Both are stocky fish; the female is dark blue and is completely covered with white dots. The male is covered with fewer dots that are white above and orange on the flanks and below, and he has a much bluer body than his mate.

At one spot along the reef a number of boulders were piled together, creating a submarine cave. At the entrance, settled in the fine sand, was a giant hawkfish. This large fish was a mosaic of shape and color, its gray-brown body covered with dark brown wavy lines edged in blue. The caudal fin was also trimmed blue, and the fish's dark eye was ringed with gold.

I swam on, beginning to turn back toward the shore. We had been in this otherworldly place for almost an hour, and it was time to return to that terrestrial existence bound by the laws of gravity and physics, laws that in the water, if not broken, certainly seem to bend.

The water was beginning to feel cold, and many snorkelers had already returned to shore, and then to the ship to prepare for the afternoon hike. I held my arms across my chest, trying to stay warm as I swam and watched, enthralled and not willing to return to my landlocked existence.

One of the last fish that I saw before I planted my feet on the sand was a guineafowl puffer. This thirty-centimeter-long, chubby fish was a fitting highlight to end my watery excursion. It was a suitably unsubtle creature upon which to hang thoughts about an alien world. It had a dark black body that was almost invisible behind the tiny white dots that encompassed the fish and disrupted its outline, providing surprisingly effective camouflage against the shadows and crev ̣ ̣s of the reef.

I surfaced and ͓̣epped back on shore, dripping wet, cold, and immensely satisfied. Barriers do exist between land and sea, but there is a narrow band where we can easily trespass into the aqueous world of fin, scale, and polyp. Other parts of the deep can be investigated with greater effort and money, but these often involve the explorer encompassing herself in tanks, suits, and submersibles. Only the snorkeler and the free diver are uncluttered and thus closer to being true participants in the ebb and flow of currents and life in the ocean.

We returned briefly to the *Don José* and then began to investigate terrestrial Isla San Francisco. The island's plant, animal, and bird life revealed itself to us in thickets and bushes, on the sandbanks and the hillsides, punctuations of life amid the desert. The colors were more sporadic and subdued than their marine counterparts just a few hundred meters away, but such undersea visions were now hidden from sight, and we were back with the familiar movements, sights, and sounds of our terrestrial heritage.

The high tide line revealed the creatures of the reef in mummified form, their bones bleached by the sun and picked at by scavengers. Spotted porcupine fish and reef cornetfish were just debris on the beach now, whereas only hours earlier they had been embodiments of grace, color, and movement in the liquid sustenance of the ocean. The occasional piece of driftwood cast upon the shore hid crabs and scurrying amphipods. All across the beach were strewn the large carapaces and slender legs of spider crabs. Each crab shell was whole, but empty and missing pincers. Some were spotted with sand, while others were clean and placed so carefully that the still life had the appearance of manipulation or design rather than the random casting of flotsam upon the beach.

The vegetation on the sand dunes was infrequent, mainly dune grass and bursage. Black-throated sparrows began their slow, plaintive calls that ended in a trill crescendo as we climbed the dunes, our feet sinking deep into white sand.

Beyond the dunes the typical Baja desert vegetation was spread out before us. Ice plant and pickleweed dominated the near flats, while a few small elephant trees dotted the hillside, their yellow leaves imparting a glowing aura to the twisted tree. The dusty ground revealed blooms of intense color: red flowers of the fishhook cactus, yellow of morning glory, and white of the desert daisy.

We began to search the boulders and stones beneath the jojoba and pitaya agria for signs of lizards and snakes. Our search flushed side-blotched lizards and their zebra-tailed compatriots. But we were searching for something a little larger. Eventually one of the large red volcanic boulders was overturned, and there, shading itself from the late afternoon sun, was a chuckwalla. It was not a very large specimen, but it filled our hands. Chuckwallas frequent the cracks and crevices between and under boulders; when threatened they squeeze into a suitable crevice and puff themselves up, making it virtually impossible for a predator to force them out. Of course, we subverted such defensive posturing by simply removing the boulder altogether.

The lizard was dark gray, with darker speckling all over its body. It was noticeably darker above than below, and when placed back on its rock blended with the russet volcanics. Stroking the reptile was like feeling something slightly baggy, as though it had yet to fully grow into its skin. I could feel the tiny scales in the roughness of the integument. The creature's tiny feet clasped at our fingers, just like a baby. In evolutionary terms it is we who are the infants, and this saurian is the modern-day manifestation of a noble and dignified ancestry that dominated these lands long before our emergence from the cradle of humanity along the nurturing rivers and coasts in the moist tropics.

As we headed toward the flat white expanse in the center of the island, an osprey flew silently overhead. We stepped on the crusty surface and our feet sank down five or six centimeters. The material felt strange and smelled dank, as though the gentle sea breeze had been captured and magnified a hundredfold. It has been calculated that there is enough salt in the oceans to cover all the continents with a layer 166 meters thick. Several areas in the salt pan were saturated, and grasped at our feet like quicksand. In the center of the pan were four rectangular pools dug into the ground. Each pool was full of water, and the banks were white with crystalline salt. The salt pan was a natural phenomenon, born of the proximity of the ocean and the depression of the island. But the pools were built by people to take advantage of salt precipitation to cure fish.

Capillary action draws the salt water to the surface on the pan, and then the heat of the sun evaporates the water, leaving behind pure salt. Several of the pools were tinged red with algae, amazingly at home in such inhospitable concentrations, while the banks of pure salt to the side were penetrated by the bright green stems of pickleweed. When we try to imagine what might make a place inimical to life forms, a place such as this surely springs to mind. However, even here life seems to flourish.

We should value all such areas; they may lack the diversity of more conducive environments, but the very tenacity of life here and the type of adaptations that hardship spawns are of intrinsic value, perhaps one day for practical purposes, but also for their contribution to our thoughts and ideas today. They generate understanding and wonder in our own minds, and that is simply invaluable. Nothing can replace it, or compensate for it. It is there and we can look upon it. If it vanishes, we have lost what cannot be valued, or perhaps even dreamed of.

We worked our way back to the beach, through stands of jumping cholla in bloom and tiny flowering spurge. Bombardier beetles moved between stems, leaving lacy tracks across the sand. The *Don José* was anchored in front of us, and with the evening light beginning to fade behind the mainland, we left Isla San Francisco. Across the bay, two American oystercatchers probed the mud and a snowy egret stood like a ghost on the shoreline. We spent the night cradled in the bay, protected in the azure waters turned black against the quietly impressive backdrop of an island wrought of volcanoes and earthquakes.

At dawn the sun rose behind Isla San José, and we steamed along the Canal de San José which separates the island from the mainland. The morning breeze was brisk, and high cirrus clouds streaked the darkening blue sky as the sun rose ever higher, a perfect golden orb on its ascent. The mainland mountains, the Sierra de la Giganta, rose and fell with our passage, images in our memory, just as they are images in the historical memory of all people. Our experience, our vision of this world, every shape and form of the land, rise and fall of a mountain, shift and swell of the ocean, becomes transformed. What is ours now becomes everyone's tomorrow. Our thoughts and ideas are those of humanity, for humanity is built on the foundation of the individual.

As the morning progressed, the breeze faltered and the whitecaps merged with the sea. The dark squalls on the water's surface disappeared and the silvery sunlight poured through the high clouds and turned the sea a shimmering silky gray. The islands were misty illusions that strengthened and weakened with the blowing wind. A few low dark clouds molded the shape of the mainland mountains, changing the contours and creating new boundaries between the land, sky, and sea. The high cirrus clouds were streaked south as if directing the flight paths of birds to southerly climes.

The mainland plateaus were interspersed with pinnacles and domes. The rise and fall of the rock created the natural architecture of a desert cathedral. All of humanity is reflected in nature: thoughts, designs, culture, architecture, and artistry. We are reflections of what we see around us. Remove that which we draw upon to make us human, and you remove our souls.

A Bryde's whale spouted in the distance. The animal surfaced briefly, and the dorsal fin cut the surface before vanishing from sight. We know little about these elusive whales. Bryde's whales become sexually mature when about 12.5

meters in length, and grow to a maximum size of 14 meters. Considering its body length, the Bryde's whale's distinctly sickle-shaped dorsal fin is large; at 46 centimeters, it is much taller than the dorsal of a blue whale. Populations have been found near shore as well as in truly pelagic regions, and many appear to be sedentary. They do not seem to make the annual poleward migrations of the larger rorquals (something that may explain their small size). Indeed, it was the small size of the Bryde's whale that apparently protected it from the excesses of the whaling industry for so long. Only with the decline of the more profitable larger species did the focus fall on species such as this. Luckily for the Bryde's whale, this transfer of effort happened late enough that they suffered for a relatively short time before the imposition of the 1985 moratorium on commercial whaling.

Today the oceans may hold 40,000 to 60,000 Bryde's whales, close to the pre-whaling levels. It is a small population that certainly could not sustain any level of economically viable commercial hunting in the future.

A sea lion leapt next to our vessel, distracting us from the empty water ahead. The porpoising animal was closely followed by two brown pelicans that dove on the mammal, pursuing vengeance for some unknown crime. The air and water were dotted with birds. Craveri's murrelets were gathered in small groups on the surface, and a Heermann's gull and parasitic jaeger briefly alighted in the water. California and yellow-footed gulls wheeled and cawed in the misty light, and the wind began to rise again, darkening the water in squalls and creating deeper and deeper troughs until the tips of the waves rolled over into spray and whitecaps.

The morning passed quietly; occasionally black storm-petrels darted close to the water and black-vented shearwaters glided across wave tips, alternately beating their wings seven or eight times and then gliding on the wind. At ten, a huge splash on the horizon between Isla Santa Catalina and Isla Monserrate revealed the possibility of whales. The weather continued to oscillate from dark, trough-filled seas to calm waters softened by sunlight as we motored onward, scanning the horizon and water for any signs of motion.

A school of dolphins churned the water in the channel between the mainland and Isla Monserrate, and two blue whales spouted close to the island. A mobula cleared the water within meters of our bow, the sun glistening off the creamy white underside of the grinning ray; a blue-footed booby crossed our wake. Suddenly there were whales in front of us.

At first the blue whales were distant, and visible in the gray-blue seas only when the sun hit and highlighted their towering blows and blue flanks. There were four of them. As each surfaced, blew, and dove, we turned through every hour of the clock face to watch the rise and fall of whales. It soon became apparent that the routine was regular. The animals would blow eight or nine times, moving slowly along the surface, their huge, flat rostrums pushing the water off their living bow, and then they would dive, with a ponderous roll of that huge back, topped by a short, curved dorsal fin. Toward the end of the dive, the whales' thick tail stocks drew near to the surface, but only one of the animals brought its vast flukes clear of the water. The whales were down for about eight minutes and then surfaced to repeat the cycle.

Blue whales, and the other rorquals, do not normally "fluke" when diving, while humpback and gray whales commonly do so. Researchers have postulated that the fluking motion assists in deep dives by increasing the line of descent. This may be more important for the less streamlined whales. The sleek, torpedo-shaped rorquals, such as the blue, fin, Bryde's, minke, and sei, may not need the extra impetus provided by fluking to initiate and maintain their dives; their body shape achieves just that. Observations reveal that only 10 to 15 percent of blue whales fluke. Such a pattern reinforces the view that fluking is the result of a genetic predisposition that has been lost in the majority of rorquals and remains only in a fraction of the population; it may be a remnant of their close evolutionary ties to nonrorqual cetaceans.

The whales were moving fairly long distances between dives. We could differentiate between some of the animals by the shape of the dorsal fin or the position of remoras attached to flanks, and often the whale that blew in front of us reappeared several hundred meters behind eight minutes later. However, each of the four animals was staying within the same general region southeast of Isla Monserrate, just a few kilometers offshore.

Researchers who study humpback whales use the distinctive markings on the undersides of the flukes to track individual animals; those studying orca look at the markings around the saddle patch behind the dorsal fin. Blue whales have light mottling patterns over their backs, patterns that appear permanent. Photographs taken of blue whales' backs, as long as the dorsal fin is present in the photograph to act as a point of reference, are used to individually identify these magnificent creatures.

There is still so much that we do not know about blue whales—their migration routes, where the calves are born, and so much more about their mating, supposed monogamy, social structure, and communication. The blue whale produces the most powerful sound in the animal kingdom. Sounds in the frequency range of 20 to 60 hertz have been recorded, with source levels of 188 decibels and higher. Some have postulated that before the oceans became the noisy places of today, full of boats and ships and industrial noise, these whales could have been heard around the world. This is not the unlikely proposition that it may seem. Modern-day submarines use the topography of the sea bed, the undersea mountain chains and valleys to channel their acoustic signals. Whales evolved in that environment; if such long-distance communication has a positive survival benefit, for example locating mates or confirming the location of a prime feeding spot, then it may well have developed naturally over time.

We drew close to one of the whales as she surfaced off our bow, the telltale aqua shadow revealing the point of surfacing moments before the animal appeared. We could hear the rush of air as the double blowhole snapped open, and the exhalation was followed by an inrush to fill the lungs to capacity. Water rivulets ran off the broad back and were pushed forward by the rostrum as the whale plowed through the water. After the eighth blow, the whale rolled her back and dove, her tail flukes visible through the gray water but remaining covered by water.

All four of the whales were down, and the calm waters were deserted save for the occasional mobula. The twin fins of mobulas were joined by the dorsal fins of twenty to twenty-five bottlenose dolphins. With the larger distractions submerged, we played with these nautical messengers.

The *Don José* was moving at moderate speed, and José kicked the engine to provide more sport for the dolphins. Several began to weave back and forth across the bow. The water revealed their shadows beneath the ship as they raced to their places, powering themselves through the water with heavy strokes of flukes, hitting the surface with audible gasps, and then descending again, turning from side to side to look upward at the people on the bow. Those dolphins not directly on the bow waves were playing across our wake. One individual began to leap almost vertically out of the water, falling heavily back on his side, creating the splash of a breaching dolphin. He continued to do this, once, twice, four, five times, while other animals porpoised clear of the water and sounded sharp retorts as their small flukes were slapped hard across the surface. After a while the dolphins began to move off, several still leaping clear of the water, dark currents and the mountains of the mainland behind them.

After lunch we continued our search for blue whales. We had not seen them since the dolphins had captivated us. Now we began to slowly motor toward Isla Monserrate again, searching the blue water for the aqua sign of blue whales.

The first animal we saw was the fluker. The whale surfaced and blew several times before going into his slow dive. His back rounded clear of the water, the small sickle fin lifted high, and then the broad tail stock began to appear. Finally the whale lifted his silvery gray flukes clear of the water and descended on his dive until the flukes cut into the water and vanished from view. We were watching the dive from the side. The tail stock of a blue whale is incredibly thick when seen in profile. The muscles in the tail provide the propulsion that makes the blue whale the fastest of all cetaceans. Under normal circumstances the blue can swim at speeds of about twenty-two kilometers per hour (13.5 mph), but it can sustain speeds of forty-eight kilometers per hour (30 mph) if alarmed or chased. This is remarkable, considering that we usually equate size with sloth rather than speed. We could see the lines of the tendons in the tail stock; the strength of the animal was clear, the power that protected the whale from the whalers until the advent of steam evident.

From the side, the line of the flukes is almost invisible, so thin are they in comparison with the stock. But from either in front of or behind the fluking blue, the finely sculpted gray-blue flukes glistened in the sun as the leading and trailing edges sliced into the water. Unlike the scarred and barnacle-encrusted flukes of the gray or humpback, those of the blue, and the other streamlined rorquals, are clean and smooth, the perfect power thruster for such a long, sleek torpedo of an animal. The swimming speed of these animals is simply too rapid to enable barnacles and other parasitic growths the opportunity to adhere.

The second blue surfaced off our bow, and the animals continued to surface and dive in synchrony, although they were spatially separated. Each whale would surface and blow the standard eight times, then descend for precisely eight minutes before returning to the surface. Whatever communications may or may not have passed between them, it made for fascinating viewing, first on one side of the ship and then on the other. This routine continued for a little more than an hour. The light cloud cover was reducing the glare of the sun, but our slow passage made for hot conditions on the w-w deck. The whales were not moving far with each surfacing. Vast flukeprints smoothed the water before each whale broke the surface, and occasionally they came close to our vessel, permitting clear views of the remoras attached to their flanks, and the expanse of the rostrum settling the water.

While the blues were both down, we were entertained by sea lions and mob-ulas that porpoised and leapt from the water. Brown pelicans and congregations of gulls and cormorants fed prolifically on a school of fish massed near the surface. The pelicans dived with arrow-like precision on the fish, and the whales continued to surface and dive in their eight-by-eight rituals.

The whales were drawing us toward our destination for the afternoon, Bahia de Aqua Verde, just to the north of Punta San Marcial. The blues were drifting farther apart as the afternoon wore on, and their dives were lengthening. Even-tually we could see only a single whale, and with each dive up to around twelve or thirteen minutes, we left the blues and motored toward the entrance of Aqua Verde to spend the night.

Bahia de Aqua Verde is marked by a granite monolith at the entrance to the cove. The vertical rock springs from the bay like a breaching whale, and is mot-tled with the guano of the seabirds that roost on its ledges. Clouds were beginning to fill the sky, and the hills behind the cove were set in recession plains of light and dark.

A small spit at the mouth of the bay was crowded with brown pelicans, Cali-fornia and yellow-footed gulls, Brandt's cormorants, and great blue herons. In the water bobbed a Heermann's gull, and a few stood on shore, their soft gray coloration and blood-red bills beautiful contrasts on the black shoreline. Turkey vultures flew high overhead, gliding on the rising air, and an osprey perched on its eyrie, protruding from a pinnacle of rock on the cliff face.

Three sailboats were moored in the bay, nestled between the red rocks and green water. The rocky cliffs that spread in an arch about the bay were sparsely covered with vegetation. Cardon cacti and elephant trees stood out like sentinels looking toward the sea, but the sporadic vegetation only seemed to add to the desolate desert colors: red, russet, and dusty brown.

The afternoon was passing, and as soon as the *Don José* was safely anchored we took to the pangas. We motored over toward the rocky cliff and watched in silence as the ospreys flew to and from the eyrie. The two birds ducked and cooed to each other as only fish eagles can, gently clicking their hooked beaks together and offering sticks and twigs to further fortify the substantial structure upon which they perched.

The pangas slowly turned back toward the vertical rock. This behemoth of stone held a multitude of birds and intertidal life betwixt surf and shore. Brown and blue-footed boobies clung to tiny ledges and flew out overhead, the blue feet of the latter fantastically visible in flight. There were about half a dozen great blue herons around the rock. A few stood out on the lower perches, near to the shore through which they would stalk, silhouetted against the blue sky. Higher up, four nests hung from the rock, draped in the living green of fig trees. It seemed incongruous that these large, slender birds would choose such a narrow and precipitous nesting location, but there they stood, elegant gray-blue birds decked in black plumes and a superior attitude.

Toward one side of the rock, a group of five double-crested cormorants stood on a broadly rounded rock bespeckled with mussels. At their apex was a single brown pelican in full breeding plumage with his head tucked into his long, slender neck. An American oystercatcher roamed the surf line with a striking spotted sandpiper, and sally lightfoot crabs rushed back and forth with the waves.

The pangas turned toward the beach, and we leaned over the side to watch the fish ebb and flow with the movements of the boat. Gazing down, we suddenly saw a chocolate chip star. This creature has to be one of the most aptly named of all animals. It has the five legs of traditional starfish, but each arm is thick, short, and stubby, so that the animal is roughly star-shaped but does not have the distinctive long arms we tend to associate with starfish. The coloration is unmistakable. The star is rimmed in black or chocolate brown, with brown lines emanating from the center and running down each arm. The upper part of the body is spotted with "chocolate chips" on cream, giving the Echinoderm every appearance of a chocolate chip cookie. In contrast to the pleasing nature of the animal's appearance and its English name, the star's scientific name is *Nidorellia armata,* which roughly translates to "small reeking one who is armed"—a perplexing contrast between casual observation and science. Perhaps if the English name matched the content of the scientific, we would not be so ready to look upon the star with delight.

We landed on the beach among gangling turkey vultures picking at flotsam and fish heads. It was close to five, and we had an hour or so on shore before the light faded and the vultures became eerie ghosts rather than ungainly scavengers.

A small fishing village hugged the shore among the palm trees, and violet-green swallows darted along the cliff face, clinging to the rock and taking to the air with the ease of the weightless. The turkey vultures were omnipresent. They roosted in the black mangrove trees and in the palms. They watched our passage with indifference, landing in the topmost branches of the trees with a flurry of black wings, then perching in silhouette as though adding cancerous growth to the trees.

A dry, narrow creek bed bisected the village, and pigs rooted through the mud while chickens ran between them. Under a huge tree a goat herd found shade, their tiny bells jangling with motion. We passed pitaya agria, bearded cactus, and elephant trees. A pair of hooded orioles alighted on a palm tree, the bright orange and black coloration of the male standing out clearly against the lush green vegetation. He called from the undergrowth, *wheet, wheet, wheet,* the intense sound growing in strength with each whistle. A vermilion flycatcher hopped along the dusty ground, its red plumage as deep in color as blood. The flycatcher took to the air as we approached, and began feeding on the insects hovering in the cool evening air. The bright red bird flew straight up, then slowly downward, repeating the action again and again as it stripped insects from the air.

We meandered between the trees, occasionally flushing a bird with our steps, but attempting to move in silence and stealth to see the desert birds close and unharassed. A male phainopepla fluttered from one of the trees nearby, alighting back on its perch as we passed. The shiny black bird cocked its crested head but remained silent. The black and white bars on back and wings revealed a female Gila woodpecker on one of the tree trunks, and we watched as the bird skillfully negotiated the bark up and down, probing and digging with her slender bill. As we were returning to shore, our path was crossed by the delicate wings and colors of a Costa's hummingbird. It briefly hovered ahead of us before disappearing in a blur of red and vibrating wings.

Back along the shoreline, two turkey vultures squabbled over a fish head in the surf, while a yellow-footed gull stood by ready to pick up the pieces left behind. The clouds had rolled in during our walk, and the sea and sky were an equal shade of soft silvery gray. As darkness fell, the vultures dispersed, returning to whence they came until the morning light resurrected them again. The stars were blocked from view, and the moon only occasionally lit the night sky with its luminous glow. Everything was calm and serene. The evening was spent talking of blue whales and blue-foots, of the colors encompassed in the water and on land, by fish and by birds, of the smallest and the largest of forms, and of us, seeing all but understanding so little.

We left our anchorage at Aqua Verde after breakfast. It was just after 8 A.M., and light clouds filled the sky. However, the day held promise of sun, and the clouds were high and slight enough to burn off within hours. As we passed the granite monolith, the breeze began to rise, whipping about the w-w deck as we watched the osprey on its eyrie and passed brown pelicans and snowy egrets on the sand spit.

Ten minutes later we had seen five blue whales. Two were out toward Isla Santa Catalina. They were making shallow three-minute dives, followed by brief surfacings that sent three tall blows shooting into the morning air. The whales were moving slowly through the dark water, their color matching the waves. For forty minutes we watched the animals roll at the surface, their throat grooves expanding with the massive intake of water that can triple the whales' volume with a single gulp. The vast extension of the whale was visible in shadow below the water. It was as though this leviathan had swallowed the world. Jonah would have been no problem—save for the twenty-four-centimeter esophagus!

The whales continued to feed leisurely at the surface when a school of common dolphins appeared. For twenty minutes they gave a show off our bow that merits more than a "common" nomenclature. The sea around us was boiling with the motion of dolphins. Some three to five hundred churned the water, leaping clear of the waves, reflecting their beautiful flanks in parallel, traveling in pairs as though mirror images of each other. The blue whales continued to feed, and several dolphins peeled off our bow or wake to play around their larger relatives. The creamy white flanks of the dolphins flashed up at us as they wove through the water. These creatures seemed to have such enthusiasm for life.

The structure of dolphin schools is fluid. We are only just beginning to unravel the design, but it appears that the larger schools divide into small parties to feed during the afternoon and night, regrouping at dawn. School sizes vary dramatically from several tens of animals, to hundreds, to a thousand or more. One astounding report tells of 300,000 animals grouped over concentrations of fish in the Black Sea, while another tells of 2 million animals seen in the eastern tropical Pacific. Smaller schools seem to dominate in the spring and summer, and there may be a segregation of sexes between mating seasons, which in this region occur in January–April and August–November. Although actual breeding may be season-dependent, observers have witnessed dolphins mating throughout the year. We do not know whether mating associations and schools are permanent, or whether there are core groups in the schools, while more transient animals come and go over some variable time scale. We know even less about dolphins' communicative skills or the social interactions that go on within a school.

As they rode the pressure wave on our bow, the dolphins sent up streams of salt spray that caught the sunlight and imprisoned it in the droplets, patterning the air with rainbows. Henry David Thoreau wrote: "It was a lake of rainbow light, in which for a short while, I lived like a dolphin. If it had lasted longer it might have tinged my employments and life." For those on board the *Don José,* watching dolphins bowriding blue whales and our own wooden leviathan, the moment did tinge our lives.

The dolphins briefly accelerated away from us, their small forms generating whitecaps where the wind now failed, and their commotion adding a dramatic foreground to the blows of blues behind. The tales of multi-armed sea serpents told by mariners over the centuries may be explained by the porpoising motion of thousands of dolphins.

When the rainbows vanished and the air became clear and uncluttered, the blows of the blue whales had dissipated and grown distant. Our radio sputtered to life. Another whale-watching vessel was positioned several kilometers to the north of us, close inshore at Punta Candeleros, just to the south of Isla Danzante. They had fin whales.

The *Don José* began to follow the coastline, passing Isla Monserrate, our horizon filled with Isla Del Carmen. The islands were deeply carved, like the buttress trunks of tropical trees. Such erosion is a clear visual indication of wetter times in this desert, when water was channeled down the grooves from high in the mountains, perhaps once supporting lush vegetation where now there was desert mottling. The clouds were breaking up, the sunlight dispersing them until blue exceeded white above us as we drew close to our destination.

It was 11:30 when we saw the blows, so like those of the blue whales, tall white plumes lacking the shape of humpback or gray. Tall white exclamations of what it is to be cetacean.

It is often said that fin and blue whales are difficult to distinguish in the field. That may be true from a distance, where only the tall, slender white breath provides evidence of a large rorqual beneath the waves. But given sign of the animal's fin and back, there is no mistaking this majestic whale. Blue whales are much lighter in color, the bluish sheen to the skin so apparent, and their dorsal fins tiny in comparison to those of fin whales.

The two whales surfaced and dove together. Their dark frames were clearly visible. The large dorsal fin, which may be up to sixty-one centimeters high (compared to thirty-three centimeters for the blue), cut through the water's surface and was raised high upon the animal's back as it prepared to dive. Fin whales, *Balaenoptera physalus,* are typical rorquals. They share their rorqual character with four other species: minke, Bryde's, sei, and blue (leaving for a moment the question of pygmy whales and various geographic subspecies that may exist within these classifications). Fin whales are found in all the oceans of the world, but are rare in the tropical or polar waters.

The fin whale can reach a staggering twenty meters in length when fully grown, and some specimens have been recorded at twenty-seven meters. As with other rorquals, the female is larger than the male, in both length and weight. Precise weight measurements have never been conducted on fin whales, but it is estimated that a twenty-five-meter animal would weigh more than 70,000 kilograms. A blue whale of equivalent size would probably weigh 150,000 kilograms, clearly demonstrating that although the fin can be more than a match in length, its build is slighter. We stayed with these fins for almost an hour, watching as water cascaded off flat rostrums and broad gray backs with each surfacing.

Fin whales also suffered at the hands of whalers. As with the blue, it was the fin whale's speed that protected the animal for so many years. It can sustain speeds of thirty-seven kilometers per hour, and in the early years of whaling that was sufficient to outrun the longboats. However, with the arrival of the harpoon gun in the 1860s, fin whales began to fall to the lance, first in the Atlantic, and then in Antarctic waters. When blue whales were found, they became the focus of the whalers, but as their numbers declined, the next-largest whale succumbed. In the 1937–38 Antarctic whaling season, 28,009 fin whales were taken, twice the number of blues. Following the war years, the take of fin whales exceeded 10,000 animals annually until 1965, averaging more than 30,000 annually in the decade 1952 to 1962. The pre-whaling population in those waters was estimated at 400,000 adult whales (with only an additional 70,000 adults believed present in the Northern Hemisphere).

It does not take a mathematical genius to determine that a 400,000-animal population cannot sustain an annual decline of 10,000 to 30,000 animals for very long. In the period 1937–1962, more than 450,000 fin whales were killed, taken from a population in which mature females probably give birth every two or three years, carrying their single calf for eleven months.

The International Whaling Commission, the organization with the management oversight of whale stocks, acted too late, and despite the quotas implemented to protect the fin whale, the structure of the IWC made it a paper tiger; nations that wanted to continue whaling did so. Only when the species was commercially extinct did the whaling nations bow to the will of the majority and suspend whaling for fins. However, today fin whales are still hunted in some areas for subsistence, and for "scientific purposes." In fact, in the early 1990s, Iceland continued to call for a resumption of fin whaling in the North Atlantic, claiming that the whales were eating too much fish. Current population estimates of fin whales range widely. In 1989 the U.S. National Marine Fisheries Service estimated the fin whale population at 105,200 to 121,900, of which 85,000 were in southern waters; also in 1989 the International Whaling Commission reported that direct counts had led to a new estimate of only 2,000 to 3,000, and no more than 5,000, fin whales left in the Southern Hemisphere. Such are the uncertainties of counting whales.

As the animals' rostrums hit the surface, we could make out the asymmetrical color pattern typical of this species. The lower jaw of the fin whale is white on the right and dark on the left. It is the easiest way to tell the difference between fin and blue, assuming, of course, that the observer is on the right side of the whale. The white flash along the fin whale's jaw is believed to act as a fish-scaring tactic, its sudden appearance causing a school of fish to clump into a bite-size group (fish-eating minke possess a white flash on one pectoral flipper, while fish-eating humpbacks often have whitish "wings"). The whales continued to send tall plumes of condensed air and water skyward. As the expanse of back rolled at the surface, the flukes were visible beneath the waves, six meters broad, curved under the water as the animal descended in a steep but flukeless dive that took it below for six minutes at a time.

It was early afternoon, and the fin whales had drawn us toward Isla Danzante, a tiny island sandwiched between mainland Punta Candeleros and the southern point of Isla Del Carmen. The waves were tossed higher and higher by the strengthening wind, and whitecaps dotted the sea as we left the whales and entered the quiet sandy cove, washed by aqua water and backed by towering cliffs. The entrance to the bay was marked by guano-covered volcanic red rocks, and desert colors punctuated the landscape.

The pangas ferried us to shore, and as we waited for the rest of the ship's complement, we watched white butterflies dance in the breeze, alighting on the ice plant that gave the beach verdant coloration where all else was lacking or thorn-covered.

A movement on the great boulders at one end of the beach drew our attention. When stationary the creature was invisible, but as it moved slowly across the light gray rocks, its form and delicate colors were revealed. Clinging to the vertical side of the boulders was a banded rock lizard. It was an impressive beast about thirty centimeters in length. The lizard had a bluish-green head and tail, with its midsection more distinctly yellow. The entire animal was banded with light black stripes, beginning with a much darker black stripe across the back of its neck. As the lizard clung motionless on the sunlit rock, it was almost impossible to point it out to the others who were now on the beach. As we closed in, it remained still, and we approached to within a few meters without eliciting any reaction.

We began to hike along the trails leading into the narrow island. The path and hillsides were heavily colonized with cardon barbon cactus and tiny *Mammillaria* holding up their red blooms. Side-blotched lizards scurried for cover, and small elephant trees reflected gold off their yellowy leaves as the sun beat down on the shadeless trail with unrelenting heat.

Black-throated sparrows called from the undergrowth, and the occasional raptor flew overhead, while high above turkey vultures wafted on the upcurrents. We scrambled up one of the cliff trails and were rewarded through the sweat and dust with exquisite views of the bay laid out before us. The hills of the mainland and Isla Del Carmen were visible on every side, and the sun set shimmering patterns in the waters below. A small stand of red mangrove was nestled to one side of the bay, and the surrounding beach was home to a brilliant white snowy egret.

Pairs of yellow-footed gulls stood against the stunning backdrop of this wilderness, cholla bloomed in yellow, and side-blotched lizards continued to offer the only testament of terrestrial animal life in the desert. From the clifftop we could gaze down at the reef beckoning from below. We could pick out fish through the green waters and the reflections of sun and sand patterns. Watching fish from thirty meters above sea level—snorkeling from dry land with binoculars.

We did not continue our terrestrial observations for long. The sun was too hot and the waters too close to delay snorkeling. As we descended to the beach and began to suit up, four kayakers appeared from beyond the bay. In sharing tales of our respective adventures, I found that all four were from Anchorage, Alaska, my adopted hometown. It really is a small world.

We immersed ourselves in the warm waters, wading out from the sandy beach and heading to the cliff face, where the sandy bottom was replaced by boulders. The shallow waters dropped off precipitously, revealing a shadowy place beyond the ability of our senses to penetrate. We watched Panamic sergeant major fish and puffers, parrotfish and reef cornetfish, the occasional small moray, and comical boxfish and wrasses swim over the boulders and tempt us out of our depth. The conditions were not as ideal as in earlier locations, and our foray into the water was relatively short. The boulders cluttered the water, and many of the fish were hidden. The sudden drop beyond the reef seemed to present water with little visible life beyond the minutiae that we beheld in captivity in front of our masks.

We were soon back aboard the *Don José* and left Isla Danzante about an hour before sunset. We returned to Aqua Verde to anchor for another night beyond the granite. Dusk hit the mountains, and the sun set fires among the pinnacles and precipices. The sky was transformed from a light shimmering yellow to the deepest gold, from rose to the most intense red, and then to fading purple as the sun disappeared and its strength and power were darkened by the passage of the planet. As the waters reflected this palette of color, common dolphins briefly hit our bow, and a blue whale swam by.

The *Don José* was soon enveloped in the darkness of night; bioluminescence lit the waves as we plowed onward. The wind picked up steadily as the evening progressed, and by the time we pulled into the protected cove at Aqua Verde, our vessel had seen the heights of the tallest waves and the depths of the deepest troughs. We were ready for the relief offered by a safe and secured anchorage. But even beyond the granite monolith, we felt the swells generated from far off in the ocean. We spent the night beneath an illuminating night sky, the sparks of bioluminescence beneath us, restless amid the power of wind and wave.

We left Aqua Verde just after 8 A.M. Wednesday morning. The water was calm, although a slight swell remained from the previous day's winds. High cirrus clouds streamed sunlight over the land and sea as we cruised past the breaching rock. We planned to spend the day cruising the waters to the south of Isla Santa Catalina, in the area punctuated by the islands of Santa Cruz and San Diego, until we reached Isla San José and our overnight anchorage, just to the north of the tiny island of San Francisco.

We were only fifteen minutes from Aqua Verde when a blue whale surfaced near the ship, brought her broad silvery flukes up to where the water cascaded about them, and dove. We waited, scanning the water around us, looking to where the monolith stood out just a couple of kilometers away. Two brown pelicans flew close to the w-w deck, their wing beats setting up a silky, soft feathery sound in the air. The whale resurfaced ten minutes later, about three hundred meters from our vessel. The silver animal blew four times in quick succession, sending nine-meter white plumes into the air. She then went into a steep dive, bringing her flukes clear of the surface, as though in slow motion. She remained below for another eleven minutes, then came up close to our position. She blew four times and rolled her back steeply upward; the small dorsal fin, some thirty centimeters high, rose and fell as she raised flukes clear of the water. We were sideways to the animal, and her thick tail stock was beautifully visible in descent.

While the fluking blue was below the water, a second animal appeared some distance away, and we watched the emission of blows and the rise and fall of the broad back. We stayed with the fluking whale while keeping careful watch for the maneuvers of other whales in the area. North of our position, we watched a v-shaped blow blast clear of the water close to a fishing panga. It was a small humpback whale. We waited for our fluking blue whale to resurface, but after thirteen minutes with no sign, and the second blue still distant, we decided to investigate the humpback and skiff.

The humpback dove and then resurfaced sharply next to the panga. The two fishermen in the skiff were frantically drawing in net; then the whale dove again, and the net was stripped from their hands and meter after meter of line plummeted into the depths. The skiff jerked in the direction of the whale and then stilled. The humpback surfaced and lay motionless. The water was translucent, and we could see the length of the whale inches beneath the water, its blowhole drawing air into tired lungs. The animal was still for the longest time, and the fishermen continued to draw in line as rapidly as they could. Our eyes followed the line to the whale.

The thick green nylon fishing net was wrapped around the whale's flukes. A red buoy floated at the surface about halfway between the panga and the whale.

The humpback was small, probably 11.5 meters in length, and likely one to three years old. He dove again, his back rounding, his flukes reaching the surface, but the strain of the line was apparently too much to bring them all the way up. The fishermen lost hold of the line and threw their hands up in frustration. We stood on the w-w deck watching as more and more line was lost overboard as the whale dove deeper and deeper, trying to shake the unwanted hangers-on.

We began to shout instructions to the fishermen, offering suggestions on how and when to cut the net. They told us that the net had been laid the night before, and that they did not know how long the whale had been fighting to free itself. They did not want to lose their net, but they were running out of options. The obvious thought went through our minds: we could suit up and enter the water to free the whale from the net ourselves. But it was simply too dangerous. Other such rescue missions have ended in near-disaster when well-meaning divers have tried to free entangled whales or dolphins only to suffer the same fate in the tearing, cutting nylon line.

The only hope for this whale was to gather as much of the line in the panga as possible and then cut the net, so that he could leave with as little line tied to his flukes as possible. With the whale diving so frequently, and so deeply, this would be no easy task.

The humpback surfaced just off our bow. We could see the line just below the surface, and the whale lay still, tired from his exertions. The huge flippers of the *Megaptera* were clearly visible below us, as though the whale were simply hovering in midair. The fishermen began to haul in the line. The skiff drew close to the whale, until it was within three meters of the animal's flukes. Just as the clippers were raised and the line was held taut, the whale dove, ripping the cutting line from their hands. We all let out long breaths. Tens of meters of line poured over the side of the skiff, and the fishermen looked up at us on the w-w deck, pleading for some suggestion or action to settle their predicament.

A few minutes later the whale surfaced about thirty meters from the panga. The fishermen hurried to pull in the line, pick up the slack, and pull themselves closer to the animal. The whale lay at the surface, breathing quietly, the line still firmly tied around his flukes. This time they were successful. When the panga was within five meters of the whale, they cut the line.

For a moment the whale remained motionless. Then the young animal seemed to realize that he was no longer restrained by the skiff, and began to move slowly away. His flukes, still wrapped in line, powered the whale forward. His back rounded as he prepared to dive, the sun glinting off dark flanks. The whale completed his dive, flukes raised to the surface but not clearing the water. We followed the whale at a distance for the next half an hour, watching as he surfaced and blew, and as each dive was accompanied by a failed attempt at fluking.

We were hopeful for this young whale—the kind of hope that should lie with the next generation. Although the line around his flukes and the trailing five meters of line were obviously impeding his diving, he was able to swim and move about without too much difficulty, unlike animals entangled about the head or mouth. Watching the whale swim, it seemed likely that in time the line around the flukes would break or degrade, freeing him. Even if the whale was finally set loose, the line that he shed would undoubtedly entangle some other maritime traveler, and continue to do so with all the tenacity of the artificial.

In one sense this whale was lucky. The fishermen took their time trying to free him, and the entanglement did not seem to pose an immediate threat. Others, many others, are not so lucky. The drift nets and gill nets that bisect our oceans kill literally millions of these so-called "nontarget" species, from sharks and rays to whales, dolphins, and porpoises. When these nets are retrieved, the unwanted carcasses are simply thrown back into the sea. When nets break loose from their moorings, they continue to fish the ocean, with no one to maintain them or re-cover the catch. They continue to kill, year after year, animal after animal.

How many marine mammals die in this way, victims of the so-called "inci-dental catch"? In 1990, the U.S. Marine Mammal Commission estimated that 25,000 miles of drift nets were in use around the world—enough to encircle the earth. The "by-catch" for one Japanese neon squid fishery in 1990 was 26,000 marine mammals, 406 sea turtles, 270,000 seabirds, 700,000 blue sharks, 25,000 other nontarget species of squid, 141,000 salmon, and 39 million other fish of various species. Even these staggering figures are probably underesti-mates, since the "dropout" rate for marine mammals, seabirds, and turtles as the nets are hauled on board is believed to approach 50 percent. In the North Pa-cific, some 20,000 Dall's porpoise die in drift nets every year. In Baja, 25 to 35 of the rare Gulf porpoise, the vaquita, which probably numbers no more than a few hundred animals, are killed annually by the gill-net and shrimp-trawling fisheries. It is an increased mortality that the species is ill equipped to deal with and that Mexican fisheries' laws seem unable to reduce. The numbers of great whales killed by drift nets is even harder to estimate. Several species of smaller cetaceans are also believed to be in decline because of this destructive fishery, including the northern right whale dolphin and Pacific white-sided dolphin. For many species, already depleted by commercial whaling, any enhanced mortality could potentially have serious population-level impacts.

Cetaceans may attract most of the attention, but the myriad of other species involved are integral to the food chain, to the health and balance of the marine ecosystem. In June 1991, the U.S. government issued a blunt statement regard-ing the use of drift nets: "The sheer numbers of individuals and species involved strongly suggest the potential for serious disruption of the ecosystem of the North Pacific Ocean."

We can abhor such catches on a number of levels: distaste at the loss of so many animals, a horror at the wanton waste of a resource, or simply a repulsion at the destruction of creatures for no purpose. Whatever the reason for our condemnation of such wasteful destruction of life, mammalian or piscine, we must translate that condemnation into action. What good does it do to protect the marine through international moratoriums if those creatures are caught in "walls of death" strung between buoys far from shore, to become by-catch statistics in fishery journals and resource management institutes?

If we are serious about protecting the riches of the oceans, then we have to do so through international treaties to protect calving grounds, feeding and breeding grounds, migration routes, and all those areas in between, through which whales swim, dolphins play, and porpoises ride the bow in sleek form reflecting sunbursts and rainbows.

I can't imagine a world without whales, where the song of the humpback whale is silent, the immensity of the blue whale is seen only in the halls of museums, and the bow-riding exuberance of dolphins is a memory of the few. I also don't want to imagine a world where the whales are scared by encounters with humans: drift nets, outboard motors, harpoons, bullet holes, and the insidious unseen scarring of pollution deep within muscle and tissues and reproductive organs. We are within sight of the former world and on the border of the latter.

We left the young humpback to swim on, trailing the fishing net but beginning to have more success at maneuvering his broad flukes. The blues were still in the area, including the fluker, and we sought out the blows amid the blue of the ocean.

The Baja sun beat down on us, baking the surface of the w-w deck, and we shifted seating on the hot surface and cooled our throats with icy sodas and beers. The calm waters parted to reveal four blue whales nearby. One swam close to the *Don José,* surfacing for extended periods of time, her throat grooves distended as she drew in vast mouthfuls of water. When she dove she vanished for eleven to thirteen minutes, but always surfaced close by, preceded by the blue-green aura so characteristic of these whales, and providing excellent views of her rostrum and multi-pleated throat. We could see the length of the animal, rounded flippers a third of the way down her body, and immense gray flukes which, more often than not, the behemoth lifted from the water, streaming white rivulets from the edges, and cutting into the water like a knife.

At one surfacing, the whale slowly circled our vessel, within twenty meters, checking us out as though assessing our motives. She remained off our bow for the next hour, surfacing and descending four times in those sixty minutes. The humpback whale was still nearby, and a Bryde's whale blew off our port side. We were just off Isla Monserrate. The events of the morning had served to keep us close to Aqua Verde, where our morning excursion had begun. We had been so inundated with whales that our movements had been largely circular as the morning had progressed.

We had been idling for more than an hour now, and it was nearing midday. The sun was high above us, and the w-w deck was still scorching. We scanned the water beyond the blue whale looking for more telltale signs of whales. To the southeast was Isla Santa Catalina. One of the observers on the deck yelled of a sighting close to the island. Something big, black, and triangular had surfaced and then vanished close to the island. The rest of us atop the vessel had missed the sign, but we headed toward the shore, eager to investigate the possible orca sighting that the fin appeared to herald.

For the next two hours we cruised toward the island. The sky remained clear and hot, a light breeze adding some relief, but tiny flies harassing those who stayed on lookout. As the cruise continued, the wind began to build, and the swells lifted our vessel amid the whitecaps. The small mobulas flung themselves clear of the water as we passed by, their sad faces a welcome sight after a few days' absence.

No whales blew as we neared the island; only the mobulas and the occasional shark broke the surface. At 1:30 P.M. we made anchor at Isla Santa Catalina. The rounded rocky beach ahead of us curved serenely about the cove, and to our starboard side a huge rock jutted from the granite cliffs, looking every bit like the head and trunk of an elephant. The line and crevices of the rock carved the head and ears of the animal, and protruding downward, fused at the base, was the elephant's trunk.

We landed onshore, stepping across the huge gray boulders rounded by time and waves. Beyond the boulders, cardon cacti were closely grouped, each green pinnacle topped by the glossy black coat of a common raven. Beyond the cacti, the lay of the land rose dramatically, typifying the desert with the mottling of vegetative color against the dusty hillside.

A movement across one of the round boulders revealed a green-tailed uta. The brilliance of the lizard's green tail cut a dash of color through the rock, then merged softly with the brown and gray of the upper parts of its body. This uta is found nowhere else in the world; this island is its only home. This sanctuary washed by the Sea of Cortez is the entire world as far as this ancient species is concerned. Here, amid the cardon and the barrel cactus, the ravens and the oppressive heat, a tiny lizard, a unique packaging of genetic material, is at home beneath the rocks and in the cool shade under a spine-laden plant.

We hiked into the interior of the slender island. Giant cardon cacti were everywhere, their green ribs adding symmetry to the desert, and their columns towering eight meters or more above us. The intense green of these cacti was a beautiful match for the vivid sky. They are the desert colors that add a simple reality to a stunning vision.

Some of the tall cardon columns were constricted near their apex, so that the new growth had the appearance of a giant green football. The vegetation below the cardons was dominated by pitaya agria, and at intervals across the hillsides, the giant barrel cactus, another Baja California endemic, towered upward as much as four meters, its spiny ribs undulating down the length of the plant, as though the cactus were wriggling in slow, vegetative motion. A few of the giant barrels held brilliant red flowers at their points; others showed the remnants of old flowers or potential bloomings still to come.

A whip-tail lizard darted into the tangled mass of tendrils that formed one of the pitaya agrias. Black-throated sparrows called out warnings of our passing, while ravens and turkey vultures wheeled over our heads on the strong upcurrents generated by the heat of the rising desert air.

We returned to the *Don José* at about 5 P.M., and while we were still at anchor a school of 100 to 200 bottlenose dolphins rounded the point and swam by our stern. At rest we offered no sport, and the dolphins continued on their way. As soon as the large group had passed out of sight, a second, smaller group of some 50 to 75 animals passed by, a few of them electing to swim around our ship before continuing on along the unmarked trail that their predecessors had taken moments earlier.

The sun was low in the sky, and as we left our anchorage it went through transformations from gold to red, and from russet to purple, until the light faded completely, leaving only the intense colors in our minds. We were cruising to our nighttime anchorage at Isla San José, approximately seventy kilometers to the south. As the ship plowed through the black waters that reflected the points of light above, other lights lit up the bow waves. The bioluminescence began softly, turning the white crests turquoise, then the lights began to reach a silent crescendo, as the invisible life in the water was revealed in motion by dashing colors and streaks of bioluminescent light. Schools of fish rushed from our path, lighting up their wakes in greens and reds. Suddenly the dark waters were teeming with life, as every motion was transformed into visible colors.

We leaned over the bow as the pinpoints of light rose and faded as the ship scared fish and other watery creatures from their paths or resting places on the surface. It was as though we were witness to a marine aurora borealis, or some submarine fireworks display. Lights shot from our bow into the darkness, shooting stars captured in the waves, precipitated by our passage but integral to this fantastic watery world.

I forget how long we stayed there, watching the shifting motion of waves and fish through reflected images. We did not leave our places under the cool night sky until the lights dimmed and the colors returned to foaming white crests of waves off the bow. When that happened, we turned our faces upward, to those other lights revealed by darkness, above our heads and under our feet, the lights of heaven and earth, and of the living.

It was late when we pulled into Isla San José, and we slept in eager anticipation of birds and whales on the morrow tide. At dawn we headed into the mangroves that rim the inlets and coves of this island. As we entered the meandering green maze, we passed close to a sandbank crowded with brown pelicans and snowy egrets. The pelicans took to the air as we motored by, their wings beating in sequence.

Once in the red mangrove complex, reflected images of green and blue greeted us. The deep, luxurious green of the mangroves was mirrored in the clear waters. The reflected image resembled the delicate brush works of a Matisse or Monet. The blue sky and soft clouds added further texture and depth to the scene.

As we moved closer to some of the impenetrable green banks of vegetation, we could see the tangled mass of roots and stems descend beneath the water line. They created a maze beneath us, through which swam bull's-eye puffer fish and rays and schools of tiny fish, spawned in these waters and protected from the rigors of the ocean until mature.

We motored on, occasionally cutting the noisy outboard motor to sit in silence among the mangroves and listen to the movements of creatures deep within, but hidden by the stems and the green and yellow oval leaves. We could hear the rustle of leaves and twigs, caused by both wind and avian motion.

A belted kingfisher darted out of the all-encompassing green, its brilliant blue drawing the eye to the brashness of this punk-crested bird. The red mangrove trees were dotted with slender and elegant birds high up in the canopy. A reddish egret and white ibis stood like frozen pinnacles projecting from the top of the vegetated ceiling.

The pangas motored softly into an open lagoon, bounded on three sides by the mangroves, and ahead by a desert island. A lone black mangrove stood out, isolated by water in the middle of the shallows. We looked over the side of the pangas and watched the bottom shift and change with the light, and as fish darted for cover, startled by our passage.

The banks changed suddenly from tropical green to desert browns. The sloping shoreline was home to the slight-legged waders, curlew, spotted sandpiper, and willet. The cacti had a hold on this part of the cove, and the untidy nest of a turkey vulture was precariously placed at the juncture between two of the towering columns. A group of elegant terns stood at the apex of a small, rocky spit, their feathers ruffled by the light breeze, and behind them yellow-footed gulls joined in raucous debate.

We turned back toward the main mangrove concentrations, and slowed to watch the delicate maneuverings of a snowy egret. The bird was moving slowly, trying to avoid detection by the fish it was evidently stalking in the shallows. It looked so obvious to us, white against green, that it was hard to imagine such deception being rewarded. But as we watched, the egret struck and raised its bill full of fish.

A yellow-crowned night-heron looked back at us, at eye level with those in the panga. All herons have an air of elegance about them, imparted by the slender neck, long bill, and graceful movements. Their breeding plumage is often particularly eye-catching, for example the black plumes and neck patterns of the great blue heron, or the long white plumes of the heron that was in front of us now. The bird flew as our panga drifted too close to its perch, leaving us to look again into green banks, trying to detect further color and movement among the living tangled mass of stems and stalks and roots that make up a mangrove thicket.

The expanse of the lagoon spread out in front of us, the green borders just a short distance away. We motored forward, occasionally skimming our hands in the cool water, and watching the terns and ospreys wheel and dive overhead. As we neared the center of the expanse, three brown pelicans flew past in formation, their wings beating in unison. They turned as one, flying low over the water, the downturn of their wings almost catching the surface. They flew upward, again as though in a single motion. They turned and repeated their flight over our heads. Then the pace seemed to pick up, and their wings beat faster. Still moving as one, joined by some invisible thread, they banked steeply over and dove toward the water. The moment before impact their wings were drawn back tight against their bodies, so that they plummeted with the precision of an arrow shot into the water from a crossbow. All the birds entered simultaneously and they surfaced together, shaking heavy bills and streaming water from their gaping mouths.

We returned to our vessel anchored just a short distance away. Light clouds filled the sky, and the breeze began to pick up as we left the enclosed, protected boundaries of the mangroves. We headed south toward exquisite Isla Espiritu Santo and the sea lion colony of Los Islotes, islands that were becoming so familiar to me now that I looked to the horizon with a feeling of homecoming.

The rest of the morning passed quietly. We lay across the w-w deck taking in the heat, while murrelets tripped across our bow and the occasional bottlenose dolphin crossed our path. The sound of sea lions on nearby islands was brought to us on the light ocean breeze. It was a soft accompaniment fitting to our mood and direction. The cloud cover began to increase as the morning progressed, but the sun was unimpeded. Fortunately the wind began to pick up, providing some relief to the whale-watchers thirsty under the sun, but not sufficient to generate whitecaps or the troughs into which we would fall and rise in undulating motion. A lone Bryde's whale surfaced to our starboard, providing a clear if brief view of its sickle-shaped dorsal fin before the animal vanished into the seemingly barren ocean that surrounded us.

The remainder of the morning was almost devoid of life: no whales, and few birds. Our wake was investigated by a few Bonaparte's gulls and black storm-petrels, and a small group of phalaropes winged their way by, but otherwise we were alone with our thoughts and the desert sun. With the trip so close to its completion, we began to think of homes and arrangements that had little connection with our current situation. They were thoughts that we would have been pleased to dispel with the simple cry of "Whales off the bow."

The sloping plateaus of Isla Espiritu Santo were laid out before us. The sight never fails to inspire me. The undulations simultaneously inform the observer of the power of planetary forces, the immensity of time, and the limits of human perception and understanding. But they also do something else: they demonstrate that it is human perception that makes them what they are; it is our view of them that gives them value.

Landscapes, objects, and individual organisms or collective species all have intrinsic value, regardless of any value that we arbitrarily place upon them. But we are able to see and interpret the visions in front of us, and by doing so we transform ourselves, our perceptions, and our thoughts. If we could not witness, and therefore value, these places, we would be the poorer in spirit and in mind, because we would lack the foundation upon which to achieve such a transformation. To put it in simpler terms, we would lose our ability to imagine, and our ability to dream.

The ship continued its quiet passage toward Espiritu Santo, and we prepared for our afternoon hike. Out of the water ahead of us were precipitated the forms of whales. We watched the blows exhaled from the mass of blubber surfacing back toward the mainland. There were two whales, blue whales, a cow-calf pair.

If there is anything that makes whale-watching an inspirational experience, it is the sight of a blue whale cow and calf. It is difficult to explain, and perhaps it is difficult to comprehend. To those already consumed by the moment and the ideal, it is obvious. The blue whale epitomizes so much: hope, tenacity, stubbornness, and resiliency. In a modern world where conservation is pitted against the power of governments with short-term aspirations and private agendas, those are the characteristics that we need to perpetuate. Add the fact that the blue whale is the largest animal ever to have graced the Earth, that we know so little of what it does with its immense brain, and that we almost lost the species amid the greed and intransigence of nations during the midpart of this century, and I hope that you will begin to see the attraction. The blue whale is, simultaneously, the symbol of everything that we can do, right and wrong alike, in our treatment of the natural world.

The cow surfaced first, to our port side, closely followed by her calf. The female, at twenty-three meters in length, probably weighed about 80,000 kilograms. When she surfaced and rolled to dive, her skin was taut and drawn. The toll of raising a calf in these desert waters had dramatically reduced her body weight. After a winter feeding in the cold California current or in the Gulf of Alaska, she would probably weigh in excess of 120,000 kilograms. Even so, in length and mass she still dwarfed our vessel.

Both whales were making short, shallow dives, each lasting no more than a couple of minutes. When the female surfaced, she blew four or five deep, long exhalations and then dove. The calf surfaced more infrequently, and often the female appeared two or three times before her youngster broke the surface. The calf was about six weeks old, and the area around his dorsal fin was crowded with remoras. It remains a mystery where the calves of this small population of blue whales are born. Some believe that they are born in the warm and protected Sea of Cortez, while others have hypothesized that they may be born along the California coast before the whales enter the gulf. Our captain, José, offered his view: the remoras that adhered to the calf were not from the gulf. Wherever the calf had been during its short life, at some point it had been outside the gulf, and that is where it must have picked up its maritime hitchhikers.

Blue whale females probably reach sexual maturity at between five and ten years of age. They give birth to one calf every two or three years following a ten- or twelve-month gestation period. Some researchers have speculated that the whales may live to ages comparable to the upper end of human survival, 100 or more years. What is certain, however, is that few 100-year-old blue whales exist today.

As we followed the whales, watching them weave back and forth making their shallow, brief dives, a Bryde's whale intercepted their path. The blues did not react to the appearance of one of their mammalian cousins, and the Bryde's whale did not deviate from its path toward the island. It would be intriguing to know whether the acoustics of these whales are compatible. They are both rorquals and use sound to varying degrees to learn more about their environment. Their abilities mean that they were probably aware of each other's presence long before they were in close proximity. From our poor vantage point there was no obvious interaction between the leviathans, but in the sounds beneath the waves something may have been communicated that our evolution has yet to prepare us for.

We stayed with the blues for three hours. We watched in silence the relaxed routine of mother and baby, wondering at the communications between them, the learning phase that all creatures go through, the trials and tribulations that they would face in the future, and whether through the perfect salt medium that encompassed both, they were in unseen dialogue with whales tens of kilometers or even oceans away.

Thoughts of hiking evaporated with the blows of the whales. Only as the afternoon grew late, and the low angle of the sun sent starbursts off the backs of the whales, did we leave and head toward Los Islotes. We had plans to swim with the sea lions before the sun was doused to the west and the water chilled. The wind picked up briskly as we motored toward the guano-encrusted islands, and for a while it seemed as though the whales would move with us, but as the whitecaps steepened they vanished from sight, leaving us alone on the ocean.

In 1989 the water at Los Islotes had been too cold for snorkeling, but this year we were not to be denied by the weather. We rounded the island in the pangas, watching the scurrying sally lightfoots and the dashing motions of sandpipers and oystercatchers. I love the scientific name of sallys, *Grapsus grapsus*. It is a name that translates the fleeting motion of the crabs, precipitating images in the mind of Steinbeck and all those who came after him, trying to capture, to grab, the elusive, evaporating sally. Above our heads the resident magnificent frigatebirds and brown and blue-footed boobies circled the pinnacles of rock or perched on the narrow ledges marked by guano.

Circling the rocks in the pangas, we could see sea lions marked by the teeth of sharks—terrible wounds that had healed to scars in huge oval bites on flanks and backs. Other sea lions wore different scars, those from encounters with fishing line and nylon nets. Several of the animals wore these "necklaces of death." Some seemed unaware of their burden, while others were being slowly strangled, and their eyes looked glazed and sickly.

An elegant white-crowned male sea lion barked at us from the water. His sagittal crest gave him a distinguished air, and his thick, muscular neck imparted the strength to command the rocks. Other sea lions basked in the late afternoon sun; cows nursed pups, and young males jostled each other for the most comfortable places to doze.

We motored over to the far island, which was rimmed in part by a low rocky outcropping. We stepped ashore and completed our preparations for snorkeling. With fins and wetsuits we moved to the edge of the rocky shore, walking across the sharp granite rocks with oversized feet and giant footsteps. The rocks fell off over the side, descending into the depths. The surfaces of the rocks were dotted with spiny red urchins, sea anemones, and barnacles. It was awkward maneuvering, sitting with feet dangling over the side, then pushing forward to swim away from the projections that threatened to cut and dig flesh. As I pushed myself in, I felt my left leg lightly bump one of the rocks.

The water was freezing, and for a few moments the only thing I could hear was my own deep breaths and the odd involuntary shiver at the cold. We began to move off the ledge, and the bottom dropped down precipitously. The water was wonderfully clear, but beyond the ledge it was impossible to make out the bottom. The blackness appeared impenetrable. We headed back toward the shore of the second island, and as we began to move more in tune with our adopted environment, the fish and the colors of this remarkable world were revealed to us.

The rounded rocks were alive with branching stony corals colored a delicate green. Spiny sea urchins seemed to fill every crevice, and in places the distinctive multi-armed crown of thorns was half hidden by the boulders. Four of us swam together, keeping watch on the surface as well as below, trying to see where the sea lions were. We hoped to engage some in play, but also wanted to avoid the mature males, who would likely see us as an invasion into their territory, and respond accordingly with mock, and sometimes not so mock, charges. That was not a sight that I wished to be on the receiving end of.

Several young females entered the water and began to circle us, diving and twisting and turning over and over beneath us, looking skyward with open mouths. We dodged and weaved with them, playing games of tag as they dashed about, infinitely faster than we, but apparently entertained by our clumsy actions and attempts at imitation. Bubbles streamed from their nostrils and fur, creating tiny swirling lines of silver that raced to the surface and burst into the air.

One of the sea lions broke off weaving through the water and swam directly beneath one of the snorkelers, then lay on the bottom, looking up at him. There followed a game of chicken. The snorkeler dove down toward her, and the sea lion raced skyward; only at the last moment did she swerve out of the way with all the dexterity of motion of a subaqua acrobat. After several repeated dives, the last game of chicken did not go quite as planned; as the two divers raced toward each other, one up and one down, the sea lion swerved, but her open mouth and teeth grazed the snorkeler's mask, almost lifting it from his face. The incident had all the appearance of mischievousness rather than miscalculation.

We continued to swim across the dappled red boulders, watching the fish swarm with the movements of the currents, and breaking off to play with the sea lions as they approached. King angelfish, Cortez rainbow wrasse, and whitetail damselfish swam over the reef. Stunning azure parrotfish with bright green bodies and turquoise fins picked their way across the boulders, and distinctive iridescent blue juvenile giant damselfish, each marked by four bright blue spots on its flanks, stood out clearly on the reef. The scientific name of the giant damselfish, *Micropathodon dorsalis,* refers to a small sheath tooth on the fishes' back used as a defensive mechanism.

A large, dark form caught our peripheral vision. The four of us were at the surface, in a star formation looking downward at the schools of fish and a yellow-spotted star laid out on one of the boulders. The dark form approached. Very rapidly it had our undivided attention. Evidently it was only a young bull, but he had already gained something of a white sagittal crest, and he was an order of magnitude larger than any of the animals that we had been playing with during the last hour. The bull swam underneath us, and we hovered over him, breathing shallow breaths and watching him roll over and over as he observed us closely, his mouth agape and his well-developed canines clearly visible.

The bull satisfied his curiosity, presumably determining that these ungainly creatures enclosed in blubbery black skins were harmless enough. As soon as he had vanished from sight, we all stood upright and began to tread water, yelling at the top of our lungs from exhilaration. Those on the ship had been watching the entire episode, and had seen the male enter the water and approach us. We yelled over to them: "Did you see the size of that thing!?" Our arms and hands were held out wide apart above the surface. Those on the deck laughed and responded by reducing the size of our "fish" a hundredfold with their imitation of the exaggerating fisherman. We returned to the shore and pulled ourselves back onto the rocky ledge to await the pangas. Only then did I notice what I had done to my leg diving in. My left leg from the knee down was covered in blood, and the wounds were flowing freely. The barnacle-encrusted rocks had cut deep, and the salt water had evidently kept the wounds open throughout the snorkeling expedition. Some figures and statements just seem to cling to the mind; the one about sharks detecting 1 part of blood in 100 million parts of water is one of them. Shark bait is not something that I would like to be in my future.

The snorkeling session was an incredible experience. We were flying with the sea lions in a medium in which they are so at home, and we are clumsy transgressors. And yet, weaving back and forth with the chocolate-colored sea lions, for a few moments we did feel as if we belonged, even perhaps that we were accepted. My leg healed quickly, but I still have the scars to denote my snorkeling experience at Los Islotes. They are a tangible reminder of the intangible.

Our final night beneath the Baja sky was at Isla Partida at the north end of Isla Espiritu Santo, rocked by the gentle ocean currents. We watched quietly as the sky turned brilliant red, and the embers of the desert faded and died until resurrected the following day.

We left Isla Espiritu Santo while the early dawn light was still permeating through the morning haze. Within the hour we had approached and landed upon Isla Ballena, Whale Island. Named for its shape, from a distance it looks like the broad back of a whale. Perhaps this was an island of old, where Christian people set foot to say mass, only to find their footing slip and move as the island turned and rolled into a living, breathing whale. Then Almighty God in His wisdom transformed the shape of the whale into land, enshrining it as a place of God, for prayer and hope. Such an island was found by Saint Brendan when he sailed from Ireland in search of the New World centuries ago. The island no longer graces the maps or minds of modern people, and that is perhaps something to be regretted, for those were the days of miracles and otherworldly aspirations, something that would light the modern world and transform those who inhabit it.

Tiny isopods ran between the black rocks of the shoreline on this our transformed island, and the brash carapaces of the sally lightfoot crabs caught the sun in a variation of a thousand colors. The sky was filled with the silent wing beats of brown pelicans, who blocked out the light as they flew overhead, like a resurgence of the pterodactyls that long ago lifted their bodies into the weightlessness of the air.

On the ground, the pelicans were nesting everywhere. We could see the slender necks and bills of the birds protruding from the mass of thorns and tendrils of the pitaya agria, cholla, and in the larger cardon. Upon closer inspection, the nests were actually perched in the branches of small elephant trees that were dwarfed and hidden by the surrounding and all-encompassing cacti.

Bird life swarmed between thorns and leaves: purple finches, the green verdin, black-throated sparrows, and Costa's hummingbirds, and dogging the wings of the pelicans, Heermann's gulls. However, despite the numerous birds that we could see moving through the vegetation, the island was surprisingly quiet. Only the black-chinned sparrows offered vocal accompaniment to the rustling of pelican feathers in the hot air.

We moved through a landscape dotted by the skeletons of cacti and pelicans alike, around which scorpions and bombardier beetles scurried and hid. These were places where both had fallen, and now offered silent testimony to this penetrating place, where we talked in hushed voices, or not at all. It was a reverent place, where all around us seemed to have respect. The birds added color to this desert whale, now hallowed land, but perhaps out of reverence or sanctity they too were silent. Perhaps this was the Whale Island of eons past, when people set foot on the whale, and God made land out of the living animal.

We spent a couple of hours on Isla Ballena and then were on our way again. All too soon we were entering the confines of Bahia de la Paz. The emissions of the Pemex refinery were already visible on the horizon. It was not the sort of guide we wanted home, but perhaps it was fitting. The contrast between natural and artificial could not have been better illustrated. We were surrounded by the flowing landscape of the Sierra de la Giganta and Isla Espiritu Santo, washed by the shores of the Golfo de California, and contaminated by the outpouring of technology without which our modern lives would grind to a halt (and the very ship that we traveled in would cease to move). It is perhaps a dichotomy without answer.

As we looked to the horizon distorted by smoke, a Bryde's whale surfaced off our bow. Instead of disappearing after a couple of blows, in typical Bryde's fashion, this whale remained. For forty minutes the small rorqual weaved back and forth leisurely across our bow, surfacing regularly, sometimes within tens of meters of the ship.

La Paz was only a few hours away, but the distance seemed immense as we were joined by hundreds of common dolphins. They rushed our bow and wake waves in huge numbers, gliding back and forth with abandon. After about twenty minutes, they suddenly accelerated with a show of speed that was astounding. They powered ahead of us, churning the water, and creating bow waves off their own small, lithe bodies. Lines of crashing waves accompanied them. The animals accelerated in unison, as though they were all powered by the same force, the same motivation. Common dolphins typically swim at speeds of ten kilometers per hour, but can quadruple that under the appropriate encouragement. Just as suddenly the pod slowed and waited for us to catch up. They resumed their bow-riding and raced about us, giving no indication of what had driven them forward moments earlier.

It was late afternoon when we entered Bahia de la Paz, and then the harbor. In contrast to 1989, the waters were quiet. No gray whales entered the bay this year. Our passage was heralded by seagulls and sea lions rather than the blows of whales and the rounding of broad backs. I stood on the deck, remembering the parting of the waters two years earlier—remembering the sound and the sight of whales, the scent of the ocean, and the thrill felt in the heart and soul when faced with all that is cetacean, in them and in us, for we share more than an evolutionary heritage.

Hopefully we also share a future, an understanding, and an attitude to life. Another voyage had ended, but it was a prelude to more voyages to come, another piece in the puzzle of seeking understanding of what it is to be cetacean, as well as what it means to be human. The latter has more responsibility that we realize. Continuing to watch the whales will help us attain that realization.

Every voyage heralds new discoveries. Even my tentative excursions had demonstrated that. Imagine what we could learn with just a little more time. And time is the one thing that may run out sooner than we think.

Humpback whales are the most aerial of the great whales.

Humpbacks are often seen slapping their flukes repeatedly on the water's surface, a behavior known as lob-tailing.

Only 10 to 15 percent of blue whales routinely lift their broad flukes clear of the water when they dive.

Nothing can beat touching a gray whale, here seemingly at the whale's request.

Whales seem to breach for many different reasons, and like this gray whale calf may even do it just for fun.

The heavily barnacled rostrum of an adult gray whale contrasts with the as yet unblemished snout of her calf.

California sea lions share a moment on the rocky outcrop of Los Islotes.

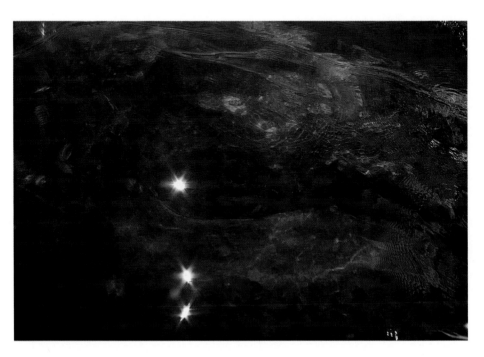

The first time I saw a whale, I looked into its eye and saw myself reflected.

Friendly gray whales greet whale-watchers in Laguna San Ignacio, giving a whole new meaning to the term "touchdown."

The largest blue whale ever measured was 107 feet in length. A blue can weigh in at up to 190,000 kilograms, and a small child could crawl through its arteries.

At the cape of Baja stand the Friars. The monolithic granite rocks are home to sea lions and a multitude of scurrying life.

Humpback whales migrate from the warm waters of Baja to the cold feeding grounds of Alaska. These three whales were feeding in Icy Strait, near Glacier Bay, Alaska.

Common dolphins porpoise along the surface.

With mud and water streaming from its open mouth, this young gray whale seemed to be in the middle of a lesson on bottom-feeding.

On Isla Santa Catalina, cardon cactus reach skyward and barrel cactus grow to gigantic proportions.

Lizards like this banded rock lizard abound in Baja. Lizards such as this one can reach 30 centimeters in length.

The sally lightfoot crab, the bane of John Steinbeck, inhabits the shores and tidepools of Baja.

Elegant white ibis feed along the shores of Baja.

On the beaches of Isla San Benitos, curious elephant seals punctnate the sand.

Our anchorage at Isla Santa Catalina was marked by the distinctive form of the elephant rock.

Elephant seals often seem to deserve the slightly derogatory term "beach maggots."

Hoser the gray whale enjoying a backrub at the end of a long-handled broom in Laguna San Ignacio.

A breaching humpback whale demonstrates its power and shows off its throat grooves.

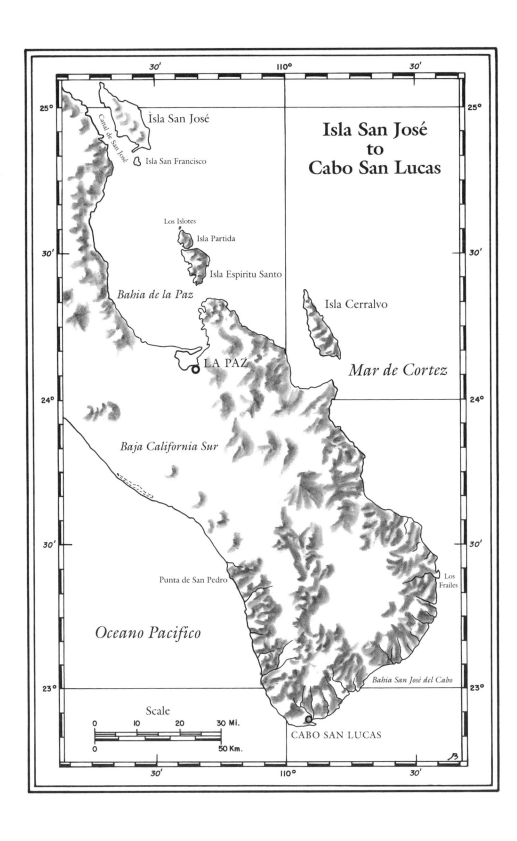

Isla San José
to
Cabo San Lucas

Ìsla San José

Canal de San José

Isla San Francisco

Los Islotes

Isla Partida

Isla Espiritu Santo

Isla Cerralvo

Bahia de la Paz

Mar de Cortez

LA PAZ

Baja California Sur

Punta de San Pedro

Los
Frailes

Oceano Pacifico

Bahia San José del Cabo

Scale

0   10   20   30 Mi.

0   50 Km.

CABO SAN LUCAS

30'

110°

30'

25°

25°

30'

30'

24°

24°

30'

30'

23°

23°

30'

110°

30'

4

La Ballena, El Niño

Straddling each a dolphin's back
And steadied by a fin,
Those Innocents re-live their death,
Their wounds open again.
The ecstatic waters laugh because
Their cries are sweet and strange,
Through their ancestral patterns dance,
And the brute dolphins plunge
Until, in some cliff-sheltered bay
Where wades the choir of love
Proffering its sacred laurel crowns,
They pitch their burdens off.
                              —W. B. Yeats, 1938

The most intense El Niño of the twentieth century began in mid-1982 and ended a year later. Sea surface temperatures in the eastern tropical Pacific and the equatorial zone were five to ten degrees Celsius above normal, affecting fisheries throughout the region and beyond. Australia suffered drought, Tahiti was hit by typhoons, and Chile was deluged under record rainfall and flooding. An El Niño event in 1986 again altered fisheries and allowed tropical species to increase their range, while decreasing overall marine productivity.

In the winter of 1992 I returned to Baja to recapture the moments of my first voyage. I should have realized that those moments and events evaporate as soon as one experiences them. They exist only to precipitate memories and dreams. Our plan had been to take the *Don José* from Bahia Magdalena around the cape into the Sea of Cortez and then to La Paz, a voyage identical to that of three years earlier.

When we arrived in La Paz, it was clear that this voyage would be very different. Nineteen ninety-two was an El Niño year. It was not as intense as the

1982–83 event, but the water temperature in the Sea of Cortez was two degrees Celsius warmer than normal, and the effect on the climate and the whales was to prove dramatic.

What exactly is El Niño? Most people have heard of this phenomenon, but few understand its causes. The world is trying to come to grips with the possibilities of global warming, something that may be manifested to date by temperature increases of 0.5° C. El Niño can generate temperature variations ten to twenty times as great over very short periods of time. Increasing our knowledge of the effects and ramifications of these relatively short-term temperature anomalies may help us deal with global problems and changes as, or when, they arise.

El Niño is Spanish for "The Christ Child." It refers to an oceanographic anomaly that generates unusually warm ocean conditions off the west coast of South America. El Niño was first named by Peruvian fishermen in the nineteenth century. They noted the annual flow of warm equatorial waters southward at Christmas, and named the condition after the Yuletide. Later, Peruvian scientists recorded intense oceanographic changes that occurred at intervals of several years and noted that violent climatic associations, such as flooding, often accompanied the warm waters. These more pronounced events were also given the name El Niño, and the name continues to reflect this unusual event.

The first recorded El Niño was probably in 1525, when the Spanish conquistador Francisco Pizarro landed in northern Peru to be faced with strange desert rains and blossoming vegetation. It has even been suggested that El Niño rains, the unusual ocean temperatures, and the verdant vegetation may have facilitated the conquest of the Inca empire by the Spanish. The widespread disruption of natural cycles and the attendant collapse of agriculture and fisheries may have weakened the empire, or given the Spanish more time, better conditions, or simply better omens to allow for a successful expedition. So this oceanographic anomaly, which in modern times makes deserts bloom, fisheries crash, and typhoons destroy towns and cities, may well have contributed to events that changed the course of South American and European history for centuries.

We are still unraveling the precise causes and ramifications of El Niño. We know that it is related to a similar interannual change in the tropical atmosphere known as the Southern Oscillation. These events are coupled to form a single large-scale climatic and oceanographic interactive force, the El Niño/Southern Oscillation, or ENSO. During the warm phase of ENSO, the South Pacific trade winds shift dramatically.

Under normal conditions, high-pressure systems over the eastern South Pacific and low-pressure systems over northern Australia and Indonesia maintain strong westward trade winds. Northward-blowing winds off South America cause nutrient-rich waters to upwell from below the shallow, warm surface layer. This upwelling makes essential nutrients, principally phosphates and nitrates, available to the photosynthetic plankton, and then to the zooplankton, and so on up the food chain.

However, during El Niño the pressure systems change, weakening the trade winds. The result is warm surface water that moves east along the equator from the western Pacific, thickening the warm surface layer. This thick layer acts as a barrier to upwelling by the coastal winds. Photosynthetic plankton are limited by the availability of essential nutrients. Without those nutrients productivity declines, with a domino effect on the zooplankton and their associated fish, mammalian, and avian predators. Fish populations in the affected areas undergo a precipitous decline as they migrate to other areas in search of food. Fisheries around the world have been severely affected, often for several years, by the onset of an El Niño.

So, what did El Niño mean for us when we arrived in Baja in search of whales? During mid-March, we could expect to see gray whale cows and calves in Bahia Magdalena. Most of the males would already have begun their northward migration, but the cows and calves remain in the bays and lagoons longer, building their strength for the arduous journey to Alaska. We could also plan on seeing blue whales and humpbacks in the Pacific and into the Sea of Cortez.

When we arrived in La Paz, however, the news was not encouraging. A vessel cruising Bahia Magdalena the previous week had not seen a single gray whale; other ships came back with news of a handful of whales, two or three seen in the entire lagoon complex. Perhaps the water temperature was a trigger to the whales—when the temperature reached a certain level, that was their cue to begin the move north so that they arrived on their Alaskan feeding grounds in time to take full advantage of the summer productivity. An El Niño event would accelerate the warming and initiate the migration weeks earlier than usual.

Whatever the cause, we could not plan on seeing gray whales in Bahia Magdalena, and our itinerary was changed. Instead of taking the *Don José* from Magdalena to La Paz, we would cruise from La Paz through the waters of the lower Sea of Cortez, north to Isla San Francisco and south to Los Frailes and Cabo Pulmo, plying the waters in between in search of whales and dolphins. El Niño was to have a hand in our voyage from the outset. Almost everything that we saw, or did not see, we could point to the rain clouds, the winds, and the warm water, and blame El Niño.

The *Don José* was docked in the marina, surrounded as in years previous by bustling bird life and the raucous boatyard activities. A great blue heron and a willet waded along the boat slip, and magnificent frigatebirds and California and ring-billed gulls swooped overhead. Along the shoreline weaved western sandpipers, reddish and snowy egrets, and a tricolored heron. The delicate footsteps of the waders and the harsh calls of the gulls were linked by the subtle clicking of metal boat stays against masts. Brown pelicans flew low over the water, their wing tips almost trailing along the surface, and above them circled the omnipresent turkey vultures, silhouettes against the azure sky.

Since our itinerary had been changed, we had an extra day in La Paz before cruising out of the harbor and into the gulf. We left the loud streets and colors of the city and headed into the desert to see some of the plants blooming following recent rains. We drove north toward Bahia Pichilingue, a beautiful cove set on the east side of Bahia de la Paz. The leisurely drive took us past luxuriant mangroves and dusty red desert soils.

The brittlebush, desert mallow, rock daisy, and elephant trees were all in bloom, as were the thorny ocotillo, cholla, pitayas, and the elegant towering cardon. But even now, so short a time after the water had anointed the dry land, it had been absorbed into the living, organic flesh of the plants. Many of the flowers had already faded, returning the powerful colors concentrated in their petals to burgeoning fruit and seed, dropping their spent leaves and sepals to litter the desert floor until scavenged by scurrying herbivores or blown by the wind. So it is that the benefit of the rains is felt, absorbed, and passed on to the new generation, a transitory passage, but further evidence both of the tenacity of desert life and of the tenuous threads upon which it hangs.

On our return into the port of La Paz, we stopped to look at four tuna seiners tied at the dock. They were massive ships. Their decks were crowded with skiffs and net, and above them towered tall and erect crow's nests. On elevated platforms above the wheelhouse were the helicopters. The tuna business is big business. The tuna fishery can afford such hefty overhead and material costs because the returns are so large. Unfortunately, the successful tuna fisherman has also been a successful dolphin catcher.

Dolphins, particularly spinner and spotted dolphins, are regularly found in association with yellowfin tuna, apparently feeding on the same underlying food resource. By having their lookouts watch for the boiling cauldron of water that surrounds a dolphin school, the fishermen were able to find their tuna. When the nets were set around the fish, the dolphins were also caught. Between 1959 and 1972, it is estimated that 4.8 million dolphins were killed. Fishing nations eventually got together to try to limit the kill. Nets were modified and methods changed that would allow the dolphins to escape while retaining the tuna. The dolphin kill by U.S.-flagged vessels dropped dramatically. The reason, though, probably had more to do with the fact that the dolphins that regularly associated with the tuna were already dead, and fishing vessels that were unable or unwilling to introduce the new technology raised the flags of other nations on their masts and continued as normal. Official figures now put the annual kill at 20,000, but in reality it is probably still around 100,000 animals per year.

We returned to our vessel to prepare for the morning departure. Several members of the crew were familiar faces. Captain José, Felix, Luis, Hernan, and Roberto had returned for another season with the whales, and they were joined by Enriche. Ron LeValley, the enthusiastic co-owner of Biological Journeys, was to be our shipboard naturalist, assisted by Diane Gendron, a French-Canadian biologist from Montreal, now living in Baja to study blue whales, and Heather Angel, a British wildlife photographer.

The night was spent aboard the *Don José* regaining familiarity with the wooden boards of an old friend who revealed whales from the blue waters of the gulf, and joined with them like some artificial whale adopted into their midst. The night was far from peaceful. The sounds of barking dogs and music from other vessels penetrated any silence we could have hoped for. We fell asleep with the raucous sounds of people in our ears and awoke with the piercing shrieks of cockerels while the sun was still lighting embers far beyond the horizon.

We were ready to leave this port. As much as I love La Paz, the smells and sounds, the colors and the setting of this city nestled into the gulf and backed by desert, there were whales to see. With the cockerels now joined by a dawn chorus of dogs, we left the dock escorted by pelicans and elegant terns. Out in Bahia de la Paz the wind lifted small waves into billowing whitecaps, and a light front of clouds impeded the horizon.

Two blue-footed boobies crossed our bow, flying low over the water, and the twin fins of mobulas began to reveal themselves at the water's surface in small groups of three or four. Occasionally our passage spooked these submarine bats, and one would leap from the water, the sunlight reflecting off its creamy white underside before the ray splashed down heavily in the water.

The mainland peninsula stretched out along our starboard side, the lines of rock etched by time and revealed by erosion. The wind rose and died as the morning passed, alternately lifting the waves and flattening them to silky smoothness. California and Heermann's gulls followed our wake or darted across our bow, their antics watched by the soaring frigatebirds overhead, avian pirates waiting for other birds to catch a meal for them to claim following an aerial battle of wits. An adult laughing gull landed in the water to retrieve a scrap of fish, and other gulls mobbed the site. We had cleared the mainland peninsula, and now Isla Espiritu Santo was to our starboard, its impressive formations topped by light clouds and surrounded by dark water held by a building squall.

We were cruising quietly across Bahia de La Paz, the magnificent Sierra de la Giganta in front of us, rising from the sea like the walls of some ancient city. Once our passage scared up a lone needlefish that propelled itself across the surface as if an arrow had been let loose from a bow. It was still early, but the waters seemed subdued and the atmosphere peaceful. The sun streamed through the cloud-dotted sky to turn the water silver.

A group of perhaps two hundred common dolphins surfaced nearby. They did not seem to have any interest in our presence, and only a couple joined our bow for a fleeting flirtation. The majority of the animals remained in close groups, surfacing and breathing quietly as though asleep. We followed them for about ten minutes before turning due north and continuing to scan the waters ahead for signs of great whales. The dolphins moved slowly south, their gray bodies merging softly with the sea around them, and their shallow breaths evaporating in the breeze.

It was 10:30 A.M. when we spotted the first blow on the horizon. It was the elegant, tall white exclamation mark of a blue whale. We watched closely through binoculars. The whale blew six times and dove, a slow, flukeless dive. The *Don José* changed course smoothly, and we headed toward Espiritu Santo. Twelve minutes later the whale burst through the surface, sending five plumes high into the air. The animal arched its broad, blue-gray back, and the tiny dorsal fin rose and fell as it slid beneath the water a hundred meters in front of us. We moved forward slowly and saw a red stain build and spread across the water where the whale had been. The water was dotted with clouds of red carapaces. Gulls swooped on the spot, picking at the remains. The blue whale had defecated as it dove, providing clear visual evidence that these behemoths do indeed feed in the warm waters of the gulf. Within seconds, the diluting nature of the water and the scavenging gulls had eradicated the evidence, and we plowed on through the water, waiting for the whale to resurface.

The whale moved gently through the water, erupting from the deep to blow five or six times, water running in white rivulets off its broad, flat rostrum, and descending beneath us for eight to ten minutes at a time, probably making shallow feeding dives in leisurely fashion. It is so tantalizing to view a whale from such a vantage point, to witness the power of the animal through short visions of exhalation, inhalation, and the momentum of the dive. How much about these animals do we infer from such cursory intrusions into their lives? We have so many statistics from the days of whalemen and catcher boats, but of the important information we know so little—thoughts, emotions, the stuff of our humanity, and perhaps of theirs. Beneath the waves we can learn more, but still we are imprisoned and restricted. Even in submersibles and wetsuits our incursions are short. We simply cannot keep up with these animals except on the surface, and then we see only fractions of a life. How can we expect to gain more than a fraction of understanding? In the distance another blow punctuated the horizon. The whale lifted its distinctive flukes clear of the water and sounded in the manner typical of humpbacks. Two towering blows revealed more blues toward Espiritu Santo, and then the sickle-shaped dorsal fin of a Bryde's whale was highlighted in the sun. We were surrounded by whales: blue, humpback, and Bryde's. Only the blues approached closely, their bodies lighting the water from below and their rorqual shape settling the water's surface with the force of leviathan mass.

The sun was glaringly hot and reflected patterns and shades of light and dark across the rippling currents. Although the water was filled with whales, they were elusive. To the north the humpback and two blues surfaced infrequently, while some two hundred meters away the Bryde's whale swam to starboard and the other blue whale to the south, keeping their distance and eventually merging with the water. Finally they vanished, no longer revealing their presence with the expulsion of moist, cool air.

In the distance were the familiar towering guano-stained pinnacles and the barking, playful sea lions of Los Islotes. It took us almost two hours of steady passage to reach the islands. The water was perfectly calm. It was ideal whale-watching weather, save for one rather important fact: there were no whales. Under such conditions we had hopes of seeing dwarf sperm whales; incredibly unusual creatures, they are Moby Dick in miniature. They hardly create a ripple when they surface, bobbing a few times before returning to the deep for long, drawn-out dives, necessitating conditions such as these to even hope of seeing them.

During such quiet times atop the w-w deck we could contemplate the majesty of the islands around us: Espiritu Santo set in undulating static form, each cove alternately light and dark, the mainland to starboard set in receding shadows, and that to port highlighted in the bright, if hazy, desert sun. As we neared the white islands, three black-vented shearwaters flew low over the water, their feet barely clearing the surface. The cloud cover was intermittent, and the cool breeze generated by our motion chilled the w-w deck to well below the ambient temperature.

The sun reflected off the white, billowing sails of a boat on the horizon. The vessel vanished in the swell of the sea and the diffuse light, reappeared, and vanished again. This marine apparition continued to alternate between real and phantom until we passed to the other side of the rocks. Perhaps such natural visions explain the phantom ships of mariners' tales—the *Mary Celeste,* the *Flying Dutchman,* the *Fellowship,* and the *Leon.* Real visions can, as a consequence of some natural phenomenon, take on the role of phantom in the predisposed and the expectant, or the tentative and the scared.

As we prepared to drop anchor off Los Islotes, two humpback whales sounded, bringing their flukes up high and clear of the water in synchrony. We watched for a resurfacing, but just as the sailboat had vanished, so had the whales, and again we were left with the feeling that what seems real in this changeling land may so often be phantom, and the phantom real.

The sun was reflected brightly off the contortions of the islands. Brown and blue-footed boobies crowded the ledges. There were more blue-foots this year than in previous visits—a good sign. Other sights around the islands were not so encouraging. Numerous sea lions were wearing nylon necklaces that were cutting into flesh and slowly strangling their victims. As we motored by in the small pangas, the sea lions looked up at us with lazy, plaintive eyes running with tears. Females were suckling large pups along the rocky beach, and sally lightfoot crabs raced the waves along the shoreline.

Our small craft took us close to a rocky outcrop crowded with sea lions. In the center of the group was a mature bull, complete with the white sagittal crest that imparted such an aristocratic air to the animal. As our craft drifted a little too close to the rocks, some of the sea lions slid silently into the water, swimming under the panga and surfacing to look at us. The sea lions were inquisitive and their eyes curious. Those animals that had been a golden tan color on the rocks were jet black in the water.

The aqua world beneath us was alive with striped sergeant major fish, bright red sea anemones, and multilegged starfish. Along the shore a wandering tattler picked its way across the boulders, while sally lightfoots scurried about with some important purpose in mind. The guano-covered rocks encouraged tiny black flies to swarm and congregate, and our panga was soon a center of activity for these irritating, though fortunately nonbiting, insects. The flies settled on camera lenses, glasses, and irritated skin. We were glad to enter the water to escape their persistence.

We slid into the water from the stern of the *Don José,* thus avoiding the potential for injury from the sharp rocks along the shoreline (something that I did not wish to repeat). Always when entering such a new world there is the feeling that we are aliens in this element. The sound of our breathing resonates through the water, through the snorkel, and through our bodies. We could be astronauts instead of aquanauts for all the familiarity that this medium holds to our kind.

Every color of the rainbow was captured in the submarine life before our eyes. Movements in the green water revealed Mexican goatfish and Panamic sergeant major fish in shimmering schools. The yellow horizontal stripe of the goatfish gave the impression of complete synchrony of movement. The boulders below were crowded with colonial animal growth, punctuated by tan stars, spiny red sea urchins, and the form of the flower sea urchin that had the appearance of a thousand tiny flowers held together in a delicate bouquet. Other fish, familiar from previous watery excursions, darted for cover as we passed overhead, or moved with ease through the water inches from our hands: king angelfish, Cortez, scissortail, and giant damselfish, the stunningly green azure parrotfish, and the bright golden-tailed yellow surgeonfish. A large leopard grouper hugged the bottom, while the sunlight created dappled patterns across the boulder-strewn surface.

Moving inshore, we began to see ghostly figures just beyond our field of vision. The sea lions were checking us out from a distance, cruising the waters with adept body movements that seemed to reshape their torpedo-like forms with every turn. In the water these creatures are the embodiment of grace and sleek form; on land they are cumbersome, blubbery animals ill treated by gravity.

Several young sea lions, probably young females, began to approach. They swam underneath us, rolling over and over looking upward at our ungainly forms silhouetted above them. One of the sleek animals approached, and we began to weave back and forth together. With my oversized flippers and less than flexible spine, my movements were a sorry imitation of this lithe being, but I did my best to copy the sea lion move for move. We continued this submarine dance for what seemed the longest time. At intervals the sea lion dashed behind me, so that I had to turn 180 degrees to see where my dance partner had gone. Although my breathing still seemed incredibly loud, I felt at home in the water, dancing with the sea lion. At length the music in my mind stopped and the dance came to an end. The sea lion hovered inches from my mask, her friendly face inquisitive and her mouth slightly open, revealing well-proportioned teeth. I found myself talking to her, the sort of initial pleasantries with which one might begin a conversation with another species. She continued to hover in front of me, her head tilting from side to side. I smiled as warmly as I could with a snorkel in my mouth.

She flexed her body and swam so close that I could feel the displacement of water against my own body. Once she was behind me, her flippers powered down, clipping my own flippers before she vanished into the murky waters beyond the penetration of light, leaving me quite alone.

Too soon we were steaming south on our way to Los Frailes and Cabo Pulmo. We stood out on the stern as the time approached when the sun would disappear behind the desert mountains. The mountains provided a perfect display for the sunset. At 6:30 P.M. the sun began its final descent. As the last portion of it dipped to vanish from sight, we raised our binoculars and watched as the golden orange orb was transformed by the green flash as the visible light spectrum passed before our eyes. In a handful of seconds the green flash vanished, and the evening sky was backlit and deepened from orange to red to purple as the sun set further beyond the horizon.

The wind had picked up, and our small vessel began to pitch and toss through the darkening evening. We were experiencing the Coromuelo winds, named after a pirate, Cromwell, who used to ply these waters, disappearing far to the south after his raids, driven by the seasonal winds out of the reach of the authorities. We continued to be jostled by the waves throughout the evening, and Los Frailes was beginning to look further and further away. As the hour neared midnight, we cut our losses and anchored at Ensenada de los Muertos, Cove of the Dead.

During the evening we pored over the offerings of the galley, taking down and inspecting every remnant of the sea that the vessel had collected over the years. We ran our hands over common dolphin skulls and delicate vertebrae, feeling the projections of each spinous process. We felt the teeth in the jaw of a bottlenose dolphin, traced the lines of sea lion ribs, and felt the rise of the sagittal crest on the skull of an adult male California sea lion. We cradled a coyote skull, held the head of a yellow-footed gull, and weighed the skull and bill of a pelican. We mused over the shell and fused ribs of a green turtle, and held up pilot whale and gray whale vertebrae, imagining the living animal wrapped around these inanimate forms. A multitude of cartilaginous and calcareous offerings were among the remnants in front of us: puffers and cornetfish, a moray skeleton, the heads of parrotfish and triggerfish, the sail of a marlin, the jaw of a barracuda, and the plant-like form of the delicate gorgonian.

We looked over all of them, touching them and talking about the shapes and forms of the many life forms we could see in this wondrous world—toothed and baleened, mammalian and piscine.

Dawn broke over another St. Patrick's Day afloat on the warm waters of Baja California. We were continuing on our way south, trying to make up for the time lost by our dash for cover into Ensenada de los Muertos. The bright Baja sky was cloaked in clouds, but the waters were calm, a welcome change from the night before, when even at anchorage our vessel had been raised and dropped as though in a nautical game between Greek gods and goddesses atop far-off Mt. Olympus.

We were just settling in to eat a lavish breakfast when we were roused by a cry from the helm. The water was filled with whales. About two hundred and fifty shortfin pilot whales blackened the silky gray surface.

Whales surfaced and blew repeatedly to port, to starboard, and directly in front of our bow. The black rounded shape of the dorsal fins cut through the surface, followed by the broad protruding melon of each animal's head. The circular, single blowholes snapped open to take in fresh, clean, maritime air.

The animals were grouped in fairly cohesive units. One large animal with a distinctive nick in his dorsal fin hit the surface and then dove. We began to count as other animals surfaced. One, two, five, ten. We counted sixty-nine whales before the identifiable animal surfaced again. Other small units within the larger pod contained similar numbers.

Three herd types have been identified among pilot whales in the Pacific: (1) the traveling-hunting group, a large and well-organized unit, much like the one in front of us, that may be divided into harems of females and young led by one or more large adult males, with other smaller subgroups also divided by age and sex; (2) the feeding group, which consists of a loose aggregation of animals; and (3) the "loafing group" of twelve to thirty animals that group together in one area forming a nursery for young animals, or perhaps permitting mating between adults.

We followed the whales back the way we had come, watching females keeping close to tiny miniatures of themselves, and youngsters tailslapping the surface with pistol shots. The sun reflected off jet dorsals, and we could hear the sound of blows magnified a hundredfold. The pod was spread over a large area, but each animal's surfacing seemed synchronized. We would be watching the entire school, and suddenly we could see only ten animals across the open expanse of water. Then, just as suddenly, the whales resurfaced after a few minutes, their blows hitting the air like the firing of so many cannons.

The movements of the pod were certainly not random. Certain "point" animals seemed to have control over direction, and as those animals changed direction, the rest of the pod fell into line and followed, responding to commands to which we were deaf.

We do know something of these animals. Each individual has a "signature" whistle, and they use a variety of sounds for communication. Pilot whales are highly social animals. The pilot whales' society, like that of the orca, is matrilineal; young males may move to other pods, but females remain in their maternal group for life. Their tie to the pod seems to be very strong. Calves are born in July and August following a fifteen-month gestation period, and although they take solid food at between six and twelve months of age, they continue to suckle for up to two years. Life expectancy for these animals may sometimes exceed sixty years. They have few natural enemies, except possibly sharks that may attack young animals, orca, and of course people.

Pilot whales have been among the more intensively harvested of the small cetaceans. In the past, active fisheries were found in Japan, throughout the Caribbean, the northeastern United States, Newfoundland, Ireland, Norway, and several islands in the North Sea, most notably the Faeroes. Only the Faeroe "harvest" continues on a large scale. The cumulative kill attributable to these small islands has been estimated at 117,546 between 1584 and 1883. And the kill continues.

It has to be said that the "harvest" appears to be in balance with the northeastern Atlantic population. But anyone who has witnessed the carnage of the slaughter, seen the waters turn blood red as men, women, and children walk through the shallows with huge curved scythes slicing into living whale flesh, who among them can justify such a hunt? Justification is even harder when it is learned that government authorities recommend limited human consumption of the meat because of pollutants such as mercury, lead, and PCBs. The result is that "tradition" continues the hunt, but use of the resource is minimal. In a modern European community that is unforgivable, and it is certainly insupportable.

The animals were moving quietly. They did not join our bow as did their smaller, more playful cousins, although occasionally they slapped the surface of the water with sculpted black flukes. These "blackfish" sleep during the day and actively feed at night. So we were probably with a dozing traveling-hunting group that had only just finished a busy night on the prowl for squid and small fish, perhaps diving to depths of more than six hundred meters.

Pilot whales also have a rather sad reputation of being the whale species most prone to mass stranding. Strandings seem to occur when an animal leads the pod onto a beach for some unknown reason, perhaps sickness, or an inability to distinguish shallow sloping beaches with its echolocation. Whatever the cause, the resulting cries of the stranded animals seem only to draw more animals into shore, and even dragging them out to sea does not prevent those animals from rebeaching themselves. Some have reported that if an animal is sick and soon dies, then the other animals can be refloated and gradually leave the area, but until it dies, they seem bent on joining it on some sympathetic suicidal mission to die under the same unyielding pressures of terrestrial gravity.

We stayed with the dozing black animals for almost an hour, our vessel moving with them as they shifted course, hovering above them like benign and watchful guardians. In the distance a larger blow caught our eye. Five brief blows cut the water, followed by the sickle dorsal fin of a Bryde's whale. The morning light streaked through the light clouds, hitting the silvery sea with diffuse patterns and lighting the buttress flanks of the mountains with shapes that shifted and changed with the breeze.

We returned to our southerly course, the cloud cover almost total, but clearer weather was coming into the region beyond the mountains. The gray sea tipped into occasional white as we plowed down toward the cape. On the horizon a large white splash focused our attention. The whale, if indeed that was what it was, was still eight or ten kilometers ahead of us, and we pushed on, eager to meet such exuberance "up close and personal."

A black storm-petrel darted across our bow as José slowed the ship almost to a full stop. We had seen no blows since the splash punctuated the horizon thirty minutes earlier, and now we idled off the southeastern point of Baja under a cloudy desert sky. We sat in silence on the w-w deck, staring at the quiet and seemingly lifeless waters. I raised my camera to take a sea-state picture. The waters were calm and gray; hardly a breeze ruffled the surface. I lowered the camera, and suddenly the lifeless, empty waters were filled with the curving, arching body of a breaching humpback. The animal filled the silky spot that I had taken the photograph of moments earlier. The whale disappeared in a cauldron of foaming surf, and we held our breath hoping for another breach. After a couple of minutes the whale surfaced and blew three times before arching his back and diving a slow and flukeless dive beneath the surface.

We waited for the whale to resurface, but when he did so he was far to the north, and we watched him leave as we returned to our southerly heading. I have no idea how José saw the whale. Several of us were on the w-w deck, all scanning the water with binoculars looking for any telltale signs of whales, from blows, flukeprints, and flukes to the sun glinting off backs and fins and congregations of seabirds, and still none of us knew that there was even a whale nearby until he breached.

The peninsula stretched away from us, north and south in receding depth shadows. We motored on, pausing briefly to watch a marlin surface next to the ship, its sail reaching high into the air. A few fishing boats dotted the water ahead of us, each trying to catch one of these magnificent game fish. The people in those vessels were following a motivation that will always elude me. I would much rather enjoy the sights, sounds, and feel of the land and its inhabitants without making a permanent dent in their survival and thus marring the enjoyment of those that come after me, not to mention the supreme sacrifice made by the unsuspecting marlin or swordfish or shark. It is possible to enjoy everything in the hunt with a camera, save the moment of killing, and that is something that should not be enjoyed. It should be done only because of necessity or threat, never for fun or pleasure. The taking of a life should not be done lightly.

The black flies that we had picked up at Los Islotes continued to plague the w-w deck, and we waved away their insistent buzzing while watching the boats lay out their lines and fish jump in the sunlight.

A large fin protruded from the water ahead of us. Then we saw a second fin, obviously belonging to the same animal, some six meters behind the first. The dorsal fin was triangular and lightly dappled with white dots on a steely blue-gray background, while the second caudal fin was slender and trailing. The caudal fin was vertical: this was no mammalian whale, this was a whale shark, *Rhiniodon typus,* the only living representative in the family Rhiniodontidae. We maneuvered to within thirty meters as the shark basked at the surface. As we tried to approach, it moved imperceptibly so that our distance remained constant.

We strained our eyes to penetrate the water made gray by the clouds. With polarizing lenses we could occasionally make out the shadow of the animal beneath the waves. It was probably ten or twelve meters in length. It has been estimated that these sharks may reach eighteen meters, equivalent to a humpback whale, certainly larger than a gray, and more than three times the size of the great white. Unlike most species of sharks, which are either coastal (such as the bull shark or tiger shark) or oceanic (such as the oceanic whitetip), whale sharks have one of the broadest distributions of any shark and are found in all warm temperate and tropical seas, coastal and pelagic.

They are incredibly distinctive sharks, and despite their size should not impart terror into the fearful. Whale sharks are filter-feeders, baskers that strain algae, crustaceans, and small fish from the water as they swim at sedate speeds of three to five kilometers per hour filtering water through their gill slits. The name *Rhiniodon* means "file tooth," and the shark has more than three hundred of these tiny teeth in its cavernous mouth. Whale sharks have been seen rising vertically through a school of fish until their heads are clear of the surface, allowing the mouth to drain before sinking back to refill. Such episodes are strikingly similar to descriptions of lunge-feeding whales. Indeed, these sharks can be viewed as truly analogous to the baleen whales in their mode of feeding and pose no threat to the diver, save through the impact of a misplaced fin or tail thrust. It is even believed that these sharks are oviparous, giving birth to live young.

The whale shark has a broad, flat head and no noticeable snout, but rather a truncated and rounded "rostrum." The gill openings are immense, and the entire animal is dappled with light spots and faint vertical lines against a blue background. Whale sharks are not usually found in the Sea of Cortez until well into the summer; the warm water of the season brings them north, to the delight of snorkelers and scuba divers. Our shark was yet another reminder of the effects of El Niño and the warm water that it had precipitated so early in the year.

Every time we thought we had drawn close to the fish, or that the light had improved sufficiently to reveal the shark in its full length to us, we were wrong. If only the water had not rolled with a swell that occasionally collapsed into a whitecap, throwing spray across our bow and even onto the w-w deck, and especially if the sky had been clear and reflected in the water below us, we would have suited up to swim with this shark. We would have experienced playing tag with the largest shark in the world, and have been able to compare this "whale" with the familiar cetaceans through which coursed the hot blood of common ancestors.

We continued on as the distance between us and the lounging shark increased and as the light continued to play across the water's surface, barring penetration by curious terrestrial eyes. The wind built, and the whitecaps became more frequent. Toward lunch the strong winds were replaced by a brisk breeze and the waves calmed. A blow to our starboard, toward shore, suggested that a blue was in these waters, while ahead a v-shaped blow and rounded back revealed a humpback amid a congregation of fishing boats plying the currents across Gorda Bank.

The lunch bell rang as two humpback whales surfaced directly in front of us, just twenty meters away. They blew twice, the sound of their exhalation carried to us, along with the smell of the salt moisture atomized with each breath. Water cascaded about their broad rostrums, double blowholes were held open to incoming fresh air, stovebolts (the bumps on whales' heads) glistened in the soft light, and then the animals rounded their backs, drew those familiar humps upward, and dove, simultaneously lifting dark, ragged flukes clear of the water.

We idled, awaiting the whales' return, when two bright yellow fishing boats, probably from the coastal resort on the mainland, buzzed our position. They split up and passed us on either side, their speedboat motors revving and criss-crossing the area where the whales had been moments earlier. The tiny yellow vessels reminded me of the persistent flies that were plaguing the w-w deck, and we desperately wanted to brush them away before the whales were spooked and left the area.

The little boats got bored after about ten minutes and left, but the whales had vanished. The intrusion was probably sufficient to drive them away. Twenty minutes later they surfaced some distance off on our starboard side, blew one brief exhalation, fluked, and dove. They were not going to offer any close encounters, and we continued our search.

The afternoon weather was ideal. The morning clouds had largely dispersed, and the water was glassy calm. The sun baked the w-w deck and the breeze was almost nonexistent. A few fishing boats were lined up ahead of us, following the pattern of currents in the water, and two large tuna seiners were at anchor along the coast. The cape at Los Frailes was visible in the distance, beyond the recession plains and set between the silky blue-gray of the sea and the sky.

A blue whale surfaced ahead of us, her blows hanging in the still air so that as she blew four times, each atomized exhalation was added to the first. The whale dove after four blows, her back rounding to reveal a neatly shaped and tiny dorsal fin, the sun glancing off silver flanks. For twelve long minutes the waters were barren, then the telltale aqua shadow beneath the surface foretold another surfacing. She blew four more times, her double blowhole wide open, then repeated the diving motion. This time as the whale swam forward under the surface, we could trace her movements by the appearance of huge flukeprints that settled at the surface with each downward power thrust of her flukes.

The water was calm and we idled in the heat. A magnificent frigatebird circled above us, and black storm-petrels darted across our wake. We could see the whale beneath the water long before she surfaced, the blue-green shadow outlining body, pectoral flippers, and flukes, as well as the broad shape of the animal's head. She surfaced after sixteen minutes, remaining at the surface for five and generating four huge flukeprints.

Once more we watched the whale dive, resurface thirteen minutes later, blow four times in rapid succession, then round her back and dive with such impressive speed that the water swirled white about the spot where she disappeared. We did not see her surface again. What a world this creature inhabits. This thirty-meter animal could glide like a fragile bird beneath us, moving with all the ability of the black storm-petrel off our bow, her body withstanding pressures that would crush our terrestrial forms, her lungs sustaining her for longer than we can imagine, and 15,000 pints of blood coursing through her massive veins. Blues swim vast distances during the year, perhaps moving from poles to equator, using sound as we use light, following subsea channels and mountain ranges as birds use landmarks. They sense the currents, feel the temperature and salinity changes with the passing year, and can hear the life of oceans far away.

We can gain a sense of the animal in our snapshot visions, but they are so short, so incomplete, that I wonder whether it will ever be any different. And if we were to answer all of our questions, would the vision of the diving whale lose its captivation and majesty, or would our appreciation simply grow with knowledge?

A dozen bottlenose dolphins were spread out ahead of us. Two briefly joined our bow, but the widely scattered group was dozing and slow. They drifted off, leaving us to look inshore at the distant blows of the humpback that had been swimming south with us for some distance, and farther offshore at the surfacing of a blue whale that may have been our whale, or some other.

The weather was that of long-remembered Baja—cloudless, calm, and hot. One of the tuna seiners that had been anchored along the mainland shore crossed our bow. The nets and skiffs were drawn up high across the stern, and the lookout in the crow's nest used a high-powered spotting scope to scan the waters ahead. As we cruised by, he briefly trained his scope on us, before turning back to the task at hand. I wonder how many . . .

We were to spend the afternoon hiking and snorkeling around Los Frailes and Cabo Pulmo. José took the ship in toward shore, along the rocky outcrops upon which were silhouetted goats, and we prepared to anchor on the reef. The water had built a swell here, and our vessel was buoyed along toward the rocks. José turned the ship. The swells were making passage unsteady and would make anchorage, as well as snorkeling, far from calm. We turned instead to Bahia de los Frailes and the protected waters on the other side of the cape. This was the same location hidden by fog three years earlier. This time the weather was perfect, and we eagerly awaited the moment when the colorful array of underwater life would be lit for us by such ideal Baja weather. El Niño would not dominate this afternoon.

Most of our group elected to head straight to shore and hike along the hillside trails and creeks. Six of us suited up, took to one of the pangas, and began to look for an appropriate place to enter the water. The backs of my hands were sore and sunburned from the last couple of days' diffuse though intense sun, and Ron handed me a pair of bright orange diving gloves to protect them in the water.

It was distinctly chilly as we slipped over the side of our panga, sharp intakes of breath serving to delay those who followed. Once we were in the water, however, all thoughts of cold evaporated, and with heads down we began to watch the movements and designs of the creatures below us. We were snorkeling along a rocky beach, backed by high granite cliffs, and the waves crashed severely on the black rocks. We watched the swells carefully lest they raise us up on the shore. The panga moved with us along the shore, giving us a level of security amid the white crashing waves, and welcome warmth should the cold become too oppressive.

Schools of Moorish idol fled from our path. Panamic sergeant major fish weaved back and forth over the rocks, and Cortez damselfish, rainbow and sea-green sunset wrasses, and giant damselfish, showing both juvenile fluorescent blue and adult gray coloration, darted ahead of us. We gazed at the tiny comb jellies before our eyes, and hovered above the corals and clumps of vegetative animalcule life crawling over rocks and stones. We could just lie atop this world, looking down, allowing the swell of the ocean to move us, and only occasionally propelling ourselves forward with clumsy black flukes.

Swimming slowly over the reef, I watched the familiar black-striped, yellow-tailed, and azure-blue fish. Then, standing out brilliantly against the dark rocks, was a fabulously different fish. It was luxuriously golden and moved slowly along the bottom. I had seen this fish before, with its plump body, large dark eyes, and pouting features, but the last time it had been polka dot, white on black. It was a guineafowl puffer, but this was the rarer golden color phase of the species, an intense golden-yellow punctuated by infrequent black smudges. I stuck my head up above the surface to see where the other snorkelers were, and waved for them to look beneath.

We continued to move along the reef. The water was thick with life. It was enthralling just to remain stationary and focus within inches of the mask, instead of far below; in that way you developed an appreciation for the tiny, and the seemingly inconsequential. It is these tiniest of aquanauts that take hold of the light as though capturing it, reflecting it without and within. They pulsate with life, and give one a feeling of completion and intense beauty that is usually beyond our eyes.

The panga had gone, and I looked around to see where the other snorkelers were. Ron and Heather were behind me, two of the other passengers, father and son, were slightly ahead, and the final snorkeler was out of sight. We pushed on, toward the beach. The water was getting increasingly murky, and the light reflected and highlighted forms that defy explanation and imagination—who knows, they may even still defy classification.

Yellowtail surgeonfish filled the water below us. I swam near to the shore, always keeping an eye on how close I was getting to the jagged rocks. The panga was still out of sight. Suddenly there was a commotion in the water. Father and son were treading water. Their faces looked panicked, and the boy was pulling at his face mask. There was nothing visible in the water, and I swam over. He had been stung across his face, which was now reddened and sore. We couldn't see anything. I raised my bright orange gloves and began to wave—to anybody who happened to be around. I could see Ron turn toward us, but the panga was nowhere near. Then my neck and arms began to burn. The sensation intensified. I looked around. Nothing. I put my glove to my neck, and when I brought it back, there was the culprit highlighted against the bright orange neoprene.

The tiny air sac was no more than two centimeters across. The transparent flotation sac was bluish gray, and from it hung almost invisible tendrils that clung to the skin and fired darts that stung and paralyzed. It was a Portuguese man o' war, *Physalia utrilculus*. Now that I knew what I was looking for, I scanned the water's surface. There were hundreds of them scattered around. We had swum right into their midst.

The five of us were now treading water together, watching the currents and waves move the painful jellyfish around us. Only Ron and Heather, who arrived later on the scene, escaped being stung. We were soon to learn that the sixth snorkeler had headed toward the beach earlier than the rest of us, and had been the first to feel the effects of the man o' war. The panga had gone to pick her up; now it returned to us. We were ferried back to the *Don José* to apply lemon juice and baking soda to the stings. They were a soothing remedy. A man o' war victim should always soak the wounds with juice before taking to a freshwater shower, which only serves to set off any stings not yet discharged.

The pain eventually dissipated, but it took a surprisingly long time. For such tiny colonial creatures they pack quite a punch. Our skin was marked by long, thin red lines, punctuated by small red blotches where each nematocyst had fired its neurotoxin.

The Portuguese man o' war is classified in the phylum Cnidaria. The minutiae of life that we could watch right before our eyes while snorkeling, moving in pulsating fashion and refracting all the colors of the rainbow, are all contained within this phylum. Cnidarians, which encompass hydrozoans (the class that includes the Portuguese man o' war under the order Siphonophora), scyphozoans (the typical jellyfish), anthozoans (soft corals and anemones), and cubozoans (box jellyfish), are the only creatures that manufacture the microscopic intracellular stinging cells known as nematocysts or cnidae.

Cnidarians have two body forms during their life cycle: the polyp and the medusa. The cnidarian life cycle is truly astonishing. All are capable of sexual reproduction, which usually occurs when the animals are medusae, but many also reproduce asexually, as polyps. During asexual reproduction the animal forms new individuals simply by budding pieces of tissue from its body, or by dividing lengthwise or crosswise to form two identical animals. The colonies of polyps that form corals, sea pens, sea fans, and anemones are made up of genetically identical animals; essentially they are all clones. However, despite their genetic uniformity, they do show polymorphisms; that is, they are morphologically distinct in form, structure, and in some cases physiologically.

Thus, the Portuguese man o' war is a colonial jellyfish, which means that it is not a single entity but a "city" of cooperating organisms. It consists of millions of individual, though genetically identical, animals that act like individual cells, incapable of independent existence. Some are the stinging cells, the protectors and procurers of food for the colony, while others are reproductive (gonophores) or floatation cells (pneumatophores). These jellyfish do not actively pursue prey, but wait for their food to drift into their stinging tentacles, where the discharging nematocysts paralyze the victim, and the tentacles draw the creatures up to be absorbed by the specialized gastrozooids that are the digesters of the collective.

As an aside, it is noteworthy that the scientific names of the fin whale and the Portuguese man o' war share a commonality: both use the root *physalia*, Greek for "sail." For the Portuguese man o' war the rationale is obvious—the gas-filled sac serves as its "sail." But what about the fin whale? The scientific name refers to the prominent fin on the baleen whales' back; although functionally more like a keel, it seems reasonable to refer to such a large fin as a sail.

When the hikers returned, we had quite a story to relay, and scars of combat to show off. It was quite an experience. El Niño had struck again. The warm water had brought the jellyfish into the Sea of Cortez, and to Los Frailes, where they had not been sighted before so early in the year.

As the moon rose high overhead we stood out on the stern, looking at the reflections of moonlight in the dark waters. The stings were still evident, but the discomfort had lessened considerably. Four pelicans flew low to the water, their wings catching the silvery light, and then two humpbacks double-breached in the moonlight. To think of the vision, to replay the movement in the mind's eye, is to feel the heart lift and the pulse race. We were witness to plays and actions that are so far removed from the everyday that they might as well have occurred on another planet or in our own imaginations, so separate, so unreal, do they appear in hindsight. Whales breach in moonlight in our dreams, not in reality—except here, it seems, where the warm ocean laps desert shores, and thoughts are transformed into physical realization.

The generator was kicked into life at precisely 5:21 A.M. The same could not be said for the passengers. An hour later people began to emerge from their bunks, and the smell of coffee and breakfast resurrected the remainder. The stings from the previous day had faded, although fine red lines were still visible across our necks and arms. The pain had passed, and now the event was simply a curiosity.

We left our anchorage and headed back out onto Gorda Bank. The sea was perfectly calm, and the sky above was almost mirrored in the blue waters; only a few clouds cluttered the horizon. A marlin leapt clear of the water half a kilometer distant, then leapt again, demonstrating that even the piscine can show some of the leviathans' exuberance.

The morning was just getting started when two humpback whales surfaced a couple of hundred meters away. They fluked following a long exhalation, and for twenty minutes we watched the waters around us for any sign of their passage. A pink-footed shearwater skimmed the water near our bow, but the whales had vanished far beneath us and we continued on.

Gorda Bank was marked by a number of currents that collected flotsam and debris in long lines between the major flowing bodies of water. The currents had the appearance of marine highways along the sea surface, and this impression was reinforced as we watched two coffee-and-cream-colored whales surface three times in the slipstream. Their indistinct blows hung momentarily in the air, then they dove a quick, flukeless dive. Precisely twenty minutes and thirty seconds later they resurfaced in the same water current some distance behind us. Their blows were brief and their surfacing was short, but this time we got a clearer view of the animals.

The whales were smaller than the other great whales that we had been seeing. We estimated their length at six meters. Their backs were heavily scarred, and the small dorsal fin was a distinctive shark shape. We were looking at one of the more unusual of the whales, a member of the family Ziphiidae. Ziphiids, of which there are about eighteen species, are medium-sized toothed whales that have a pointed beak and a single pair of grooves that converge on the throat.

Identifying these animals at sea following brief sightings turns into a process of elimination rather than a categorical confirmation. Numerous Ziphiids can be eliminated purely on their geographical range (although caution must be used because in many cases we simply do not know the complete range of these species). There are six recognized genera in the family: Tasmacetus, Hyperoodon, Indopacetus, Berarduius, Ziphius, and Mesoplodon.

Despite the caution, it was with some confidence that we could dismiss the genera Tasmacetus, Hyperoodon, and Indopacetus based on their known geographic distributions. That left us with Baird's beaked whale in the genus Berarduius (since the other species in this genus is the southern variety, Arnoux's beaked whale); Cuvier's beaked whale, the lone species in the genus Ziphius; and the two or possibly three species of Mesoplodon that could conceivably be found in the Sea of Cortez: the arch beaked whale, the ginkgo-toothed beaked whale, and Blainville's beaked whale.

On the basis of the observed distributions of these whales in polar, temperate, or tropical waters, we could eliminate Baird's beaked whale and both the arch beaked and ginkgo-toothed beaked whales since they do not favor truly tropical waters. That left us with Cuvier's beaked whale (also known as the goosebeak whale) and the Mesoplodon Blainville's beaked whale (identified by some as the dense beaked whale).

Blainville's beaked whale is believed to average between 4.5 and 4.8 meters in length, quite a bit smaller than the estimate we had made of our whales. However, it is probably unwise to base an identification solely on size when the discrepancy is one meter on a moving subject half a kilometer away. Both Cuvier's and Blainville's beaked whales have a prominent dorsal fin and an indistinct blow. However, it was the coloration that ultimately convinced me that our two whales were Cuvier's. Blainville's beaked whale is regularly a dark blue-gray color, while Cuvier's beaked whale shows great color variation throughout its range, and has often been seen in this coffee-brown form.

It is a remarkable way to whale-watch: observing a fraction of the animal's life and then playing twenty questions trying to identify it. When you finally come to a conclusion, it is with a feeling of resignation rather than the exhilaration of seeing a new species. For the remainder of the day you convince not only others but yourself. After all, the books that you are relying on say that the distribution of the whales is this, the usual coloration is that. And the books are never wrong. Right? Does it really matter that we, as amateur whale-watchers, identify the animal to species level? Is it not enough that we say it was a member of the family Ziphiidae? Probably not. But the debate that we went through on the w-w deck of the *Don José* should at least serve to demonstrate that our knowledge of these whales is more than incomplete. We have difficulty identifying the animals in the wild; our only knowledge of them comes from the destructive harvesting done by whaling vessels, or the sorry analysis of stranded corpses.

A case in point is Cuvier's beaked whale. When Raymond Gorsse collected a skull near the mouth of the River Galegeon in France in 1804, he sent the specimen to Baron Cuvier at the Musée Nationale d'Histoire Naturelle in Paris. Cuvier studied the skull and mistakenly identified it as a fossil, because of the densely ossified rostrum. He published a description of an extinct whale for which he created the genus Ziphius, from the Greek *xiphos*, "sword," and the species *cavirostris,* from the Latin cavus, "hollow," and *rostrum,* "beak."

Throughout the 1800s there was a proliferation of newly described "beaked whales." In 1826 *Delphinus desmaresti* appeared, in 1850 *Hyperoodon doumetii,* in 1865 *Petrorhynchus capensis* and *Delphinorhynchus australis,* and in 1872 *Epiodon chathamensis.* Detailed work by a number of cetologists, most notably T. H. Huxley and Sir William Turner, succeeded in stemming the flood of "new" species, and clearly established the genus Ziphius. It was also clarified that *Ziphius cavirostris* was alive and well, and far from being permanently imprisoned in rock. However, the highly individual coloration of Cuvier's beaked whale continued to result in "new" species being proposed well into the twentieth century.

More is known of Cuvier's beaked whale than most other Ziphiids, because it seems to strand more frequently than other species in this family, and because the Japanese take three to thirty-five animals annually as part of their Baird's beaked whale fishery. Information that has been collected from such fisheries and strandings puts the average length of Cuvier's beaked whale at between 5.5 and 6.1 meters, with maximum lengths of 6.7 to 7.0 meters, with no apparent difference in size between the sexes. The whales are cigar-shaped and appear to weigh in at between 3,000 and 4,500 kilograms. Their flippers are small and narrow and can be tucked into a slight depression or "flipper pocket" on the flank (a characteristic typical of Ziphiids).

Cuvier's beaked whale has a blunt profile and a small, poorly defined rostrum. It is this profile that has led some to give the animal the descriptive name "goosebeak." Interestingly, teeth erupt only in adult males, and then they have only two, which project forward beyond the rostrum. The bodies of all Ziphiids are heavily scarred, with the oval white marks of cookie-cutter sharks and the parallel striations that are apparently made by the twin teeth of males, presumably during fighting for mates. We know little of their reproductive behavior, or even when they reach sexual maturity. Japanese researchers have reported that males reach sexual maturity at 5.5 meters and females at 5.8 meters, but other researchers have suggested that this is too high. No clear calving season has been identified, and rough estimates of age indicate that if the techniques used on other odontocetes are appropriate for Ziphiids, Cuvier's beaked whales live thirty to thirty-six years.

Cuvier's beaked whales appear to be distributed worldwide except for polar waters. Stomach analysis indicates that they feed on squid in waters under 1,000 meters and fish below that. There is no information available on population size. And not surprisingly, little is known about the whales' behavior; they have occasionally been seen to breach, but seem to avoid vessels, a feature that obviously complicates study. In fact, some have commented that the best place to see them is from the stern of a vessel. It is unlikely that these whales have many natural enemies. Orca probably hunt them on occasion, and so far the human take is small and largely opportunistic. One worrisome factor is the occurrence of potential toxins in their tissues. Tissue analyses have noted DDE, DDT, DDD, and mercury in measurable amounts. The long-term effects of such contaminants are unknown.

We continued to watch the water currents for a reappearance of these intriguing animals. Thirty minutes passed, then forty, and we saw no sign of the Ziphiids. We were simply confirming one of the negatives associated with this species: they avoid vessels.

We were not without entertainment for long. A pod of several hundred bottlenose dolphins was moving through the area. The group was widely scattered, so that as far as we could see were spread the gray backs and erect dorsal fins of dolphins. The pod was fluid in time and space. Animals linked by sound do not need to be linked by sight. They were moving slowly, and only briefly did one or two join our bow.

The dolphins moved ahead of us, and their gray bodies rapidly merged with the silky gray surface of the ocean. We could see a collection of boats on the horizon, congregated over a foaming cauldron of water. The bottlenose dolphins were engulfed in a feeding frenzy over tuna, which were also the focus for the fishermen. The air was filled with birds. A red-billed tropicbird flew over the waves, cutting a dashing figure of white trimmed with black and splashed red. Magnificent frigatebirds, black-vented shearwaters, and parasitic jaegers flocked over the fish. The distinctively beautiful Sabine's gull tripped over the waves, and a lone California sea lion was facing the brunt of the gull's aggression as it surfaced with a large fish gripped between strong jaws. The birds mercilessly mobbed the sea lion, forcing it to dive repeatedly to avoid its persecutors.

Whitecaps covered the area, as dolphins leapt and slapped the surface with flukes, and the fishing boats let out lines and drew in their catches. A thresher shark leapt clear of the water four times in succession, and beyond the mass of animals two humpback whales blew four times, then dove without raising their flukes.

We moved toward the whales. Two minutes later they were both up; they blew twice, then fluked and dove again, leaving swirling flukeprints to mark the point of disappearance. Almost ten minutes later they reappeared, heading toward the mainland. The whales stayed close together, continuing to make shallow rolling dives for the next twenty minutes, each time disappearing for five or six minutes, surfacing and blowing three or four times, and then sinking beneath the silky surface with a single downthrust of their flukes, creating vast flukeprints of smooth water across the surface. On a number of occasions we could track the animals by the appearance of flukeprints at the surface, and more than once we watched the green shadow of the long, tapering flippers build and fade as the whales neared the surface and then descended out of sight.

At one surfacing, the animal with an almost entirely black fluke brought his heavy tail stock across the water's surface in a side-sweeping action at the initiation of his dive. Water was raised up in a curtain of spray and a resounding crash as the flukes slapped on the surface. There followed another brief dive, and the animals continued their heading toward the mainland, the mountains creating a picturesque backdrop to the maneuverings of the mountainous creatures.

The whales were moving steadily, surfacing and diving in synchronized fashion. Occasionally they seemed to speed up, their flukes and tail stocks side-slapping the surface and whipping the water white with activity; then they returned to their routine and continued passage toward the mainland. The short, shallow dives and side-sweep fluking actions suggested that the animals were shallow-feeding, and this was confirmed when one of them swirled the water white at the surface then appeared vertical at the surface, its mouth open and water streaming from its open maw.

A third humpback surfaced at our one o'clock position several hundred meters away. The whale logged at the surface, blowing softly. He then dove steeply, fluking high and vertically. It was the characteristic behavior of a lone singing male. We slowly began our approach so that we might get to a position where we could listen to the whale. The lone animal surfaced after ten minutes and again blew four times while logging at the surface, before lifting his largely white flukes high out of the water as a prelude to another steep, long dive. Mare's tails streaked overhead billowing white against the azure sky, and we continued to monitor the maneuverings of the other two whales so that we could catch up with them later in the day.

A manta leapt next to our vessel as we cut the generator, silencing the ship, and lowered a hydrophone over the side. A few pairs of bottlenose dolphins swam close by, and we listened to the sounds of the ocean percolate up from the depths. The song of the humpback whale grew louder and louder. We could hear the tones, the rise and fall of notes and phrases, the intonation of an artist in the deep. The water was ideally calm, and we drifted under the scorching sun and gently shifting mare's tails that drifted with the wind as we drifted with the current. Everyone on board was quiet, and we sat listening to the sounds, trying to guess at a meaning, but also listening simply for the pleasure of hearing the sounds from the heart and mind of a leviathan.

The hydrophone provided a clear and penetrating vision of the animal hanging motionless beneath our vessel, but we were still removed from the event, reliant on technology to provide a conduit for our appreciation of the song. I wanted to hear the song for myself—without impediment, without cables, wires, and speakers. Five of us suited up and slipped into the water from the stern of the *Don José*. We were floating in about six hundred meters of water. Visibility was poor, and the water was rich with life.

We hung at the surface, spread-eagled at the interface between aqueous and atmosphere. I stared downward into the blue darkness highlighted by starbursts from the sun above me. My breathing sounded so loud as I stared at the tiniest of life forms float by my mask, focusing on the minutiae in deference to staring at the bottomless blackness beneath. It was such a strange feeling, like falling into nothing, hovering over an unseen world, tied to the periphery, limited in every sense, by every sense, from experiencing this new world.

As we swam back and forth from the stern, Luis, the ship's first mate, simply shook his head and said, "tiburon," shark. Only five of us entered the water; the rest remained on board to listen to the whale through the hydrophone. With the exception of our guide, Ron, everyone who entered the water to listen to the whale had been stung the previous day by the Portuguese man o' war. I'm not sure whether that means that we simply wanted to "get back on the horse that threw us," or whether one of the side effects of the neurotoxin is warped judgment.

I held my breath and attempted to dive, but the wetsuit buoyed me upward and I succeeded in lowering my head only a few feet beneath the surface. But in the controlled silence I could suspend my own life and begin to hear, or sense the presence of, that other life far below us. I began to hear the squeaks and groans and whistles. Or rather I could feel them; I could almost feel my body resonate with sound. Moans and cries, yups and snores, ees, oos, whos, and woos—the sound of a humpback whale looking for love.

Humpbacks are the most vocal of the great whales, and although bowheads, blue, and fin whales also sing, it is the humpback that produces the most beautiful sounds. The humpbacks' song is the longest and most complex produced in the animal kingdom. It can last anywhere from six to thirty-five minutes and is often repeated many times in succession, each song identical to the one preceding it. The song is heard principally in the breeding season, although some singers have been heard in Alaskan waters and the feeding grounds, and it is only the male who sings, presumably to impress and attract a mate or exert dominance over other males. Variations have been identified between songs in different whale populations, and mysteriously the song changes annually, with each whale singing the new song that may differ only in slight phrasing style, but differs nonetheless.

It was a nerve-racking experience. Holding my breath, I could feel my blood flow, hear and feel my heart pump. As I stared into the cloaking darkness, I wondered what other inhabitants were below. We are so vulnerable in these waters, buoyed up by the life-giving waters of the planet, but as helpless as the fetus buoyed by the uterine fluids of the mother. However uncomfortable we feel in the water, we also feel an affinity with it, a sense of union that seems to transcend our tentative seaside excursions as children. Perhaps our enthrallment with the aquatic is more visceral than intellectual; perhaps we remember long-forgotten links with our distant ancestors in the deep.

Seeing a reflection of humanity in the whale's eye is not so unlikely a proposition when you remember that we share a common evolutionary heritage that far outstrips our recent terrestrial endeavors. If our ancestors had taken a slightly different route, we might have found ourselves swimming alongside our marine cousins with our arms molded to flippers and legs to flukes. We all tend to have a view of our distant evolution leading us on to our current position, as though *Homo sapiens* were somehow an inevitable product of evolution. We were not inevitable, but the result of a culmination of chances and errors and luck.

When we pulled ourselves back on board the vessel, the hydrophone was silent; the singing had stopped. The rush of adrenaline precipitated by the experience, the fear and the exhilaration, stayed with me for the remainder of the day, and could be revived on subsequent days by visualizing the starbursts of light reaching out beneath, and remembrance of the resonating song within my bones. For one brief moment we had been aquanauts exploring a dark world where the stars are living and the planets sing.

After lunch we were on the move again. Within moments of reviving the engine, we were in the company of four humpback whales, three adults and a calf. In the distance a marlin jumped behind a fishing boat, and we could see the activity as the sport fishermen began to reel in the unfortunate fish.

The whales were incredibly active, and we stayed with them for the next three hours. Two of the adults plus the calf swam close together, blowing, fluking, and diving in unison. The fourth animal was off to port.

The whales were not moving far with each surfacing or dive. They were concentrated within a fairly small area, which made our task a great deal easier. José brought the ship to idle, and we gathered on the w-w deck to witness the interactive spectacle before us. It was possible that two of the adult whales were the (presumed) males that we had been following earlier. Their flukes were fairly distinctive, one largely black and marked by oval barnacle scars as well as the striations of orca, and the other with each paddle of the fluke white surrounded by black and highly scalloped around the edges. Each fluke probably measured three or four meters across.

The humpback whale is largely oceanic in nature, but enters these shallow tropical seas during the winter breeding season. Besides Baja, other North Pacific breeding areas include Hawaii and the region around Taiwan and the Ryukyu Islands. Baja's humpbacks have been identified in southeast Alaska in the Frederick Sound region, and although they seem to show fidelity to their breeding grounds, occasionally a whale from Mexico (principally from Isla Socorro in the Revillagigado Islands) shows up in Hawaii during the same or a subsequent breeding season. The Southern Hemisphere populations of humpbacks are geographically separate from the northern populations, feeding in Antarctic waters during the southern summer and wintering near the equator. As with most other great baleen whales, feeding is largely seasonal and practiced only opportunistically during the breeding season.

There was a great deal of swirling motion in the water between the animals. We watched as flukes were sideslapped across the surface, and as the whales seemed to twist and turn over and over under the water, their flukes or flippers breaking the surface. The whales may have been shallow-feeding on a concentration of fish, the activity designed to corral prey. However, the actions of the female suggested that the two males had more amorous intentions. Every time one of the males approached the female and her calf, the female sped away, frequently blowing a wall of bubbles between herself and her pursuers. On several occasions the calf was on a direct heading toward the *Don José,* and the female intervened in similar fashion to prevent her offspring from approaching us too closely.

The timing of mating and birth in the humpback ensures that pregnant females spend the maximum time in the food-rich northern waters, and that the newly born calf spends the longest period possible in the cradling warmth of the tropics. Humpbacks give birth every one to three years following an eleven-month gestation period, and at birth the calf may weigh in at 1,350 kilograms and measure four to five meters in length. They probably suckle their young for just under a year. The young calf itself will be ready to breed when four or five years old.

As the males and female continued their acrobatic dance around each other, the calf lifted its head clear of the water, showing the barnacles that were already adorning its head and jaw. One such high head up turned into an energetic slap on the water's surface as the calf played around our vessel. Occasionally one of the adults joined in this behavior, pushing its flat rostrum high above the surface so that the sun highlighted the tubercles or stovebolts.

The whales shifted positions around us. The blows and dives were remarkably synchronized, and the sound of the exhalations reached us on the w-w deck—powerful sounds suggestive of combat beneath the waves. The sun was getting low in the sky, and the sunlight was beginning to light starbursts on the surface and silhouetting the actions of the whales. One of the males, the one with white paddled flukes, launched into a tail-slapping display, sending cannon shots of sound through the water before diving out of sight. He repeated this exercise at intervals during the afternoon, apparently attempting some one-upmanship on his competitor.

Our observations of the whales were temporarily distracted as a shark swam across our bow, but the resurfacing of the second male with the orca scars in front of us refocused our attention. The whale brought its huge, broad black flukes high out of the water in a steep dive, swirling the water slick.

The whales were unbelievably close to each other, and at times it was hard to see how they could avoid physical contact as they fluked and dove just a few feet apart. Then, when they returned to the surface, all three adults released their immense exhalations in unison, magnifying the effect in our eyes and creating a cataclysmic air of conflict.

The mainland mountains provided a beautiful backdrop to the dance of these animals, and if the day had been longer we would have stayed with them to see the conclusion to this stirring spectacle. But with sunset less than an hour away, we were forced to pull ourselves away from the humpbacks and begin to head to Los Frailes and our overnight anchorage. Our heading took us into the wind, the whitecaps built, and the temperature dropped dramatically. Only a couple of us stayed on the w-w deck to watch as the land grew larger and larger on the horizon, as the occasional mobula jumped clear of our path or a shark swam across our bow. The updraft off the w-w deck provided sport for an immature California gull and we watched, captivated by this common bird, marveling at the wonder of flight superbly demonstrated by a species that most discount and largely ignore. With such a cursory or dismissive glance, we forget the fantastic phenomenon that is flight.

It was almost dark by the time we dropped anchor. The stars were out in force, reflected beneath us, as was the full moon that rose from behind the mountains and lay a linear silver light across the black waters.

Dawn was just over an hour old when we stepped ashore at Los Frailes to hike in the desert before the sun made such passage unbearable. Those of us who had been sidetracked by the Portuguese man o' war were now able to see the desert in bloom. Light clouds filled the sky, providing a welcome filter to the sun and reflecting the water silver.

We landed on the familiar broad sandy beach backed by a cliff topped with the spiny tendrils of pitaya agria. The sand at our feet was crowded with the tiny prostrate form of the spurge *Euphorbia leucophylla,* which in Spanish is known as golondrina. The tiny white flowers filled with yellow centers spread out across the sand, forming mats of delicate and minute perfection. This attractive little plant is used by the locals as a wash to clean cuts and soothe rashes. It is also used in traditional remedies, often as a tea, to cure rattlesnake bites, kidney problems, and even cancer. The name golondrina means "swallow."

Between the golondrina mats swarmed thousands of ants, all hurrying purposefully across the sand dunes in search of the conical entrances to their nests or some tasty morsel to return to the collective. Tangles of milkweed along the beach revealed the delicate homes of orb-web spiders suspended between long, thin green stems, and lower down on the beach the familiar flotsam of Baja littered the drift line—porcupine fish and the grinning heads of hammerhead sharks.

As we walked further inland, the scene was startlingly different from the one that had greeted me during my first visit three years earlier. The vegetation was verdant and towering. Even the shrubs reached one or two meters high. Turkey vultures circled overhead and settled in the trees above us. A loggerhead shrike let out a long buzzing call, and a verdin repeated its plaintive three-note whistle.

Hooded orioles seemed to dominate the vegetation. Everywhere we looked we could make out the black and orange form of these delightful birds, their presence revealed more than once by *weep, weep, weep* calls from the undergrowth. A pair flew among the intense green of the palm tree fronds, calling and displaying to each other, flashing orange and black with avian affection. Occasionally an orange and black bird turned red, and we realized that cardinals were also at play among the fronds.

The lower story of vegetation was crowded with prickly pear and spiny acacias, and a green-tailed towhee flushed from beneath one of the prevalent lomboy bushes. We were moving into more typical dry desert vegetation, with widely spaced plants and large clearings of dusty red-brown soils. The omnipresent lomboys were rapidly losing their leaves now that the rains had passed, and elsewhere the ground was covered with the euphorbias, whose red leaves provided the tiny plants with protection against the harsh ultraviolet light from the sun.

A jackrabbit was feeding on the slope above us, its huge ears almost cartoonish in character. A white-winged dove called sorrowfully from a cardon at the top of the ridge, and a crested caracara flew close by, giving us a clear view of this impressive large, hawklike bird with white dappling about its wings, a black cap, white neck, and buff-streaked breast.

A cactus wren darted between cholla and pitaya agria while butterflies were lifted and blown across our path, at the mercy of errant winds and currents beyond their control. The cactus wren continually dogged our path. It is a bird that does not fit my idea of what a wren is supposed to look like. My bird-watching experience is founded in the Old World. But here, so many species carry the names of the Old but the form of the New. Often it seems that their similarity was more in the mind of the homesick observer than in the familiar ties of avian relatives.

A short distance off the trail, a pitaya agria presented a tangled mass of spiny tendrils. On one prickly projecting arm was a mass of dried vegetation, straw-like, carefully gathered and fabricated into a cozy dwelling. We stood back and waited for the architect of this structure. We waited five minutes, which length-ened to ten. The group dwindled as people began to investigate other attractions along the trail, but a few of us remained. A movement in the bushes beyond the pitaya drew our attention. We could see a bird darting about, as though assess-ing whether it was safe to return to the nest. We could hear the distinctive chattering of the wren and see the flash of black and white bars across its wings and tail. Finally, after assessing the situation for a few more minutes, the cactus wren landed on the spiny arm in front of the entrance to the nest. The wren's beak was filled with the broken bodies of insects, whose legs and abdo-mens were tangled together in a mass that could be attractive only to the open maws of the fledglings held inside the nest. At least the mass of food was con-firmation that this was indeed a nest, for the cactus wren also constructs these bulky structures for roosting. The wren dipped forward, looking through the el-ongated passage, and darted in. Within seconds the bird reappeared, a fecal sac in its bill. The bird dropped the sac and wiped its bill against its perch. The cactus wren is an attractive bird. In size it is considerably larger than other wrens, measuring up to twenty-two centimeters in length, but it is slim in build, and stands erect and slender on a branch. The bird looked over toward us as it wiped its bill again. In addition to the heavy black and white bars on wings and tail, the bird has a darkly stippled breast and a broad, white eyebrow that stands out even at a distance. The wren flew off, chattering, into the undergrowth. We stayed to watch it return with further offerings to hungry offspring, then de-parted to see what else the trail would reveal.

Before the trail turned back toward the beach, we stopped to look at the tow-ering countenance of the garambullo, or old man cactus. The plant was a mass of vertical, ribbed stems, each topped by hairlike gray spines that give the cactus a bearded appearance. The plant was at least six meters tall, and can grow to more than eight meters in height. The small red fruits are often made into a tea by the locals to treat ulcers, and sliced fruits can be used to ease stingray wounds. To one side of the ancient cactus stood an exotic intruder. It was fa-miliar in shape and color. In gardens back in England, these "red-hot poker" plants are immensely popular. Here in Baja they have spread and multiplied, lifting their yellow and red poker flowers high off the desert floor. Farther down the trail, the furry fruits of the cardon barbon topped the cactus ribs, and nu-merous holes reflected the presence of Gila woodpeckers.

We were in a true desert environment now. Costa's hummingbirds darted about the bright red flowers of the palo adán, antelope ground squirrels peered at us from the tops of boulders, two red-tailed hawks circled on hot desert up-currents far above our heads, and a merlin flew past us like a bullet shot from a gun. Behind us, ridges of exposed sandstone were baked red under the sun, and beyond the ridges were the rounded dry hills of interior Baja. But the trail was taking us down onto the floodplain. This was a face of the desert that I had never seen before. As we entered the floodplain, we came to a lake. The basin depression was completely flooded. It was the first time that standing water had been here since the 1950s. Locals vividly remembered the last time that water had flowed here, as though it were yesterday. The desert demands a long memory from its peoples.

The vegetation was dotted with parasitic dodder that clung to stems and leaves with an asphyxiating cloyingness, and at our feet, nightshade, known in Spanish as Ojo de Liebre (a name taken by one of the gray whale lagoons on the Pacific shores of Baja), lifted purple flowers above the herbaceous layer. Black crab spiders speckled white hid among the leaves, and gray flycatchers stripped insects from the lakeside air. Snowy egrets and cinnamon teals paddled along the shore, the white of the egrets contrasting with the dark mud and occasional sprig of green emergent vegetation. At the far end of the lake, magnificent frigatebirds were diving into the water, momentarily bathing with a flourish of feathers, then taking to the air again. It was like watching an aerial ballet, as the birds dove and splashed and took to the air with such exuberance of spirit that one could almost forget their piratical lifestyle.

The edge of the lake was cluttered with saltbush and jojoba-like plants whose small oval green leaves were thick with the succulence of desert flora. The lake-shore was washed by the gentle motion of breeze-induced waves, the mud and shallows dotted with green algae and tiny cress-like plants. Crouched by the shore, drinking long and hard at the water's edge, was the brilliant blue form of a tarantula hawk wasp. We could see the movement of the wasp's abdomen as it drew in the cool, refreshing water. Its body glinted turquoise and blue in the sunlight, its long legs and antennae almost black, and its wings, folded neatly across its back, an intense orange crisscrossed by the veins and scales of arthropodal ancestry. These wasps feed on spiders. They possess painful stings that paralyze their prey to varying extents. The unfortunate spiders are then fed, often in a comatose state rather than dead, to the wasps' young. When the wasp had finished drinking, it cleaned off its antennae with a gentle, controlled motion of its forelimbs, and then, with an audible buzz, its wings opened and the large insect took to the air and disappeared into the light breeze.

We had walked to the far end of the lake, and now followed the outlet stream down to the beach. The mud flats dominated by saltbush now shifted to golden sand bisected by linear strands of morning glory. The stream channel was heavily colored by green algae that caught tiny air sacs among its single-cell masses, causing light to refract and glisten, so that it appeared tiny rainbows had been captured within the stream. As we reached the beach where our hike had begun, the *Don José* was at anchor in the bay, framed by the rocky cliffs that protected the fragile reef out of sight below. We could see far beyond the anchorage, and whitecaps rose and fell in the distance. It looked as though the wind had picked up, and we returned to the ship anticipating a rough morning out in the gulf.

We left Bahia de los Frailes around midmorning. Toward noon a humpback breached several kilometers ahead, and we changed course so that we would rendezvous near where the whale had last surfaced. When we reached the spot, two whales surfaced close by; both were heading south, and we turned back into the sun so that the wind pounded at our backs. It was a preferred position. Despite the desert sun, when traveling into the wind all warmth was stripped from the air, leaving us breathless and gasping.

The two whales stayed close together. They surfaced, arched their distinctively humped backs in a seemingly exaggerated manner, and dove simultaneously. Neither animal lifted its flukes clear of the surface, although we could see them swirl the water into smooth flukeprints. The animals were moving slowly, almost lethargically, as though dozing. Only once did one of them slap the surface of the water with its fluke and speed ahead of us. The reason for such an acceleration was unclear; perhaps it was due to our proximity, but whatever the reason, both whales returned to their leisurely pace, surfacing briefly with one or two blows before arching their broad backs and shallow-diving, swimming forward under the water, their passage marked by flukeprints and the occasional aqua shadow of their long, tapering pectoral flippers.

It was their seeming curiosity about vessels and their slow swimming speed that made humpbacks an early target for the whalers. The fact that they favor nearshore regions during the breeding season also cast the die for this majestic species. The very place for procreation and continued surety for the species became translated to killing grounds. Coastal fisheries began in the Far East, around Japan, in the 1600s, and had spread to eastern North America by the 1700s. Two hundred years later, the killing had reached the North Atlantic population. However, it was not until the early twentieth century that intensive whaling for humpbacks was initiated. Whaling stations near Antarctica rapidly reduced the southern humpback population as the whales spent the summer in the nutrient- and resource-rich Antarctic waters. The total kill for the Southern Hemisphere from 1904 to 1939 is recorded as 102,298 animals. The impact on the humpback population was inevitable. Humpbacks constituted 96.8 percent of the catch at the South Georgia whaling station in the 1910–11 whaling season, but only 9.3 percent in the 1916–17 season, despite an equivalent or even increased effort by the whalers. The reduced population, however, did not end the kill. For every season from 1948 to 1964, the humpback kill was above 2,400.

In 1966 the International Whaling Commission, under intense pressure from conservation groups and nonwhaling nations, was forced to place the humpback whale on the protected list, and commercial whaling for the species was suspended. Pre-whaling population estimates put humpback numbers at 100,000 animals in the Southern Hemisphere, 15,000 in the North Pacific, and 10,000 in the northwestern Atlantic. The current worldwide estimate for humpback whales is between 10,000 and 15,000 individuals.

The whales in front of us maintained their slow southbound heading, and just after noon we left them to continue our passage north. The *Don José* turned back into the wind, dropping the temperature on the w-w deck and sending spurts of salt spray up onto the deck. A few whitecaps began to appear across the water's surface, and the high cirrus clouds remained the only cover, so that out of the wind the conditions remained hot and desert-like.

We had ninety kilometers to travel by nightfall, and the *Don José* was soon up to speed, taking us toward Isla Cerralvo. We saw a few distant humpbacks heading south, but we needed northbound companions, and they were absent. As the afternoon progressed, the windy w-w deck drove the whale-watchers below, and we relaxed in the galley or "staterooms." It was a long and peaceful, but whaleless, passage.

It was almost six by the time we drew in close to Isla Cerralvo. It is a large island, set parallel to the mainland due east from La Paz just beyond the mainland peninsula. As the crow flies, Isla Cerralvo is less than forty kilometers from the city. At one time, before the birth of the gulf five or six million years ago, the island would have been connected to the mainland. Today the thirty-three-kilometer-long island is just eleven kilometers from the mainland shore.

It had been a long afternoon aboard the *Don José,* with no sign of whales, and we looked forward to setting foot on the island to stroll as the sun died beyond the distant mountains. We landed on a broad, sandy beach backed by hills of scattered low-lying vegetation and tall cardons. The beach was covered with tiny pebbles rounded by wave action, and with shells discarded by the surf. Driftwood littered the high tide line, the crevices between the timber filled with the movements of tiny silverfish. Between the driftwood and shells lay porcupine fish and reef cornetfish, unreal manifestations of the living creature now caught in the permanence of death.

Beyond the sand dunes, various species of euphorbia began to take hold, along with bursora, cholla, and the pitaya agria. The sandy ground between the plants was dotted with piles of droppings from the prevalent black-tailed jackrabbit. Ocotillo plants blocked our way along the trail, living up to their reputation as living barbed wire, and at our feet were the perfectly spherical holes of ghost crabs. High on the hillside stood a few giant barrel cacti—not the true giants of Santa Catalina, but nevertheless undulating mammoths of thorn topped by red flowers. Further along the trail we came across acacia plants, one-meter bushes that were heavy with huge seed pods fifteen centimeters long and more than three centimeters thick. Each pod was constricted at quarter or fifth intervals along its length, and they were curved at either end and very hard; it was impossible to break them open, and even a penknife was blunt against them. The pods belonged to the palo chino (*Acacia peninsularis*), a species endemic to Baja California.

It was quiet out on the trail; only the sound of the surf crashing on the distant rocks and the occasional call of a black-throated sparrow invaded our thoughts, or rather seemed to give them substance. It was somehow refreshing to be out in the desert at the time when the last embers of the sun's light create shadows among the cacti, douse the few brash colors, and bathe everything in a silver monotone that defies capture on film. We could walk, and meander between thorns and ghost crab burrows, unencumbered by the cameras of daylight, just allowing ourselves to drift in quiet contemplation of this desert land so different from the places where most of us are from, and to which we shall return.

On the other side of the cove stood two tall towers. One flashed at intervals of several seconds, warning passersby of rocks off the point (although, sadly, the point was also marked by a white cross, the sign of a death in the waters, perhaps the very event that led to the construction of the light). The second tower was even with the first, and was the former light. Now it was home to a towering osprey eyrie, and as we watched, the flashes of the new light illuminated the birds sitting tight on their nest. Through the spotting scope we could see a single chick. With each flash of light we watched the delicate maneuverings of the adults. What a strange world for the chick to be born into, all of its nights illuminated by a solar-powered lighthouse. When the bird grows up and leaves its towering home, I wonder if the night will look different cloaked in permanent darkness, and whether it will remember the security of the nest and the power of the light that watched over them.

The evening was beautifully cool. The mainland was passing through a multitude of recession planes as the light faded visibly and rapidly with each passing minute. Five pelicans winged their way overhead, flying in formation until they merged with the darkness, and an ash-throated flycatcher gave its rasping call in the cool, gray night.

It was so peaceful on the shore. It would have been wonderful to stay on the beach and fall asleep while the guardian light flashed its protective message, while ospreys clicked bills under the yellow beam, flycatchers danced in the dusk air, and the calls of songbirds were slowly silenced by the night to be resurrected at dawn. The light was fading behind the mainland, and the cacti became ghosts against the hillside, images of the island's past when unknown people stepped ashore and made these rich waters their home.

We returned to the *Don José* in the dark, the waves crashing against the rocks beneath the osprey eyrie. We watched the luminescent trail left by the passage of our panga, and saw stars reflected in the black waters below us, as well as stars that moved and shifted overhead as we passed.

We anchored at Isla Espiritu Santo for the night, and now as dawn broke across the peninsula we continued our northward heading toward the russet rocks and white-crusted salt pans of Isla San Francisco. The week was drawing rapidly to a close, and we were all feeling the tiredness born of exhilaration. The sea was calm, and the cloud cover overhead gave everything a silvery gray, soft appearance. Some of the clouds looked distinctly dark, heavy with moisture, while others were backlit by the sun and sported the classic silver lining. In places the sun was beginning to break through gaps in the clouds, and the mainland mountains caught the rays, magnifying the deep desert colors.

We sat on the w-w deck, savoring the feel of the early morning air. A sea lion porpoised past the ship, and we watched the patterns of the water, marked by slicks of color and tone where the currents of the sea merged and mingled, or split and divided with shifting tides and winds. Isla San Francisco rose in sloping, red grandeur from the gulf in front of us surrounded by a sea of shimmering gray.

A black-tip shark crossed our path, and suddenly we saw more fins slice through the surface, first five, then ten, twenty, fifty. Two or three hundred common dolphins powered over to us. They joined our bow and wake, flinging themselves clear of the water and crashing heavily with massive body slaps. They hit the shimmering surface with pistol shots from flukes, and weaved across our bow with an ability born of millennia in a fluid environment that merges with the body and permits maneuvers and actions denied those of a terrestrial existence. We cheered our responses, trying to convey our thoughts and our excitement as we leaned over the bow listening to the whoosh of exhalations, the snap of the blowhole, and watched the eye of the dolphin looking back at us. No sooner had these protean messengers left, as quickly as they had arrived, than the blows of great whales appeared in the distance and further delayed our arrival at San Francisco.

Three blows rose from the water back toward Isla Espiritu Santo. Slate-black bodies cut the surface, arching huge backs and lifting large sickle fins clear of the water. The cloud cover was complete and unbroken, and the wind was beginning to roll the seas around us. Still, we changed course and began to close on the great whales.

Ten minutes after our first sighting, the whales surfaced. There were four of them, three adult fin whales and a calf. The cow and calf were slightly separated from the other whales, but all were heading toward Espiritu Santo, and we followed at a distance. The whales blew three or four times and then dove. The water bubbled with surface schools of mackerel, and occasionally fish leapt from the water, perhaps fleeing the very whales that we were awaiting. After ten minutes, just like clockwork, the whales surfaced, cutting through the silence with bursts of exhaled air. Three blows and they were down again in perfect synchrony. Mobulas lifted their twin fins from the water as we motored slowly forward, the white ventral side clearly visible and contrasting neatly with the dark water. The cow and calf fin whales surfaced again to our starboard. The other whales were more widely dispersed now, and we stayed with the youngster and its mother. The cow was easy to identify. As she rounded her back, she had distinctive black spots on her flanks, markings that were missing from each of the other whales.

We had been slowly following the fin whales for about ninety minutes. Fish continued to race across the surface, creating a slight feeling of tension in the air. Half-beaks skimmed the surface in panic, and the mackerel continued to mass and swarm below us. It was as though something incredibly traumatic were happening beneath us, something shielded from our eyes, made invisible by the surface layer of water upon which we traveled. If the whales were feeding, then there was panic in the water, as the object of their fervor attempted to escape. And what does that do to our usual interpretation of these animals? Whales are the gentle giants, remember? We do not tend to think of the great whales as hunters seeking out their prey. Perhaps because of their size and our vulnerability, it is something that we do not dwell upon. Or perhaps because the object of their predatory instinct is piscine, such avaricious predation does not bother or offend us. If they were preying on the cute and the cuddly, that is, the mammalian, perhaps they would not be assigned such benign dispositions. Still, we watched as the fish raced back and forth, frothing the water white, jumping clear and descending into darkness, with a slight feeling of foreboding for them, and perhaps a little regret.

We were now back near Isla San Francisco. The meanderings of the fin whales had led us back to where we had started earlier in the morning. The clouds were beginning to spit rain, and all four fin whales were still surfacing with clocklike regularity. In the distance beyond San Francisco a splash echoed across the water. The motion caught our eyes, but the cause escaped us. We watched closely. The tiny form—well, tiny relative to the whales in front of us now,—of a humpback calf cleared the water and delivered another massive crash of white water. The calf breached repeatedly. The cow was surfacing alongside her calf, and the small whale gamboled with clear enthusiasm about its dam. The humpbacks were swimming through a channel marked by small rocky projections above the surface. A skiff was tied to one of these small islands, and the barking of sea lions reverberated across the shallows. The fin whales were heading in the same direction. With the cow and calf fin whales positioned to our port at nine o'clock, we began to approach the two hump-backs. The wind was picking up and beginning to whistle about our ears. The rain was falling steadily, and the wind cooled the w-w deck. The climate was be-ginning to feel more Alaskan than Mexican.

With the fin whales following the same currents that were moving us, we tried to get near the humpbacks. As we maneuvered to parallel them, or waited ahead for them to catch up to us, they surfaced in a different position or di-rection. They didn't seem to be deliberately avoiding us, but they also were not curious enough to approach. The humpbacks continued to tempt us, and the fin whales offered their routine in the background. It was rapidly nearing noon, and we finally pulled into the sculpted harbor of San Francisco as the rain fell and the winds drove us below.

Isla San Francisco is an exquisite island. The rain had dampened the red, green, and brown volcanics of the island, but the ash strata were still clearly vis-ible, and the colors were deepened by the rainfall. As we pulled into the curving, sandy cove, two blue-footed boobies stood out on a rock at the entrance to the bay, their feet in dramatic contrast to the red boulders that served as their perch. An osprey circled overhead, then landed on its elegant eyrie, greeting its mate with a bow of the head and clicking of bills. Previous rains had made the vege-tation on the volcanic hillsides rich and verdant. It was not the vision of desert that I had seen the year before.

The red pebbled beach was trimmed with aqua-colored water and bespeck-led with low-lying plants. The red cliff face on the other side of the bay was evenly dotted with "velcro" plants sporting distinctive yellow flowers and an off-putting smell. Black-throated sparrows darted around the saltbushes that dominated the dune rise beyond the beach. The tiny, colorful euphorbias and iodine bushes were everywhere, imparting a typical desert feel to this recently rainwashed island. The ground between the scattered saltbush, or jellybean plants, was dappled with red and white pebbles, creating a wonderful abstract effect of color and texture. As we meandered between the bushes, a small hermit crab crawled from beneath a saltbush, and rapidly retreated into its red and white speckled shell to hide from us. We waited patiently, sitting silently and still, until the crab poked out stalked eyes, gradually emerged one leg at a time, and continued its seemingly uncoordinated and clumsy walk across the pebbles.

We wandered along the lower part of the hillside. Spiders were strung on webs between the rising fronds and tendrils of plants, and above us the hillsides seemed to be dotted with plants of every shade of green, spatially separated by the demands for water and scarce nutrients from the spartan desert soil. We walked to the heart of the island where the carefully crafted salt pools were tinged red with algae, and the tiny sprouts of salicornia were pushing upward from beneath the mounds of salt. The surface of the water was filled with mosquito larvae, floating in the briny water, lifting their spiracles above the surface to breathe. Our feet sank into the salt as we walked. This island, more than any other that we had visited, really felt its union with the sea. Everything about the land is tied to and the result of the sea—its waves, the salt-laden breeze, and the percolating infusion of water from beneath its very foundations.

We stepped through prickly bursage to reach warm sand back on the beach. Bursage thorns were embedded in our shoes, and we pried them off with penknives and hardened fingers. As we awaited the pangas we waded in the cool, shallow water, savoring the soothing lap of water against dry, sunburned skin. We returned to the ship and were then back on the water to watch the birds in the bay wheel and dive on the dark shadow of sardines that were massing in the green waters.

The rocky shoreline was crowded with brown pelicans in full breeding plumage. Hundreds of them stood proudly on the dark rocks, feathers lightly ruffled in the breeze. Interspersed between these large, comical birds were the equally impressive Heermann's gulls with their blood-red bills, and the magnificent blue-footed boobies with their slicked-back head feathers and blue feet. The small spit projecting from the rocky shore was filled with Caspian, royal, and elegant terns, providing us with the perfect opportunity to see the birds side by side and clearly distinguish them from each other: the slender elegant, the stocky Caspian, and the white-crowned royal that had yet to acquire its breeding plumage. Yellow-footed gulls were parading the shoreline, bullying other birds from the rocks, and brown boobies circled our panga.

The sardines were drawing the birds from their perches. They rose into the air with silent wing beats, circling the bay several times, either in pairs, in small groups, or singly. The birds flew round and round, their speed building until they turned and plummeted into the mass of fish, submerging themselves with a flurry of activity, then rising back into the air like the phoenix rising from the ashes, bills filled with wriggling fish.

It was our final afternoon aboard the vessel, and it was late when we left the protected cove. Our night anchorage would be at Isla Espíritu Santo to the south, and we traveled across the calm gray ocean, topped by dark clouds that occasionally spat rain. The light was fading fast, partly due to the hour and partly due to the poor weather conditions. At one instance we were joined briefly by a dozen bottlenose dolphins who played across our bow, but it was just after five when we saw the spout of a great whale rise in the distance, barely visible against the silver-gray sea. The whale blew four times and then sank beneath the surface, its blue-gray coloring mirrored by all around it.

We idled and waited. Ten minutes passed, then fifteen, and we were sure that we had missed a surfacing against the silky background, light breeze, and rapidly fading light. Exactly twenty minutes and thirty seconds after we had seen the animal dive, the blue whale surfaced off our bow. We were literally looking straight down the animal's blowhole and watched as the rorqual's huge, flat rostrum settled the water and pushed a small wave ahead of it, just like the bow of a vessel. The whale blew three times in leisurely fashion, then dove. We played the waiting game, and like clockwork, after twenty minutes and thirty seconds, the whale surfaced to port.

Blue whales in the St. Lawrence River in Canada (one of the only other places where blues can be seen so close to shore) are well known for their long dives, and those of twenty minutes are not unusual. In Baja, ten- to twelve-minute dives appear to be the rule, but this whale was certainly the exception. We could see a humpback blow and fluke way in the distance, almost at Isla Espiritu Santo, and we waited for our whale to return. It became a running joke on the w-w deck. We went below to collect beers and food, while those on deck kept all apprised of the time. At nineteen minutes everyone was gathered on the deck, and ninety seconds later the whale surfaced, in position, right next to our vessel. Despite the poor light we could see the entire animal under the water. We stood on the w-w deck and looked over the side of the *Don José* to see the length of the whale no more than ten feet from our ship. The whale hung next to us, logging and breathing gently, and then with a slow roll of its gargantuan back, it dove.

Of the many injustices done to the blue whale, one of the most damning on conservation grounds was the implementation of the Blue Whale Unit (BWU). It was a strange concept whereby one blue whale was deemed equivalent in oil production to two fin whales, two and a half humpbacks, or six sei whales. In simple terms, a BWU quota assigned to a whaling nation encouraged whalers to concentrate on the largest whales. In 1950–51, a quota of 16,000 BWU was set for Antarctic waters, a quota that was satisfied by a catch of 32,566 whales from twenty factory ships. Blue whales were the ultimate prize for the whalers. With the International Whaling Commission both unable and unwilling to protect the species, any blue whale that crossed the bow of a whaling vessel was fair game. Regulations regarding length or to protect cows with calves were openly flouted, and species discrimination was undoubtedly suspect. The blue whale continued to suffer until 1966, and even then, pirate whalers, nonmembers of the International Whaling Commission, and unscrupulous official whaling nations continued to take blue whales.

What now of the fate of the blue whale? Whaling was suspended almost thirty years ago, and still blue whales are few. Of the great whales, only the California stock of gray whales appears to have rebounded to its former numbers after intense whaling pressure. For the blue whale, the right, and countless others, numbers remain pitifully low compared to pre-whaling levels. Today, as we sail the oceans, we are lucky to see whales blow on the horizon and occasionally catch closer glimpses of these giants. With the numbers of many species still heavily depressed because of whaling activities a generation ago, future population growth is dependent on our treatment of coastal regions, our control of fisheries and pollution, and our development and use of alternatives for whale-derived products. But even more important to the long-term survival of cetaceans is our change of attitude and culture. It must become unacceptable to kill whales commercially, in the East and in the West, in developed and undeveloped nations. It must become morally and ethically aberrant to condone the killing of cetaceans for oil and meat, meat that rarely finds its way to the dinner table but is more usually ground for animal feed and pet food. This should be so not because whales are necessarily more deserving than a multitude of other species, but because our treatment of them becomes symptomatic of our treatment of the environment in general, and of human and nonhuman animals alike.

The light was painfully poor. We motored slowly forward, watching the water around us, gray on gray becoming ever harder to spot. When the whale surfaced again after the standard twenty minutes and thirty seconds down, we knew that this would be the last surfacing we would see. We also knew that this was probably the last whale.

The blue lay next to us, like a magnificent lover waking from the deep. With an entire ocean to choose from, it is remarkable that for three surfacings, over an hour spent beneath us, the whale should choose to remain so close. We could have reached out and touched this whale, and we did, at least in spirit if not in body. As the whale dove for the final time, we cheered its passing, thanking Poseidon for allowing us such a close look at this spirit of leviathan.

The helm was adjusted and we began our final approach into Candelero Cove on Isla Espiritu Santo. I stood on the stern, watching for the blue to resurface, and as we moved further and further away, I saw the spout rise and the gray body catch the last light of day before both faded from sight.

Nature

O nature I do not aspire
To be the highest in thy quire,
To be a meteor in the sky
Or comet that may range on high,
Only a zephyr that may blow
Among the reeds by the river low.
Give me thy most privy place
Where to run my airy race.
In some withdrawn unpublic mead
Let me sigh upon a reed,
Or in the woods with a leafy din

Whisper the still evening in,
For I had rather be thy child
And pupil in the forest wild
Than be the king of men elsewhere
And most sovereign slave of care
To have one moment of thy dawn
Than share the city's year forlorn.
Some still work give me to do
Only be it near to you.
—*Henry David Thoreau*

Our final day aboard the *Don José* was spent in quiet contemplation as we neared La Paz. The sky above us was gray and overcast, the horizon obscured by clouds. A few of us sat on the w-w deck, hoping to spy whales in the final traverse of these rich waters. The sea's surface was calm and silky gray, but as the desert rains began to fall, our final reminder of El Niño, we took refuge inside, after initially allowing the warm droplets to cleanse our minds and souls.

We pulled smoothly into harbor and I gathered my camera equipment and notebooks. I ordered pages and dog-eared corners that I read and reread, trying to recapture moments that now seemed so distant in time and memory as to fade from reality and enter imagination. The rain-splattered pages, marked by sand and salt, would be my guide in the weeks, months, and years to come. I hope that the memories will never fade. I can look back over every voyage that I have ever undertaken and remember moment by moment what unfurled in front of my eyes. But if I ever need some reinforcement, I have the ink-stained pages and species names taken down as the images flashed before me under the desert sun, on top of the rolling sea, or washed by the uplifting buoyancy of the reefs and coves.

There is an arrogance in the written word—an assumption that what you write is going to be of sufficient interest to justify the amount of paper being used, as well as the time and effort of the reader. I know that what I saw in Baja was, and is, important. The sights and sounds of a wilderness stocked with devilfish and blue whales will always be of value in our world. I write for those who will never see the eye of the whale or feel the pliant skin beneath their hands, watch the soaring frigatebird and osprey, or rescue a sea hare. And I write for those who think that they will never care. Because one day when the mountains and ocean stand empty and silent, everyone will care. I write these words so that some may realize what they have now that is too precious to lose. So when children ask, "What is a whale?" let them see for themselves in Baja, or Alaska, or New England, or Australia, or Patagonia, or Ireland. In the Atlantic, the Pacific, the Antarctic, the North Sea, the Indian Ocean, or the Mediterranean. Let them experience another world, peopled by other than people.

Many people are drawn to a different life, wishing to experience something that is apart from the everyday, the usual. For some this means leaving the world that they know and wholeheartedly adopting a new lifestyle, while others are able to do exactly the same thing without ever leaving their home ports. It is all a state of mind, a desire and willingness to change ourselves more than our surroundings.

It is our mental state, our intellectual capacity, that allows us the luxury of consideration. There are certain things that we believe and think because of what we are: human. But what is it that makes us human? It is not our arms and legs, our bodily form. It is our hearts and minds—our souls. If this is true of us, then it is also true of the other animals with which we share this planet. If it is how we think and act that makes us what we are, then we should be able to make a similar allowance for those other animals, particularly other mammals that share our evolutionary heritage and a common historical gene pool.

Our modern-day achievements are the result of a culmination of evolutionary pressures on our ancestors and on their ancestors, down the chain of life that spawned the sea hare and the side-blotched lizard, the osprey and the devilfish. We are not the pinnacle of evolution, simply one of many emergences that have flourished upon the face of the Earth in a flash of geologic time insignificant in the grand order of the planet. Other forms have seen more, experienced more, and survived infinitely longer.

We are fortunate in being able to stare at the fossils of life long since vanished and consider things past, present, and future. It is a gift to be able to see what others have only dreamed of. On the shores and in the waters of Baja California, we can behold Guy Murchie's *The Seven Mysteries of Life:* The *abstraction* of wind, waves, and sun on the silica shores of this changeling desert. The *interrelation* of life, plant, and scurrying animal on the shore, of life larger than life in the pristine clear waters of lagoons and bays. The *omnipresence* of the whale, seen and unseen, on land and in the waters at our feet. The *polarity* of predator and prey, the electrical pulse of hearts and minds, the survival and continuation of life and thought. The *transcendence* of the expression of life. To look at Baja or any natural system is to have the impression of life, thought, and continuous existence above and beyond the created universe about us. In the animalcule and plant we see the *germination,* the creation of new life following life. Barren ground yields green, clear waters that reveal a microcosm world out of sight, and the sky above transports the golden warmth of life to the Earth's surface. And finally, the *divine* nature of the world around us, all-powerful, all-seeing. Cold and hot, forgiving and unyielding. Life itself on a blue-green planet in a single universe among many universes, a single planet among many planets. A single home alone.

Abstract, interrelated, omnipresent, polar, transcendent, germinating, and divine Baja. Behold all the wonders of life on the beaches and in the eye of the whale, for these are the sights of the world and the emotions of humankind—*Homo sapiens,* the ultimate destroyers and the ultimate altruists, the environmental schizophrenics whose ability to protect is immense but whose seeming desire to destroy polarizes our lives and threatens those seven mysteries that sustain our very existence.

With whales we can see what such polarity in view does—how within the space of one hundred years the waters of Baja were transformed from red tides of commercial harvest to the outreaching of hands into warm, life-supporting waters. But how easily such polarity of effort could be reversed, and the actions of mothers and calves once again lead them to fall to the lance to be rendered on the decks of vessels.

We can ensure that such a dichotomy never returns again to the whale, and perhaps avoid such a fate for ourselves. We understand our own actions; we have no knowledge of whether other animals understand either their actions or ours. It would be fitting to begin with the premise that we and they are equal under the vision of this abstract universe.

The Human Problem

We are as much strangers in nature
as we are aliens from God.
We do not understand the notes of birds.
The fox and deer run away from us;
the bear and tiger rend us.
We do not know the uses of more than a few plants,
as corn and the apple, the potato and the vine.
Is not the landscape, every glimpse of which
hath a grandeur, a face of him?
Yet this may show us what discord is between
man and nature, for you cannot freely admire
a noble landscape if laborers are digging
in the field hard by.
    The poet finds something ridiculous
in his delight until he is out of the
sight of men.
           —*Ralph Waldo Emerson,* Nature, *1836*

In 1974, William E. Schevill edited a book entitled *The Whale Problem: A Status Report.* The book arose out of a 1971 conference of experts gathered to assess whether a future existed for whales at the hands of humans. I have taken the title of that book and turned it around, for the "whale problem" is founded not in the oceans but on land. The problem with whales is human.

The human problem is multifaceted. It includes an ever-expanding population, encroachment on coastal regions, and increased exploitation of marine resources—mineral, oil, and biological. It encompasses monetary issues of industry and government. And because of our cultural evolution and sentience, it includes issues of morality and ethics. The final sections of this book address

"The Human Problem"—why it exists, and how, or even whether, we should attempt to correct it.

We need to step back in time to understand the apparently innate fascination that people have with whales. In the seat of human society, among the ancient Greeks and Romans, cetaceans were viewed as something other than convenient packages of meat and blubber. We can relive some of that history in the pages of Aristotle, Plato, the tales of Delphi, and the Book of Job.

The beginning of human-whale relationships saw gods reflected in the whale. The word for "dolphin" in Greek is delphys, closely related to delphis, meaning "womb." Greek mythology tells of Apollo Phoebus, the sun god, and his defeat of Delphyne, the dolphin or womb monster. The Oracle at Delphi is one of the most important in Greece, and was continuously inhabited from the fourteenth century B.C.E. According to legend, it was originally a temple to Gaea, the Earth goddess. When Apollo defeated Delphyne, he went to the temple of Gaea, then known as Pytho, and killed her serpent child, Python, to found his own oracle. The symbolism to the Greeks was clear: Apollo defeated the Earth and leapt from the womb of creation, the sea, in the guise of a dolphin. To kill a dolphin was to unleash the wrath of the gods: dolphins were the reincarnated souls of the dead; you could go out to sea and hear them singing. To kill a dolphin was to silence the song, and offend the gods. Dolphins adorn the temple of Knosso (which dates to the late Minoan II period around 1400 B.C.E.) and the palace of Phaestos. Artists, sculptors, and minters used the form of the dolphin, often surprisingly accurate renditions, to decorate frescoes, pottery, and coins. With the rise of Christianity, the roles of the dolphin and whale in creation remained. Christian myths and legends incorporated much that had been written in earlier times. Dolphins saved St. Martian, St. Basil the Younger, and Callistratus from martyrdom, and when the martyred St. Lucian of Antioch was thrown into the sea, a dolphin bore his body to Drepanum for a Christian burial. Early Christians saw the dolphin as a symbol of rebirth just as the Greeks had, and some historians believe that it was the dolphin, not the fish, that led to the secret symbol that marked the meeting place for persecuted Christians.

The affinity that people had for dolphins was always more muted when considering the great whales. These leviathans were simply too large and too threatening to be treated with the love shown their smaller cousins. But the whale did instill awe and fear into the people. The whale, often depicted with scales and gills (although Aristotle had identified whales and dolphins as mammals around 344 B.C.E.), was held up as the messenger and servant of God. The words of the Book of Job are some of the most powerful ever written about leviathan, and the story of Jonah takes the whale as the instrument of divine will, against which humankind is powerless.

Many early societies based their myths and legends on the form of the whale: Haida, Maori, Aborigine, Chinese, Inupiat, Polynesian, Celtic, Norse, and Classical. Subsistence cultures tied the whale to the welfare of their society. Without the whale they would cease to exist. Their stories reflect this duality of thought: hunting and killing the animal on the one hand, and raising it up as all-powerful on the other. You could kill a whale only if the animal willingly gave itself to the hunter—if you showed disrespect for the animal either before or after the hunt, then future hunts would be barren, and the animals would no longer give themselves to the people. In 1979, Eben Hopson, a Native Alaskan from Barrow, stated, "The whale is the focal point of our life and culture. We are the People of the Whale. Catching and distributing whale is our Eucharist and our Passover. The feast of the whale is our Easter and Christmas—an ancestral celebration of the mysteries of life."

In Islamic mythology, Allah lifted the Earth onto the back of the whale for stability. In Vietnam, the people believed that whales were sent by the "God of the Waters" to watch over fishermen and sailors and to carry the shipwrecked back to shore. Tradition told that anyone finding a dead whale or dolphin was the eldest son of that animal, and was responsible for leading the mourning and depositing the animal's remains in a sanctuary. They believed that whenever a whale or dolphin died, the rain would pour and the wind rage for three consecutive days. In ancient Japan, the hunters also revered the animal that they wrought from the ocean with spear and harpoon. The dead whales were honored with religious services, a Buddhist name, and shrines set up looking out to sea in the hope that other whales would come forth to offer themselves to the whaler. In western Africa, whales were the ruling spirits of the sea, and to find a dead whale was the portent of widespread mourning, since the people knew that their destiny was one with the ocean and its rulers.

As societies changed and grew over centuries, our innate reverence and fascination with the natural world changed. Increasing urbanization, industrialization, and the fading power of myth and legend, as well as the adoption of a Christian creed that lauded domination over the nonhuman, all served to divorce humankind from a close, balanced association with the world that spawned them. We can trace this change, prophetically, to some of those early myths and legends.

In 109 C.E., Pliny the Younger spoke of a human-dolphin encounter on the coast of Africa. A young peasant boy was befriended by a dolphin called Simo who had saved him from drowning. The two were inseparable. They played in the bay, the boy riding on the dolphin's back. People began to hear of this remarkable friendship and came from afar to witness it for themselves. The town grew and became crowded. The local people began to realize that they could make a great deal of money from the visitors. However, the influx soon became so great that the town could no longer cope. Too many people wanted to see the dolphin. Arguments broke out among the townspeople. The elders realized that something had to be done quickly to save the stability of their community.

They killed the dolphin.

> There is something extremely painful in the destruction of a whale . . . yet the object of the adventure, the value of the prize, the joy of the capture cannot be sacrificed to feelings of compassion.
>
> —Captain William Scoresby, Jr., 1820

Somehow we shifted from that time when hunters prayed to the whale for permission to kill, when gods took the form of dolphins, and boys rode upon their backs, to a time of easy destruction. The earliest hunting of whales is still a relatively recent occurrence in the history of the human race. Evidence suggests that whales were being hunted five thousand to six thousand years ago, perhaps as far back as eight thousand years ago in Alaska. The focus, however, would have been on stranded animals, or those blocked by ice. Large-scale hunting was simply impossible. Before the arrival of "civilization," only the slow whales could be pursued by canoe, kayak, and open rowboat, and then the whales had to float when dead, or the prize was lost. Other people caught entire pods of whales by driving them ashore, a method that continues to this day in the Danish Faeroes, to the north of the British Isles.

In Europe, early whaling was practiced by people of Stone Age Norway as far back as 2200 B.C.E., and in the twelfth century the Basques were hunting the slow right whale in the Bay of Biscay and possibly into the North Sea. Whaling slowly spread throughout Europe, but the hardships and limitations kept the whaling industry small-scale and largely coastal. Although the numbers of right whales taken by the Basques were small, the population apparently could not support even that level of whaling, and the animals soon became scarce. The Basques began to look farther afield.

In 1585, the English captain John Davis found the straits between Greenland and Newfoundland that now bear his name. The following year, the Dutch explorer William Barents rediscovered the Svalbard region, and the whalers flocked north to Spitzbergen. This was the turning point. For four hundred years, until the imposition of the temporary whaling moratorium in 1985, the great whales were hunted and rendered in all the oceans of the world—1585 can be seen as the transition from reverence and ideology to commercial and industrial fervor. In 1610, the first major whaling enterprise to Spitzbergen was dispatched by Queen Elizabeth I. The Dutch and British continued to send whalers north, battling each other over rights to the spoils of the harpoon.

As the population of northern right whales declined under the attention of the whalers, the catcher boats shifted their sights to the bowhead whale of the high Arctic. Both right and bowhead whales were rapidly depleted, and are still among the most threatened of the great whales. Spitzbergen declined in importance as the whalers moved their vessels to Greenland and the Davis Straits in the early part of the eighteenth century.

American coastal whaling had seen its start in the closing years of the seventeenth century around Nantucket and Long Island. By the beginning of the eighteenth century, whaling was well established but still coastal. Then, in 1712, an unfortunate occurrence opened the alongshore whalemen's eyes to the bounty of pelagic whaling, when a vessel was blown far from land and encountered sperm whales. With the right whales seemingly in their final decline, the realization that whales were offshore for the taking was welcomed by whalemen, and they outfitted ships to take them far from land. Besides sperm whales, humpbacks were taken whenever the opportunity presented itself.

By the mid-eighteenth century, whaling ships were making voyages to the equator and beyond. The 1760s saw a significant advance in the technology of the time, with the invention and installation of brick ovens to rend blubber to oil on board ship. The use of ovens allowed the ships to stay at sea longer, and to reach into tropical waters that had previously been out of reach to vessels trying to keep their catches cool. Alongshore whaling off the American coast declined in the early nineteenth century as the whales vanished, but pelagic whaling, particularly for sperm whales, increased. During the earlier days of whaling, the sperm whales had been largely left alone, since many considered their meat unpalatable. However, the eighteenth century saw escalating demand for oil for candles and lamps, and the unfortunate sperm whale held oil that was ideally suited for this purpose. Sperm whaling expanded rapidly during the first half of the nineteenth century to meet that demand.

Southern Hemisphere whaling grew to take the southern right whale, and back in northern waters American whalers reached the Pacific Arctic in 1848 to finish off the remaining stocks of northern right whales and bowheads. Southern Hemisphere whaling occurred off Brazil, Argentina, and the Falklands, with the British at the forefront of the decimation. Despite the 1859 discovery of petroleum in Pennsylvania, whale products were still in strong demand. Petroleum lessened the demand for whale oil as an illuminant, and toothed sperm whales were hunted less intensively, but their oil was still used as a lubricant. The mysticete whales continued to be taken for their baleen (also known as whalebone), used for many "essential" products, such as umbrellas, whips, crinolines, and shoehorns. As the Arctic waters were depleted, baleen whales in the North and South Pacific suffered as the whalemen relocated their efforts.

In 1864, Svend Foyn invented the explosive grenade harpoon, and that marked the beginning of the modern whaling era that ultimately robbed the oceans of the whales and sent species to the brink of extinction. Perhaps the transition should not have been surprising. The whales might have been able to survive the pressures of whaling as long as the whalers were restricted by distance from port, and by the speed of their vessel. But the combined introduction of brick ovens, explosive harpoons, and steam-driven vessels allowed the intensive and prolonged hunting of the faster-swimming rorquals after the slower-swimming Balaenidae had already been depleted. With no international cooperation between whaling nations, whaling replayed the classic interpretation of the "tragedy of the commons." No one nation had any incentive to rein in its take of whales to ensure a long-term sustainable industry. Each nation was in business solely for itself, and that led to a free-for-all. Since no single nation owned the resource, no single nation could protect it.

Perhaps the whalers didn't realize what they were doing (although the fate of the right whales and bowheads should have been clue enough), perhaps they thought that the Pacific and Antarctic waters held so many whales that even uncontrolled whaling could never deplete the numbers, or perhaps the companies involved were so concerned with their own profitability that they really didn't care. The result was entirely predictable: too great a demand for whale products, too many whalers, and not enough whales.

Svend Foyn's harpoon gun ushered in a massive change of pace in the whaling industry. The whalers were suddenly too efficient for their own good. They were now truly international, and in 1904 they began to exploit the richest whaling grounds in the world—the Antarctic. The whalers focused on the fast-swimming rorquals—the blue, fin, and sei whales. The whales could no longer outswim the whaling ships, and with the introduction of machinery for inflating a dead whale by injecting air into the carcass, the new era of whaling was well established. The vessels rendered whales with staggering efficiency. Early whaling in the Antarctic, from 1904 to 1924, was characterized by land-based operations, principally on South Georgia and the South Shetlands. Norway led the way, closely followed by Great Britain.

The 1920s heralded vast ships fitted with stern chutes to haul the whale on board for flensing and rendering to oil. These factory ships could operate at sea for months at a time, with no need to pull into land-based stations. The size of the vessels was astounding. One of the first ships to ply the Southern Ocean was the British *Southern Empress,* with a cubic capacity of more than 12,500 tonnes. Demand for whale oil was escalating rapidly. Although no longer used as an illuminant due to the use of petroleum, whale oil could now be converted to solid fats, leading to a flourishing soap and margarine industry. Even before the widespread introduction of factory ships in the twenties, the Antarctic whale populations were in rapid decline.

During the 1910–11 Antarctic whaling season, humpbacks accounted for more than 95 percent of the total catch. In 1917–18 they constituted just 2 percent of the catch, despite increased effort and a greater number of catcher boats plying the waters. However, the only thing that the decline in humpback numbers did was to redirect efforts toward other whales that were more numerous. Of course, the ultimate prize was the blue whale. Pelagic whaling peaked in the early 1930s, and the blue whale was the focus. In the 1930–31 season, whalers took 29,000 blues. Following seasons saw the catch drop to 19,000, then 14,000, 9,000, 7,000 in 1950–51, 2,000 in 1960–61, and finally zero in 1965 following international protection for the species. The blue whale was commercially extinct.

Earlier I said that perhaps the whalers did not realize what they were doing. In the face of statistics such as those above, that is clearly too kind an assessment. In 1911, the British Museum of Natural History called for research into the southern slaughter. Protective measures were demanded from the Colonial Office. We can find statements made as early as 1912 prophesying the future of whaling: "Foyn's harpoon gun still pursues its march of death through the oceans. . . . With so limited a power of reproduction the stocks of whales will inevitably be reduced."

In 1924, the research ship *Discovery* began making voyages into Antarctic waters. But as one researcher was later to write: "As all the world knows, the immense expenditure of time, effort and money was futile, for the information that should have guided the whaling industry was constantly disregarded, the populations of whales were severely reduced and the whaling industry, once profitable in material and money, was ruined."

The Bureau of International Whaling was established in Norway in 1929 to record whale catch statistics, and in 1931 the League of Nations (the forerunner of the United Nations) drew up the International Convention for the Regulation of Whaling, which came into force in 1935. Japan and Germany failed to ratify the treaty. The convention was a paper tiger; few countries adhered to it, and whales were afforded little protection. In 1937, the International Agreement for the Regulation of Whaling was signed in London, but once again Japan failed to ratify. The whaling nations attempted to manage stocks with the infamous Blue Whale Unit (BWU), but that was a dismal failure that simply placed the focus on the largest whales. The 1937 agreement did impose minimum lengths for blue and fin whales and set opening dates for the whaling season. The agreement also tried to protect females with calves and to form a sanctuary in the Pacific sector of the Antarctic. Both right whales and gray whales were given complete protection, and the humpback was protected south of 40° south latitude. Despite these advances, total catches continued to exceed 30,000 whales a year, with the exception of the brief breathing space during the Second World War.

In 1946 the International Whaling Commission (IWC) was founded, and fourteen whaling nations signed the International Convention for the Regulation of Whaling. The aim of the organization was to achieve the maximum sustainable yield of whale stocks, and thus to protect the future use of the resource. The history of the IWC has been mixed and of dubious value to the whales—just as the League of Nations failed to enforce its convention, so the IWC lacks the teeth to protect its charges. During its early days, the IWC incorporated the previous agreements into its structure, so that right and gray whales continued to be protected, as did Antarctic humpbacks. The IWC also continued use of the Blue Whale Units to regulate whaling activities rather than treating each species individually. Species after species declined under this "management," the largest going first. To read the catch statistics is to be left with a feeling of helplessness. In the 1950s the blue whale catches crashed, and whalers turned to the fin whale. In the 1960s the fin whale catches crashed, and the whalers turned to the sei whale. In the 1970s the sei whale catches crashed, and the whalers turned, finally, to the smallest of the rorquals, the minke whale.

Perhaps it is wrong to blame the International Whaling Commission. It could only suggest to its members what course should be taken, and the convention was written in such a way that a nation could veto a decision, and thus avoid compliance. But the IWC was established to regulate whaling activities to maintain maximum sustainable yields—that was its *modus operandi*. If it could not do that, then it should perhaps have questioned its own future. Too often, until the imposition of the moratorium in 1985, the IWC was forced by its very structure to appease the whalers. In 1949, the IWC reneged on its protection of humpback whales in the Antarctic, despite the seriously threatened nature of the stock, and permitted a quota of 1,250 animals (actual catches ranged from 1,500 to 2,100—a blatant violation of even this dangerously generous allowance). A similar blatant disregard for species survival was shown to the blue whale. Despite clear evidence that the blue was being depleted to levels that courted extinction, the IWC failed to act, and permitted whaling on a scale that probably ultimately sealed the fate of the largest animal to grace the planet. The politicking surrounding the blue whale deserves to be repeated, simply because it almost defies belief. George L. Small detailed the International Whaling Commission's official treatment of the blue in his 1971 book, *The Blue Whale*. It makes for sober reading.

When the IWC was established in 1949, the blue whale was already in trouble, and everyone connected with the organization knew it. The first three years of the organization's life were concerned with finances, rulemaking, and committees. The blue whale was not even addressed.

In 1953, in the face of clear evidence of stock collapse, the Scientific Subcommittee recommended that blue whale catches be substantially reduced. However, one whaling nation, the Netherlands, objected, and the catch-reduction recommendation was dropped under threat of a veto. In 1954 the IWC met in Tokyo. Again the Scientific Subcommittee proposed drastic measures to protect the dwindling stocks of blue whales; still the Netherlands objected, and the threatened veto prevented the plan from being formally presented. In 1955 the IWC met in Moscow. The catch levels were not reduced; only the opening date of the blue whaling season was delayed for ten days. Incredibly, the 1955 meeting also opened the "Whale Sanctuary" to the factory ships. This small region of Antarctic waters had been protected since 1937. Rather than protect the few remaining whales in that region, the IWC agreed to let even more fall to the lance.

The 1956 meeting was given the catch statistics for the 1955-56 whaling season to review. The catch of blue whales had continued its precipitous decline. Only 3 were taken at South Georgia, a station that had taken 3,689 thirty years earlier. Still, the IWC was forced to deal with the financial realities that had taken hold of the whaling nations—the number of factory ships was increasing; if the whale quota was reduced, the whalers would make less money. That soon there would not be enough whales to continue whaling at all did not seem to be of concern. In both 1956 and 1957, the focus of debate was on the fin whale, not the blue. The reason was simple. Blue whales were so rare that many whaling nations now considered them irrelevant. It was the fin whale that was supporting the whaling industry—if the fin whale population collapsed, whaling as a viable concern would probably disappear.

In 1958, the Netherlands forced the IWC to increase, not decrease, the catch levels permitted in Antarctic waters. The drive to protect the blue whale was going backward. The number of factory whaling ships operating in the Antarctic continued to increase. The IWC was powerless to do anything about it. A central tenet of the IWC had been to respect the "freedom of the seas." That meant the commission had no power (or right) to limit the lawful activities of any nation on the high seas. Such an inability to act made the IWC worse than useless in protecting whales. It was supposedly established to secure a future for whales as well as whaling. It was about to fail on both counts.

The 1959 meeting was subverted by internal bickering between the remaining pelagic whaling nations (the Soviet Union, Norway, Japan, the United Kingdom, and the Netherlands). The whalers threatened to pull out of the IWC and go their own way, taking what they wanted from the last whales. Both Norway and the Netherlands did walk out, with the Netherlands stating that they would not abide by any whaling regulations. The Dutch set their own quota in the Antarctic and quadrupled their catch of blue whales.

In 1960, the IWC decided that it needed more information about the rate of decline of each species, and it established a "Committee of Three" scientific experts. Meanwhile in the Antarctic, South Georgia catcher boats managed to find only five blue whales during the whole season. The clear decline of the blue led the IWC to table a motion simply delaying the start of the blue whale "harvest" by two weeks (it was the only protection that they could offer). Japan objected to the delay and the motion was voided. The reason? Norway and the Netherlands, as nonmembers, would not be bound by the delay, and that would place Japanese whalers at a disadvantage. Once again, short-term economics took precedence over sound judgment.

The IWC tried to tempt Norway and the Netherlands back into the fold by suspending all quotas in Antarctic waters. Norway did return, but the Netherlands held out. The result was that for two years there were no quotas in effect to control whaling levels. To appease the whalers, the whales were sacrificed, again. The 1960–61 season took 41,289 whales, the highest catch since World War II, and the second-highest catch in the history of Antarctic whaling. So much for trying to control the whalers.

The Netherlands had rejoined the IWC by 1962, and the Antarctic quota suspension came to an end. The pelagic whaling nations agreed to split up the quota between them, and the whaling continued. For the first time in whaling history, not a single blue whale was taken by South Georgia whaling stations. The Scientific Committee recommended complete and immediate protection for the blue; Japan refused to withdraw its previous veto of the delayed opening in the season. The 1962–63 whaling season in the Antarctic took about 1,000 blue whales. Researchers estimated that those 1,000 animals represented 60 percent of the remaining population. In 1963, it was estimated that only 600 blue whales remained in Antarctic waters.

The "Committee of Three" reported back to the commission in 1963, and they recommended that the total Antarctic quota for all species be reduced to under 5,000 Blue Whale Units. Japan refused to consider such a reduction, and demanded no less than 10,000 BWUs. Since a veto by Japan would have returned the quota to the previously imposed 15,000 BWUs, the IWC was forced to accept the Japanese proposal. For the blue whale itself, the "Committee of Three" recommended complete protection. It was beginning to be a familiar cry at IWC meetings; unfortunately, so was the response. Japan objected. A compromise was reached whereby all blue whales in Antarctic waters were protected, except for those found between 40° and 55° south latitude from 0° to 80° east longitude. During the preceding whaling season, 75 percent of all blue whales killed had come from this exempted area. Japan had won again, and the killing continued.

Surely by now the time was approaching when the blue whale would get the protection it deserved. At the 1964 meeting it was reported that Norwegian whalers had seen only eight blues during the entire 1963–64 season. The IWC passed a motion banning the blue whale hunt in the exempted area. Japan and the USSR vetoed and the killing continued.

Although twenty blue whales were taken in the 1964–65 season, none were taken by the Japanese fleet. The commission made one final appeal, asking its members to agree to total protection for the blue. For the first time all agreed, and the blue whale was given full protection in 1966. The reason for the agreement now was obvious: the whalers were no longer catching blue whales; it no longer mattered to them whether they were protected or not. The blue whale was history. It had taken the whaling industry just sixty years to destroy what evolution had taken millennia to create.

And what of the blue whale now, after almost thirty years of complete protection? The 1989 Comprehensive Stock Assessment released by the IWC estimated that only 500 blue whales survived in the Southern Hemisphere, perhaps 1,600 in the North Pacific, and a few hundred in the North Atlantic. The total world population was certainly no more than 2,500, out of a pre-whaling population of perhaps 230,000 animals. Some recovery has been reported since the 1989 figures were released, and the North Pacific population may number as many as 3,000 animals. But, as with the disparate figures given for the fin whale, the truth is we really don't know how many whales there are.

The British and Dutch both pulled out of Antarctica in the early 1960s, with Norway following some years later. Only Japan and the Soviet Union remained as major players in the Southern Ocean. Fin and sei whales continued to be the focus of their activities. The total world catch of baleen whales between 1956 and 1965 was 403,490; during that period, 228,328 of the toothed sperm whales were killed. It was not until 1972 that the Blue Whale Unit system of stock "management" was abandoned, and individual quotas were set for different species. It was a change of management technique that came too late. By 1975 the blue, humpback, and right whales were under complete protection, but quotas were still being set for fin, sei, minke, and sperm whales.

Nineteen seventy-five also saw the introduction of the so-called New Management Policy. This policy divided the different species of whales into stocks based on their abundance. The International Whaling Commission was trying to live up to its original objective: to establish whaling based on the principles of Maximum Sustainable Yield. Maximum Sustainable Yield comes from the idea that wild populations produce a certain annual surplus that can be culled without causing the decline of the main stocks—like removing the interest on a bank account while leaving the principal in place to continue generating funds. Protection Stocks were defined as whale stocks that were more than 10 percent below the level giving Maximum Sustainable Yield (MSY); Sustained Management Stocks were defined as stocks that were between 10 percent below and 20 percent above the level giving MSY; and finally, Initial Management Stocks were defined as whale stocks that exceeded 20 percent above Maximum Sustainable Yield.

Unfortunately for the whales, there were two major flaws in this plan. First of all, it was the whaling nations who were still entrusted with the oversight and implementation of the scheme. Secondly, the maintenance of Maximum Sustainable Yield presumed that we already had enough information to make those assessments, primarily just how many whales there were and what factors influenced their population levels. Even with near-complete information, the various ways available to calculate the MSY level also led to widespread criticism of the technique as a management tool. If estimates of the total number of whales were in error, even by as little as 10 percent, there was a very real danger that these "management techniques" would simply lead to an accelerated decline in numbers.

Whaling in the later part of the twentieth century had more to do with politics than biology. As the 1970s rolled around, the plight of the whale was taken up with a vengeance by conservationists. Suddenly, the "Save the Whale" cry became the banner of the environmental movement. The early 1970s saw the gradual rise of environmentalism in the United States and Europe, a rise that would continue for the next two decades. In 1972, the United Nations Conference on the Human Environment convened in Stockholm. The conference called for a ten-year moratorium on commercial whaling. The motion was formally adopted by the United Nations General Assembly and by the International Union for the Conservation of Nature and Natural Resources (IUCN, now known as the World Conservation Union). The International Whaling Commission turned down all such appeals.

In the United States, 1972 saw the passage of the Marine Mammal Protection Act, which made it a federal offense to "hunt, harass, or kill, or to attempt to hunt, harass, or kill any marine mammal" in U.S. waters, with the exception of a small subsistence take in Alaska. The same year also saw the publication of the Club of Rome environmental treatise, *The Limits to Growth*. In 1973, the Convention on International Trade in Endangered Species of Wild Fauna and Flora (CITES) was signed to control the trade in endangered animals and plants. Environmental awareness and legislation were proliferating around the world, but more important, there was the growing realization that public opinion could change the policies and actions of corporations and governments. Friends of the Earth was founded in 1970, Greenpeace in 1971.

The image of a small zodiac inflatable courting destruction in front of a huge Soviet whaling ship to protect a whale is among the most powerful footage collected by any environmental group. The role of the media in presenting those images to the general public was vital. Unless the people could see for themselves what was happening, it would be virtually impossible to force change. The direct though nonviolent campaigns that have become Greenpeace trademarks had the desired effect. People saw whales spouting blood with their dying breath; they saw the flensing on the decks, the fetuses cut from pregnant females; and they saw the products that resulted: fertilizer, pet food, cosmetics, soap, margarine, candles. The public was presented with the reality of whaling. And they universally favored the whale. All that was necessary now was for the whaling nations to catch up with international public opinion.

The economics of whaling were looking increasingly poor. With declining whale numbers, whaling nations were simply not making the profits that they once did. So, why hunt whales? The traditional products were of declining value. Japan and the Soviet Union were the only pelagic whaling nations left, while Norway and Iceland had smaller coastal fleets. The Soviet Union caught sperm whales for their oil, while Japan took baleen whales for human consumption. Alternatives have now replaced most of the products that once came from whales: vegetable and fish oils replaced whale oil; jojoba oil and various synthetics provide all the lubricant qualities of sperm whale oil. There is simply nothing contained in the whale that justifies killing them anymore. The Japanese argument about the cultural importance of whale meat to their diet is also spurious. In 1972, whale meat made up less than 1 percent of the total protein consumption in Japan. Today it is a fraction of that. Intransigence over whaling has become another political power play without regard for, or consideration of, either the whale or the insignificant products that result from its demise.

If the alternatives to whale products are not a sufficient argument to stop whaling, then what about humanitarian considerations? The proponents of whaling have often stated that whales are no different from cows or fish, and that our defense of them is based purely on emotion. But whales are the only wild mammal killed on a large, i.e., commercial, scale, either for food or for other "products." Despite the qualms that many of us have with respect to cattle ranching and intensive farming in general, at least cattle are domesticated animals which are not suffering from declining numbers, and their slaughter is, to some extent, controlled and relatively humane; they are also "property," and thus owned (the debate about whether one living thing can ever "own" another is better dealt with elsewhere). The slaughter of whales is far from humane, with the death typically taking anywhere from four to fifteen minutes. No one owns the oceans, or their inhabitants, so no one has the right to exert such base control over the riches contained within.

We can feel an affinity with whales because they are mammals, regardless of their intelligence (in fact, it is probably dangerous to espouse intelligence as a basis for protection, considering how fickle humans can be, and the difficult task of measuring intelligence in human terms); we can feel an affinity because they are wild; and we can certainly feel an affinity because they have been wronged for more than four hundred years. These arguments are by no means unique to whales. I am perfectly happy to make the equivalent case for elephants, gorillas, rhinos, lions, and tigers, and for the nonmammalian crocodiles, sharks, and tuna. The issue is not that whales are somehow apart from the rest of nature, deserving special treatment from us, but that they present us with an image of the natural world and our treatment of it. If we decide that the materialistic gains from whaling are not so important as to override the value of the living whale, then the leap to include other living organisms that have been trivialized by a possession-hungry world should be easy.

The economics of whaling and the alternatives available create an inhospitable environment for whaling activities. Even if we concur with those who claim we must treat whales no differently from any other wild animal, do we not decry the wasteful take of other species, mammalian and piscine? We deplore the headhunting of walrus for ivory, or killing elephants for their tusks. We are horrified by the killing of gorillas for ashtrays and skins. We cry out against the wasteful use of any resource. What greater waste of a living resource can there be than the slaughter of a great whale for minimal economic reward and obsolete products? If human beings are so intelligent as to have the power of choice, then we have a clear one to make here.

These are the arguments that galvanized the environmental movement and finally turned the tables on the whaling members of the IWC. During the late 1970s, the IWC expanded its jurisdiction to the medium-sized whales (such as beaked whales and orca) that had so far been slipping through the control net. At the 1978 IWC meeting in London, a reduction in the total whaling quota was imposed, and by the 1979–80 whaling season, more than three-quarters of the total catch was being sustained by minke whales, with sperm whales making up most of the remainder. The 1979 meeting saw the foundation of a whale sanctuary in the Indian Ocean to protect an important breeding area for the sperm whale. Calls for a complete moratorium on commercial whaling continued and were gaining strength.

In 1982, three-quarters of the IWC's members voted for an indefinite moratorium on commercial whaling, to take effect in 1986. Norway, Japan, and the Soviet Union all formally objected. From 1982 to 1986, the IWC imposed strict quotas on those species still open to hunting: minke, fin, sei, and Bryde's whales. The objections filed by the Soviet Union, Norway, and Japan exempted them from compliance with the moratorium, and they made frequent statements about setting their own quotas and maintaining their whaling fleets. However, the pressure of public opinion was now so forceful that it became a political liability to continue the slaughter on a large scale. By 1987 the whaling nations had pulled most of their whaling fleets from the water, but maintained vessels for so-called "scientific whaling." The whaling nations used the loophole allowance for "scientific whaling" to keep their whalers active and prepared, as well as supplying some product to market. They grudgingly agreed to the commercial moratorium with one hand and flagrantly violated it with the other. Whales continued to be killed.

The moratorium came under intense pressure at the July 1990 IWC meeting. Iceland, Japan, and Norway all threatened to walk out of the IWC unless commercial whaling was resumed for minke whales in the North Atlantic and the Antarctic. The IWC, which was now dominated by nonwhaling countries, held firm and rejected all proposals to lift the moratorium. The so-called "gang of three" whaling nations threatened drastic action if the 1991 meeting did not accede to their demands. The machinations of the IWC were drawn out for another year until they culminated at the 1992 meeting. The moratorium was only six years old, hardly enough time to let the whales catch their breath, let alone recover from four hundred years of hunting pressure.

Norway, Iceland, and Japan went into the meeting demanding that commercial whaling be reinstated. Once more they reiterated their stand: if whaling was not resumed, they would pull out of the IWC and establish their own whaling organization, one that would not be subverted by the "anti-whaling conservationists." On the table in Glasgow was the Revised Management Procedure (RMP), which if implemented would set annual commercial catch limits for stocks of baleen whales, beginning with the minke whale—the only rorqual to remain in large numbers, simply because during the height of whaling it was too small to be of interest; now it was all that was left.

The meeting was barely open when Norway announced, unilaterally, that it would resume commercial hunting of minke whales in 1993, and Iceland walked out of the IWC saying that the organization had been taken over by a "rabid" minority who were against whaling even though scientific fact no longer supported the prohibition. Furthermore, stated the Icelandic representative at the meeting, "'Save the Whale' is an antiquated demand." Whose "scientific fact" they were referring to is unclear. The 1989 IWC Comprehensive Assessment of Whale Stocks had revealed population figures worse than even the most pessimistic of conservationists had expected, with some estimates being revised down by as much as 90 percent. Japan also used the 1992 meeting to state that it wanted to resume hunting minke whales, but did not push its position as aggressively as Norway or Iceland, letting its whaling colleagues take most of the heat for a change (and perhaps wanting to avoid the threat of U.S. trade sanctions). The IWC stuck to its guns, supported by its European Community members and the U.S. delegation, and so far the moratorium remains in place. However, its days seem to be numbered. In 1994 Norway began limited takes of minke whales, and the Icelandic and Japanese fleets are not far behind.

Whaling is not the only threat to cetaceans, although it is certainly the most immediate. Incidental catches in fisheries, the impacts of coastal development, pollution, and disturbance all have the potential to affect cetacean populations. To "Save the Whale" you have to do more than simply stop the direct slaughter, you have to protect the waters in which they swim, the organisms upon which they prey, the lagoons and inlets in which they breed. In the long term, these are the more insidious threats that could, slowly and almost imperceptibly in some cases, seal the fate of species already laid low by whaling.

The incidental catch of cetaceans is large. In many areas, coastal fishermen see dolphins as a nuisance. River dolphins, common dolphins, orca, belukha, and false killer whales, to name just a few, have all felt the persecution that comes from eating fish that people wish to catch for themselves. Cetaceans may also be suffering in some regions because overfishing is taking away their food supply. In the Bering Sea, the collapse of the pollock fishery has been implicated in the decline in marine mammals (particularly Steller's sea lions) and sea ducks (such as the spectacled eider). The expansion of the capelin fishery in eastern Canada and its subsequent collapse is believed to have affected fin whales, while industrial-scale fisheries around the Shetland Islands appear to be adversely affecting the distribution of harbor porpoise and minke whales. Antarctic waters are notorious for their whaling history, but the future is equally uncertain, particularly given the growing interest in krill fisheries. If krill is taken in large quantities, the recovery of certain whale stocks may be in question. You cannot expect the recovery of a population if you remove its food source.

As fishing expands, the incidental catch of cetaceans may also increase if precautions or standards are not imposed. The best-known incidental catch is that associated with the tuna fishery, where millions of spinner and spotted dolphins were caught along with the yellowfin tuna with which they associated. "Incidental catches" of hundreds of thousands of dolphins per year were not unusual during the 1960s and 1970s. The catches were so severe and so concentrated that the eastern Pacific stock of spinner dolphins was estimated to have declined by 80 percent. Public outrage at the slaughter, galvanized by video footage shot by environmental activists, forced fishing corporations to try alternative methods to allow the dolphins to escape before bringing in the catch, and these "dolphin-friendly" tuna boats seemed to work. The current dolphin catch is still believed to number several tens of thousands annually. However, the reduced number caught may have more to do with the relocation of fishing vessels under alternative flags that do not enforce the regulations, as well as the fact that most of the dolphin schools that regularly associated with the tuna are already dead. It remains to be seen whether the Pacific spinner populations will recover.

Gill-net, trawl, purse-seine, set-net, and long-line fisheries all take their toll on marine mammals. It is the small coastal cetaceans that have been hardest hit in many cases. Some 10,000 to 20,000 Dall's porpoise are killed in Japanese gill-net fisheries annually, not to mention the more than 39,000 Dall's that were killed commercially in Japanese coastal waters in 1989. The small cetaceans are not regulated by the International Whaling Commission, and some pro-whaling nations have been effectively trying to blackmail the IWC into permitting commercial whaling of the great whales by threatening unregulated harvest of dolphins and porpoises. By the time the IWC manages to push through expansion of its jurisdiction to all cetaceans, many species and stocks may already be severely depleted.

While the deliberate or accidental catches of the small toothed cetaceans are of concern, the incidental catch of baleen whales is potentially devastating to these already massively depleted stocks. Humpback, minke, right, and fin whales have been caught in nets off New England and eastern Newfoundland. Observers estimated that by 1980 up to 50 humpback whales were dying each year. Fifty may seem an insignificant number, but we are talking about a North Atlantic population of perhaps 5,800 individuals (and a worldwide population of no more than 10,000 to 15,000). If at least 50 animals per year are dying in a single fishery, it does not take too much extrapolation to estimate ten times that number by including other regional fisheries, and the likely reported or observed rate of actual entanglements. Increased mortality on that scale could have serious population-level impacts.

Besides encroachment on cetaceans from fisheries, there is the issue of direct habitat destruction. Many cetaceans are coastal in range, and rely on protected waters for breeding and raising their calves or feeding in the outpouring of marine estuaries. As the human population continues to grow at an ever-accelerating rate, our encroachment on limited coastal habitats for fisheries, industry, housing, and recreation leads to increased pressure and stress on cetacean populations.

The river dolphins are probably the most endangered of all cetaceans. Their narrow range and clearly restricted habitat place them directly in conflict with humans, and under that scenario it has traditionally been the nonhuman that loses. The baiji river dolphin of the Chinese Yangtze may number only a couple of hundred animals. The baiji is completely protected under Chinese law, but such protection extends only to the animal itself; the law is a "paper tiger" that does nothing to protect the animals' habitat. The Indus susu number around 600 animals, while the several-thousand-strong Ganges susu are also being depleted as pollution, dams, and incidental catches slowly take their toll. In the Sea of Cortez, the vaquita is only a few years from extinction as incidental catches continue to take the last few remaining animals. Laws that protect the individual and the species are next to useless if the protection does not encompass habitat.

Many of the great whales have specific, critical habitat requirements, and return year after year to areas that meet those needs. Thus, the gray whale travels from its breeding and birthing lagoons in Baja California to summer feeding grounds in the Chukchi Sea, and humpback whales travel from the rich southeast Alaskan and Central California feeding grounds to their calving areas off the Hawaiian Islands or southern Baja. These locations are under various levels of threat—from tourism and increased recreational use of the seas, to pollution that accompanies greater boat traffic, offshore oil and gas exploration and development with attendant potential for oil spills and acoustic disturbance, to changes in water regimes and nutrient outflows following hydroelectric developments. The degree of adverse impact in many of these instances is unclear, and evidence in many cases is lacking. Unfortunately, by the time that evidence becomes available, the damage will likely already have occurred.

The issue of pollution is a case in point. In certain instances, when a pollutant is released into the environment it is taken up by organisms and concentrated in the tissues. As those organisms are consumed up the food chain, the concentration of the pollutant increases. The result is that those species at the apex of the food chain (such as marine mammals) become most vulnerable, since they are concentrating the maximum amount of the contaminant. Of course, the pollutant may be biologically inert, so that regardless of its concentration in the animal's tissues, it has no biological effect. Unfortunately, the pesticides and heavy metals that have been detected in the blubber, muscle, liver, and brain of many cetacean species are far from being biologically inert. Toxic chemicals of concern are the insecticides DDT and its derivative DDE, dieldrin (and its many relatives), PCBs, and trace elements such as mercury, lead, cadmium, zinc, and copper. PCBs, DDT, and DDE are insoluble in water but soluble in lipids (fats). This means that they are taken up by the animal and stored in the blubber and other fatty tissues; when this fat is metabolized, the chemicals enter the system with potentially damaging effects. DDT is a stomach poison that also affects the reproductive system. PCBs cause liver and reproductive organ damage, and dieldrin affects the nervous system. Trace elements such as mercury, cadmium, and copper do not concentrate in the blubber but enter the organs, particularly the liver and kidneys. There they can enter the bloodstream with toxic effects. Lead, zinc, magnesium, and chromium are found in blubber and organs in equal measure, and when metabolized, these too are highly toxic.

The nature of oceanic and atmospheric circulation has resulted in the transportation of our chemicals and products around the globe. No region of the world or the world's oceans has escaped. A review of recorded contaminant levels is deeply worrying. New Zealand once suggested to conservationists that they campaign to have jurisdiction for whaling passed over to the United Nations' Food and Agricultural Organization, because the FAO would likely ban human consumption of whale meat based on the level of contamination alone!

Many researchers have examined cetaceans to try to understand which species may be most vulnerable to this invisible threat. They have found that levels of DDT, PCBs, and mercury are highest in those coastal species that feed on fish and squid, such as harbor porpoise and bottlenose, common, and striped dolphins. High levels of heavy metals have been found in fin whales, bottlenose and common dolphins, and Cuvier's beaked whales. Baleen whales and the sperm whale seem to be less susceptible, although sampling has been admittedly small-scale.

We know the potential effects of these contaminants on biological systems—such as liver and neural damage and infertility or reduced viability of fetuses. However, it is difficult to extrapolate to actual environmental conditions. If the contaminants remain in the blubber, then it is unlikely that the individual will be damaged. However, if the blubber is metabolized during times of food short-age, pregnancy, or lactation, then the anticipated impacts on internal organs could occur. Studies with captive harbor seals have shown sublethal effects of both DDT and PCBs on reproduction, and continuing studies may be able to extrapolate these data to cetaceans. The presence of high levels of PCBs in the St. Lawrence Estuary population of belukha whales has been linked with poor reproduction and a high rate of disease, while abnormal hormone levels have been seen in other small cetaceans with significant contaminant levels. Animals have been found with DDT levels of more than 2,600 parts per million (bottle-nose dolphins off California), and PCB levels of 840 ppm (long-finned pilot whale in the western Mediterranean), suggesting that the effects could be more serious, and of a more long-term nature, than we may have imagined.

Oil is probably the most obvious form of marine pollution. However, oil pol-lution and its potential effects on marine mammals are only just beginning to be examined in depth, and early indications are that its effects may be less det-rimental than general industrial pollution or the more insidious effects of the chemicals previously discussed. There have been a few cases of oiled cetaceans being washed ashore following a spill, but there has never been direct confirma-tion of oiling resulting in the death of a cetacean, and we have little experimental information on how whales, dolphins, and porpoises deal with oil in their en-vironment. Observations suggest that bottlenose dolphins do detect and avoid oil slicks, even in the dark. Gray whales have been seen swimming directly through natural oil seeps off the California coast, while humpback and fin whales have been seen surface-feeding in the middle of an oil slick off Cape Cod. In 1990, Joseph R. Geraci and David J. St. Aubin edited a book entitled *Sea Mammals and Oil: Confronting the Risks*. It sets the state of knowledge to date on this vital subject.

It has been estimated that 10,000 to 15,000 tonnes of petroleum enter the marine environment every day. The National Academy of Sciences estimated the annual figure at 3.2 million tonnes. The sources for this frankly incredible figure are broad; only some 200,000 tonnes (or about 6 percent of the total) comes from a variety of natural sources, principally oil seeps. The most important anthropogenic source is associated with marine transportation, along with mu-nicipal and industrial wastes, offshore oil production, atmospheric deposition, runoff from rivers and urban areas, and ocean dumping. The U.S. Coast Guard estimates that there are more than 10,000 oil-spillage incidents in U.S. waters annually. So, what happens to this oil? Where does it go, and what does it do to those cetaceans that encounter it?

After oil is released into the marine environment, it undergoes weathering. Weathering includes a number of processes, such as spreading, evaporation, dissolution, dispersion into the water column, oxidation, the formation of emulsions, biodegradation, adsorption to suspended particles in the water, stranding on the shore, or settling into the sediments on the sea floor. The speed and proportion of oil affected by each process will determine how much of an oil slick will remain in a state of potential danger to cetaceans.

Marine mammals by their very nature are closely associated with the water's surface. Whales may spend up to 70 percent of their time below, but they have to return to the surface to breathe. This means that if there is a spill, whales, dolphins, and porpoises would be exposed to oil while swimming, and particularly when surfacing to breathe. Cetaceans are certainly less at risk than other marine mammals such as polar bears and sea otters. Their lack of an insulating layer of easily fouled fur and the fact that they do not ingest oil on their bodies by grooming lessen their exposure in a couple of important ways. However, baleen whales are likely to be vulnerable to fouling of their baleen plates that would reduce their feeding efficiency and potentially result in the ingestion of some quantity of oil. Furthermore, since all cetaceans are carnivores, they are at risk of feeding on oil-contaminated food, such as fish, squid, or zooplankton.

Both zooplankton and benthic invertebrates accumulate petroleum hydrocarbons. However, studies have shown that marine carnivores are inefficient assimilators of petroleum hydrocarbons, and marine food chain biomagnification does not occur. Thus, the main threat to cetaceans from oil appears to be from direct surface contact, inhalation, baleen fouling, and direct ingestion. Even here, though, the risks do not seem excessive. If directly oiled, cetaceans do not lose the insulation capabilities of their blubber, and cetacean skin is nearly impenetrable to the components of oil (even contact with wounds does not result in lasting damage). Fouling of baleen can occur, but its suppression of feeding efficiency is minimal and not sustained. Inhalation could be potentially damaging to a cetacean in the midst of a spill, but evaporation of the highly volatile fractions occurs in the first few hours of release, so the likelihood of a cetacean being trapped near highly volatile compounds is not great.

The information available on the effects of oil on cetaceans is certainly more encouraging than any of the data on toxic chemicals that have found their way into the food chain. The effects of oil appear transitory, and in the event of an incident are certainly localized. The unknowns do still exist. We do not know whether there are significant sublethal effects that may appear in the future, or what the long-term effects would be if a spill impacted a population at a particularly sensitive period, such as calving, or in a critical habitat area, such as the humpback feeding grounds in southeast Alaska or the calving grounds off Hawaii or Baja.

The final potential threats to cetaceans that I want to address here are disturbance and harassment. Cetaceans live in an acoustical world where sounds travel great distances through the water, and they use sound to communicate and to gain information about their surroundings. Acoustical disturbance—the input of additional noise into the environment as a result of human activities—threatens to disrupt this process. The proliferation of boat traffic in areas frequented by whales could also threaten to drive them from traditional areas and critical habitat.

Over the past twenty-five years, the ambient noise level of certain marine regions has increased by as much as ten decibels as a result of increased vessel traffic. Researchers expect that this trend will continue, with noise levels rising an additional five decibels over the next twenty-five years. What do, or could, these heightened noise levels mean to whales?

The sounds generated by human activities have the potential to interfere with frequencies used by cetaceans. It is the baleen whales that are the main receivers of artificial noise, which tends to be of low frequency (below 1 kHz), and therefore outside the hearing range of most toothed whales. The sounds transmitted by artificial structures or vessels may be benign and the animals may ignore them, or they may be of a loudness and frequency that interferes with communication and/or echolocation signals. Anthropogenic noise may initiate a startle reaction in the animals followed by habituation, and the reaction to noise may be confounded by the reaction of the animals to the noise source, for example a moving vessel.

Research has demonstrated that some cetaceans, often naive populations that have not previously been exposed to such noise levels, will exhibit avoidance reactions from major noise sources (such as particularly loud moving vessels) at distances of more than six kilometers (and even more than forty kilometers from seismic survey vessels), while reacting at distances of less than one kilometer if the noise source is stationary or moving very slowly. Whales have been observed to react most notably toward erratically moving vessels with varying engine speeds and gear changes, as well as vessels in active pursuit.

In many respects, cetaceans are probably "preadapted" to a great deal of this acoustical interference, since the oceans are naturally noisy and highly variable environments. Behavioral observations support this view, with severe reactions usually noted only in response to extremely loud and intermittent sounds. However, many behavioral changes may be subtle alterations in the surface-dive-respiration cycles, a gradual movement away from the noise source, or more overt responses such as aerial displays and complete avoidance of an area. The level of behavioral reaction appears to be closely related to the activity of the animal before the disturbance event. Animals engaged in active behaviors, such as feeding or socializing, appear less likely to show overt responses to sudden noises.

The potential disturbance resulting from whale-watching activities has received a great deal of attention in recent years. As people have become more interested in the environment, as ecotourism has become big business, and as many of the locations frequented by whales become more accessible, there are concerns that whale-watchers may literally be "loving whales to death." The animals in three areas in particular have been the focus of interest: the humpback whales of Glacier Bay in southeast Alaska, those around the Hawaiian Islands, and the gray whales of Baja California.

Before 1978, the Glacier Bay National Monument was consistently the summer feeding ground for ten to twenty-four humpback whales. In 1979 the bay was used by only three individuals, and fewer than ten used it over the following three years. Those studying the area proposed two hypotheses: (1) the uncontrolled increase in vessel traffic had altered the behavior of the humpbacks and forced them to leave the bay, or (2) the departure of the whales was due to the natural decline in the availability of their prey in the bay, or to some other natural phenomenon.

Vessel traffic had increased by 120 percent in the bay between 1976 and 1978. The result was that the number of whale-vessel interactions increased from 38 percent of all vessels in 1976 to 67 percent in 1978. Researchers looked at the reactions of the whales to vessels, and at the distribution of prey. What they found was that the whales consistently concentrated in areas of high prey density. In 1982, a group of whales spent the summer in the busiest and noisiest part of Glacier Bay, over a great concentration of prey. This is not to say that vessels do not disturb humpbacks. Vessels that pass close to whales have an effect on their surface-dive ratios, although this is probably insignificant to the individual whale. Vessel traffic that is not oriented toward the whales, does not actively pursue them, or does not rapidly change gears does not appear to elicit any visible reaction, and humpbacks appear to habituate to regular boat traffic.

The U.S. National Marine Fisheries Service imposed boat quotas for Glacier Bay in the early eighties, and humpbacks have been returning to the bay in increasing numbers. However, they also frequent Icy Straits, the region just outside the bay, where boat traffic is not controlled. This is the region that I am most familiar with, having spent a great deal of time plying those waters in search of bubble-net-feeding humpbacks. This region is well known for the frequency of close encounters with humpback whales, encounters that are almost reminiscent of the friendly gray whales of Baja. I have been on the receiving end of several distinctly curious encounters with these whales, who have closely approached the vessel and spy-hopped within feet of the boat. The only overt response from a humpback whale that I have witnessed in Alaska, and been convinced of its cause, was in Frederick Sound in the southeast. I watched a humpback whale breach 112 times in response to the distant passage of a ferry. The reason for such an exaggerated aerial display is difficult to determine; perhaps as one humpback whale researcher working in Glacier Bay stated, there are wooden whales, aluminum whales, and real whales, but as far as humpbacks are concerned, they are all basically whales. Humpbacks often breach and perform other aerial acrobatics when joined by other whales, perhaps as a means of communication or a method of expressing one animal's dominance over another. If a large vessel passes through an area, the elicited behavioral response may be increased to meet the scale of this "aluminum whale."

The Hawaiian Island winter population of humpback whales has been intensively studied by those trying to determine whether increased human activity has affected whale distribution and numbers. Some have suggested that humpbacks have abandoned certain areas because of disturbance. Whales used to be common near Koko Head on Oahu during the 1940s and 1950s. The whales were so numerous that they received extensive press coverage and a whale-watching association was founded. Today, humpbacks are found only infrequently along that stretch of coastline. Since the 1930s, southeast Oahu has seen a drastic increase in human activity, including marine construction and boating. However, it is difficult to infer a causal relationship, because during the early 1960s, heavy whaling was initiated on the Aleutian summering grounds used by many of these animals. However, other islands in the Hawaiian chain have also voiced concerns about the potential effects of vessel traffic and whale-watching activities on humpbacks. Volunteers have set up stations to track whale movements between the islands so they can warn the inter-island jet-foils of whales in their path, and thus avoid boat-whale collisions, and the National Marine Fisheries Service introduced regulations for whale-watching etiquette to give the whales more room.

However, it is the California gray whale that offers the most astonishing testament to the potential of whale-watching and human-whale encounters. The Baja lagoons and the coastal migration routes of gray whales provide a perfect natural laboratory for trying to determine whether boats or industrial activities adversely affect whales.

Vessel traffic and other human disturbances have been implicated in the abandonment of San Diego and Mission Bays as breeding lagoons, although some researchers question whether these bays were ever as important as the more southerly lagoons. It has also been suggested that human disturbance may have caused an increased tendency for gray whales to migrate farther offshore. It is likely that there was always an "offshore component" of the gray whale migration, but it is unknown how many more whales are moving offshore as general vessel traffic and industrialization of the coasts and seas continues.

It has been hypothesized that gray whales may be vulnerable to human activities in the confines of the lagoons simply because they cannot readily flee from disturbance as they can in the open ocean. Furthermore, given the critical nature of the lagoon habitat necessary for successful reproduction, exclusion from one or more lagoon areas could cause overcrowding in the remaining sites or force the whales to seek alternative and suboptimal areas in which to breed.

Between 1957 and 1967, there was intense industrial salt-mining activity in Laguna Guerrero Negro in Baja California Sur. This lagoon was favored by gray whales, and the number of animals using it had been increasing steadily as the population recovered from the toll taken by the whalers. With the salt mine in operation, vessel traffic was heavy and whale use of the lagoon declined to zero. When mining operations stopped in 1967, the whales returned to the lagoon in substantial numbers. The mining operation was transferred to another lagoon in 1967, Laguna Ojo de Liebre, but the whales did not abandon that site. Laguna Ojo de Liebre is larger than Guerrero Negro and has a wider entrance, leading some to suggest that the whales felt less crowded and so were less disturbed by the operations. Since the 1970s, Baja California and its gray whales have become something of a mecca for whale-watchers. As the numbers of vessels have increased, plying the coast and entering the lagoons, fears have been raised about the potential for increased harassment to result in cow-calf separations, strandings, and abandonment of favored lagoons. There is currently no evidence to support these fears, and it is hoped that the management system set up by the Mexican government will ensure that the pressures never get out of hand. The increasing number of friendly whale encounters is further evidence that whale-watching can be compatible with whales even at the most sensitive times (such as post-calving).

The increasing phenomenon of "friendly gray whales" certainly confounds the argument that all whale-watching activities harass whales. Some observers have suggested that the whales have habituated to the activity, and that the sounds produced by the skiffs' outboard motors actually serve as an attractant. It is also possible that the friendly behavior is the result of simple curiosity by the whales, naiveté toward boats, the teasing behavior of some of the vessels that tempts the whales closer, and the tactile stimulation that results when the whales rub themselves against the boats or are touched by the whale-watchers.

Most whale-watching vessels in the lagoons split their day, much as ours did, so that skiffs are on the water looking for whales half the time, or even less. The Mexican government controls the number of vessels that can enter a lagoon and the number of skiffs that are permitted in the water at any one time. In Laguna San Ignacio, the areas within the lagoon are managed separately so that vessels are not permitted into the upper reaches where the calves are born, but are allowed to frequent the more open stretches of the lower lagoon where the older calves can be found. This automatically controls the amount of disturbance that will occur during any one day, and which animals are exposed to it.

However, there is a very real concern that uncontrolled whale-watching activities could harass whales. These activities could drive the whales from the very areas that people flock to see them in. As I have mentioned, whale-watching in the lagoons of Baja is strictly controlled, and vessel operators harass whales at the risk of losing their permits. In U.S. waters, the Marine Mammal Protection Act of 1972 makes it a federal offense to "hunt, harass, or kill, or to attempt to hunt, harass, or kill" a cetacean. In a world where recreational use of the sea and coastal regions is increasing, and where "ecotourism" is expanding into ecologically sensitive areas, it is vital that those people participating in such trips and the tour operators are aware of the type of regulations that exist, not only in their own country but in the countries they are visiting.

Whale-watching vessels in all waters should operate under guidelines to ensure that their presence does not affect or potentially harm the very resource that they are seeking to enjoy. I have been on vessels where the captain's technique around marine mammals has been questionable, and the day has seemed to be one of pursuit rather than passive observation or controlled interaction. Such actions should not be condoned or permitted to continue. If a vessel flouts the rules, an objection can always be made through official channels. In U.S. waters, the Marine Mammal Protection Act provides all the necessary recourse required, as does the permit system in Mexico. All those who take to the sea in boats, ships, and skiffs, whether to watch whales or to simply enjoy the open ocean, lagoons, or inlets, should be aware of whale etiquette. Just as all vessels are aware of the international regulations regarding dumping garbage, sewage, or plastic at sea, so they should be aware that in the ocean, whales have the right of way, and that appropriate penalties are in existence for those who refuse to honor that right.

As the number of vessels operating in whale waters increases, we must ensure that the whales are not excluded from these waters. Evidence from Hawaii, Baja, and Alaska suggests that it is possible to have both—an active, sometimes interactive, whale-watching industry, and a growing whale population that returns year after year to the delight of whale-watchers everywhere. This will continue to be the case only if boat operators are considerate of the animals that maintain their industry. It has been well documented that other species, particularly terrestrial birds and mammals, will avoid areas where they are actively and continuously hunted, where the level of disturbance is irregular, infrequent, or of such a nature that habituation is not possible, or where the disturbance occurs at a particularly sensitive period in the life cycle. If whales are to avoid this fate, a potentially serious one considering the coastal nature of many species during the winter breeding and summer feeding seasons, then the whale-watching industry must ensure that disturbance levels are kept under control.

Whale-watching takes people close to animals that few would previously have had the opportunity to see. "Friendly encounters" between whales and whale-watchers should be monitored, and perhaps even encouraged, because the more we see of them, "up close and personal," the more distant become the days of commercial harvest. As whaling attempts to resurrect itself around the world, the role of the whale-watcher will become increasingly important. Whales are a living resource, and to the whale-watcher and the whale-watching industry, the whale is worth infinitely more alive than dead. If whale-watching imparts some level of disturbance to the whales, it is, I believe, a reasonable trade to ensure that enough people get to see the animals for themselves, and just perhaps become more vocal in their opposition to the return of a very real and very direct threat.

> Nature is the opposite of the soul, answering to it part for part. One is seal and one is print. Its beauty is the beauty of his own mind. Its laws are the laws of his own mind. Nature then becomes to him the measure of his attainments. So much of nature as he is ignorant of, so much of his own mind does he not yet possess. And, in fine, the ancient precept, "Know thyself," and the modern precept, "Study nature," become at last one maxim.
>
> —Ralph Waldo Emerson

What basis is there for applying a human ethical system to our treatment of the human/whale problem? Is it reasonable to expect the human race to protect the nonhuman, especially when profits are involved? Can ethics even be applied to the nonhuman? If it were shown that whales could be "harvested" sustainably, according to proven management procedures, should whaling be allowed? Or does our ethical and moral responsibility transcend what is possible, and instead concentrate on what should rather than could happen?

We can find some answers to these perplexing problems in the development of ethical and moral values through human history. How did *Homo sapiens* become ethical beings? We can trace the evolution of kin selection, reciprocity, and ethical judgment until it becomes apparent that as a society matures and evolves, the formulation of ethical and moral values is inevitable. We are currently at the crossroads where it will be decided whether to allow those values to transcend species barriers and become equally applicable to the nonhuman, and perhaps even the inanimate.

Ethics is defined as "the philosophical study of the moral value of human conduct and of the rules and principles that ought to govern it." Everyone within our society has ethics of some sort. Ethics is concerned with decision making, choices by which we can determine the difference between right and wrong. Some choose to ignore those differences and act for personal gain—but still they know that what they do is wrong. Thus, people murder for money; they know that murder is wrong, but the object they hope to gain motivates them to ignore the ethical restraints that usually temper our actions.

Ethics must have developed hand in hand with human evolution and sociality. Our use of ethics and our application of ethical principles affect our relations with other people, and that is the foundation of society. We can see the probable origins of human ethics by examining the developing ethics of nonhuman animals. We are social animals; we live in groups and we have rules regarding how we interact and treat other members of our group. We can see the emergence of these rules in other primates as well as in animals further removed from us on the evolutionary scale.

Animals that live in a group must show a certain level of behavioral restraint, otherwise cooperation within the group will break down. It would be impossible to maintain a group if the most powerful animal always fought the other members for food or mates, and in doing so maimed or killed those individuals. Social animals either must refrain from attacking members of their social unit, or must have some sort of restraint to prevent altercations from escalating into fatal or injurious acts. We can see this type of restraint in many animals, where the weaker animal shows submissive behavior to the stronger, and the stronger recognizes the submission and does not pursue the attack. Wolves, dogs, chimpanzees, vervet monkeys, baboons, and rats all show this intrinsic ethical code of conduct.

Evolutionary theory, at its most basic, states that each individual is striving to perpetuate its genes, and in a world of survival of the fittest and "nature red in tooth and claw," it may be supposed that natural selection would be working in opposition to the development and adoption of ethical codes. After all, altruistic behavior, on the surface, appears to contradict the "evolutionary purpose": if you help someone else to mate or feed, or protect them from harm, you are ensuring the survival of their genes, not your own. Natural selection, we are told, is selfish. But close social groups in the animal kingdom are usually family groups. So the individuals that you feed or protect are in all likelihood kin; and kin selection can be a powerful force. Obviously, the greatest benefit comes from protecting and helping your own offspring, but the offspring of your sister or brother also have some of your genes, as do more distant relatives, although the actual proportion of genetic similarity drops off rapidly the farther from the family tree that you move.

None of this is necessarily conscious, but the actions of most species tend to be allied with the general rules. The introduction of human culture, foresight and hindsight (the human consciousness, if you like), tends to complicate the rules as they may be applied to *Homo sapiens*. But these differences can be tied back to when we passed a certain point in our own evolutionary development and it became we ourselves rather than the random and blind processes of natural selection that began to shape our lives, our future, and our thoughts.

As social groups grow in size, the members will not always be kin. So then what controls the type of interaction that occurs between members? The answer may lie in reciprocity. I may help someone else on the understanding that at some point in the future she will reciprocate. Obviously this relies on trust, and it suggests that the individual initially offering the assistance is at a disadvantage, because in the long run there is little to prevent her being taken advantage of again. But is that really what happens?

Reciprocity depends on a couple of important factors. Both parties must be able to recognize each other, and remember that a "bargain" was made. If the individual that offered the service does not receive either the same or equivalent service in return at some point in the future, then that individual must be able to make the connection and deny the second animal future favors. It would further reinforce this "blacklisting" if the transgression were made known to the animal's kin so that they too would blacklist the animal that had taken advantage of their relative. In this way, reciprocity develops within the group based not on mutual mistrust but on the basis of recognition and group support. Such controls have been observed in baboons, vervet monkeys, chimpanzees, wild dogs, and dolphins.

It is likely that as our pre-human ancestors first began to settle in family groups, and then larger social units, kin selection and reciprocity were the beginning of our ethical treatment of others. Even today, our ties to family members are stronger than any others, while our treatment of non–family members is often based on reciprocity. On a larger scale, our societies have become segregated by religious, racial, or national divides—the groups we have created for ourselves are peopled by those whose religions, race, or national background is similar to our own. Outsiders are viewed with suspicion and prejudice, and tensions can develop based on issues that are irrelevant to the fact that we are all people. Nations develop strategies to deal with other nations; politics becomes the forum for debating and maintaining reciprocity between groups. When that reciprocity breaks down, we can find ourselves at war.

Since the beginning of written history, people have tried to understand and explore the basis for ethical and moral behavior. Why is one thing acceptable in one society and unacceptable in another? Are there ethical universals, basic rights and wrongs? Just what are our responsibilities in an ethical world? Why should we do the "right thing"? Is the "right thing" an immutable constant, or does it change with interpretation, with society?

Ancient seats of civilization set forth their interpretation of ethics. Since that time the "science of ethical thought" has matured and evolved in its own right, but still many of the original tenets of ethical thought remain, suggesting that ethical judgment is more than choice and interpretation, but that we all know, intuitively, the difference between right and wrong. However, the ethical philosophies of east and west have, historically, been very different.

Among eastern philosophical traditions, Indian Vedas, Buddhism, and Jainism encompassed human and nonhuman alike in their treatise on "moral order." In China, Lao-tzu's Tao tells readers to be true to themselves and return good for good, and good for evil, the universal principles that were later adopted by Christians. But it was Confucius who had a much wider appeal, applying ethical principles to common life. Confucius was once asked by a student to say the one word that could serve as a guide for personal conduct throughout one's life. He replied: "Is not reciprocity such a word? What you do not want done to yourself, do not do to others." Considering this assessment of the beginnings of ethics in human and nonhuman, reciprocity is more appropriate than even Confucius may have realized. The key is perhaps to recognize that reciprocity need not be confined to our own species.

The classical Greek ethical theorists developed ethical and moral views that were espoused by Socrates, Plato, Aristotle, and later by Stoics and Epicureans. These philosophers were concerned with what made an act good or bad, and how did people know which was which? If people knew what was right and what was wrong, why did some still choose to do wrong? They wanted to know whether self-interest was bad. Was lying acceptable under certain circumstances? If no one would ever find out that you behaved unethically, would you have any motivation to behave justly? Aristotle's interpretation of ethics even led him to support slavery (because non-Greeks were "less rational" than Greeks) and killing animals for food (because they were "living tools"). As the Christian faith rose in prominence through the Classical world, many of the ethical treatises that had been developed five or six centuries before the present era were adopted into the Christian fold. People were told to do what was right or risk the eternal fires. The basis for why certain things were good and other things evil was not explored. In other words, there were many ethical injunctions but no ethical philosophy.

As we move closer to modern times, the development of ethical philosophy becomes more distant from theories of "divine will and retribution." The British ethics theorist Thomas Hobbes (1588–1679) gave us a first look at human ethics based solely on human nature. He believed that people were concerned only with self-pleasure and self-preservation. But Hobbes saw that some people did act altruistically, and he saw such acts as fulfilling some "object of desire." Thus, he gave alms to the poor because it "pleased" him to see another pleased. The late seventeenth century saw a reaction against this view. The opposition was led in part by Henry More and Samuel Clarke. But it is interesting that the same tenets of ethical behavior appear time after time, brought forth by people divorced from each other by time, culture, and motive. Clarke built on the so-called Golden Rule that is central to all ethical theory: "Whatever I judge reasonable or unreasonable for another to do for me, that by the same judgment I declare reasonable or unreasonable that I in the like case should do for him."

How similar in thought is this to Confucius's statement "What you do not want done to yourself, do not do to others." However, despite the similarities with eastern thought, only a few philosophers in the period from the seventeenth to the nineteenth centuries considered broadening their statements to include the ethical treatment of the nonhuman. Not until Jeremy Bentham (1748–1832), the father of modern Utilitarianism, was the view that everything that was pleasurable was good and everything that resulted in pain was bad extended to nonhuman animals.

In the twentieth century, the ethical debate developed further. Herbert Spencer tried to build an ethics around Darwin's theory of evolution by arguing that ethical behavior was "more evolved," as did the biologist E. O. Wilson. Other sociobiologists rejected this claim, using Darwin's theories of natural selection and subsequent notions of "selfish genes" to show that inequality was inevitable.

Perhaps these arguments need to be reconsidered under the increasingly broad banner of environmental ethics. This new ethics is more closely tied to eastern ethical treatises than the anthropocentric ethics of the 1600s to 1800s. We are reaching the stage where ethical theory must go beyond simply trying to ascertain why we act in certain ways and not others, or why we should take responsibility for our actions. We must translate general ethics theory to a practical system of applied ethics that contribute to, and not merely explain, our actions.

As the number of people on this planet increases and our resources become increasingly limited, we are all faced with very real problems, not least escalating species extinctions and human inequality. We use resources to feed ourselves, to manufacture products, and to improve our standard of living. But we are also part of an ecosystem. We cannot hope to survive without protecting the fabric of the natural world, upon which we rely for our food, our oxygen, and thus our continued ability to perpetuate our genes. If we believe that human ethics arose out of kin selection and reciprocity, then our actions toward the nonhuman and the inanimate have a precedence. Our ethical treatment of other people is based on family and societal values, a belief that right and wrong are definable, that pleasure is better than pain, and that to act justly is in our best interests, as well as in the best interests of society. We must begin to view reciprocity on a global scale. If we protect others, human and nonhuman, in return we secure our own future. In these terms, ethical judgment and the adoption of ethical principles are an evolutionary progression.

We are capable of exerting such profound changes on our world, in such a short space of time, that without some sort of restraint on our behavior (our use of resources and our population growth), the restraint that comes with implementing an environmental ethic, we will condemn ourselves to extinction just as surely as the maladapted do. We must learn the ultimate lesson, that altruism is a positive evolutionary step forward, because if we don't extend it to ourselves or to other living organisms, survival becomes tentative rather than assured. For highly prolific, social animals, the development and implementation of ethical reasoning in all aspects of our lives and our interactions becomes essential to the continuation of the species, and therefore should be selected by the evolutionary process we have come to know as natural selection.

The next section is going to examine some, although certainly not all, of the specifics behind environmental ethics based on the existing foundation of ethical thought. We must consider why it should be of concern if a species becomes extinct. Does it matter if we dam a river and flood a valley? Is our responsibility to the individual, to the species, or to the ecosystem? What happens when these responsibilities are in conflict? Do we meet our responsibility if we protect animals in zoos and parks? Are we part of, or apart from, nature? Do we protect species and systems because they have value to us, either monetarily or aesthetically, or do they possess an intrinsic value outside our appreciation? And since we are what we are, can we ever hope to attain a true ethical relationship with nature when we seem incapable of attaining one with our own species? Will we ever realize that one is impossible without the other?

> To speak truly, few adult persons can see nature. Most persons do not see the sun. At least they have a very superficial seeing. The sun illuminates only the eye of the man, but shines into the eye and the heart of the child. The lover of nature is he whose inward and outward senses are still truly adjusted to each other; who has retained the spirit of infancy even into the era of manhood.
> —Ralph Waldo Emerson

In the development of human ethics, we have the foundation for an ethical treatment of the nonhuman. We can consider global reciprocity, respect for life, the universal avoidance of pain, and the lives of future generations who will pick up what we leave behind. But the human race seems to have enough trouble applying equivalent ethical values to other members of our own species, so how do we even attempt to show those values to species with whom we cannot debate or reason or see an affinity? The previous pages have shown that ethics can be applied to others; the question now is whether they should be. We can argue that something is either ethical or it is not. What about badger or bear baiting, dog and cock fighting, headhunting for walrus, killing something just for the fun of it—the enjoyment of watching something die in fear and in pain? Surely these must be unethical behaviors based on our previous assessment of what should or should not be acceptable behavior. If they are true for humans, why should they not also be true for the nonhuman? On what basis do we make the distinction? Sentience? Similarity? Language? Understanding? Imagined necessity?

Every characteristic that we see in ourselves can be found in other species. What is it that we have to see in them before we show them the respect that we are supposed to show to each other? Is it simply easier to refuse to see, because otherwise we have to admit that so many of the things we have done were truly unconscionable? Isn't that a reflection on our character rather than theirs?

There have been many arguments put forth to explain our selectivity in the application of ethical principles, arguments that are being voiced today as strongly as ever:

People come first.
People are more important than . . . (insert animal of choice)
Why should we spend money on animal species when people are starving?
We cannot save everything.

Some species are more important than others; we should be selective.

Some animals are just curiosities; they don't really matter.

We can preserve what we need in zoos.

Extinction is a natural process.

Humans are part of the natural process.

You can't expect developing countries to protect instead of develop.

You can't expect developed countries to pick up the tab for protection.

We have to protect our jobs, our future.

The environmentalists are alarmists.

Animals don't feel pain the way we do.

Animals don't think the way we do.

One more species extinct, what does it really matter?

That these arguments are still voiced with all the assuredness of those who believe they are walking on firm ground, only to find that their next step takes them over the precipice, is astounding. They are the anthropocentric optimists who refuse to see the image of their own future in their present actions. Some see no further than their next paycheck; others (who should certainly know better) see no further than the next four-year term. Few take the generational view, thinking of their children's children and far beyond. Many of the arguments are simply blatant misrepresentations of the views of conservationists, made by those seeking only to pass the blame for worldly problems onto the shoulders of others.

The statements that I have listed above are certainly not all that are used against those who would seek to preserve and protect, but they are some of the most widely stated. They are questions that we should all consider, because our elected representatives are making decisions based on their interpretation of the answers. If their answers differ from yours and mine, we may be in trouble.

The "people come first" argument is always a gem to deal with. People are more important than animals, more important than plants. How can we even think of spending millions to protect them when people are starving, dying, in need of medical treatment, jobs, a better future for themselves and for their children? Are people really so blind that they cannot see that without the natural world we would not have the very lives we seem to cherish so much? Our future is connected with theirs in more complex ways than we can even imagine at this point in our limited intellectual evolution.

Do we need to be reminded that of the estimated 5 to 30 million species believed to inhabit this planet, we have named and identified just 1.4 million? And does it bear repeating that since 50 to 90 percent of these organisms live in the tropical rainforests, we risk losing 25 percent of all species by the year 2050 if we continue to raze the tropical forests at current rates? But people come first, right? People need land upon which to farm, and raise cattle to sell. People need land to mine, and land upon which to live and procreate. We need to flood valleys, drill into geological chasms, and tap into the atom to create power. But what power are we relinquishing by doing all of this in the name of meeting immediate desires? Do we risk losing our ability to make choices in the future? Every time we make a decision that eliminates a species or drives one closer to the edge, we are denying ourselves (and our children) choices. It is as though we are walking down a corridor that is getting narrower and narrower the farther we walk. The corridor is lined with doors, but each one is locked, and the only way we can go on is to continue to move down the ever-narrowing corridor, until we can go no further.

Of the 75,000 species of known edible plants, we use only 5,000 for food. Western civilization uses even fewer, perhaps 30 providing the majority of our sustenance. Our reliance on a few grass species is staggering. Wheat, barley, and corn form the foundation of our diet. Should this be of concern? With shifting temperature patterns, either natural or human-induced, we are limiting our adaptiveness in the future by relying on extremely limited gene pools in the few species that we use commercially. We took the original plants and bred them to supply our needs—high productivity at the expense of genetic variability and disease resistance. We have selected what we need now, but what will we need in ten years, or twenty, or one hundred years from now? If climatic or water regime conditions alter so that the varieties of wheat, barley, and corn that we use are no longer appropriately adapted, then we are up the proverbial creek without a paddle. Unless, of course, we have access to the wild varieties from which we originally selected such narrow attributes. If we still have the original gene pool in place and gradually evolving in tune with shifting conditions, then we also have access to new varieties adapted to the very conditions that we now need. Preserving a few of the original plants in a refrigerator somewhere does not preserve the necessary variety. We need viable and vibrant plants that are adapted to a broad range of conditions that only exposure can generate. We need the plants and we need the ecosystems that support them.

If this scenario does something else, it should demonstrate that protecting the cute and the cuddly isn't what conservation and preservation is all about. We need to conserve the grasses, the invertebrates, the bacteria, and the viruses. Less than 1 percent of all tropical plants have been screened for medicinal use, while scientists have estimated that one out of ten plant species contains compounds with ingredients active against cancer. If people come first, then so does everything else. We are what we eat and drink and breathe—and if our ecosystem does not provide us with food, water, and air, where is it going to come from? Of course, if our concern is with this generation and this generation only, look no further than your own needs and desires. But if you are concerned with your children, and their children, ad infinitum, then think carefully before you presume to say that conservation is a luxury that people cannot afford, because the species you condemn to an early extinction may be your own.

So, why should we spend money on preserving species when people are starving or sick? Because we want a future in which people have enough to eat and have access to the best medicines available. And we can't get there alone.

Five to 30 million species on Planet Earth, and a human population of more than 5 billion. The United Nations estimates that eventually our population will stabilize at around 12 billion people, with 95 percent of all population growth taking place in developing countries. The argument goes that people have immediate problems and immediate needs; perhaps we should be selective. There are so many species, some must be redundant; after all, only 1 percent of all life on Earth is bigger than a bumblebee! What would it matter if we lost a few of the smaller ones, the less important and the expendable? Our resources are limited; all we need is direction, a plan to protect ourselves over the long term while minimizing the amount of effort we have to expend today. That's it! Some animals are simply curiosities, they don't really matter. We can keep a few in zoos, but we don't have to protect them in the wild.

Okay. You have a plan. How do you intend to implement it? How do you begin to choose, and what criteria do you use to decide? Some sort of global species triage system, based on economics, feasibility, "value"? You have names for only 1.4 million species; what about the other 95 percent of all species that you haven't even gotten around to yet—are they going to factor into the equation, or is the premise that if we don't know what they are by now, they don't really matter? Before you decide, you need to know the organism's life cycle, how it fits into the ecosystem around it, what species are linked to it. You wouldn't want to eliminate an insect that then turns out to be the only species that can pollinate plant A, which is the only food source for animal B, which of course is the major prey of animal C—unless you decide that A, B, and C are also expendable. It's not easy, is it, playing God?

Species become extinct all the time. It is a natural process. Evolution works through a process of natural selection whereby "the survival of the fittest" ensures the perpetuation of genes to future generations based on their adaptation to existing conditions. Species can be roughly defined as specialists and generalists. At any given time we may find many specialists in a habitat, species that have evolved to take advantage of a particular narrow resource where competition is limited. There will also be generalists; these species are not so well adapted to specific conditions, but can get by in a number of different situations. If there is change, the specialists are much more likely to die out, while the generalists often adapt and flourish. We can see examples in our own world—the rat, dog, and cat are generalists, the giant panda, mountain gorilla, and orangutan are specialists. If you take the rat, dog, or cat out of its usual environment, it tends to adapt to the new surroundings. Do the same to the specialists and, to coin a phrase, you have a "fish out of water," and fish out of water don't last too long. Perhaps you would be happy in a world of rats, dogs, and cats that was devoid of giant pandas, mountain gorillas, and orangutans? It wouldn't be so bad; we could have a few sequestered away in zoos and the odd park or preserve, enough that the chosen few could see them. And we can always just replay those wonderful wildlife documentaries so that we can forget what it was that we lost.

The view that we may lose species in the wild, but zoological parks and preserves are forever, is a sad fallacy. In most countries, zoos and the associated parks and preserves are commercial ventures. They are in business to make money, and although many contribute to species survival and reintroductions, primarily they are about putting animals on show (usually the cuter and cuddlier the better). Most institutions do not have the resources to maintain large, viable stocks of animals. Geneticists agree that at least 500 breeding individuals are required to provide a large enough gene pool to secure a species' future (I'd like to see the zoo that could hold 500 cetaceans!). Zoos have a role to play in education and awareness, and in certain special cases can be used to assist in species survival, but they will never be the answer. If a species becomes extinct in the wild and survives only in zoological collections, then its days are clearly numbered.

As the tropical rainforests are razed to make way for ranching, human settlements, agriculture, and mining, it is estimated that we are losing 50 to 150 individual species each day. Most are invertebrates that have never even been looked upon by the human eye. Where is the cure for cancer, or AIDS, or a multitude of other human afflictions? Perhaps in those unique packages of DNA that are being so casually discarded for transitory profits and short-term solutions to intrinsic problems of human society.

The rate of extinction today is more rapid than at any other time in the natural world since the vast geological upheavals of the ancient past. Furthermore, extinction is not the random process that we are now allowing to gather momentum. Natural extinction excludes the maladapted from the gene pool and permits the well-adapted to go forth and multiply. What are we doing? We are throwing the nonhuman species on this planet a curve ball where adaptiveness has nothing to do with the ability to survive. We are destroying entire habitats and altering ecosystem relationships. We are accelerating processes that have been fine-tuned for eons, and forcing changes in decades instead of millennia. Humans evolved by a process of evolution, but we are no longer doing so. Our special nature, our sentience, and our intellectual capacity have removed us from the "natural" world simply because we now possess the ultimate power and foresight over our and others' development. Evolution is a blind process— it has no desire or goal; it is a process that works on the natural variability of a population, weeding out the weak from the strong, and then moving on. But we are not blind, and we are no longer permitting natural evolution to shape us. Therefore, while we are no longer part of that "natural system," we retain

complete power over its other components. To permit our power to go un-
checked solely because we are a product of evolution is to ignore the very
"differences" that we use to separate us from other species, and thus justify our
treatment of them.

We have been told throughout history that other animals do not feel pain or
think in the ways that we identify with, as though that excuses our behavior
toward them. In many religions this has been expanded to say that nonhuman
animals have no souls and are thus undeserving of either our pity or our assistance. This argument has no foundation biologically or ethically. We evolved out
of the same primeval soup that gave rise to the rest of life on Earth—we are not
unique in that respect. We may be unique in our ability to *express* feelings of
pain or pleasure through the medium of language (although even here, the supposed human monopoly is one of degree rather than absolutes). There is no
reason to presume that other species do not experience similar feelings to ours
simply because we are not able to understand them.

Earlier I posed the question, "Is our responsibility to the individual, to the
species, or to the ecosystem?" This dilemma is a perplexing one. We often assign
arbitrary values to different species—mammals over fish, "higher" mammals
such as primates over "lower" mammals such as rodents. All living things may
be imagined to rather like the "idea" of living, and few animals willingly go to
their deaths. We know that animals feel pain; we can recognize that they have
an intrinsic value in being alive—even if that value is beyond our ken.

When we seek to conserve a species or habitat, we often seem to be conserv-
ing our ideal of that system. The ideal is usually how that system was before we
altered it in some fashion, either deliberately or accidentally. Thus, although
many of us are uncomfortable with mass extermination programs that seek to
eradicate an introduced "pest," we know in our hearts that "the ends justify the
means." Thus, feral goats on California's Channel Islands or the Galapagos, or
rats and mongooses on the Hawaiian Islands are killed to preserve those that
were there before them. We have made a value judgment that the system that
evolved *in situ* is superior to the altered or degraded system that has replaced it
(or is threatening to). These programs have, as their ultimate goal, the restoration
of the system to what it was before, in the knowledge that upon completion, the
system can be left alone. But herein lies the problem: What do we do when the
issue is not removing an intruder, but dealing with the absence of an integral
part of the system—namely the large predators?

Many of the so-called wilderness areas in the world are in fact sad reflections of the true wilds. They lack the pinnacle of their food chains—the wolf
and mountain lion, the cheetah and lion, the tiger and grizzly bear, the hunting dog and hyena. Many of the "wildlands" are surrounded by human
settlements, and excursions outside of the "preserve" by predators are not ap-
preciated. It is simply impossible to conserve a system in balance when the

balancing act has been destroyed. Where the predators once controlled the numbers of herbivores and omnivores, now the game wardens have had to take over—culling animals so that the habitat is not degraded to the detriment of the entire species. The absence of natural predators has forced humans to become the "controller" in the very areas that we were trying to preserve *because* they existed outside of our influence! In some cases we can reintroduce the predators and thus restore the balance; in others the size of the preserve may prevent that avenue, simply because the land may not be large enough to support a predator population of sufficient size to maintain genetic diversity and minimize inbreeding. Where people have had to take over the role of predator, we end up with a system managed to conform with the human ideal of what the system should be, not the system that natural selection crafted. It is a sad commentary that when we have finally recognized the value in these lands and their inhabitants, we find our hands forced to exert basic control over the numbers and interactions of the animals we seek to protect. And by exercising that level of control, we are altering the very fabric of what we profess to value.

Why should we decry the artificial management of populations that attempt to inflate prey animals at the expense of their predators, or policies that seek only to domesticate the wilds? Because such policies and practices reflect the way that we view everything that is nonhuman. They send a message of control and manipulation, a message that the "wilds" and "wilderness" can be allowed to exist only in certain forms, forms that are acceptable to humans. Such policies are symptomatic of our inability to look at natural systems and realize that evolution has crafted them and made them what they are. If we interfere, we invariably destroy what has taken millennia to develop. Do people defend the wolf, the mountain lion, and the eagle against their detractors because such animals epitomize "wilderness" in our mind's eye? Perhaps. But they also know that a system is only as healthy as its predators. There is a balance in nature, amid all of the seemingly random motions of population cycles and environmental fluctuations, a balance between predator and prey, between prey animals, and between animals and the vegetation upon which they graze. It is a balance to which we too often seem blind. None are so blind, it would seem, as people who believe that along with our humanity we bring absolute power and control over our world, and the right to exercise that control wherever and whenever we choose. It is a short-sighted and selfish vision that already exists in too many places. The wolf is no less a wolf, the whale no less a whale, simply because we happen to be human. And, since a person cannot make a wolf or a whale, or turn him- or herself into one, those that *just are* wolf or whale deserve a little more respect from evolutionary latecomers such as ourselves.

I hope those who say the environmentalists are alarmists are right, because to think otherwise is truly frightening. Our knowledge of global warming and ozone depletion is still developing; perhaps the balances of the world will win out, and we will not be faced with escalating temperatures and increasing ultraviolet light exposure. But do we really want to play Russian roulette with our own futures? Can we be so cavalier about the implications if we are wrong? Unfortunately, the uncertainty that surrounds global warming and ozone depletion does not fill the debate on species extinctions.

Our population is expanding, and it will continue to grow. If the United Nations estimates are correct, we will have to deal with 12 billion people, and people need space and resources. The rainforests are being felled, the oceans and rivers are being polluted and overfished. We know this to be true. Is the sky falling? Not yet—but we can keep it up there only a little longer. Some people believe that the world is overpopulated today; what will conditions be like when it doubles? The issue of overpopulation is critical to our survival, and more than that, it is critical to the *way* that we wish to live in the future—the standard of living that we hold so dear. But the issue is not solely one of numbers, it is also about consumption and the way that we use both renewable and nonrenewable resources. Population growth may be higher in developing countries, but consumption by the few in the developed world is also escalating out of control. If population growth must be curbed, perhaps more important, so too must the wasteful use of valuable resources and the industrial pollution of what remains—something that is very much a Western world problem. We cannot in truth look at our present situation and say that there are too many people. The problem is that the few have almost everything, while the majority have next to nothing. It is distribution and materialism, not shortage, that is the problem today.

The environmentalists are not the alarmists; it is those who choose not to see who are blindly allowing the human race to stampede toward a future that no one wants to imagine. We can change our future—there are no absolutes here, no predestined end for our species. We can shape our own destiny, recognize what we are capable of, the good and the bad, and select the good. The developed world has the technology, and the developing world has the biological resources that we need to survive. However, we must remember that technology is not a panacea, and that inappropriate technology transfer created many of the problems that the developing world is now facing.

Recent environmental conferences were designed to bring the two parts of the world together in harmony, so that what neither can do alone can be achieved in concert. If the 1992 Rio conference did anything, it showed how difficult it will be to get the countries of the developed world to realize that they cannot work alone, and that they must take the responsibility for many of the serious and potentially irreversible problems that we are faced with. We in the developed world must be willing to work with others to secure a future in which development and conservation are not mutually exclusive but intimately tied, each impossible without the other. We must recognize that the way things have been done in the past may not be the most appropriate in the future, and that the genetic diversity that we value so highly in the tropics comes with a price tag.

Some people in the West speak of protecting their jobs at the expense of the environment. Environmentalists are held up as the Luddites of the twentieth century. But our future, the future for all of us, is on this planet—unless you have something else in mind. It's the only real home we can ever expect to have.

These issues are all vital to our basic survival, as much as they are to the survival of the nonhuman. They include the view that as ethical beings we should protect species whenever we can simply because they exist. There is the economic argument that without self-sustaining systems, our fisheries, forests, and agricultural industries would collapse, and that the natural world offers some of the best chances for large-scale medical advances to battle old diseases and new ones. And there is the ecological argument that we are unraveling systems that we know too little about, and that we are as yet incapable of putting back together.

But the last argument is, I believe, the most compelling. It is an argument based on emotion. First and foremost we are emotional creatures; our ethics, and therefore our actions, are dictated by those emotions. We can be rational and irrational, and what makes us human may be the unpredictable balance between the two. Our emotions and how we act on them are vitally important to our characters. If we ever try to divorce ourselves from our emotions, we will lose our capacity to care, and it is that capacity that drives us to act for the better in all things.

What have we lost with the passing of the dodo, the passenger pigeon, Wendell's and Steller's sea cows, the moa, the quagga, and the Tasmanian wolf? We may have lost a part of the gene pool that one day could impart characteristics that we may live or die for; we may have lost some wonder drug or crop to feed the world. But these are intangibles; they may have been lost, or they may never have been there—we will never know. But I do know that with their passing, we have lost something else—beauty and imagination in the natural world. What have we lost with the damming of Hetch Hetchy Valley and the degradation of countless more landscapes and vistas? We have lost a vision of the natural world that we can never recreate.

Ralph Waldo Emerson linked people with the transformative power of nature. He called nature "the vehicle of thought" and the "symbol of spirit." In Emerson's eyes the world was "the mirror of the soul," and the universe its "externalization." We cannot seek to understand ourselves without beginning to understand nature. Emerson's contemporary and student Henry David Thoreau also spoke with a wonder about nature:

> We can never have enough of Nature. We must be refreshed by the sight of inexhaustible vigor, vast and Titanic features, the seacoast with its wrecks, the

wilderness with its living and its decaying trees, the thundercloud, and the rain which lasts three weeks and produces freshets. We need to witness our own limits transgressed.

Emerson wrote that beauty in nature was central to us as individuals:

> The simple perception of natural forms is a delight. . . . The presence of a higher, namely, of the spiritual element is essential to its perfection. There is still another aspect under which the beauty of the world may be viewed, namely, as it becomes an object of the intellect.

Emerson saw the value of nature in our ability to use our perception of it to heighten our understanding, to reason, and to *know* ourselves. But it is also something more, something more intimately tied to our own humanity. The value of nature is translated to our capacity to feel emotion. Humanity is defined as "the quality of being human," or showing "kindness or mercy." I firmly believe that our humanity is founded in our imagination, our ability to transform a situation to a personal level, to experience pleasure at a sight, and to feel compassion, injustice, and love. Without nature we cannot imagine, and the ability to look outside ourselves or place our own thoughts in the mind of another is the stuff of imagination. If nature and imagination are intimately tied, then without nature we have no humanity, and we cease being human. There is nothing in the ability to imagine or dream that can be seen as uniquely human, and it may just be possible for us to catch a glimpse of burgeoning humanity in our fellow animals.

There are many places that harbor the flavor revealed in the waters of Baja. In their inhabitants we can see ourselves. If we are lucky, we see it in the eye of the whale or the flurry of an osprey's feathers. We can travel and immerse ourselves in a place distant and alien, and marvel at creatures separated from us by water and linked by air. If we desire to light a flame under our imaginations, then we need those who allow us the privilege to imagine. People live by their dreams.

To transgress our limits, to see the mirror of our soul and to go beyond our humanity, we need to go beyond what is human. You do not have to read Emerson or Thoreau to know this; all you need to do is watch those who are outside yourself.

In later years I have continued to be awed by leviathans of all shapes and sizes—bowheads and southern right whales, spinner dolphins and dwarf sperm whales. Aerial spectacles and feeding displays, bowriding and flipper slapping. Exclamations of life and power thrusts from the strongest muscles in the world.

Baja is a wilderness that stokes the imagination with the barren heat of the desert hiding greenery and propagules behind thorns, with the vivid green of impenetrable mangroves hiding garish birds, and azure seas hiding behemoths. To see, all you have to do is look behind the obvious and allow your mind to wonder at the sights revealed. Things that are worth seeing, and worth protecting, are often hidden from view, while others are invisible in plain sight. "We see what we want to see" becomes a vital precept.

If basic survival is what we desire, then perhaps we can lose much of the wilderness and its inhabitants and still retain our "human nature." But if we look upon art with pleasure, and look to the future in hope, then we owe it to ourselves to want more than the basics of life. When we have the ability to protect, we must, simply because through indifference or design we also have the ability to do otherwise.

Conservation is about choice and ability. In recent times we have heard a great deal about the reasons to save, or not save, a species. Every few years the IUCN–World Conservation Union issues the "IUCN Red List of Threatened Animals." The next few pages list all animal species classified by the IUCN as either extinct (within the last fifty years), endangered, vulnerable, or rare. The 1990 list obviously includes only the 5 percent of endangered animal life on this planet that we have named. The countless unnamed and unknown are not represented; neither are plants.

Some of the names are descriptive; some are taken from the names of those who first looked upon them; others are still steeped in Latin and Greek. Do you still think that there is no problem? Do you want to choose which lives and which vanishes forever—a unique organism that we can never recreate—and explain to your children why?

While I was preparing this list, I accidentally deleted one name. I had already completed the list, and I had no idea which one it was. I could have left it out— one more species, what does it really matter; no one would miss it. Then, the more I thought about it, the more I realized that is the problem. So I sat down with both lists and pored over them until I found the spotted loach, *Lepidocephalichthys jonklaasi,* an endangered fish from Sri Lanka. I doubt that anyone would have noticed if I had left it out. But I would have known, and I don't want to forget any species that one day may vanish because someone else left them off a list. So to protect the likes of the Sri Lankan spotted loach, please remember the names of some of those that today are few in number, and some of those who will never come again.

Going: Abbot's booby, Abbot's duiker, Abruzzo chamois, acorn pearly mussel, *Acraea hova, Acraea sambavae, Acrothele calpeiana,* addax, Ader's duiker, Adriatic salmon, *Aeschrithmysus dubautianus, Aeschrithmysus swezeyi, Aeschrithmysus terryi, Aeshna meruensis, Aeshna persephone,* African blind barb fish, African elephant, African giant swallowtail, African green broadbill, African lammergeyer, African wild ass, African wild dog, akepa, akialoa, akiapolaau, ala balik, Alabama beach mouse, Alabama cavefish, Alabama lamp pearly mussel, Alabama red-bellied turtle, Alabama sturgeon, *Alaena margaritacea,* alagoas curassow, alaotra grebe, alaotran gentle lemur, *Alasmidonta raveneliana, Alasmidonta robusta, Alasmidonta wrightiana,* albertine owlet, alcon large blue, Aldabra giant tortoise, Aldabra warbler, Aleutian Canada goose, Algerian nuthatch, alligator snapping turtle, Almeda striped racer, *Aloeides caledoni, Aloeides dentatis, Aloeides egerides, Aloeides lutescens,* alvord chub, amami rabbit, amami sunbird, amami thrush, *Amanipodagrion gilliesi,* Amargosa vole, Amargosa pupfish, *Amauris comorana, Amauris nossima, Amauris phoedon,* Amazon River dolphin, Amazonian manatee, amber darter, ambon yellow white-eye, American burying beetle, American crocodile, American earthworm, Amsterdam albatross, Amur sturgeon, *Amychus candezei, Amychus granulatus,* Anastasia Island beach mouse, Andaman leafwing, Andean cat, Andros ground iguana, Anegada ground iguana, *Anetia briarea, Anetia cubana, Anetia jaegeri, Anetia pantheratus,* angonoka, Angula ciega, ankober serin, *Antanartia borbonica mauritiana,* Anthony's wood rat, Antipodes parakeet, *Antipodogomphus hodgkini, Antiponemertes allisonae,* Anyayukaksurak char, Apache trout, *Apaturopsis kilusa, Apaturopsis pauliani, Aplothorax burchelli,* Apolinar's marsh wren, Apollo, Appert's greenbul, apricot-breasted sunbird, *Apteromantis aptera,* aquatic box turtle, Arabian oryx, Arabian sand gazelle, Arabian tahr, Archey's frog, *Archon apollinaris,* Argentinian pampas deer, *Argiocnemis solitaria, Argonemertes australiensis, Argonemertes hillii, Argonemertes stocki, Argyrocupha malagrida malagrida, Argyrocupha malagrida paarlensis, Arigomphus maxwelli,* Arkansas darter, Aruba Island rattlesnake, Ascension frigatebird, ash meadows bug, ashy darter, ashyheaded laughingthrush, Asian dowitcher, Asiatic black bear, Asiatic buffalo, Asiatic cheetah, Asiatic lion, Asiatic wild ass, asper, asprete, Atiu swiftlet, Atlantic ridley, Atlantic saltmarsh snake, Atlantic sturgeon, Atlantic walrus, Atlantic whitefish, *Atrophaneura luchti, Atrophaneura schadenbergi,* Attwater's prairie chicken, Audouin's gull, Australian grayling, *Austrocordulia territoria,* axolotl, aye-aye, ayumodoki, azure-breasted pitta, babirusa, Bachman's warbler, bactrian camel, bactrian deer, Baer's pochard, *Baetica ustulata,* bagre de Cuatro Cienegas, bagre de Muzquiz, bagre de Rio Verde, bagre de Yaqui, bagre del Panuco, bagre lobo, Bahamian hutia, baiji, *Balea perversa,* Bali starling, balkash perch, Baluchistan bear, bamboo sylph, banded bog skimmer dragonfly, banded cotinga, banded dune snail, banded green sunbird, banded hare-wallaby, banded wattle-eye, Banggai crow, Bannerman's turaco, Bannerman's weaver, banteng, bar-winged rail, Barbary deer, Barbary hyena, Barbary macaque, Barbary sheep, Barber's ranger, bare-eyed myna, Barens topminnow, Barnard's rock-catfish, barrens bluet damselfly, Barrington land iguana, Bate's weaver, battling glider, bay checkerspot butterfly, bay colobus, Baykal teal, bayou darter, beach vole, Bear Lake sculpin, bearded goby, beautiful nuthatch, beautiful shiner, bee hummingbird, *Belenois orgygia,* Belkin's dune tabanid fly, Belle's sand clubtail, beloribitsa, Bengal florican, bent wing swift moth, Berg River redfin, Biak flycatcher, Biak monarch, Biak paradise kingfisher, Big Bend gambusia, big pine key dung beetle, big thicket emerald dragonfly, bigeye jumprock, Bigger's groundwater planarian, bighead redhorse, Bimini boa, birdwing pearly mussel, Bishop's oo, black and rufous elephant-shrew, black bog ant, black buntingi, black caiman, black colobus, black dorcopsis wallaby, black gibbon, black lemur, black lion tamarin, black muntjac, black petrel, black rhinoceros, black ruby barb, black shama, black sicklebill, black soft-shell turtle, black spider monkey, black stilt, black toad, black wildebeest, black-banded barbet, black-banded flycatcher, black-capped petrel, black-cheeked lovebird, black-faced impala, black-faced lion tamarin, black-faced spoonbill, black-footed ferret, black-fronted piping guan, black-fronted tern, black-headed uakari, black-hooded antwren, black-masked nuthatch, black-necked crane, black-shanked douc monkey, black-spotted cuscus, black-winged lory, blackfin sucker, blackish cuckoo-shrike, blackmouth shiner, Blakiston's fish-owl, bloater, blotchside logperch, blue chaffinch, blue ground beetle, blue jewel copper, blue lorikeet, blue shiner, blue sucker, blue whale, blue-billed curassow, blue-breasted flycatcher, blue-capped wood kingfisher, blue-headed quail-dove, blue-streaked lory, blue-throated parakeet, bluebarred pygmy sunfish, bluehead shiner, bluenose shiner, bluestripe darter, bluestripe shiner, bluntnose shiner, bog turtle, Bogota rail, bold characodon, Bolson tortoise, Bonin Islands honeyeater, bontebok, bonytail chub, Borax Lake chub, border barb, Bornean Bay cat, boulder darter, Bouvier's red colobus, bowhead whale, *Brachyaspis atriceps, Brachythemis fuscopalliata,* Brasilia lyrefin, bridled nailtail wallaby, bristle-thighed curlew, broad-nosed caiman, broad-tail beaver, bronze clubtail dragonfly, brow-antlered deer, brown cross sphecid wasp, brown-eared pheasant, brown howler monkey, brown hyena, brown lemur, brown mesite, brown teal, brown-backed flowerpecker, brown-backed parrotlet, brown-chested jungle-flycatcher, brown-headed spider monkey, brush-tailed bettong, buffy-headed marmoset, buffy-tufted-ear marmoset, *Bulimulus* sp., bull trout, Bulwer's pheasant, Bunker's wood rat, Burchell's redfin, *Burmagomphus sivalikensis,* burrowing bettong, bush dog, bushy-tailed hutia, Cabot's tragopan, Cabrera's hutia, cachorrito de dorsal larga, cachorrito boxeador, cachorrito cabezon, cachorrito cangrejero, cachorrito de media luna, cachorrito de Mezquital, cachorrito del Aguanaval, cachorrito enano de Potosi, cachorrito gigante, cachorrito lodero, caddo madtom, *Caecocypris basimi,* cahaba shiner, cahow, Calamian deer, California condor, California freshwater shrimp, California tiger salamander, calnwilliam sandfish, *Calopteryx syriaca,* Calvert's emerald, *Cambarus zophonastes, Canariella fortunata, Canariella leprosa, Canariella pthonera,* cane turtle, Canterbury mudfish, Cape Fear shiner, Cape Mountain zebra, Cape platanna, Cape vulture, cape whitefish, caprivi killifish, *Capys penningtoni, Carabus olympiae,* caracara commensal scarab beetle, Caribbean monk seal, carinated striate banded mountain snail, Carolina madtom, Carolina northern flying squirrel, Carolina pygmy sunfish, *Caseolus calculus, Caseolus commixta, Caseolus sphaerula,* Cassini periodical cicada, *Castor fiber bindai,* Cat Island turtle, *Catabasis acuminatus,* caterpillar searcher, cauca guan, Caucasian viper, cave catfish, Cedros Island mule deer, Celebes rainbow, *Celeriio wilsoni perkinsi,* Central American river turtle, Central American squirrel monkey, Central American tapir, Central Asian cobra, Central Asian monitor, central rock-rat, *Cephalaeschna acutifrons, Cephalokompsus pachycheilus, cerambyx longicorn,* chaco sideneck turtle, chaco tortoise, chacoan peccary, Chapin's flycatcher, charal de Alchichica, charal de la Preciosa, charal de Quechulac, charal del Valle de Mexico, charalito, charalito chihuahua, charalito saltillo, charalito sonorense, *Charaxes cowani, Charaxes karkloof capensis, Charaxes marieps, Charaxes usambarae, Charaxes xiphares desmondi,* Chartreuse chamois, Chatham Island oystercatcher, Chatham Island petrel, Chatham Island robin, checked goby, cheer pheasant, cheetah, chequered elephant-shrew, chequered skipper, *Cherax crassimanus,* Cherokee clubtail dragonfly, cherry barb, cherry-throated tanager, chestnut Rajah, chestnut-headed partridge, chestnut-necklaced partridge, Chilean pudu, Chilean woodstar, chimpanzee, Chinese alligator, Chinese egret, Chinese monal, Chinese paddlefish, Chinese three-tailed swallowtail, Chinese water-deer, chittenango ovate amber snail, *Chlorolestes draconicus,* Choctawahatchee beach mouse, Christmas frigatebird, Christmas imperial-pigeon, cicek, cima discula, cinereous vulture, cinnamon-banded kingfisher, cisco, clanwilliam redfin, clanwilliam rock-catfish, clanwilliam yellowfin, Clarence galaxias, Clarion wren, Clarke's weaver, Clear Creek gambusia, clouded leopard, cloven-feathered dove, coachella fringe-toed lizard, coahuilix de Hubbs snail, coconut crab, cocos cuckoo, coelacanth, coldwater darter, collared lemur, collared mangabey, Colorado chipmunk, Colorado River cotton rat, Colorado squafish, colorless shiner, *Coluber cypriensis,* Columbia River tiger beetle, Comanche Springs pupfish, combtail, common sturgeon, comoro black flying fox, conasauga logperch, concentrated snail, Concho water snake, conchos pupfish, conchos shiner, conondale gastric-brooding frog, Cook's petrel, copper redhorse, coppercheek darter, Coquerel's dwarf lemur, *Cordulegaster mzymtae,* corncrake, Corsican fritillary, Corsican red deer, Corsican swallowtail, cottonball marsh pupfish, cottontop tamarin, cracking pearly mussel, cream-banded swallowtail, Creaser's mud turtle, crested argus, crested eagle, crested fireback, crested honeycreeper, crested ibis, crested parrotbill, crested shelduck, *Crocidura zimmermanni,* Cromwell chafer, crowned lemur, crystal darter, cuatro cienegas shiner, Cuban crocodile, Cuban gnatcatcher, Cuban ground iguana, Cuban parakeet, Cuban solenodon, cui-ui, Culbra Island giant anole, Cumberland bean pearly mussel, Cumberland monkey-face pearly mussel, Cumberland pigtoe, Curiers' hutia, Curtus's mussel, cutthroat trout, Cuvier's gazelle, *Cymothoe amaniensis, Cymothoe aurivillii, Cymothoe magambae, Cymothoe melanjae, Cymothoe teita, Cynolebias constanciae,* Cyprus mouflon, Dakota skipper, Dalmatian barbelgudgeon, Dalmatian pelican, dama ciega blanca, dama gazelle, Damara tern, Dangs giant squirrel, Danube salmon, dapple-throat, dardo de conchos, dardo de cuatro cienegas, dark serpent-eagle, dark-rumped petrel, dark-tailed laurel pigeon, decim periodical cicada, decula periodical cicada, Defillippe's petrel, Deignan's babbler, Delmarva fox squirrel, delta green ground beetle, delta smelt, *Dermogenys megarramphus, Dermogenys weberi,* Des Moulin's snail, desert dace, desert pupfish, desert slender salamander, desert tortoise, *Deudorix penningtoni, Deudorix vansoni,* Devil's River minnow, Devil's Hole pupfish, dhole, diablotin, diademed sifaka, Diana monkey, dibatag, Dickson's brown, Dickson's copper, Dickson's sylph, Dickson's thestor, dikume, diminutive clubtail, *Dinomys branickii, Discoglossus jeanneae, Discoglossus montalentii, Discula leacockiana, Discula tabellata, Discula testudinalis, Discus defloratus,* Discus scutula, Djibouti francolin, Dominican hutia, dorcas gazelle, *Dorcus auriculatus, Dorcus ithaginis,* Doria's tree-kangaroo, drill, dromedary pearly mussel, duck-billed buntingi, dugong, Dunn's mud turtle, durangonella de coahuila snail, *Durbania limbata,* dusky friarbird, dusky greenbul, dusky hopping-mouse, dusky large blue, Duthie's golden mole, dwarf hutia, dwarf wedge mussel, *Dynastes hercules, Dynastes hercules hercules, Dynastes hercules reidi, Dytiscus latissimus,* East Coast akalat, eastern cougar, eastern freshwater cod, eastern giant eland, eastern indigo snake, eastern lowland gorilla, eastern province rocky, eastern red colobus, eastern sand darter, *Ecchlorolestes nylephtha, Ecchlorolestes perengueyi, Economidichthys trichonis,* egg-carrying buntingi, Egyptian tortoise, eight-spotted skipper, el segunda blue, elegant sunbird, Elizabeth Springs goby, Elk River file snail, Elliot's pheasant, Emei Shan liocichla, *Engaea subcoerulea,* enos stickleback, *Epargyreus antaeus, Epargyreus spana, Epioblasma brevidens, Epioblasma capsaeformis, Epioblasma metastriata, Erebia annada annada, Erebia narasingha narasingha, Erikssonia acraeina, Eriogaster catax,* escargot de Quimper, Eskimo curlew, Espada de Clemencia, estuarine crocodile, Ethiopian bush-crow, *Eucrenonaspides oinotheke, Eumaeus atala florida, Euploea albicosta, Euploea blossomae, Euploea caespes, Euploea configurata, Euploea cordelia, Euploea dentiplaga, Euploea doretta, Euploea eboraci, Euploea eupator, Euploea euphon, Euploea gamelia, Euploea lacon, Euploea latifasicata, Euploea magou, Euploea martinii, Euploea mitra, Euploea tobleri, Euploea tripunctata,* European bison, European leaf-toed gecko, European marbled polecat, European mink, European otter, European red wood ant, *Euxanthe madagascariensis,* Everett's thrush, fairy pitta, fairy shrimp, falanouc, false dewy ringlet, false gharial, false ringlet, false water-rat, fat pocketbook, Fatuhiva monarch, fawn-breasted thrush, Fea's muntjac, Fernando Po Speirops, fiery redfin, Fiji crested iguana, Fiji petrel, Filfola lizard, fin whale, fine-rayed pigtoe pearly mussel, finescale saddled darter, Finn's baya weaver, fire-maned bowerbird, fissi, flame chub, flame-templed babbler, flat-spired three-toothed snail, flattened musk turtle, flax snail, flax weevil, flinders gudgeon, Flores crow, Florida atala hairstreak, Florida cave shrimp, Florida cougar, Florida gopher tortoise, Florida saltmarsh vole, Florida spiketail dragonfly, fluminense swallowtail, Fly River grassbird, forest ground-thrush, fork-marked dwarf lemur, *Formica aquilonia, Formica lugubris,* Formosa serow, Formosan sika, fountain darter, four-horn sculpin, frecklebelly madtom, freckled darter, freira, freshwater mullet, freshwater pearly mussel, Fresno kangaroo rat, Frey's damselfly, Frigate Island giant tenebrionid beetle, fringe-backed fire-eye, Fuerteventura stonechat, Galapagos giant tortoise, Galapagos flightless cormorant, Galapagos hawk, Galapagos land iguana, Galapagos marine iguana, Ganges susu, Gardiner's Seychelles frog, *Garra barreimiae, Garra dunsirei,* Garrido's hutia, gaur, Geelvinck Bay leaf-nosed bat, gelada baboon, Geoffroy's spider monkey, geometric tortoise, *Geomitra moniziana, Geonemertes rodericana,* Georgia pearly mussel, Germain's peacock-pheasant, Ghana cuckoo-shrike, gharial, ghost bat, ghost walker beetle, giant anteater, giant armadillo, giant catfish, giant clam, giant Columbia River spire snail, giant freshwater crayfish, giant garter snake, giant Gippsland earthworm, giant golden mole, giant ibis, giant imperial-pigeon, giant nuthatch, giant otter, giant panda, giant sable antelope, giant stickleback, giant sunbird, giant torrent midge, Giffard's sphecid wasp, Gila chub, Gila monster, Gila trout, giluwe rat, ginger pearlfish, *Girardinichthys multiradiatus,* Glacier Bay wolf spider, *Glaucomys volans guerreroensis, Glaucomys volans oaxacensis, Glossogobius intermedius, Glossogobius matanensis,* glutinous snail, Goeldi's marmoset, golden bamboo lemur, golden cocqui frog, golden-crowned sifaka, golden Kaiser-I-Hind, golden leaf monkey, golden lion tamarin, golden parakeet, golden sleeper, golden takin, golden toad, golden-fronted fulvetta, golden-headed lion tamarin, golden-shouldered parrot, Goldie's bird of paradise, goldline darter, goldsteifiger, goliath frog, *Gomphurus flavipes, Gomphurus graslini, Gomphurus lynnae, Gomphurus ozarkensis,* gon-gon, *Goodea gracilis,* goodeid, Goodfellow's tree-kangaroo, Goose Lake sucker, gorgeted wood-quail, gorilla, gough bunting, gough moorhen, Grand Comoro drongo, Grand Comoro flycatcher, Grants' golden mole, granulated Tasmanian snail, *Graphium alebion chungianus, Graphium idaeoides, Graphium levassori, Graphium mendana, Graphium sandawanum, Graphium stresemanni, Graphoderus bilineatus,* Grauer's gnatcatcher, gray redhorse, Gray's monitor, great bustard, great Indian bustard, great Indian rhinoceros, great peacock moth, great raft spider, greater adjutant, greater bamboo gentle lemur, greater bilby, greater large blue, greater prairie-chicken, greater stick-nest rat, green avadavat, green labeo, green peafowl, green racquet-tail, green turtle, green-billed coucal, green-blossom pearly mussel, green-breasted bush-shrike, green-faced parrotfinch, Grenada dove, Grevy's zebra, grey bat, grey imperial-pigeon, grey wolf, grey wood-pigeon, grey zorro, grey-backed sportive lemur, grey-crowned greenbul, grey-headed quail-dove, grey-necked picathartes, grosbeak bunting, ground parrot, Grune Keiljungter, Guadalupe bass, Guadalupe fur seal, Guadalupe junco, Guam flycatcher, Guam rail, Guam tree snail, Guayacon bocon, Guayacon de cuatro cienegas, Guayacon de hacienda Dolores, Guayacon de San Gregorio, Guayacon pinto, Guizhou snub-nosed monkey, gulf clubtail, Gundlach's hawk, Gunther's gecko, Gurney's pitta, *Hadramphus spinipennis, Hadramphus stilbocarpae, Hadramphus tuberculatus,* Haeakala sphecid wasp, Hahnel's Amazonian swallowtail, hairy-eared dwarf lemur, Haitian solenodon, hamadryas baboon, Hamilton's frog, hangul, harpy eagle, Harris' mimic swallowtail, Hartmann's mountain zebra, Hastings River mouse, Hawaiian click beetle, Hawaiian crow, Hawaiian duck, Hawaiian goose, Hawaiian hawk, Hawaiian monk seal, Hawaiian proterhinus beetles, Hawaiian snout beetles, Hawaiian sphecid wasp, hawksbill turtle, heath rat, Heck's macaque, Hector's dolphin, *Heliconius charltonius peruvianus, Helix subplicata,* helmeted myna, helmeted woodpecker, *Hemicycla adansoni, Hemicycla inutilis, Hemicycla mascaensis, Hemicycla modesta, Hemicycla plicaria, Hemicycla pouchet, Hemiphlebia mirabilis,* Henderson Island rail, henna-tailed jungle-flycatcher, Herekopare Island weta, Herman's myotis, Hermann's tortoise, hermit beetle, *Heteramphus filicum, Heterexis seticostatus,* Hierro giant lizard, Higgin's eye pearly mussel, Hinde's pied babbler, Hispaniolan hutia, hispid hare, Hochstetter's frog, Hodge's clubtail, Holsinger's groundwater planarian, Homerus swallowtail, honey blue-eye, hooded crane, hooded grebe, hooded treepie, hook-billed hermit, Hoolock gibbon, horned coot, horned guan, Houbara bustard, Houston toad, houting, Howe's midget snaketail dragonfly, Hualapai Mexican vole, *Hubsina turneri,* Hume's pheasant, humpback chub, humpback whale, Hunter's antelope, *Hydraecia petasitis, Hyles hippophaes, Hylogomphus parvidens, Hypolimnas antevorta,* Ibadan malimbe, Ibiza common genet, Ibiza wall lizard, *Ictinogomphus dobsoni,* Idaho banded mountain snail, *Idea electra, Idea iasonia, Idea malabarica, Ideopsis hewitsonii, Ideopsis klassika, Ideopsis oberthurii, Iguanognathus werneri,* imitator sparrowhawk, imperial eagle, imperial parrot, imperial pheasant, imperial woodpecker, inaccessible rail, Inagua Island turtle, Incomati rock catlet, Indian egg-eating snake, Indian elephant, Indian python, Indian wild ass, Indiana bat, Indochina featherback, indri, Indus River dolphin, *Insulivitrina mascaensis, Insulivitrina reticulata, Io arwigera arwigera,* Iowa pleistocene snail, Iphis monarch, *Iranocypris typhlops,* Iringa ground robin, iriomote cat, Isabela oriole, Island Night lizard, island grey fox, Italian agile frog, Italian spadefoot toad, ivory-billed woodpecker, jaguar, Jamaican boa, Jamaican ground iguana, Jamaican hutia, Jamaican kite, James River spiny mussel, Japanese crane, Japanese crested ibis, Japanese giant salamander, Japanese murrelet, Japanese night-heron, Japanese serow, Japanese white stork, Japanese yellow bunting, Jasper longnose sucker, Javan and Bawan warty pigs, Javan cochoa, Javan coucal, Javan gibbon, Javan hawk-eagle, Javan leaf monkey, Javan rhinoceros, Javan scops-owl, Javan white-eye, Jay's River snail, Jemez Mountains salamander, Jenny Creek sucker, Jentink's duiker, Jerdon's babbler, Jordan's swallowtail, Juan Fernandez firecrown, Juan Fernandez fur seal, Judge Tait's mussel, juil ciego, junin grebe, kabobo apalis, kagu, kakapo, kaluga, kamao, Kanawha darter, Kanawha minnow, Kaplan's thestor, Karok Indian snail, Kasier-I-Hind, *Katechonemertes nightingaleensis,* Kauai creeper, Kauai flightless stag beetle, Kauai oo, Kauai sphecid wasp, Kauri amber snail, Kedestes chaca, Kerguelen tern, Kern brook lamprey, Kern Canyon slender salamander, kern primrose sphinx moth, Kerry slug, Key deer, Key Largo cotton mouse, Key Largo wood rat, key silverside, Kilimanjaro swallowtail, killifish, Kinabalu serpent-eagle, king shag, Kirtland's warbler, Kitti's hog-nosed bat, *Kiwaia jeanae,* kiyi, Klamath Lake sculpin, Kloss's gibbon,*Knipowitschia punctatissima, Knipowitschia thessala,* Knysna seahorse, Kocevje subterranean spiders, kokako, Komodo dragon, konye, *Koonunga cursor,* korrigum, kouprey, Kozlov's pika, Kuhl's deer, Kuhl's lorikeet, kululu, kungwe apalis, *Kupea electilis,* Kuril seal, L'Hoest's guenon, La Plata otter, Lake Eacham rainbowfish, Lake Lerma salamander, Lake Magadi tilapia, Lake Patzcuaro salamander, Lake Victoria cichlids, lake lamprey, lake sturgeon, Lancelin Island skink, Lange's metalmark, Larch Mountain salamander, larche ringlet, large blue, large blue lake mayfly, large copper, large green-pigeon, large-billed bushwarbler, large-eared hutia, largescale pupfish, *Laticauda crockeri,* Latifi's viper, Laysan duck, Laysan finch, Leadbeater's possum, leaf-nosed lizard, Lear's macaw, least chipmunk, least chub, leatherback, lechwe, legless skink, leka keppe, lemon-throated white-eye, Leon Springs pupfish, leopard darter, *Lepidochrysops ariadne, Lepidochrysops loewensteini, Lepidochrysops lotana, Lepidochrysops methymna dicksoni, Leptonemertes chalicophora,* lesser adjutant, lesser florican, lesser kestrel, lesser white-fronted goose, *Lethe dura gammiei, Lethe europa tamuna, Lethe gemina gafuri, Lethe margaritae, Lethe ocellata lyncus, Lethe ramadeva, Lethe satyavati, Libellula angelina,* Liberian mongoose, Lilford's wall lizard, limestone salamander, lion-tailed macaque, Little Colorado spinedace, little bittern, little blue macaw, little bustard, little earth hutia, little long-nosed bat, little spotted cat, little spotted kiwi, little winged pearly mussel, loach minnow, long-beaked echidna, long-bearded melidectes, long-billed apalis, long-billed rhabdornis, long-billed white-eye, long-fingered bat, long-haired spider monkey, long-tailed ground roller, long-tailed paradigalla, long-tailed prinia, long-wattled umbrellabird, longhead darter, longnose dace, longnose darter, Lord Howe rail, Los Angeles pocket mouse, Lost River sucker, Lotis blue, Lower California pronghorn, Lower Keys rabbit, lowland anoa, lowveld largemouth, Luth turtle, *Lutodrilus multivesiculatus,* Luzon redstart, Macabe Forest skink, *Macromia margarita, Macularia saintyvesi, Maculinea teleius, Maculinea teleius burdigalensis,* Madagascan emperor swallowtail, Madagascar fish-eagle, Madagascar plover, Madagascar pochard, Madagascar serpent-eagle, Madagascar teal, Madeira laurel pigeon, Madeiran land snail, Madison Cave isopod, magenta petrel, Maharasthra giant squirrel, Malabar civet, *Malacolimax wiktori,* Malagasy civet, Malagasy narrow-striped mongoose, Malayan tapir, Malaysian peacock-pheasant, maleo, Malheur Cave planarian, Mallorcan midwife toad, Maluti minnow, *Mandibularca resinus,* mandrill, maned sloth, maned wolf, mangaia kingfisher, manipur brow-antlered deer, manipur bush quail, Mansfield's three-tailed swallowtail, manus green tree snail, marbled teal, margay, margined tortoise, Mariana fruit-dove, Marianas crow, Marianas megapode, Marianna flying fox, marine otter, markhor, maroon wood-pigeon, maroon-fronted parrot, Marquesas ground dove, Marquesas imperial-pigeon, Marquesas kingfisher, Marquesas monarch, marsh crocodile, marsh deer, Marshall's mussel, Martinique oriole, Marunga sunbird, Maryland darter, Masafuerae raydito, masked finfoot, masked titi, Matalote cahita, Matalote conchos, Matalote del Bavispe, Matalote opata, Matinan flycatcher, Maui parrotbill, Mauritian flying fox, Mauritius bulbul, Mauritius cuckoo-shrike, Mauritius fody, Mauritius kestrel, Mauritius olive white-eye, Mauritius parakeet, Mayotte drongo, Mayotte lemur, meadow jumping mouse, *Mecistogaster asticta, Mecistogaster pronoti,* Mediterranean monk seal, Meeks' graphium, *Megacolabus sculpturatus, Mehalennia pallidula,* Melones Cave harvestman, Mentawai leaf monkey, Mentawai macaque, Mentawai palm civet, Menzbier's marmot, *Metatrichoniscoides celticus,* Mexcalpique, Mexican darter, Mexican flying squirrel, Mexican golden trout, Mexican long-nosed bat, Mexican prairie dog, Mexipyrgus de Carranza snail, Mexipyrgus de Churince snail, Mexipyrgus de East El Mojarral snail, Mexipyrgus de Escobeda snail, Mexipyrgus de Lugo snail, Mexipyrgus de West El Mojarral snail, Mexithauma de Cienegas snail, *Micraspides calmani, Microcryptorhynchus orientissimus,* microdon sportive lemur, Micronesian scrubfowl, *Microtus pennsylvanicus chihuahuensis,* Mikado pheasant, milky stork, Millar's buff, Miller's snail, millerbird, Milne-Edwards' sportive lemur, Milos viper, Mindanao gymnure, Mindoro imperial-pigeon, Mindoro scops-owl, Miss Waldron's bay colobus, mission blue butterfly, moapa dace, modoc sucker, mojarra, mojarra caracolera, mojarra caracolera de Media Luna, mojarra de bulha, mojarra de cuatro cienegas, Mojave rabbitbrush longhorn beetle, molly del Teapa, Moluccan scrubfowl, Mona blind snake, Mona boa, *Monardithemis flava,* mongo, Mongolian wild ass, mongoose lemur, monkey-eating eagle, Montserrat oriole, moor macaque, Moorean viviparous tree snail, Morelet's crocodile, *Morimus funereus,* Morro Bay kangaroo rat, Mortlock flying fox, *Mortonagrion hirosei,* Mount Cameroon francolin, Mount Donna Buang wingless stonefly, Mount Graham red squirrel, Mount Karthala white-eye, Mount Kosciusko wingless stonefly, Mount Nimba viviparous toad, Mount St. Helens grylloblattid, Mountain Blackside dace, mountain anoa, mountain gazelle, mountain gorilla, mountain nyala, mountain tapir, mountain zebra, Mrs. Moreau's warbler, *Mugilogobius latifrons, Mugilogobius* n.sp., myaka myaka, *Mylothris carcassoni,* Myrtle's fritillary, naga hedge blue, Nahan's francolin, naked characin, Namaquab barb, *Napaeus badiosus, Napaeus nanodes, Napaeus propinguus, Napaeus roccellicola, Napaeus tarnerianus, Napaeus variatus,* Narcondam hornbill, narrow-billed antwren, narrow-bridged mud turtle, narrow-mouthed whorl snail, Nashville crayfish, Natterer's longwing, Nauru reed-warbler, negros babbler, nekogigi, *Nemacheilus smithi, Nemacheilus starostini, Nemacheilus xiang-*

gensis, Neosho madtom, Neosho pearly mussel, *Neptis decraryi*, *Neptis metella gratilla*, *Neptis nycteas*, *Neptis sankara nar*, *Nesithmysus bridwelli*, *Nesithmysus frobesi*, *Nesithmysus haasi*, *Nesithmysus swezeyi*, *Nesomimesa scipteryx*, Nevada blue, New Britain sparrowhawk, New Guinea eagle, New Zealand greater short-tailed bat, Newel's shearwater, niangua darter, Nicklin's pearly mussel, nicobar pigeon, nicobar scrubfowl, nihoa finch, Niihau vespid wasp, Nile crocodile, Nilgiri leaf monkey, Nilgiri tahr, Nilgiri wood-pigeon, nimba otter-shrew, no-eyed big-eyed wolf spider, noble crayfish, noisy scrub-bird, non-parasitic lamprey, noonday snail, North Andean huemul, northern bald ibis, northern bottlenose whale, northern cavefish, northern hairy-nosed wombat, northern right whale, northern sportive lemur, northern spotted owl, northern square-lipped rhinoceros, *Nososticta pilbara*, *Notarthrinus binghami*, *Nothaldonis peaci*, nsess, nueva dama ciega, nukupuu, numbat, nymphophilus de Minckley snail, Oahu creeper, Oahu nesiotes weevil, Oahu tree snail, ocelot, *Ochotona muliensis*, *Oclandius laeviusculus*, Ogilby's duiker, Ohio emerald dragonfly, Okaloosa darter, Okinawa rail, Okinawa woodpecker, olive colobus, olm, olomao, Olympic mudminnow, *Onthophagus furacatus*, *Onychogomphus assimilis*, *Onychogomphus macrodon*, oopu, oopu alamoo, oopu nakea, oopu nopili, opal goodeid, opalescent pearlfish, Opeonogo whitefish, *Ophiogomphus acuminatus*, *Ophiogomphus anomalus*, *Ophiogomphus incurvatus*, orange-banded thrush, orange-bellied parrot, orange-fringed largemouth, orange-spotted emerald, orange-throated whiptail, orange-fin madtom, orangutan, Oregon chub, Oregon giant earthworm, *Oreohelix jugalis intersum*, *Oreonectes anophthalmus*, *Orestias cuvieri*, Oriental white stork, Orinoco crocodile, ornate paradisefish, *Ornithoptera croesus*, *Ornithoptera meridionalis*, Orsini's viper, *Orthetrum poecilops mijajimaense*, *Orthetrum rubens*, Ortmann's pearly mussel, *Oryzias marmoratus*, *Oryzias matanensis*, *Ospatulus palaemophagus*, *Ospatulus truncatus*, otjikoto tilapia, Ottoman brassy ringlet, Otway stonefly, ou, Ouachita Mountain shiner, Ouachita madtom, Owens pupfish, owl-faced guenon, Ozark cavefish, Pacific damselfly, Pacific lamprey, Pacific ridley, paddlefish, *Padogobius nigricans*, pahrump poolfish, painted snake-coiled forest snail, painted terrapin, Pakistan sand cat, Palas's fish-eagle, Palau megapode, Palawan peacock-pheasant, pale hockeysticker sailer, pale lilliput pearly mussel, pale-capped pigeon, paleback darter, palila, pallid sturgeon, paludiscala de Oro snail, *Pantinonemertes agricola*, *Papilio acheron*, *Papilio benguetanus*, *Papilio carolinensis*, *Papilio chikae*, *Papilio esperanza*, *Papilio grosesmithi*, *Papilio himeros*, *Papilio mangoura*, *Papilio maraho*, *Papilio moerneri*, *Papilio neumoegeni*, *Papilio osmana*, *Papilio toborio*, *Papilio weymeri*, Papillion la pature, Papua New Guinean cuscus, Papuan dorcopsis, papyrus yellow warbler, paradise parrot, *Paragomphus sinaituicus*, *Parantica albata*, *Parantica clinias*, *Parantica crowleyi*, *Parantica dannatti*, *Parantica davidi*, *Parantica garamantis*, *Parantica kuekenthali*, *Parantica menadensis*, *Parantica milagros*, *Parantica nilgiriensis*, *Parantica philo*, *Parantica pseudomelaneus*, *Parantica pumila*, *Parantica rotundata*, *Parantica* schoenigi, *Parantica sulewattan, Parantica taprobana, Parantica tityoides, Parantica toxoperi, Parantica wegneri, Parantica weiskei, Pararge menava maeroides, Paratherina cyanea, Paratherina labiosa, Paratherina striata, Paratherina wolterecki,* pardel lynx, *Parides burchellanus, Parides coelus, Parmacella tenerifensis, Parnassius apollo vinningensis, Parnassius autocrator, Parnatica marcia, Parnatica phyle, Partula hebe, Partula langfordi, Partulina confusa, Partulina fusoidea, Partulina perdix, Partulina splendida, Paryphanta compta, Paryphanta fletcheri, Paryphanta gillisesi, Paryphanta hochstetteri, Paryphanta lignaria, Paryphanta rossiana, Paryphanta traversi,* Parzefall's stenasellidi, Pawnee Montane skipper, Pecos assiminea snail, Pecos gambusia, Pecos pupfish, pedder galaxias, Pemba flying fox, penitent mussel, Pennant's red colobus, *Pentarthrum pritchardias,* Perdido Key beach mouse, Père David deer, perrito de bolson, perrito de carbonera, perrito de cuatro cienegas, perrito de Potosi, Persian fallow deer, *Phalanta philiberti, Phildoria wilkesiella,* Philippine eagle, Philippine tarsier, Philippines crocodile, Philippines tube-nosed fruit bat, *Phylolestes ethalae,* pied tamarin, *Pieris krueperi deuta,* pig-tailed langur, pileated gibbon, pindu, pine barrens tree frog, pinewoods darter, pink mucket pearly mussel, pink pigeon, pink-footed shearwater, pla thapa, *Placostylus ambagiosus, Placostylus bollonsi, Plagithmysus* sp., Plant's gulella snail, *Platcnemis mauriciana,* platy cuatro cienegas, platy de Muzquiz, platy Monterrey, *Plebejus icarioides missionensis, Poblana ferdebueni, Poecilmitis adonis, Poecilmitis endymion, Poecilmitis rileyi,* Pohnpei flying fox, Point of Rocks spring snail, polar bear, Pollen's vanga, Polynesian ground dove, Polynesian imperial-pigeon, Polynesian scrubfowl, *Pomatias raricosta,* Poncelet's giant rat, poo uli, poor knights weta, Popta's buntingi, poso bungu, poso half-beak, prairie sphinx moth, predatory bush cricket, Predra Branca skink, Preuss's guenon, Preuss's red colobus, Prigogine's greenbul, Prince Ruspoli's turaco, Principe Speirops, proboscis monkey, *Proserphinus proserpina,* proserpine rock-wallaby, proserpine shiner, *Protoploea apatela,* Przewalski's horse, puaiohi, Puerto Rican boa, Puerto Rican nightjar, Puerto Rican parrot, Puna sphecid wasp, pungu, *Puntius amarus, Puntius asoka, Puntius baoulan, Puntius cataractae, Puntius clemensi, Puntius disa, Puntius flavifuscus, Puntius herrei, Puntius katalo, Puntius lanaoensis, Puntius lindong, Puntius mamalak, Puntius palata, Puntius sirang, Puntius srilankensis, Puntius tras, Puntius tumba,* purple cat's paw mussel, purple-naped lory, purple-winged ground dove, Pycroft's petrel, pygmy chimpanzee, pygmy hippopotamus, pygmy hog, pygmy hog-sucking louse, pygmy loris, pygmy madtom, pygmy sculpin, pygmy smelt, Pyrenean desman, Pyrenean ibex, Queen Alexandra's birdwing, radiated tortoise, Raetzer's ringlet, Railroad Valley springfish, rainbow goodeid, *Rana holtzi,* Rarotonga monarch, Rarotonga starling, Raso lark, Ravoux's slavemaker ant, razorback sucker, rebel's large blue, Red Hills salamander, red and white uakari, red goral, red siskin, red vizcacha rat, red wolf, red wood ant, red-and-blue lory, red-bellied lemur, red-billed curassow, red-cockaded woodpecker, red-crowned parrot, red-eared parrotfinch, red-faced malkoha, red-fronted gazelle, red-fronted lemur, red-naped fruit-dove, red-necked parrot, red-shanked douc langur, red-spectacled parrot, red-tailed parrot, red-tailed sportive lemur, red-vented cockatoo, redband darter, Reeves' pheasant, relict dace, relict gull, relict Himalayan dragonfly, Rennell shrikebill, resplendent quetzal, reticulated velvet gecko, Reunion cuckoo-shrike, *Rhyncogonus hendersoni*, ribbon-tailed astrapia, Ridgeway's hawk, ring-tailed lemur, ring-tailed pigeon, Rio Grande beaver, Rio Grande darter, Rio Grande minnow, river pipefish, river terrapin, riverine rabbit, rivulus, rivulus almirante, Roanoke bass, Roanoke logperch, robalo de cuatro cienegas, rock-catfish, rock-dwelling rat, Rockefeller's sunbird, Rodrigues brush warbler, Rodrigues flying fox, Rodrigues fody, Rodriguez day gecko, Roman snail, rosalia longicorn, Ross seal, roswell fontelicella, rough pigtoe pearly mussel, rough sculpin, rough-faced shag, rough-haired golden mole, roughhead shiner, Round Island boa, Round Island keel-scaled boa, round-mouthed whorl snail, round-nose minnow, roundtail chub, ruffed lemur, rufous fishing owl, rufous hare-wallaby, rufous scrub-bird, rufous-headed ground roller, rufous-headed parrotbill, rufous-necked hornbill, rufous-winged sunbird, Rugged River snail, russet-eared guenon, Russian desman, Russian River tule perch, rustyside sucker, Ruwenzori black-fronted duiker, Ryukyu Islands' wild pig, Ryukyu sika, Ryukyu spiny rat, Sacramento splittail, saddleback, saddled galaxias, sail-fin lizard, Saimaa seal, Salinas pocket mouse, salish sucker, salmon-crested cockatoo, salongo guenon, Salt Creek pupfish, salt marsh skipper, salt-marsh harvest mouse, Salvadori's pheasant, Samoan flying fox, Sampson's pearly mussel, San Bruno elfin, San Francisco forktail damselfly, San Francisco garter snake, San Francisco tree lupine, San Joaquin coachwhip, San Joaquin leopard lizard, San Joaquin Valley wood rat, San Marcos salamander, San Martin Island wood rat, San Quintin kangaroo rat, sandbowl snail, sandhills chub, Sanford's lemur, sangihe hanging parrot, sanje crested mangabey, Santa Ana stickleback, Santa Ana sucker, Santa Catarina sabrefin, Santa Cruz ground dove, Santa Cruz long-toed salamander, Sao Tome scops-owl, Sarasin's goby, Sardina ciega, Sardinian grass snake, Sardinian mouflon, Sardinian salamander, sardinilla cuatro cienegas, sardinita bocagrande, sardinita de Rio Verde, sardinita de Tepelmene, sardinita del Pilon, sardinita nazas, sardinita quijarrona, sarinita de Salado, Saunder's gull, Savadori's fig-parrot, Savannah shore mussel, sawfin, scaleless killifish, scaly ground roller, scaly-sided merganser, scarce fritillary, scarce red forester, scarlet-chested parrot, scharlachkafer, Schaus' swallowtail, *Schistura jarutanini, Schistura oedipus, Schistura sijuensis*, Schneider's pitta, scimitar-horned oryx, Scioto madtom, Sclater's lemur, Semper's warbler, septima's clubtail dragonfly, Serpent Island gecko, seven-coloured tanager, Seychelles brush warbler, Seychelles flying fox, Seychelles fody, Seychelles frog, Seychelles magpie robin, Seychelles owl, Seychelles paradise flycatcher, Seychelles scops-owl, Seychelles sheath-tailed bat, Seychelles swiftlet, Seychelles tree frog, Seychelles white-eye,

Seychellibasis alluaudi alluaudi, shade-winged sphecid wasp, Shark Bay mouse, sharp-jaws buntingi, sharphead darter, sharpnose shiner, Shasta crayfish, Shasta salamander, shining macromia dragonfly, shiny pigtoe pearly mussel, shiny ram's-horn, shore plover, short-crested monarch, short-foot sphecid wasp, short-horned baronia, short-legged ground roller, short-tailed albatross, short-tailed parrotbill, short-toed coucal, shortjaw cisco, shortnose cisco, shortnose sturgeon, shortnose sucker, Shoshone sculpin, shou, Siamese crocodile, Siamese fireback, sibayi goby, Siberian crake, Siberian crane, Sichuan golden snub-nosed monkey, Sichuan jay, Sichuan partridge, sicklefin chub, side-striped barb, silver barred charaxes, silver spotted ghost moth, simien jackal, sinarapan, *Sinocyclocheilus anophthalmus,* slackwater darter, slaty cuckoo-shrike, slaty-backed thrush, slender antbird, slender chub, slender redfin, slender sculpin, slender-horned gazelle, sloth bear, slug snail, small lappet moth, small pedder galaxias, small sparrowhawk, smalleye shiner, *Smerina manoro,* Smith's blue, Smith's dwarf chamaeleon, smoky madtom, smoky mouse, snail darter, Snake River physa snail, snow leopard, snowy-throated babbler, snuffbox, sociable lapwing, Socorro dove, Socorro isopod, Socorro mockingbird, Socorro wren, Soemmerrings gazelle, Sokoke bushy-tailed mongoose, Sokoke pipit, Sokoke scops-owl, solo goodeido, Solomons sea eagle, Somali pigeon, *Somatochlora brevicincta, Somatochlora incurvata, Somatochlora ozarkensis,* Sonoran green toad, Sonoran pronghorn, sooty babbler, soror vespid wasp, South African giant earthworm, South African hedgehog, South American red-lined turtle, South American river turtle, South Andean huemul, South China sika, South Pacific banded iguana, South Pacific parakeet, Southern African Acanthodriline earthworms, southern acorn riffle shell, southern bald ibis, southern bearded saki, southern crowned pigeon, southern damselfly, southern giant clam, southern marsh harvest mouse, southern pocket gopher, southern right whale, southern river otter, southern rubber boa, southern sea otter, Spanish imperial eagle, Spanish lynx, Spanish moon moth, speargrass weevil, speckled dace, spectacled bear, Speke's gazelle, *Speleomantes flavus, Speleomantes imperialis, Speleomantes supramontes,* Spengler's freshwater mussel, spikedace, *Spindasis collinsi,* splendid pearlfish, splendid-eye pearlfish, spot-breasted white-eye, spotted darter, spotted ground-thrush, spotted loach, spring pygmy sunfish, spur-thighed tortoise, squanga whitefish, Sri Lanka magpie, Sri Lanka whistling thrush, Sri Lanka wood-pigeon, Sri Lankan five-bar swordtail, Sri Lankan rose, St. Croix ground lizard, St. Helena earwig, St. Helena plover, St. Lucia black finch, St. Lucia parrot, St. Vincent parrot, stargazing darter, starlet sea anemone, Steller's sea eagle, Stephen's lorikeet, Stephens Island weta, Stephens kangaroo rat, stirrup shell, stitchbird, Stock Island tree snail, Storm's stork, straight-horned markhor, streaked reed-warbler, streber, striated darter, striped goodeid, *Stupidogobius flavipinnis,* sturgeon chub, *Stygionympha dicksoni,* sub-Antarctic snipe, subdesert monias, sucker-footed bat, Sudeten ringlet, sula cuckoo-shrike, sula scrubfowl, Sulawesi palm civet, sulu hornbill, Sumatran rhinoceros, Sumatran serow, Sumba flycatcher, Sumba green-pigeon, Sumba hornbill, sun bear, suntailed guenon, *Sundoreonectes tiomanensis,* Suwannee bass, swamp deer, swamp francolin, swan galaxias, Swayne's hartebeest, Swinhoe's pheasant, Swynnerton's robin, Tahiti monarch, Tahiti swiftlet, tailless blue, Taita blue-banded papilio, Taita thrush, Taiwan macaque, takahe, talaud black birdwing, tamaraw, Tampico pearly mussel, tan riffle shell mussel, tan-blossom pearly mussel, Tana River mangabey, Tana River red colobus, Tanimbar corella, Tanzanian mountain weaver, Tar River spiny mussel, Tasmanian Anaspid crustaceans, Tasmanian freshwater 'limpet', Tasmanian torrent midge, Tatra chamois, tawny-breasted wren-babbler, Tehachapi slender salamander, Tehuantepec hare, *Telmatherina abendanoni, Telmatherina bonti, Telmatherina celebensis, Telmatherina ladigesi,* Temminck's red colobus, Tennessee dace, Texas blind salamander, Texas kangaroo rat, Thailand brow-antlered deer, thamin, *Thaumatodon hystricelloides, Thermophis baileyi, Thestor tempe,* thick-billed parrot, Thomasset's Seychelles frog, Thorold's deer, thyolo alethe, tidewater goby, tiger, Timor green-pigeon, Tipton kangaroo rat, *Tiradelphe schneideri,* tiro, *Tirumala euploeomorpha, Tirumala gautama,* Tokyo bitterling, tollo de Agua Dulce, Tonkin leaf monkey, Tonkin snub-nosed monkey, tooth-billed pigeon, toothless blindcat, tora hartebeest, totoaba, toucan barbet, Townsend's shearwater, Transcaucasian long-nosed viper, Travancore tortoise, Tres Marias cottontail, Treur River barb, trinity bristle snail, trispot darter, Tristan bunting, Triton's trumpet, *Troides aeacus kaguya,* trout cod, trucha de Yaqui, Truk flying fox, Truk monarch, Truk white-eye, Tsomo River copper, Tuamotu kingfisher, Tuamotu sandpiper, tuatara, tubercled-blossom pearly mussel, tui chub, Turbott's weevil, turgid-blossom pearly mussel, Turkmenian caracal lynx, Turks & Caicos rock iguana, Turner's eremomela, turquoise shiner, Tuscumbia darter, Twee River redfin, twin-striped clubtail, two-spot bard, two-striped garter snake, *Tylognathus klatti, Typhaeus hiostius, Typhdobarbus nudiventris, Typhdobarbus widdowsoni,* Uganda red colobus, uhehe red colobus, ultramarine lorikeet, Uluguru bush-shrike, unarmored threespine stickleback, *Unas piceus,* uncompahgre fritillary butterfly, unga, *Unio crassus, Uranothauma usambarae, Urothemis luciana,* Usambara eagle-owl, Usambara ground robin, Utah prairie dog, Valencia toothcarp, valley elderberry longhorn beetle, Van Dam's vanga, Vancouver Island marmo, vaquita, Vateria flower rasbora, Vegas Valley leopard frog, Verreaux's sifaka, *Vertigo geyeri,* Victoria crowned pigeon, vicuna, virgin spinedace, Virginia fringed mountain snail, Virginia northern flying squirrel, Visayan spotted deer, Visayan warty pig, vitelline warbler, vogelkop whistler, volcano rabbit, vortex banded mountain snail, Waccamaw killifish, Waccamaw silverside, Waccamaw spike, Wahnes's parotia, Waigeo brush-turkey, walia ibex, Wallace's hawk-eagle, Wallengren's copper, wandering skipper, warner sucker, warsangli linnet, Washington giant earthworm, watercress darter, weasel sportive lemur, wedge-billed wren-babbler, West

African chimpanzee, West African manatee, West Indian manatee, West Indian whistling duck, western barred bandicoot, western bearded pig, western bristlebird, western crowned pigeon, western fan-shell pearly mussel, western forest emperor, western gentle lemur, western giant eland, western klipspringer, western mountain reedbuck, western mouse, western red colobus, western swamp turtle, western tragopan, westland petrel, wetapunga, Wheeler's pearly mussel, whistling warbler, White River spinedace, White River springfish, White River sucker, White Sands pupfish, white cat's paw mussel, white cockatoo, white marmoset, white warty back pearly mussel, white-bellied bushchat, white-bellied heron, white-breasted babbler, white-breasted guineafowl, white-breasted mesite, white-breasted thrasher, white-browed bushchat, white-chested white-eye, white-clawed crayfish, white-collared lemur, white-eared night-heron, white-eared partridge, white-eared pocket mouse, white-footed sportive lemur, white-footed tamarin, white-fronted lemur, white-headed black leaf monkey, white-headed duck, white-legged duiker, white-lipped bandicoot, white-naped crane, white-necked picathartes, white-necklaced partridge, white-nosed saki, white-shouldered ibis, white-spotted sapphire, white-tailed eagle, white-tailed laurel pigeon, white-tailed swallow, white-throated guenon, white-throated jungle-flycatcher, white-winged cotinga, white-winged cuckoo-shrike, white-winged duck, white-winged ground warbler, white-winged guan, white-winged tit, whooping crane, widemouth blindcat, wild Asiatic water buffalo, wild yak, Wilken's stenasellid, wineland blue, wolverine, Wood River sculpin, wood bison, Woodlark Island cuscus, Woodruff's dung beetle, woolly lemur, woolly monkey, woolly spider monkey, woundfin, wrinkled hornbill, *Xenopoecilus sarasinorum, Xerotricha nubivaga,* Yakushima macaque, Yaqui sucker, Yaqui chub, Yarkand deer, yellow golden mole, yellow kite swallowtail, yellow tit, yellow-bearded greenbul, yellow-blossom pearly mussel, yellow-crested cockatoo, yellow-eared parrot, yellow-eyed penguin, yellow-legged weaver, yellow-shouldered blackbird, yellow-shouldered parrot, yellow-sided clubtail, yellow-spotted sideneck turtle, yellow-tailed woolly monkey, yellowcheek darter, yellowfin madtom, yoked ended banded mountain snail, *Ypthima dohertyi persimilis,* Yunnan snub-nosed monkey, Zanzibar bushbaby, Zanzibar red colobus, zapata rail, zapata sparrow, zebra duiker, zetides swallowtail, Zuñi bluehead sucker.

Gone: *Agrotis photophila,* Alabama coosa slit-shell, Alice Springs mouse, ameca shiner, American chestnut moth, amistad gambusia, Anthony's river snail, Antioch Dunes shieldback katydid, arc-form pearly mussel, arcuate pearl mussel, Ash Meadows killifish, Atitlan grebe, Babylon coosa slit-shell, Bali tiger, Barbados racoon, Bavarian pine vole, big-eared hopping-mouse, Blackburn's sphinx moth, Blackburn's weevil, blackfin cisco, bluebuck, broad-faced potoroo, bush wren, Caerulean paradise flycatcher, *Campsicnemus mirabilis,*

Canarian black oystercatcher, Cape Verde giant skink, Carelia sp., Carolina parakeet, Castle Lake caddisfly, central hare-wallaby, Chapman's fruit bat, chestnut clearwing moth, chestnut ermine moth, *Clavicoccus erinaceus,* Clear Lake splittail, *Coleophora leucochrysella,* Colombian grebe, confused moth, crescent nailtailed wallaby, Curtis pearly mussel, Darling Downs hopping-mouse, deepwater cisco, *Deloneura immaculata,* desert bandicoot, *Drosophila lanaiensis, Dryophthorus distinguendus, Dryotribus mimeticus,* Durango shiner, eastern hare-wallaby, Edmund's snaketail dragonfly, *Epioblasma biemarginata, Euthalia malapana,* fabulous green sphinx of Kauai, Falkland Island wolf, fine-rayed pearly mussel, forest owlet, Fort Ross weevil, Gauyacon ojiazul, giant African forest shrew, glaucous macaw, Gould's mouse, Guadalupe storm-petrel, Guam flying fox, harelip sucker, Hawaiian hopseed looper moth, Hilo noctuid moth, Himalayan quail, Israel painted frog, Ivell's sea anemone, Jamaican pauraque, Japanese sea lion, Javan wattled lapwing, jugorum melalagrion damselfly, june sucker, Kaholuamano noctuid moth, Kerr's noctuid moth, Ko'olau giant looper moth, Kona giant looper moth, Labrador duck, Lake Pedder planarian, *Lampsilis dolabraeformis, Lampsilis fasciola, Lampsilis hostonia,* large Palau flying fox, Las Vegas dace, Laysan dropseed noctuid moth, Laysan noctuid moth, Lefevre's pearly mussel, *Lepidochrysops hypopolia,* lesser bilby, lesser mascarene flying fox, lesser stick-nest rat, Lewis pearly mussel, *Libythea cinyras,* little longhorn caddisfly, long-tailed hopping-mouse, longjaw cisco, Lord Howe Island stick-insect, lovegrass noctuid moth, *Macrancylus linearis,* mainstream river snail, Marquesas fruit-dove, Mexican dace, Mexican grizzly bear, Midway noctuid moth, Miller lake lamprey, minute noctuid moth, Mono Lake diving beetle, Moorean viviparous tree snail, Mulokai creeper, nearby pearly mussel, Nelson's rice rat, New Zealand grayling, New Zealand lesser short-tailed bat, North China sika, *Oedemasylus laysanensis,* Ola'a peppered looper moth, omilteme cottontail, *Pacifastacus nigrescens,* pahranagat spinedace, pahrump ranch poolfish, Palos Verdes blue, Panay giant fruit bat, *Papilio phorbanta nana, Parmacella gervasi,* parras characodon, *Partulina crassa, Parulina montagui,* Pecatonica River mayfly, Pemberton's deer mouse, *Peridroma porphyrea,* perrito de parras, perritos de Sandia, phantom shiner, phleophagan chestnut moth, *Phyllococcus oahuensis,* pig-footed bandicoot, pink-headed duck, *Plectomeris dombeyana,* Pohnpei mountain starling, poko noctuid moth, procellaris grotis noctuid moth, Puerto Rican flower bat, quagga, rabbit-eared tree-rat, Raycraft Ranch poolfish, recovery pearly mussel, Robert's stonefly, robust burrowing mayfly, rough maple leaf pearly mussel, rubious cave amphipod, *Salamis angustina vinsoni,* San Macos gambusia, Sardinian pika, Shansi sika, short-tailed hopping-mouse, silver trout, snail-eating coua, Snake River sucker, Socorro spring snail, *Speyeria adiaste atossa,* Steller's cormorant, Steward's pearly mussel, sthenele wood nymph, Stone's pearly mussel, Strohbeen's clodius parnassian, stumptooth minnow, *Sym-*

petrum dilatatum, Syrian wild ass, Tanzanian woolly bat, Tasmanian wolf, Texas tailed blue, *Thaanumia* sp., thicktail chub, three-tooth caddisfly, toolache wallaby, Utah lake sculpin, Volutine stoneyian tabanid fly, whiteline topminnow, Woodford's rail, xerces blue, *Xylotoles costatus,* Yorba Linda weevil, and unnamed thousands. . . .

> To believe your own thought, to believe that what is true for you in your private heart is true for all men—that is genius.
>
> —Ralph Waldo Emerson

The closing years of the twentieth century will see a return of commercial whalers seeking their prey in the world's oceans. As much as I deplore the thought of it, I am equally certain that it will happen. Norway, Iceland, and Japan have stated intentions to resume the killing of minke whales. The catch that they take in those first few years will be small and will not further endanger the species that they chase. A larger catch would simply not be tolerated by nations and a public who see no good reason to return to the red tides of the past. But if those small catches are allowed to grow, born of greed, commercial aspirations, and a misguided perception that whale populations can be managed to give a sustainable and economic yield, then we will be on the same helter-skelter ride that almost lost us, and may still lose us, the right whale, the blue, the humpback, the fin, and the gray.

Perhaps those images of the "Save the Whale" movement of the seventies and early eighties are still burned in your mind, as they are in mine—we can never return to those times, you say. Those days are gone. Unless we act now to prevent that initial return to a "sustainable harvest," we may not be able to act later to prevent history from repeating itself, and ultimately achieving what was nearly so thirty years ago.

Throughout this part of the book, I have tried to state clearly that we live in a society and a culture that permits choice. It really is as simple as that. We have the choice to make sure that commercial whaling is relegated to the history books and case studies on how not to manage populations. We have the choice to protect and save the world's whales. We can also choose not to. Can anyone really justify such a deliberate act of environmental sabotage? But even if we do not actively pursue such a course, our inaction may yet bring it about.

Suppose that whaling could be managed and sustainable. Do we want to risk everything again? The whalers have had four hundred years to demonstrate good management techniques; all they have succeeded in doing is showing their incompetence. Even when a whaling moratorium was imposed to gather information and assess a future for whaling, the whalers disregarded the intent if not the law of the moratorium by continuing "scientific whaling."

We have seen the politicking that has taken over the IWC, how nations could veto decisions and carry on regardless of quotas or scientific recommendations; we have seen how the blue whale was used as a pawn in the game of international one-upmanship; and we have seen how a nation can simply walk out when things do not go its way. When the International Whaling Commission meets again, none of these things will have changed. The IWC was set up with these flaws written into its constitution, and it would take major revisions of its articles to remove them—and that is something to which the whaling nations will never agree.

The moratorium is already under attack from the whalers. The original purpose of the suspension of whaling activities was to allow a detailed and comprehensive assessment of whale stocks so that future quotas could be set without endangering species. The Comprehensive Assessment of Whale Stocks provides more accurate counts of the world's whales than have previously been available, and demonstrates that we are far from a "sustainable whaling industry."

There are those who argue that whaling can be regulated so that the stock declines of the past will never occur again, and that former stock mismanagement was the result of ignorance, not design. Nice try. The history of whaling tells us a very different story, and we are not even discussing ancient history. The unethical actions of the whaling nations, their blatant disregard for species and stock protection, were not something of one hundred or even fifty or thirty years ago. We are talking about attitudes and actions of the last decade, of the last meeting of the International Whaling Commission.

The figures listed below may over- or underestimate the true situation. The fact is that recent census data for most of the great whales have dramatically decreased population estimates, often to the point of critical concern. The International Whaling Commission should see the writing on the wall, and the United Nations should take up the mantle of whales and whaling. The whalers were given the power and have misused it; we should never trust them again. We have an obligation to ourselves, to our children, and to the whales. The moratorium must stay in place—indefinitely.

> Can he who has discovered only some of the values of whalebone and whale oil be said to have discovered the true use of the whale? Can he who slays the elephant for his ivory be said to have "seen the elephant"? These are petty and accidental uses; just as if a stronger race were to kill us in order to make buttons and flageolets of our bones.

> —Henry David Thoreau, 1853

Species	Pre-exploitation population (estimate)	Present population (estimate)	Year of commercial protection
Blue whale	230,000	2,500–10,000	1966
Bowhead whale	30,000	7,600	1935*
Bryde's whale	90,000	60,000	1986*
Fin whale	700,000	5,000–100,000	1986*
E. Pacific Gray whale	20,000+	22,000+	1935*
Humpback whale	115,000	10,000–15,000	1966*
Minke whale	490,000+	331,800+	1986*
Right whale	100,000	4,000	1935
Sei whale	256,000	65,000 (max.)	1986
Sperm whale	2,400,000	20,000–200,000	1985*

*"Subsistence whaling" still permitted by the International Whaling Commission.

Was it ethically and morally correct for the Basque whalers of the twelfth and thirteenth centuries to take right whales until they vanished from the area and were pushed to the brink of extinction, from which even now they have failed to return? It could be argued that the moral and ethical actions of people must be taken in the context of their time and culture. We can look back at the Basque whalers and say quite categorically that what they did was misguided; they mismanaged a resource and ultimately suffered for it. The Basques' offense was a lack of knowledge. They did not know that their actions could have such an effect. Let us hope that the passage of eight centuries has improved things.

Whales have become a symbol to all those who want to protect the natural world, not just because it has intrinsic value but also because without securing a future for them, our own becomes all the more tenuous. Perhaps by letting a few species disappear, we do not near the edge of that cliff ourselves, or perhaps we are simply blind to what lies beyond. The battle lines of conservation are drawn with the whale. The premise is simple: if we cannot save the whale with all of our knowledge, our foresight, and the commitment of so many, what hope the Earth? If we ever let the "Save the Whale" cry become just another cliché, then we will have lost the battle, and the seas will cease to sing.

Why do whales pique our interest? They lift our hearts and our minds to new heights; they are beauty wrapped in a blubbery countenance. Whales are special to us. We are compatriots in an evolutionary framework that began before any of us can even imagine. Whales are the culmination of millions of years of evolution, the result of natural selection in a unique environment. They are at the apex of the food chain. We understand so little of what that means, or of what altering that balance may mean to the delicate ecological systems on this planet that are maintained by the oceans. Whales are important to us culturally and emotionally. They let us imagine and dream. They fill us with awe. We are impressed by their size, their intelligence, their cooperation, their gentleness. No other mammal seems to search us out as the whales are now doing, pushing their calves into our outstretched arms. We have a link with them that is at once biological, cultural, ecological, emotional, and ethical.

All whale-watchers, amateur and professional, must continue to wonder whether their seasons of pilgrimage will always herald whales, or whether one day the lagoons, inlets, and oceans will be silenced. Whale populations have been pitifully reduced, far beyond the levels that even the most pessimistic of conservationists had previously believed. And still the whaling continues, commercial, pirate, "scientific," incidental, and subsistence. Other hazards such as overfishing, deep-sea trawl nets, pollution, and coastal development continue to confront the dwindling populations.

What does this mean to us? What does it mean to be human? It means being all-powerful. It means having choices and decisions to make not only about our future but about the future of others. It means being part of a society, being one of many, and having the right to voice opinions. Go out, join whatever groups reflect your philosophies, and vote. If you don't act, you throw away your chance to make a difference; and it may be your voice that makes the final impact.

I held out a hand and touched a whale. I saw myself reflected in another mammalian eye that was far from human. And I saw myself through another's eyes. Loren Eiseley referred to people as a "fantastic neurofungus." We spread and multiply and dominate our world. It will be a true test of intelligence if we can continue to do so without degrading the lives of others, as well as our own.

In the whale we have a symbol of nature, of life. So look through a child's eyes into the eye of the whale and see yourself reflected. If we lose the chance to see ourselves as others see us, then we have lost the chance to gauge our own humanity. Humankind without humanity becomes simply another failed evolutionary experiment that will disappear into the geologic prison of time to be talked about and discussed in eons to come by descendants of ancestors who today are unseen and silent.

We may be the only species to possess foresight. What a crime it would be if we should realize that only in hindsight.

> There is one thing stronger than all the armies in the world: and that is an idea whose time has come.
>
> —Victor Hugo

Appendix 1

Baja's Flora and Fauna

N.B. This appendix provides the English, Spanish, scientific, and other recognized names of the plant and animal species identified in the text. Bird and marine mammal names are presented in taxonomic order, while the other species are listed in alphabetical order. Details on other Baja species can be found in the following recommended texts: *Birds of North America* (National Geographic Society); *Walker's Mammals of the World; Baja California Plant Field Guide; Flora of Baja California; Sea of Cortez Marine Invertebrates;* and *Marine Animals of Baja California.* See Appendix 3 for full citations.

TABLE 1: Plants

Common Name	Scientific Name	Other Names/Spanish
Barrel cactus	*Ferocactus diguetii*	Biznaga
Black mangrove	*Avicennia germinas*	Mangle negro, mangle salado
Brittlebush	*Encelia farinosa*	Incienso
Broom baccharis	*Baccharis sarathroides*	Hierba del Pasmo
Bursage	*Ambrosia dumosa*	Burro-weed, huizapol
Bush snapdragon	*Galvezia juncea*	
California juniper	*Juniperus californica*	
California poppy	*Eschscholzia californica*	
California saltbush	*Atriplex californica*	Chamizo
Candelabra cactus	*Myrtillocactus cochal*	Cochal
Cardon barbon	*Pachycereus pecten-aboriginum*	Hairbrush cactus, cardon Espinosa
Cardon pelon	*Pachycereus pringlei*	
Cedros lupin	*Lupinus* sp.	Garbancillo, arroyo lupin
Cliff spurge	*Euphorbia misera*	Liga, tacora, jumeton
Coastal agave	*Agave shawii*	Century plant, mescal, maguey
Coastal poppy	*Eschscholzia* sp.	
Cochemia	*Cochemia pondii*	Biznagita
Cordgrass	*Spartina foliosa*	
Coreopsis	*Coreopsis maritima*	
Desert hyacinth	*Hyacinthus* sp.	
Desert lavender	*Hyptis emoryi*	Bee sage, salvia, lavanda
Desert mallow	*Sphaeralcea ambigua*	Desert hollyhock, plantas muy malas, mal de ojo

TABLE 1: Plants (con't.)

Common Name	Scientific Name	Other Names/Spanish
Dodder	*Cuscuta* sp.	Cochear
Dune grass	*Elymus* sp.	
Dusty miller	*Senecio cineraria*	
Eel grass	*Zostera marina*	
Elephant tree	*Pachycormus discolor*	Copalquin, torote, torote blanco
Evening primrose	*Primulaceae* sp.	
Fishhook cactus	*Mammillaria dioica*	Pincushion cactus, Mammillaria, biznagita, llavina
Four o'clock	*Mirabilis* sp.	
Gambling cactus	*Machaerocereus gummosus*	Pitaya agria/sour pitaya
Groundsel	*Lepidospartum squamatum*	
Hedgehog cactus	*Echinocereus pacificus*	Claret cup cactus, pitayita
Indian paintbrush	*Castilleja* sp.	Garanonas, hierba del Cancer
Jojoba	*Simmondsia chinensis*	Goatnut
Jumping cholla	*Opuntia bigelovii*	Teddy bear cholla, ciribe, cholla del oso
Kelp	*Macrocystis* sp.	
Lemonade berry bush	*Rhus integrifolia*	Hiedra
Lomboy	*Jatropha cinerea*	Lomboy blanco, torotillo
Ocotillo	*Fouquieria splendens*	Ocotillo
Organ pipe cactus	*Lemaireocereus thurberi*	Pitaya dulce/sweet pitaya
Parmer's frankenia	*Frankenia palmeri*	Yerba reuma, alkali heath
Pickleweed	*Salicornia bigelovii*	Ice plant, glasswort
Prickly boxthorn	*Lycium* sp.	Desert thorn, thorn bush, frutilla
Prickly pear	*Opuntia tapona*	Nopal, tuna tapona
Red mangrove	*Rhizophora mangle*	Mangle rojo, mangle colorado, mangle dulce
Rock daisy	*Asteraceae* sp.	
Sea dahlia	*Dahlia* sp.	
Sea rocket	*Cakile edentula*	
Sugar bush	*Rhus lentii*	Lentisco
Surf grass	*Phyllospadix* sp.	
Ulva	*Ulva* sp.	
White forget-me-not	*Myosotis* sp.	
White mangrove	*Rhizophora mangle*	Mangle blanco
Wild fig	*Ficus brandegeei*	Higuera, zalate, amate

TABLE 2: Birds

Common Name	Scientific Name	Other Names/Spanish
Order: Gaviiformes		
Common loon	*Gavia immer*	Great northern diver
Red-throated loon	*Gavia stellata*	Red-throated diver

TABLE 2: Birds (con't.)

Common Name	Scientific Name	Other Names/Spanish
Order: Podicipediformes		
Western grebe	*Aechmophorus occidentalis*	Zambullidor occidental
Order: Procellariiformes		
Black storm-petrel	*Oceanodroma melania*	Paiño negro
Black-vented shearwater	*Puffinus opisthomelas*	
Pink-footed shearwater	*Puffinus creatopus*	Pardela blanca común
Sooty shearwater	*Puffinus griseus*	Pardela sombría
Northern fulmar	*Fulmarus glacialis*	
Order: Pelecaniforms		
Blue-footed booby	*Sula nebouxii*	Piquera patiazul
Brown booby	*Sula leucogaster*	Piquero pardo
Brown pelican	*Pelecanus occidentalis*	Pelícano pardo
Double-crested cormorant	*Phalacrocorax auritus*	
Pelagic cormorant	*Phalacrocorax erythrorhynchos*	
Red-billed tropic bird	*Phaethon aethereus*	Rabijunco piquirrojo
Magnificent frigatebird	*Fregata magnificens*	Fragata magno
Order: Ciconiiformes		
Black-crowned night-heron	*Nycticorax nycticorax*	Garza bruja
Yellow-crowned night-heron	*Nyctanassa violacea*	Martinete cabecipinto
Great blue heron	*Ardea herodias*	Garzón azulado
Green-backed heron	*Butorides striatus*	Garcilla verde
Tricolored heron	*Egretta tricolor*	Garceta tricolor
Reddish egret	*Egretta rufescens*	Garceta rojiza
Snowy egret	*Egretta thula*	Garcita blanca
White ibis	*Eudocimus albus*	Ibis blanco
Order: Anseriformes		
American wigeon	*Anas americana*	Pato calvo
Black brant	*Branta bernicla*	
Common mallard	*Anas platyrhynchos*	Pato cabeciverde
Northern pintail	*Anas acuta*	Pato rabudo
Ruddy duck	*Oxyura jamaicensis*	Pato rubicundo
Surf scoter	*Melanitta perspicillata*	
Order: Falconiformes		
Crested caracara	*Polyborus plancus*	Caracara cargahuesos
Merlin	*Falco columbarius*	Esmerejón
Osprey	*Pandion haliaetus*	Sangual
Turkey vulture	*Cathartes aura*	Jote cabeza roja

TABLE 2: Birds (con't.)

Common Name	Scientific Name	Other Names/Spanish
Order: Gruiformes		
Virginia rail	*Rallus limicola*	Rascón de Virginia
Order: Charadriiformes		
American oystercatcher	*Haematopus palliatus*	Ostrero pardo
Black oystercatcher	*Haematopus bachmani*	Ostrero negro
Bonaparte's gull	*Larus philadelphia*	Gaviota de Bonaparte
California gull	*Larus californicus*	Gaviota California
Glaucous-winged gull	*Larus glaucescens*	
Heermann's gull	*Larus heermanni*	Gaviota de Heermann
Herring gull	*Larus argentatus*	Gaviota Argéntea
Laughing gull	*Larus atricilla*	Gaviota reidora
Ring-billed gull	*Larus delawarensis*	Gaviota piquianillada
Thayer's gull	*Larus thayeri*	Gaviota de Thayer
Western gull	*Larus occidentalis*	Gaviota occidental
Yellow-footed gull	*Larus livens*	Gaviota patiamarilla
Cassin's auklet	*Ptychoramiphus aleuticus*	
Craveri's murrelet	*Synthliboramphus craveri*	
Greater yellowlegs	*Tringa melanoleuca*	Patiamarillo mayor
Long-billed curlew	*Numenius americanus*	Zarapito piquilargo
Whimbrel	*Numenius phaeopus*	Zarapito trinador
Long-billed dowitcher	*Limnodromus scolopaceus*	Agujeta silbona o piquilarga
Marbled godwit	*Limosa fedoa*	Aguja canela
Parasitic jaeger	*Stercorarius parasiticus*	Arctic skua, págalo parásito
Pomarine jaeger	*Stercorarius pomarinus*	Pomarine skua, págalo pomarino
Caspian tern	*Sterna caspia*	Pagaza major o piquirrojo
Common tern	*Sterna hirundo*	Gaviotin golondrina
Elegant tern	*Sterna elegans*	Pagaza elegante
Forster's tern	*Sterna forsteri*	Charrán de Forster
Royal tern	*Sterna maxima*	Gaviotin real
Dunlin	*Calidris alpina*	Correlimos pechinegro
Least sandpiper	*Calidris minutilla*	Correlimos menudo
Western sandpiper	*Calidris mauri*	Correlimos occidental
Spotted sandpiper	*Actitis macularia*	Playerito manchado
Wandering tattler	*Heteroscelus incanus*	Correlimos vagamundo
Willet	*Catoptrophorus semipalmatus*	Piguilo
Order: Columiformes		
Mourning dove	*Zenaida macroura*	Paloma rabuda

TABLE 2: Birds (con't.)

Common Name	Scientific Name	Other Names/Spanish
Order: Apodiformes		
Costa's hummingbird	*Calypte costae*	Colibrí de Costa
Rufous hummingbird	*Selasphorus rufus*	Chispita rufa
Order: Coraciiformes		
Belted kingfisher	*Ceryle alcyon*	Martin pescador verde
Order: Piciformes		
Gila woodpecker	*Melanerpes uropygialis*	
Order: Passerriformes		
Black phoebe	*Sayornis nigricans*	Mosquero de agua
Black-throated sparrow	*Amphispiza bilineata*	
Common raven	*Corvus corax*	Cuervo común
Golden-crowned sparrow	*Zonotrichia atricapilla*	
Hooded oriole	*Icterus cucullatus*	Bolsero encapuchado
Horned lark	*Eremophila alpestris*	Alondra con cuernos
House finch	*Carpodacus mexicanus*	
Loggerhead shrike	*Lanius ludovicianus*	
Mangrove warbler	*Dendroica petechia*	Yellow warbler, reinita de manglar
Northern cardinal	*Cardinalis cardinalis*	Cardinal norteño
Northern mockingbird	*Mimus polyglottos*	Zenzontle norteño
Orange-crowned warbler	*Vermivora celata*	Renita olivada
Rufous-sided towhee	*Pipilo erythrophthalmus*	
Sage sparrow	*Amphispiza belli*	Sabanero salvia
Savannah sparrow	*Passerculus sandwichensis*	Sabanero zanjero
Verdin	*Auriparus flaviceps*	
Vermilion flycatcher	*Pyrocephalus rubinus*	Churrinche
Violet-green swallow	*Tachycineta thalassina*	Golondrina verde violácea
Yellow warbler	*Dendroica petechia*	Mangrove warbler, reinita amarilla

TABLE 3: Terrestrial Mammals

Common Name	Scientific Name	Other Names/Spanish
Antelope ground squirrel	*Ammospermophilus insularis*	
Black-tailed jack rabbit	*Lepus californicus*	
Cedros Island mule deer	*Odocoileus hemionus cerrosensis*	
Coyote	*Canis latrans*	

TABLE 3: Terrestrial Mammals (con't.)

Common Name	Scientific Name	Other Names/Spanish
Domestic burro	*Equus asinus*	Ass, donkey, burro
Domestic cat	*Felis catus domesticus*	Gato
European hare	*Lepus europaeus*	Brown hare, liebre moreno
European rabbit	*Oryctolagus cuniculus*	Old World rabbit, domestic rabbit, rabat

TABLE 4: Marine Mammals

Common Name	Scientific Name	Other Names/Spanish
Gray whale	*Eshrichtitus robustus*	Rip sack, mussel digger, devilfish, ballena gris
Blue whale	*Balaenoptera musculus*	Sulphur-bottom whale, ballena azul
Bryde's whale	*Balaenoptera edeni*	Tropical whale, ballena de Bryde
Fin whale	*Balaenoptera physalus*	Finback, razorback, common rorqual, ballena de Aleta
Humpback whale	*Megaptera noveangliae*	Hunchback, bunch whale, rorcual jorobado
Shortfin pilot whale	*Globicephala macrorhynchus*	Pacific pilot whale, calderón de Aletas Cortas
Cuvier's beaked whale	*Ziphius cavirostris*	Goosebeak whale, zifido de Cuvier
Bottlenose dolphin	*Tursiops truncatus*	Tursión, tonina
Pacific white-sided dolphin	*Lagenorhynchus obliqiudens*	Hook-finned porpoise, white-striped dolphin, delfin de Costados Blancos
Common dolphin	*Delphinus delphis*	Saddleback, crisscross, whitebelly, delfin común
Harbor seal	*Phoca vitulina*	Foca común
Northern elephant seal	*Mirounga angustirostris*	Foca elefante del Norte
California sea lion	*Zalophus californianus*	Lobo marino de California

TABLE 5: Fish and Marine Invertebrates

Common Name	Scientific Name	Other Names/Spanish
Anchovy	*Engraulis mordax*	Anchoa
Azure parrotfish	*Scarus compressus*	Perico

TABLE 5: Fish and Marine Invertebrates (con't.)

Common Name	Scientific Name	Other Names/Spanish
Barnacle sp.	*Cryptolepas rhachianecti*	Percebe
Bulls-eye puffer	*Sphoeroides annulatus*	Botete diana
California needlefish	*Strongylura exilis*	Agujon
Chiton	*Chiton virgulatus*	
Chocolate chip star	*Nidorellia armata*	
Cortez damselfish	*Stegastes rectifraenum*	Pez azul de Cortes
Cortez rainbow wrasse	*Thalassoma lucasanum*	Ara iris
Feather duster polychaete	*Bispira rugosa monterea*	
Flower sea urchin	*Toxopneustes roseus*	
Garibaldi	*Hypsypops rubicunda*	
Ghost shrimp	*Thalassinoius* sp.	
Giant hawkfish	*Cirrhitus rivulatus*	Chino mero
Guineafowl puffer	*Arothron meleagris*	Botete negro, botete de oro
Hammerhead shark	*Sphyrna lewini*	Pez martillo
King angelfish	*Holacanthus passer*	Angel real
Leopard grouper	*Mycteroperca rosacea*	Cabrilla sardinera, calamaria
Mexican goatfish	*Mulloidichthys dentatus*	Salmonete
Moorish idol	*Zanclus cornutus*	Idolo moro
Mullet	*Mugil* sp.	Lisa, liseta
Opal-eyed perch	*Perca* sp.	
Pacific boxfish	*Ostracion meleagris*	Pez caja
Pacific calico scallop	*Argopecten circularis*	
Panamic sergeant major fish	*Abudefduf troschelii*	Pintano
Portuguese man o'war	*Physalia utrilculus*	
Purple sea urchin	*Echinometra vanbrunti*	
Red gorgonian	*Eugorgia daniana*	
Red sea fan	*Gorgonia adamsi*	
Reef cornetfish	*Fistularia commersonii*	Pez corneta
Sally lightfoot crab	*Grapsus grapsus*	
Sand flea	*Grammarus* sp.	Sand hopper
Sea hare	*Aplysia* sp.	Liebre mar
Sea pen	*Ptilosarus undulatus*	Pluma mar
Spotted sea anenome	*Antiparactis* sp.	
Tan star	*Phataria unifascialis*	
Thresher shark	*Alopias vulpinus*	
Whale lice	*Cyamus ceti*	Piojo ballena
	C. kessleri	
	C. scammoni	
Whale shark	*Rhincodon typus*	Tiburon ballena
Yellow gorgonian	*Filigella mitsukuri*	
Yellow sea fan	*Pacifigorgia* sp.	
Yellow surgeonfish	*Prionurus punctatus*	Cochinito

Appendix 2

The Complete Whale List

Common Name	Scientific Name	Other Names/Spanish
MYSTICETI		
Family: Balaenidae		
Bowhead whale	*Balaena mysticetus*	The whale, great polar whale, arctic whale, Greenland right whale
Northern right whale	*Eubalaena glacialis*	Biscayan right whale, great right whale, ballena Franca
Pygmy right whale	*Caperea marginata*	
Southern right whale	*Eubalaena australis*	
Family: Eschrichtidae		
Gray whale	*Eschrichtius robustus*	Rip sack, mussel digger, devilfish, ballena gris
Family: Balaenopteridae		
Blue whale	*Balaenoptera musculus*	Sulphur-bottom whale, ballena azul
Bryde's whale	*Balaenopetera edeni*	Tropical whale, ballena de Bryde
Fin whale	*Balaenoptera physalus*	Finback, razor back, common rorqual, rorcual común
Minke	*Balaenoptera acutorostrata*	Piked whale, lesser rorqual, sharp-headed finner, rorcual minke
Sei whale	*Balaenoptera borealis*	Rorcual de sei
Humpback whale	*Megaptera noveangliae*	Hunchback, bunch whale, rorcual jorobado
ODONTOCETI		
Family: Ziphiidae		
Tasman whale	*Tasmacetus shepherdi*	Shephard's beaked whale

Common Name	Scientific Name	Other Names/Spanish
Arnoux's whale	*Berardius arnuxii*	Giant bottle-nosed, southern four-toothed, New Zealand beaked whale, smaller ziphid whale, southern porpoise whale
Baird's beaked whale	*Berardius bairdii*	Northern fourtoothed whale, Japanese porpoise whale, giant bottle-nosed whale, zifido de Baird
Cuvier's beaked whale	*Ziphius cavirostris*	Goosebeak whale, Cuvier's whale, zifido de Cuvier
Northern bottlenose whale	*Hyperodon ampullatus*	Bottlehead, Calderón gigante
Southern bottlenose whale	*Hyperoodon planifrons*	Flower's bottlenose whale, flatfront bottlenose, flathead bottlenose, Antarctic bottlenose
Longman's beaked whale	*Indopacetus pacificus*	IndoPacific beaked whale
Andrew's beaked whale	*Mesoplodon bowdonii*	Splaytoothed whale, Bowdon's whale
Arch beaked whale	*Mesoplodon carlhubbsi*	
Bering Sea beaked whale	*Mesoplodon stejnegeri*	Stejneger's whale, sabretooth
Dense beaked whale	*Mesoplodon densirostris*	Blainville's beaked whale, Mesoplondonte de Blainville
Gervais's beaked whale	*Mesoplodon europaeus*	Gulf Stream beaked whale, European beaked whale, Mesoplondonte Antillano
Ginko-toothed whale	*Mesoplodon ginkgodens*	Japanese beaked whale, Mesoplondonte Japónes
Gray's beaked whale	*Mesoplodon grayi*	Scamperdown beaked whale, southern beaked whale
Hector's beaked whale	*Mesoplodon hectori*	Skew beaked whale, New Zealand beaked whale
True's beaked whale	*Mesoplodon mirus*	Wonderful beaked whale
North Sea beaked whale	*Mesoplodon bidens*	
Straptooth beaked whale	*Mesoplodon layardii*	

Common Name	Scientific Name	Other Names/Spanish
Family: Platanistidae		
Amazon river dolphin (Bolivia)	*Inia boliviensis*	
Amazon river dolphin	*Inia geoffrensis*	Inia, sisi, ihui, boto, bufeo
Baiji	*Lipotes vexillifer*	Yangtze river dolphin, pei c'hi, whitefin dolphin
Franciscana	*Pontoporia blainvillei*	La Plata river dolphin, tonina
Ganges river dolphin	*Platanista gangetica*	Susuk, soosa, sisumar, hiho
Indus river dolphin	*Platanista minor*	*Platanista indi*
Family: Monodontidae		
Belukha	*Delphinapterus leucas*	Beluga, white whale
Narwhal	*Monodon monoceros*	Unicorn whale
Family: Physeteridae		
Dwarf sperm whale	*Kogia simus*	Cachalote enano
Pygmy sperm whale	*Kogia breviceps*	Lesser sperm whale, lesser cacholot, cachalote pigmeo
Sperm whale	*Physter catodon*	Cachalote, *P. macrocephalus*
Family: Stenidae		
Roughtooth dolphin	*Steno bredanensis*	Delfin de Dientas Rugosos
IndoPacific humpback dolphin	*Sousa chinensis*	Chinese or Bornean white dolphin, speckled/ freckled dolphin, lead-colored dolphin
Atlantic humpback dolphin	*Sousa teuzii*	Cameroon dolphin
Tucuxi	*Sotalia fluviatilis*	River dolphin, estuarine dolphin
Family: Phocoenidae		
Burmeister's porpoise	*Phocoena spinipinnis*	Black porpoise, Marsopa espinosa
Harbor porpoise	*Phocoena phocoena*	Common porpoise
Spectacled porpoise	*Phocoena dioptrica*	Marsopa de anteojos
Vaquita	*Phocoena sinus*	Gulf porpoise, cochito, duende
Finless porpoise	*Neophocaena phocaenoides*	Bhulga, molagan, tabi, hai-chu
Dall's porpoise	*Phocoenoides dalli*	Spray porpoise, white-flanked porpoise, Marsopade Dall

Common Name	Scientific Name	Other Names/Spanish
Family: Globicephalidae		
Longfin pilot whale	*Globicephala melaena*	Blackfish, calling whale, pothead, bagfin
Shortfin pilot whale	*Globicephala macrorhynchus*	Blackfish, Pacific pilot whale, calderón de Aletas Cortas
Melon-headed whale	*Peponocephala electra*	Many-toothed blackfish, calderón pigmeo
Orca	*Orcinus orca*	Killer whale, swordfish, thrasher, bufeo de Mascarilla
False killer whale	*Pseudorca crassida*	Thicktooth grampus, orca falsa
Pygmy killer whale	*Feresa attenuata*	Slender pilot whale, orca pigmea
Family: Delphinidae		
Atlantic white-sided dolphin	*Lagenorhynchus acutus*	
Hourglass dolphin	*Lagenorhynchus cruciger*	
Pacific white-sided dolphin	*Lagenorhynchus obliquidens*	Hook-finned porpoise, white-striped dolphin
Peale's dolphin	*Lagenorhynchus australis*	Blackchin dolphin
Dusky dolphin	*Lagenorhynchus obscurus*	
White-beaked dolphin	*Lagenorhynchus albirostris*	Squid hound
Fraser's dolphin	*Lagenodelphis hosei*	Short-snouted whitebelly dolphin, delfin de Fraser
Northern right whale dolphin	*Lissodelphis borealis*	Cicada dolphin
Southern right whale dolphin	*Lissodelphis peronii*	Tunina sin aleta, delfinliso
Black dolphin	*Cephalorhynchus eutropia*	Chilean dolphin, delfin negro, whitebelly dolphin
Commerson's dolphin	*Cephalorhynchus commersonii*	Piebald dolphin, tunina overa
Heaviside's dolphin	*Cephalorhynchus heavisidii*	Benguela dolphin
Hector's dolphin	*Cephalorhynchus hectori*	New Zealand dolphin
Irrawaddy river dolphin	*Orcaella brevirostris*	Snubfin dolphin
Risso's dolphin	*Grampus griseus*	Gray grampus, gray dolphin, mottled grampus, delfin de Risso
Atlantic spinner dolphin	*Stenella clymene*	Helmet dolphin, delfin tornillo del Atlantico
Atlantic spotted dolphin	*Stenella frontalis*	

Common Name	Scientific Name	Other Names/Spanish
Spotted dolphin	*Stenella attenuata*	Bridled dolphin, pantropical spotted dolphin, narrow snout dolphin, Cape dolphin, delfin manchado pantropical, Cuvier's dolphin
Spinner dolphin	*Stenella longirostris*	Pantropical spinner dolphin, delfin tornillo pantropical
Striped dolphin	*Stenella coeruleoalba*	Longsnout, blue-white and streaker, delfin listado
Common dolphin	*Delphinus delphis*	Delfin común
IndoPacific bottlenose dolphin	*Tursiops aduncus*	
Pacific bottlenose dolphin	*Tursiops gillii*	
Atlantic bottlenose dolphin	*Tursiops truncatus*	Tursión, tonina

N.B. This list contains eighty species of cetaceans. In the future addtional species may be officially added to the list, including the pygmy blue whale, pygmy Bryde's whale, and possibly Northern and Southern Hemisphere or Atlantic and Pacific subspecies of minke and humpback whales. There is always the possibility of more species of beaked whales being discovered, and perhaps the further splintering of those species that we currently recognize. In 1991, a new species of Mesoplodon, *Mesoplodon peruvianus,* was described from a stranded specimen found off the coast of South America. Ulitimately there may be close to, or more than, one hundred species classified in the order Cetacea.

Appendix 3

Further Reading

The books listed below vary widely in quality and readability, but they do offer a reasonable starting place for those wishing to read and learn more of this remarkable planet and our treatment of it. My particular favorites are denoted by an asterisk (*).

CETACEANS

Age Determination of Toothed Whales and Sirenians. International Whaling Commission, 1980.
Baiji: The Yangtze River Dolphin and Other Endangered Animals of China. Zhou Kaia and Zhang Xingduan. Stone Wall Press, 1991.
Biology of the Genus Cephalorhynchus, The. International Whaling Commission, 1988.
Blue Whale, The. George L. Small. Columbia University Press, 1971.
Bottlenose Dolphin, The. Edited by Stephen Leatherwood and Randall R. Reeves. Academic Press, 1990.*
British Whales, Dolphins, and Porpoises. F. C. Fraser. British Museum (Natural History), 1976.
Brother Whale: A Pacific Whalewatcher's Log. Roy Nickerson. Chronicle Books, 1986.
Delicate Art of Whale Watching, The. Joan McIntyre. Sierra Club Books, 1982.
Dingle Dolphin, The. Ronnie Fitzgibbon. Temple Printing Co., n.d.
Dolphin Dolphin. Wade Doak. Hodder and Stoughton, 1981.*
Dolphin Dreamtime: Talking to the Animals. Jim Nollman. Anthony Blond, 1985.*
Dolphin Societies: Discoveries and Puzzles. Edited by Karen Pryor and Kenneth S. Norris. University of California Press, 1991.*
Dolphins. Jacques-Yves Cousteau and Philippe Diole. A&W Visual Library, 1975.
Dolphins and Porpoises. Richard Ellis. Robert Hale, 1983.
Dolphins and Porpoises. Louise Qualye. Headline Books, 1989.
Ecology of Whales and Dolphins, The. D. E. Gaskin. Heinemann, 1985.*
Encounters with Whales and Dolphins. Wade Doak. Hodder and Stoughton, 1988.*
Falling for a Dolphin. Heathcote Williams. Jonathan Cape, 1990.*
Follow a Wild Dolphin. Horace E. Dobbs. Souvenir Press, 1990.
Friendly Whales, The. Roy Nickerson. Chronicle Books, 1987.
Genetic Ecology of Whales and Dolphins. A. R. Hoelzel. International Whaling Commission. Cambridge, 1991.
Gentle Giants: At Sea with the Humpback Whale. Tsuneo Nakamura. Chronicle Books, 1988.
Gray Whale, Eschrichtius robustus, The. Edited by Mary Lou Jones, Steven L. Swartz, and Stephen Leatherwood. Academic Press, 1984.*
Greenpeace Book of Dolphins, The. John May. Century, 1990.
Guide to Identification of Cetaceans in the North East Atlantic. P. G. H. Evans. Mammal Society, 1982.
Hawaii's Humpback Whales. Gregory Dean Kaufman and Paul Henry Forestell. Pacific Whale Foundation Press, 1986.
Humpback Whales. Francois Gohier. Blake Publishing, 1991.

Individual Recognition of Cetaceans: Use of Photoidentification and Other Techniques to Estimate Population Parameters. International Whaling Commission, 1990.

Lilly on Dolphins. John C. Lilly. Doubleday, 1975.

L'Oeil émerveillé ou la Nature comme spectacle. Samivel. Albin Michel. Paris, 1976.

Mind in the Waters. Joan McIntyre. Sierra Club Books, 1974.

Natural History of Whales and Dolphins, The. Peter G. H. Evans. Christopher Helm, 1987.*

Orca: The Whale Called Killer. Erich Hoyt. Camden House, 1984.*

Orcas of the Gulf: A Natural History. Gerard Gormley. Sierra Club Books, 1990.

Pod of Gray Whales, A. Francois Gohier. Blake Publishing, 1988.

Pod of Killer Whales, A. Vicki Leon. Blake Publishing, 1989.

Report of the Special Meeting of the Scientific Committee on Sei and Bryde's Whales. International Whaling Commission, 1977.

Reproduction of Whales, Dolphins and Porpoises. International Whaling Commission, 1984.

Rescue of the Stranded Whales. Kenneth Mallory and Andrea Conley. Simon and Schuster, 1989.

Right Whales: Past and Present Status. International Whaling Commission, 1986.

Save the Dolphins. Horace E. Dobbs. Souvenir Press, 1981.

Seasons of the Whale. Erich Hoyt. Mainstream Publishing, 1990.

Sperm Whales. International Whaling Commission, 1980.

Voyage to the Whales. Hal Whitehead. Hale, 1989.*

Whale, The. Jacques-Yves Cousteau and Philippe Diole. Arrowood Press, 1972.

Whale Nation. Heathcote Williams. Jonathan Cape, 1988.*

Whale Song: The Story of Hawai'i and the Whales. MacKinnon Simpson and Robert B. Goodman. Beyond Worlds Publishing Co., 1989.

Whale Sound. Edited by Greg Gatenby. J. J. Douglas Ltd., 1977.

Whales. E. J. Slijper. Hutchinson, 1979.

Whales. Jacques Cousteau. W. H. Allen, 1988.

Whales. Kara Zahn. Headline Books, 1989.

Whales and Dolphins. Vic Cox. Crescent Books, 1989.*

Whales and Dolphins. Dr. Anthony R. Martin. Salamander, 1990.

Whales, Dolphins, and Porpoises. Edited by Sir Richard Harrison and Dr M. M. Bryden. Merehurst Press, 1990.*

Whales of Canada, The. Erich Hoyt. Camden House, 1988.

Whales of the World. Lyall Watson. Hutchinson, 1985.

Whales of the World. Nigel Bonner. Blandford Press, 1989.

Wild Whales. Dr. James Darling. West Coast Whale Research Foundation, 1987.

Wings in the Sea: The Humpback Whale. Lois King Winn and Howard E. Winn. University Press of New England, 1985.*

Year of the Whale, The. Victor B. Scheffer. Scribners, 1969.

WHALING

Aboriginal/Subsistence Whaling (with special reference to Alaska and Greenland Fisheries). International Whaling Commission, 1982.

Arctic Whalers, Icy Seas. W. Gillies Ross. Irwin Publishing, 1985.

Balaena mysticetus: Whales, Oil and Whaling in the Arctic. Mark Fraker. SOHIO Alaska Petroleum Company, 1984.

Behaviour of Whales in Relation to Management. International Whaling Commission, 1986.

Bibliography of Whale Killing Techniques. International Whaling Commission, 1986.

Comprehensive Assessment of Whale Stocks, The: The Early Years. International Whaling Commission, 1989.

History of the American Whale Fishery. Alexander Starbuck. Castle Books, 1989.

History of World Whaling, A. Daniel Francis. Viking, 1990.

Hunting of the Whale, The. Jeremy Cherfas. Penguin Books, 1989.*

Incidents of a Whaling Voyage. Francis Allyn Olmsted. Bell Publishing Co., 1969.

Marine Mammals of the Northwestern Coast of North America, The. Charles M. Scammon. Dover Publications, 1968.˙

Narratives of the Wreck of the Whale-Ship Essex. Owen Chase et al. Dover Books, 1989.˙

Special Issue on Historical Whaling Records. International Whaling Commission, 1983.

Whale Problem, The: A Status Report. William E. Schevill. Harvard University Press, 1974.

Whale War, The. David Day. Sierra Club Books, 1987.˙

Whaler and Trader in the Arctic, A: 1895-1944. Arthur James Allen. Alaska Northwest Publishing Co., 1988.

Whales, Ice, and Men: The History of Whaling in the Western Arctic. John R. Bockstoce. University of Washington Press, 1986.

Whaling and Old Salem. Frances Diane Robotti. Bonanza Books, 1962.

MARINE MAMMALS

Diving Companions: Sea Lion, Elephant Seal, Walrus. Jacques-Yves Cousteau and Philippe Diole. A&W Visual Library, 1974.

Handbook of Marine Mammals. Vols. 1-4. Edited by Sam H. Ridgway and Sir Richard Harrison. Academic Press, 1989.˙

Pinnipeds, The: Seals, Sea Lions, and Walruses. Marianne Riedman. University of California Press, 1990.˙

Raft of Sea Otters, A. Vicki Leon. Blake Publishing, 1987.

Sea Mammals and Oil: Confronting the Risks. Joseph R. Geraci and David J. St. Aubin. Academic Press, 1990.˙

Seals and Sea Lions. Vicki Leon. Blake Publishing, 1988.

MARINE LIFE

Encyclopedia of Underwater Life, The. Edited by Dr. Keith Bannister and Dr. Andrew Campbell. Unwin Animal Library IV. Equinox, 1985.˙

Octopus and Squid: The Soft Intelligence. Jacques-Yves Cousteau and Philippe Diole. A&W Visual Library, 1973.

Sharks. Edited by John D. Stevens. Merehurst Press, 1989.

Sharks: Silent Hunters of the Deep. Reader's Digest, 1987.˙

USEFUL GUIDES

Field Guide to the Birds of North America. National Geographic Society, 1987.˙

Walker's Mammals of the World. Vols. 1-2. 5th ed. Johns Hopkins University Press, 1991.˙

BAJA CALIFORNIA

Baja California Plant Field Guide. Norman C. Roberts. Natural History Pub. Co., 1989.˙
Flora of Baja California. Ira Wiggins. Stanford, 1980.
Marine Animals of Baja California: A Guide to the Common Fishes and Invertebrates. Daniel
   W. Gotshall. Sea Challengers, 1982.˙
Sea of Cortez Marine Invertebrates: A Guide for the Pacific Coast, Mexico to Ecuador. Alex
   Kerstitch. Sea Challengers, 1989.˙

ENVIRONMENTAL ETHICS

1990 IUCN Red List of Threatened Animals. World Conservation Monitoring Centre. IUCN,
   1990.˙
Biophilia Hypothesis, The. Edited by Stephen R. Kellert and E. O. Wilson. Island Press, 1993.
Ecology in the Twentieth Century: A History. Anna Bramwell. Yale University Press, 1989.˙
End of Nature, The. Bill McKibben. Anchor Books, 1990.
Environmental Ethics: Duties and Values in the Natural World. Holms Rolston III. Temple
   University, 1988.
Gaia. J. E. Lovelock. Oxford University Press, 1987.˙
Gaia: A Way of Knowing. William Irwin Thompson. Lindisfarne Press, 1987.
Nature's Price. W. Van Dieren and M. G. Hummelinck. Marion Boyars, 1979.
Only One Earth: Living for the Future. Lloyd Timberlake. BBC/Earthscan, 1987.
Resources: Environment and Policy. J. Fernie and A. S. Pitkethly. Harper and Row, 1985.
Schumacher on Energy. Edited by Geoffrey Kirk. Abacus Books, 1982.
Small Is Beautiful. E. F. Schumacher. Abacus Books, 1973.
State of the World. Worldwatch Institute. W. W. Norton. Annual.˙
Why Preserve Natural Variety. Bryan Norton. Princeton University Press, 1987.˙

NATURAL HISTORY LITERATURE

Cape Cod. Henry David Thoreau. Penguin, 1987.
Immense Journey, The. Loren Eiseley. Vintage Books, 1959.˙
Journals. Meriwether Lewis and Christopher Clark. Mentor, 1964.
Log from the Sea of Cortez, The. John Steinbeck (1951). Penguin, 1987.˙
Maine Woods, The. Henry David Thoreau. Princeton University Press, 1983.
Moby-Dick, or The Whale. Herman Melville. (1851). Penguin, 1985.˙
My First Summer in the Sierra. John Muir. Sierra Club Books, 1988.
Natural History Essays. Henry David Thoreau. Peregrine Smith Books, 1980.˙
Portable Thoreau, The. Edited by Carl Bobe. Penguin, 1982.˙
Selected Essays, Lectures, and Poems. Ralph Waldo Emerson. Bantam, 1990.˙
Story of My Boyhood and Youth, The. John Muir. Sierra Club Books, 1988.
Travels in Alaska. John Muir. Sierra Club Books, 1988.˙
True Adventures of John Steinbeck, Writer, The. Jackson J. Benson. Penguin, 1984.
Two Years before the Mast. Richard Henry Dana. (1840). Penguin, 1986.˙
Unexpected Universe, The. Loren Eiseley. Harvest/HBJ, 1969.˙
Walden. Henry David Thoreau. Princeton University Press, 1989.˙
Whale for the Killing, A. Farley Mowat. Bantam Books, 1986.˙
Yosemite, The. John Muir. Sierra Club Books, 1988.˙

ANIMAL BEHAVIOR

Almost Human: A Journey into the World of Baboons. Shirley C. Strum. Norton, 1990.
How Monkeys See the World. D. L. Cheney and R. M. Seyfarth. University of Chicago Press, 1990.˙
King Solomon's Ring. Konrad Z. Lorenz. Time Life Books, 1980.
Social Behavior in Animals. Niko Tinbergen. Chapman and Hall, 1972.˙
Soul of the Ape, The Soul of the White Ant, The. Eugéne Marais. Penguin, 1989.˙
Study of Instinct, The. Niko Tinbergen. Oxford University Press, 1989.˙

ECOLOGY

Introduction to Ecology. Paul Colinvaux. John Wiley and Sons, 1973.
Population Ecology: A Unified Study of Animals and Plants. Michael Begon and Martin Mortimer. Blackwell Scientific Publications, 1986.

EVOLUTIONARY BIOLOGY

Blind Watchmaker, The. Richard Dawkins. Penguin Books, 1988.
Collected Papers of Charles Darwin, The. Edited by Paul H. Barrett. University of Chicago Press, 1977.
Darwin's Century: Evolution and the Men Who Discovered It. Loren Eiseley. Doubleday, 1958.
Descent of Woman: The Classic Study of Evolution. Elaine Morgan. Souvenir Press, 1985.
Essential Darwin, The. Edited by Mark Ridley. Unwin Paperbacks, 1987.
Extended Phenotype, The. Richard Dawkins. Oxford University Press, 1982.
Selfish Gene, The. Richard Dawkins. Paladin Books, 1985.˙
Voyage of the Beagle, The. Charles Darwin. Everyman's Library, 1980.

RECOMMENDED JOURNALS/MAGAZINES

Arctic
Audubon
Canadian Journal of Zoology
Cetus
International Wildlife
Journal of Mammalogy
National Geographic
National Wildlife
Natural History
Nature
Oceanus
Science

Appendix 4

Useful Addresses

American Cetacean Society, P.O. Box 2639, San Pedro, CA 90731
American Museum of Natural History, Central Park West, 79th St., New York, NY 10024
American Society of Mammalogists, c/o Department of Zoology, Brigham Young University, Provo, UT 84602
Baja Expeditions, 2625 Garnet Ave., San Diego, CA 92109
Biological Journeys, 1696 Ocean Dr., McKinleyville, CA 95521. Tel.: 707/839–0178
Center for Marine Conservation, 1725 Descales St., N.W., Suite 500, Washington, D.C. 20036.
Cetacean Research Unit, Box 159, Gloucester, MA 01930.
Cetacean Society International, 190 Stillwold Dr., Wethersfield, CT 06109
Cheesemans' Ecology Safaris, 20800 Kittredge Rd., Saratoga, CA 95070. Tel.: 408/867–1371
Cousteau Society, 930 West 21st St., Norfolk, VA 23517
Defenders of Wildlife, 1244 19th St., N.W., Washington, D.C. 20036
Earthwatch (Center for Field Research), 680 Mount Auburn St., P.O. Box 403, Watertown, MA 02272
Earthwatch Australia, 39 Lower Fort St., Sydney, N.S.W. 2000, Australia
Earthwatch California, 861 Via de la Paz, Suite G, Pacific Palisades, CA 90272
Earthwatch Europe, 29 Conniston Ave., Headington, Oxford OX3 OAN, England
Environmental Defense Fund, 257 Park Ave. South, New York, NY 10010
Foundation for Field Research, P.O. Box 2010, Alpine, CA 91903–2010. Tel.: 619/445–9264
Friends of the Earth UK, 26–28 Underwood St., London N1 7JQ, England
Friends of the Earth USA, 218 D St., S.E., Washington, D.C. 20003
Greenpeace UK, 30–31 Islington Green, London N1 8BR, England
Greenpeace USA, 1436 U St., N.W., P.O. Box 96128, Washington, D.C. 20090
Institute of Marine Research, Directorate of Fisheries, P.O. Box 1870, 5011 Bergen, Norway
International Whaling Commission, The Red House, Station Rd., Histon, Cambridge CB4 4NP, England
Japan Whaling Association, 3–2–4, Kasumigaseki, Chiyoda-ku, Tokyo, Japan
National Audubon Society, 950 Third Ave., New York, NY 10022
National Geographic Society, Box 37448, Washington, D.C. 20013
National Marine Fisheries Service, National Marine Mammal Laboratory, Northwest and Alaska Fisheries Center, 7600 Sand Point Way, N.E., Bldg. 4, Seattle, WA 98115
National Wildlife Federation, 1412 16th St., N.W., Washington, D.C. 20036
Natural Resources Defense Council, 40 West 20th St., New York, NY 10011
Pacific Whale Foundation, Azeka Place, Suite 303, P.O. Box 1038, Kihei, HI 96753. Tel.: 808/879–4253
Sea Mammal Research Unit, c/o British Antarctic Survey, High Cross, Madingley Rd., Cambridge, CB3 0ET, England
Sierra Club, 730 Polk St., San Francisco, CA 94109
Smithsonian, 900 Jefferson Dr., Washington, D.C. 20560
U.S. Marine Mammal Commission, 1625 I St., N.W., Washington, D.C. 20006
Whale and Dolphin Conservation Society, 19a James St. West, Bath, Avon BA1 2BT, England

Whale Club of the World, P.O. Box 50, Mansfield, Nottinghamshire NG18 2QX, England

Whale Museum, P.O. Box 945, Friday Harbour, WA 98250

Whaling Information Centre (Japanese), Cargreen Place, Station Rd., London SE25 5AP, England

Wilderness Society, 1400 I St., N.W., Washington, D.C. 20005

World Wide Fund for Nature—WWF, 1250 Twenty-Fourth St., N.W., P.O. Box 96220, Washington, D.C. 20077–7787

World Wide Fund for Nature—WWF UK, Panda House, Weyside Park, Catteshall Lane, Godalming, Surrey GU7 1WR, England

Worldwatch Institute, 1776 Massachusetts Ave., N.W., Washington, D.C. 20036

Endpiece

Canst thou draw out leviathan with a hook?
or his tongue with a cord which thou lettest down?

Canst thou put an hook into his nose?
or bore his jaw through with a thorn?
Will he make many supplications unto thee?
will he speak soft words unto thee?

Will he make a covenant with thee?
wilt thou take him for a servant for ever?
Wilt thou play with him as with a bird?
or wilt thou bind him for thy maidens?

Shall the companions make a banquet of him?
shall they part him among the merchants?
Canst thou fill his skin with barbed irons?
or his head with fish spears?

Lay thine hand upon him,
remember the battle, do no more.
Behold, the hope of him is in vain:
shall not one be cast down even at the sight of him?

None is so fierce that dare stir him up:
who then is able to stand before me?
Who hath prevented me, that I should repay him?
whatsoever is under the whole heaven is mine.

I will not conceal his parts, nor his power,
nor his comely proportion.
Who can discover the face of his garments?
or who can come to him with his double bridle?

Who can open the doors of his face?
his teeth are terrible round about.
His scales are his pride,
shut up together as with a close seal.

One is so near to another,
that no air can come between them.

They are joined one to another,
they stick together, that they cannot be sundered.

By his neesings a light doth shine,
and his eyes are like the eyelids of the morning.
Out of his mouth go burning lamps,
and sparks of fire leap out.

Out of his nostrils goeth smoke,
as out of a seething pot or caldron.
His breath kindleth coals,
and a flame goeth out of his mouth.

In his neck remaineth strength,
and sorrow is turned into joy before him.
The flakes of his flesh are joined together:
they are firm in themselves; they cannot be moved.

His heart is as firm as a stone;
yea, as hard as a piece of the nether millstone.
When he raiseth up himself, the mighty are afraid:
by reason of breakings they purify themselves.

The sword of him that layeth at him cannot hold:
the spear, the dart, nor the habergeon.
He esteemeth iron as straw,
and brass as rotten wood.

The arrow cannot make him flee:
slingstones are turned with him into stubble.
Darts are counted as stubble:
he laugheth at the shaking of a spear.

Sharp stones are under him:
he spreadeth sharp pointed things upon the mire.
He maketh the deep to boil like a pot:
he maketh the sea like a pot of ointment.

He maketh a path to shine after him;
one would think the deep to be hoary.
Upon the earth there is not his like,
who is made without fear.

He beholdeth all high things:
he is a king over all the children of pride.
                    —Job 41

I would that it were so.

Michelle A. Gilders *was born in Hitchin, England, and received her bachelor's and master's degrees from New College, Oxford, in Pure and Applied Biology. She is currently working as a biologist in Alaska and travels extensively in search of cetaceans as a naturalist, photographer, and guide.*